T0301754

BACKING
the
BOLD

**A Primer on Early-Stage Venture Capital
in Southeast Asia**

BACKING *the* BOLD

A Primer on Early-Stage Venture Capital in Southeast Asia

PAULO JOQUIÑO
Insignia Ventures, Singapore

EDITED BY
YINGLAN TAN
Insignia Ventures, Singapore

PRODUCTION OF INSIGNIA VENTURES PARTNERS

 **World Scientific**

NEW JERSEY · LONDON · SINGAPORE · BEIJING · SHANGHAI · HONG KONG · TAIPEI · CHENNAI · TOKYO

Published by

World Scientific Publishing Co. Pte. Ltd.

5 Toh Tuck Link, Singapore 596224

USA office: 27 Warren Street, Suite 401-402, Hackensack, NJ 07601

UK office: 57 Shelton Street, Covent Garden, London WC2H 9HE

National Library Board, Singapore Cataloguing in Publication Data
Name(s): Joquiño, Paulo. | Tan, Yinglan, editor.
Title: Backing the bold : a primer on early-stage venture capital in Southeast Asia /
    Paulo Joquiño ; edited by Yinglan Tan.
Description: Singapore : World Scientific Publishing Co. Pte. Ltd., [2023]
Identifier(s): ISBN 978-981-12-6468-9 (hardback) | 978-981-12-6469-6 (ebook for institutions) |
    978-981-12-6470-2 (ebook for individuals)
Subject(s): LCSH: Venture capital--Southeast Asia.
Classification: DDC 332.04154--dc23

British Library Cataloguing-in-Publication Data
A catalogue record for this book is available from the British Library.

For any available supplementary material, please visit
https://www.worldscientific.com/worldscibooks/10.1142/13095#t=suppl

Desk Editor: Geysilla Jean

Typeset by Stallion Press
Email: enquiries@stallionpress.com

Printed in Singapore

Acknowledgments

Backing the Bold is not a book in the traditional sense of the word. The goal of these thirteen chapters has been to guide venture fellows of Insignia Ventures Academy, Asia's first experiential venture capital (VC) accelerator, in their exploration of the venture capital industry and profession, specifically in the context of Southeast Asia's startup ecosystem and from the perspective of Insignia Ventures and its portfolio founders. For more information on Insignia Ventures Academy, you can head to www.insignia.academy.

Such an origin and context for *Backing the Bold* has inevitably made this book a kind of living organism, continuously growing thanks to every new group of people who become part of the VC accelerator, as organizers, mentors, or participants. It excites me to know that the book will never be fully complete — as the Michael Ventura saying goes, "There is no finish line, only line markers." For these very same reasons, there are people whose insignias (pun intended) will be left indelibly on this book as this version was formed over the summer of 2021 and revised continually up until June 2022 for this published first edition:

To Cwenne, who breathed color into the manuscript with her layouts and designs, and painstakingly took the time to help proofread the book cover to cover,

To Kimberly, Kha Yun, Mhyles, Melissa, Tuba, and Benita who brought concepts to life through infographics, research, and visuals,

To Verity, whose hard work opened up the time for me to be able to focus on this book over the summer,

To Weirong, Shaun, Jean-Anne and Chelsey, who came in the nick of time with the scrutiny the book needed to get in even better shape,

To Gail, whose leadership of the Insignia Ventures Academy gave *Backing the Bold* purpose and direction,

To Yinglan, who opened the doors for me to co-author *Navigating ASEANnovation* in 2020 and then invited me to pen *Backing the Bold* the following year, and whose ideas and insight into Southeast Asia's startup and venture capital landscape laid the foundation for this book,

To the Insignia Ventures Academy Cohort 1, 2, and 3 Venture Fellows who questioned the text, engaged with it, and as a result, became part of its creation,

And to the founders, startup leaders, and investors whose time, conversation, and inputs over the course of the past few years — distilled in podcasts, blog articles, and books — molded the insights in this book,

Thank you.
Paulo Joquiño
15 September 2021 — Manila, Philippines

To my mother, the first to fuel my words
To my father, the first to equip me with keyboards and laptops
To my brother, the first to read my stories

For your early investments that cannot ever be fully repaid
And yet remain to be the ones with the greatest returns

Foreword

by Yinglan Tan
Founding Managing Partner
Insignia Ventures Partners

Olympics and Venture Capital

It was the 2021 Olympics in Tokyo, in the women's 1500-meter race. The reigning world 1500m champion Sifan Hassan had less than a third of the race to go, or a mere 380 meters, when another runner tumbled to the ground in front of her, causing her to trip, fall, and roll across the track. Sifan quickly got back up and did not only catch up with the pack but overtook the front runner who had been 30 meters ahead when she fell. In the next 44 or so seconds, she had gone from trailing in the dust to winning the event.

This inspiring Olympic story, interestingly enough, is a reminder of what venture capital is about. Venture capitalists invest in rapidly changing markets and technologies that could be obsolete or redundant in a decade, but what remains constant is the ability of founders or leadership to adapt and continuously innovate. It's not an unfamiliar scenario in VC to work with a founder who finds their early-stage company hitting a brick wall due to new discoveries in the market or assumptions that turned out to be wrong. Assumptions and change are part and parcel of starting a company. But what separates the great from the rest are the founders who don't just sit back; they leverage the obstacle or challenge to unveil the next stage of growth.

Venture Capital is a Function of Talent

The story is a reminder that VCs don't invest in companies but invest in talent. In venture capital, returns are a function of talent raised to the power of capital:

$$\text{VC Returns} = \text{Talent}^{\text{Capital}} \times \text{Infrastructure}$$

It is not uncommon that for all the research and due diligence done, at the end of the day, investing in an early-stage startup can easily boil down to the investor's belief in the founder's ability to build a great company. Conversely, it is also possible to do all the work on the company, miss out on evaluating the founding team, and realize post-investment that they weren't really up to the task of making it to the finish line. In my years as a venture capitalist, I've learned firsthand that investing less capital in an "A"-team is exponentially worth more than putting more capital in a "B"-team, assuming all conditions are equal.

The billion-dollar question for the VC is then a matter of whose talent to "exponentialize", and answering that question is fraught with variables and uncertainty. It's easy to find comfort in the business models and technology, but venture capital is first and foremost a people business.

Talent in Southeast Asia Increases Long-term Investment Values

In Southeast Asia, this aspect of the so-called "gold rush" or "golden age" of the region's startup and venture capital ecosystem is easily overlooked, amidst all the new unicorns and increasingly massive funding rounds.

Gold rushes have always been coupled with an influx of talent and oftentimes, the impact of talent influx is more long-lasting and far-reaching than capital. For example, the migration of workers to California following the gold rush laid the groundwork for what we know today as Silicon Valley many times more than the actual gold they mined in the area at the time.

The influx of talent means more entrepreneurs to potentially back, and more people for these entrepreneurs to hire. Behind this talent influx are diasporas, both from other markets to Southeast Asia, or unicorns to smaller companies. You have former employees of Chinese tech unicorns looking to start the next chapter of their careers in the region. There are employees and leadership of the first generation of regional unicorns building their own startups, the so-called "startup mafia". There continues to be a stream of first-generation and second-generation turtles coming back to shore in Southeast Asia.

These diasporas do not only increase the density of the talent, but carry with them greater exposure. This in turn increases the "values" of talent in the VC returns function, making every investable dollar worth a lot more. While venture capital has fuelled startups into becoming billion-dollar companies, the real, long-term impact comes with these founders bringing in talent into their companies who then graduate and then set off to start their own businesses which are also more likely to be venture-backable. This is an important cycle for venture capital.

Apart from the increase in Southeast Asia's talent density and exposure, the tools to build enduring, powerful businesses are also becoming increasingly accessible. It used to be the case that you needed to build a factory or have a significant amount of upfront capital to start a business and grow your wealth.

Now we are at a unique point in the history of capitalism. All you need is code to get a business off the ground, and the capital injection required to scale a single startup is much lower, which means there are more businesses that can be funded by a single fund. With the creation of infrastructure layers to support internet businesses by this generation of tech companies in the region, we can expect even more asset-light or even "asset-less" tech startups in the future, with high-caliber teams that are fully remote and products that are highly scalable (i.e., more global companies out of Southeast Asia).

Equation is not Just about Startup Talent, but VC Talent as Well

Venture capital is just as much about investor talent as it is about startup talent. Just as the density and exposure of startup talent is increasing in Southeast Asia, so is investor talent in the region. We're seeing more interest in the venture capital profession and have set up Insignia Ventures Academy to cater to this increasing demand, which also led to the writing of this book. It's not just about imparting information or best practices but helping folks hit the ground running in an industry where the treadmill never slows down. There is also the underrated exodus of Chinese tech investors into Southeast Asia, and Singapore especially, be it families or individuals who are not just looking to invest capital into tech startups but are actually relocating to the region, making them attractive talent to bring in as executives or even board members.

This means that the gold rush into Southeast Asia is not just a matter of increased quantity, but of intellect or acumen as well, which adds to the velocity and decisiveness with which capital can be deployed long-term in the region.

Southeast Asia, as a region of emerging markets, has had the benefit of not being the first to the game at developing its internet economy. Initially, this only meant that there are more opportunities for founders to learn from markets with similar fundamentals but have been earlier in terms of developing internet or tech-based business models, and to an extent that remains true until today.

Now we are at a point in the region's tech roadmap where Southeast Asia is leapfrogging compared to the tech roadmaps of India and China, which in turn were leapfrogging compared to the US. What would have taken five to seven years to build and grow in those markets is now taking two to three years, especially in emerging but market-specific or niche sectors like healthcare, education, and property. The tech roadmaps are also syncing up, especially in areas like social commerce or crypto.

This is a function of the velocity at which talent (entrepreneurs) and capital (investors) are working together in the region, where it becomes faster to run and fund experiments, and at a smaller scale to reach product-market fit (PMF). It also helps that you have regulators and infrastructure in the region emerging to enable these experiments. One example is fintech, where emerging open banking solutions are enabling faster fintech-bank collaboration to drive innovation in the sector.

This velocity does not only put the development of Southeast Asia's tech ecosystem into hyperdrive; it also expands its reach, where you have a lot more opportunities for Southeast Asia companies to go global from day one. There is a case to be made for building a global company out of Southeast Asia (Singapore) rather than India or China, especially these days.

From the investor standpoint, the thesis for Southeast Asia is no longer just about looking at what worked in India or China a few years ago and how it can be adapted in the region, but also what Southeast Asia can offer beyond the region and to the rest of the world. Sea Group has already proven the fruits of doing this and now the resources or "factors of production" are here to follow suit.

The values of the VC returns equation are all increasing, and while this is no Olympics, the competition is thickening. With the ecosystem moving at this density and velocity, it is not unlikely to trip along the way. The question is, have you invested in a "Sifan Hassan"? And along with that question is another, equally important one, "Are you willing and equipped to run this race alongside your founders?"

Twenty-nine years before Sifan's miracle run, in the 1992 Barcelona Olympics, British runner Derek Redmond made Olympic history not because he finished first, or even made it to the finals, but because he crossed the finish line of the 400m semi-finals even as he snapped his right hamstring just past the first 250 meters. He painfully hopped on one leg to the very end, even when the rest of the runners had already crossed and there was technically no reason to finish the race. What's more, he had his father rush towards him halfway through the track and help him finish the race to a standing ovation of 65,000 spectators who were in awe and tears.

Venture capital is rife with stories of loss and failure, but what people will remember is how you worked with the founders through the hard times as much as you celebrated with them in the good. Will you run with them to the end even if they've fallen behind? It is a tough question, and there is no one right answer, but it is a question VCs will face often, especially in an ecosystem like Southeast Asia at this point in time.

By no means does *Backing the Bold* hold the answers to any of the questions I've asked thus far, because a lot of what makes VCs great is personal and built on relationships. Then again, as with any personal decision, it doesn't hurt to learn from the experiences of others. These pages are purposefully infused with and informed by specific experiences and perspectives meant to help you, the aspiring venture capitalist, go beyond the frameworks and equations to figure out the real billion-dollar question, "Are *you* bold enough to back the bold?"

If after reading this book, your answer is yes, then you can check out how to dive even deeper into the world of venture capital through the programs this book was written to accompany at Insignia Ventures Academy: www.insignia.academy. ß

Contents

Introduction

"It's nice to sit in the glow of your adulation, but without entrepreneurs, you're nothing. You have to have these real people, with the ideas and willingness to commit their life."

— **Don Valentine** *on Something Ventured, 2011*

Something Changing, Something Timeless, Something Ventured

The year 2021 marks 10 years since *Something Ventured* was released. The documentary traced the history of the United States' early venture capital industry starting in the 1950s through the 1980s, sitting down with some of the pioneers who recounted their entry into the VC business, recounting the chaos and hype around their earliest investments including Intel, Apple, Genentech, Atari, and Cisco, and how the industry shaped the velocity of innovation. I sat down to watch it recently and realized two things.

First, **a lot has changed** since Arthur Rock put money into the so-called "Traitorous Eight" behind Fairchild Semiconductors and when Don Valentine joined the company as Director of Marketing. At the time, it was worth noting that the personalities defining the venture capital industry were themselves "outliers". No one knew what being a venture capitalist meant, or why somebody would put money into a product without a business model.

1

Yet venture capital has changed so much on so many levels, from the people who are leading the top global firms to the founders they back and the technology they are building. Y Combinator's 2021 summer cohort has seen Southeast Asian startups triple from the previous batch, when a decade ago there were hardly any from the region to speak of. The number of venture-backed unicorns from Southeast Asia has for the first time exceeded that of China in 2021, by a long shot. And that's just a few milestones in this region alone.

Hop onto venture capital's corner of social media and it abounds with 20-something Gen-Z VC communities networking for their next investment, new firms focusing on minorities and underfunded demographics, and new investments in verticals that didn't exist a decade ago. There are arguments to be made for inertia in certain aspects of the industry, but the reality is that change is not just inevitable, but necessary in venture capital, as its future is tied to the pace of innovation and its spread globally and beyond.

On the other hand, **nothing has changed** since the likes of Kleiner Perkins and Sequoia Capital kicked off a new age of business creation, breaking off from the practices and traditions of the Industrial Revolution, redefining what it means to be an entrepreneur, and ushering the world into the Internet Revolution. The answers Don Valentine and his peers gave when asked what kind of entrepreneurs they would back echo the answers given at the most recent venture capital panels held over Zoom. Venture capital continues to be the business of building companies and creating something where nothing existed before. The struggles faced by Atari and Apple in their early days and the decisions of early venture capitalists to invest and stick it out nonetheless still offer valuable lessons for the VCs of today.

In that way, *Something Ventured* is, paradoxically, both outdated and timeless. The same can be said for this book and any similar efforts to teach or impart learnings in venture capital. By the time that you are reading this, a lot would have already changed in Southeast Asia's tech and venture capital ecosystem since the first words of this book were written. Yet, there remain principles and mindsets that VCs decades into the future will consider crucial or built upon in the context of their time.

These two seemingly opposing realities of venture capital are not mutually exclusive, but actually support each other. The timeless principles and mindsets are foundational to the kind of change the industry needs to embrace in every investment decision. This is the reality that this book aims to capture for the aspiring venture capital professional or early-stage startup investor, with the juxtaposition of "rules" against the continuously evolving context of Southeast Asia's internet economy and venture capital industry.

Backing the bold cannot be done without being bold as well. This means embracing the duality of direction and uncertainty that comes with being a VC. For example, investing in founders rather than companies or building companies rather than simply putting capital into them are in themselves timeless mindsets particular to VC but in practice, they also force the venture capitalist to embrace change and uncertainty (e.g. the company pivots). Early-stage venture capitalists are virtually investing in founders because the company can go either way. That said, you cannot go in blind and yet you will also need to be aware that the path before them is not set in stone.

Ultimately, this book is less about making sense of venture capital than it is about enabling the reader to embrace the uncertainty of it all.

Dealing with Uncertainty in Venture Capital

The venture capital industry, as with any field, will continue to unearth new insights and learnings about itself the more it is practiced, but there is a horizon where there is only so much that the growing plethora of literature, content, and programs can address or adequately equip a venture capitalist.

In quantum physics, the Heisenberg Uncertainty Principle addresses the reality that it is impossible to measure both the position and momentum of an object exactly. In venture capital, it is impossible to maximize both the company's potential returns and its momentum of growth. Creating more potential for returns means coming in early, which also means less momentum and more uncertainty around its future growth. Coming in later to invest at a point in time where the company has more momentum to work with could also lead to higher returns but that would be too expensive and impractical for the venture capital business model.

The Heisenberg Uncertainty Principle makes approximations to measure both position and momentum of a quantum object within a certain range. Venture capital also necessitates assumptions and approximations to justify valuation (price) to commit to the company and its founders. A lot of information will not be available, and the potential of a startup is not easily quantifiable.

These assumptions and approximations are built on three aspects of venture capital which the book touches upon across its chapters but ultimately leaves blanks for the reader to fill out themselves.

The first is that venture capital is a personal business and profession. Not only because it is the business of backing real people building companies, but because the decision to back these people is ultimately personal. These decisions are often counterintuitive, and they will often go against the grain of what everyone else is saying. Even when decisions are made with the consensus of an investment committee, or after the rigor of due diligence, it is still a judgment call in the heat of the moment without the luxury of foresight or hindsight.

That said, personal does not mean emotional or even devoid of logic. It means that venture capital requires conviction — the same conviction with which Sequoia Capital decided to invest in Cisco when no other VC would put their money in them at the time, or when Dick Kramlich decided to double down on Forethought Software's PowerPoint product when everyone else in the industry thought it was a ludicrous decision, even in hindsight.

Conviction is not just casual, out-of-pocket confidence. Making decisions from that end of the spectrum just puts the venture capitalist in full exposure of uncertainty (but to each their own, I guess). Conviction that minimizes the risk posed by uncertainty is built from personal experience, expertise, and connections, and sharpened by focus. This is why operator VCs or superconnector VCs are often highly considered in forming startup boards. Apple's first board of directors brought together Arthur Rock's finance background and Don Valentine's sales and distribution experience, which complemented the product and technology focus of the founders.

More importantly, the best founders can value and recognize whether or not that conviction is right for their company. Competitive rounds are fought and won based on these value propositions, and not the term sheets. **For the venture capitalist, this means building one's own value proposition is important in dealing with the uncertainty of making early-stage investments.** That is a personal endeavor, and something that no amount of content or training can make up for. In a world where venture capital is much more commonplace and even highly attractive as a profession, very different from the stories told in *Something Ventured,* developing this personal conviction is more important than ever before.

Conviction does not mean getting investments right. In fact, getting things wrong is par for the course, and arguably even part of getting things right. As a venture capitalist, if you're not getting things wrong, you're probably not thinking big enough. Conviction is also about commitment and knowing when to call it — two things that are also built on expertise and experience.

The second aspect of venture capital upon which assumptions and approximations in investment decisions are made is that VC is the art of leveraging patterns. Pattern recognition is found at every stage of work venture capitalists do. VCs will develop investment theses based on geographic, temporal, or technological patterns, then they'll also use patterns to optimize their sourcing strategy. Patterns also come into play when spotting red flags or addressing concerns with due diligence, and they also become helpful when making connections in portfolio management.

Patterns also play a huge role in how this book was put together, because a lot of the learnings we share in these pages come from patterns gleaned from companies I've worked with, founders and investors I've spoken to, and cases I've studied.

That said, leveraging patterns is not just about recognizing them, but also translating them into new contexts and even breaking away from them. This goes back to the idea that the "rules" of venture capital have their own limits. **In a lot of cases, VCs have to break their rules (i.e., preconceived notions or traditional wisdom) in order to truly find and build exceptional companies.** Venture capital finds its origins and nature in breaking away from patterns, which again ties back to the previous point that it is also a personal business, because when patterns need to be broken, more conviction is needed.

The third aspect is that **venture capital is built on perspective.** Perspective defines the parameters of investment decisions. A business model that might not work in one market could work in another due to a difference in the industry in these two markets. A portfolio company might be doing well within one's expectations but not be up to par with other investors.

In this book, we consider many characters — the founders, the venture capitalists, the limited partners, regulators, customers, and more — against the backdrop of Southeast Asia's rapidly evolving tech startup ecosystem. To make the best possible decisions, venture capitalists can focus and define their operating perspective amidst the noise. Under what parameters are we investing in this company at this point? What does the company need currently in order to get to this north star metric? Is the founder the right person to lead this company at this point in its growth?

Defining perspective and following through on decisions based on this focus requires personal conviction and the ability to leverage patterns. It's not just enough to have the big picture, "CAGR" perspective on an industry; having on-the-ground knowledge of what consumers experience adds another valuable layer of understanding that could influence what kind of companies the investor would look at. Having a track record of companies is one thing but being able to glean learnings from working with various founders makes this track record all the more valuable.

When put together, personal conviction, patterns, and perspective enable the venture capitalist to embrace direction and uncertainty when it comes to backing the bold. In this book, we share principles, mindsets, and best practices to develop this ability to navigate decisions beyond the "horizon", making the best possible approximations and assumptions in early-stage investing.

Building Your Own Black Box

As I write this book, Southeast Asia's venture capital ecosystem is becoming flush with capital as the region's first generation of unicorns look to go public and a new generation of startups join the unicorn club in massive rounds. But along with this gold rush is the influx of founders and venture capitalists where this capital is being invested into, from ex-unicorn employees starting their own ventures to investment managers looking to support family offices from China and invest their money in Southeast Asia startups.

The pouring in of talent and capital has created an interesting environment in Southeast Asia, where there are emerging opportunities especially for underrated, venture-backable sectors and increasing competition to tap into these emerging opportunities. This makes it a great but also challenging time to be a venture capitalist or to enter the industry. You're no longer first to the bus station, but there are tons of buses coming in for you to hop on. The question is, will you get on the right bus?

The nature of decision-making in venture capital as we discussed previously is such that it can be highly contextual, built on personal conviction, patterns, and operating perspective. This means that in venture capital there's a lot of black boxes, and no set recipe for winning an investment or turning that investment into a billion-dollar exit. There are similarities and lessons to be learned from various cases, which we cover in this book, but to expect a formula probably means working in the industry might not be the best fit.

Getting on the "right" bus depends on you and your own black box. Throughout the book, as we discuss the various decision-making processes of venture capitalists in their pursuit to invest in and grow startups, the hope is that you will be able to develop your own decision-making paradigm: your own personal conviction, your own ability to leverage patterns, and your own operating perspective.

The challenging thing about venture capital is that these "black boxes" inherently require experience and track records, but these track records and experience are themselves built on these "black boxes". By sharing with you some of the commonalities and differences of these venture capital "black boxes", as we see them from our corner of the ecosystem here in Southeast Asia and as we've documented on *Insignia Business Review*, "On Call with Insignia Ventures" podcast, and the book *Navigating ASEANnovation*, we're offering a boost to get at least a step ahead of this chicken-and-egg problem.

But then again there is nothing like simply dropping this book, going out there, and backing the bold.

Backing the Bold: Redefining Venture Capital

For all the uncertainties that come with being a venture capitalist and the many ways to embrace this challenge, the pursuit boils down to "backing the bold". **Entrepreneurs define the venture capital industry.** They are on the steering wheel, putting their lives on the line to lead an expedition into the unknown, and venture capitalists are just in for the ride, pitching in their special fuel to get to the destination a little bit faster, and once in a while pointing at the stars that lead the way.

In the equation of venture capital, capital is only as efficient as the talent it is invested into. A smaller check into a team capable of enduring, pivoting, and growing through the seasons can do exponentially more than a larger check into a team that breaks down at the first hiccup or cannot move fast enough. That talent begins with the founders but also encompasses the capabilities of the engineers they bring on board, the sales organization they build, the country managers and senior executives they hire, and the board of directors they bring together.

Looking at venture capital as the business of investing in talent and not just investing in companies or technology is essential to being able to understand the challenges of the industry and why it is important to be able to embrace uncertainty. Understanding and working with the complexities of people will always outweigh the uncertainties posed by investing in a rapidly evolving market or frontier technology. The most crucial decisions VCs will have to make will revolve around people, and that is where the true uncertainty lies.

Something Ventured covers the story of how Sequoia's Don Valentine and Cisco's CEO and Chairman had to fire Cisco's founders after several executives gave an ultimatum. At the time it was a decision that had to be made. Everything turned out well for Cisco, and the founders left with enough money to retire and went on to continue building more ventures. The VC industry is littered with these stories of conflict and pivotal decision-making around people, and regardless if these decisions were categorically the right thing to do, the reality is that the decisions made or influenced by VCs do not just shift percentages on a capitalization table or fund projections, they change lives and chart the course of history.

I hope this book encourages you to reconsider your view of venture capital as more than just a profession of investing, innovation, or company building. It's a profession of committing time and resources to people, from the customers and employees to founders. And that means voluntarily taking on the risk of having to make tough calls that could potentially burn bridges or lose money along the way. While the uncertainty of committing time and resources to people poses risk, more importantly, it is at the core of what drives venture capitalists to keep backing the bold. After all, who can truly say for sure what a group of college students huddled together in a dorm room, hacking away at their computers, could create for the rest of the world? Who's to say what a corporate employee can do when inspired by a compelling problem? Whether it would help a young girl in a far-flung village get access to healthcare or a business owner earn enough money to be able to send their kids to school?

For all the uncertainty that comes with backing the bold, embracing the unknown these entrepreneurs venture into can lead to positive, impactful, and enduring change, and that's the best kind of returns a venture capitalist can truly hope for.

Paulo Joquiño
15 September 2021 — Manila, Philippines

Chapter 1

Rule #1: Southeast Asia is Not Silicon Valley

What is the First Rule of Venture Capital in Southeast Asia?

The first rule of venture capital in Southeast Asia is to understand that Southeast Asia is not Silicon Valley. It is an easy concept often repeated in nearly every panel of tech founders and investors in the region, yet it remains challenging for many startups and tech companies to execute.

The companies that have been able to follow this rule were able to build the region's billion-dollar companies (unicorns). At the heart of this first rule is that **building startups in Southeast Asia requires a deep understanding of the markets in the region.** Simply bringing in what has originated from Silicon Valley and other global technology hubs will not work without this understanding.

This rule aligns with the risk-reward dynamic that venture capital inherently operates in as an investment vehicle. **Venture capital finds its success in investing in the game-changers, the disruptors, and the non-obvious.** Investing in the average and the repetitions does not result in fund-making returns.

This is because these companies are neither following the mold nor cloning the successes that preceded them, but rather building for the specific circumstances of the millions of people living in the region.

One could easily respond — isn't it obvious that an entrepreneur should build for the market they are in? This tendency to invest in clones stems from the earlier days of Southeast Asia's startups and venture capital in the 2000s, when the region largely saw capital and talent coming in from tech companies while investors had no prior experience in these markets. Despite the early influx of tech companies, there were still a lot of infrastructure gaps and inefficiencies in the region that prevented the rapid adoption of digital services.

So even if Southeast Asia's position as an emerging market naturally exposes its startup ecosystem to the influences of the success stories of more mature markets (i.e., Silicon Valley), these influences cannot easily be implemented without first addressing the need for certain infrastructure foundations or working with the pre-existing industry fragmentation.

For example, edtech startups coming into the 2020s still face challenges pushing for live streaming services in schools in rural areas with internet connectivity issues. While there is much to learn from the narratives from mature markets, there is also much to unlearn when it comes to applying these business models to Southeast Asia.

Balancing global influence and localization by unlearning — learning from what has worked elsewhere and unlearning certain aspects of that to consider what will work better for Southeast Asia — is how founders and investors can embrace this rule. This challenge will always continue to persist, especially as new waves of foreign talent and capital make their way into the region for the first time.

And these waves of foreign talent and capital making their way into Southeast Asia are part of a larger trend of venture capital investments diversifying from mature markets like the US and China into emerging markets like India and Latin America, as we see in Exhibit 1. Among these regions, Southeast Asia has been taking a larger share at an increasingly rapid rate at the turn of the decade, and we shall dive into the reasons further in this chapter.

The best venture capitalists build bandwagons

While Southeast Asia is not Silicon Valley, there is no harm in learning from Silicon Valley or any other tech hubs across the world. That much was clear to the governments trying to figure out how to jump-start the process of creating a critical mass of entrepreneurs and innovation that would attract not only more investments, but also create new jobs and usher more people into the digital age. Singapore in particular, took the time to learn from a similar city-state, Israel. Learnings from markets like Israel informed Singapore's approach to developing initiatives like the National Research Foundation (NRF) and government scholarships geared towards R&D talent, software engineers, tech entrepreneurs, and investors.

Similar to Singapore's NRF launched in 2009 and Malaysia's MaGIC (Malaysia Global Innovation and Creativity Centre), a startup ecosystem-building agency launched in 2014, many of the region's early incubators and investors were sprung out of government initiatives.

Apart from government initiatives, many of the early incubators and venture capital funds also came from the innovation teams of family-run conglomerates and corporations. An example would be Ideaspace (an incubator) and Kickstart Ventures (a venture capital firm) in the Philippines, each stemming from the two biggest telecom companies in the country. However, even with this emergence of corporate and government funds, accelerators, and incubators, it still took a lot of work to point global investors in the direction of Southeast Asia, as Yinglan reminisces in a conversation with a fellow investor, Cathay Innovation's Rajive Keshup, in a Clubhouse session in April 2021.

> "In 2010, 2011, when I was still in the government, I was trying to persuade VCs to come to Southeast Asia. You had to have come up with hundred-page slide decks introducing where Southeast Asia is, where Singapore is, how the local venture landscape is doing, and [potential] limited partners were wondering what this is exactly. Even China was very early then." [1]

This government and corporate-first approach to building local tech ecosystems provided a platform for foreign players seeing potential in the region to embrace this first rule and have greater confidence in government money putting its skin in the game.

This points to another interesting hallmark of venture capital: **the bandwagon effect**. Even if venture capitalists try to find the non-obvious and outliers, once they are found, investors quickly crowd around them and compete to get their checks in. In some cases, this effectively balloons the valuations of the companies being sought after. Following the bandwagon will have its pros and cons depending on the company in question. Furthermore, the venture capital firm's thesis also comes into question, but that's for another chapter. Another more productive way of thinking about this dynamic is that **the best venture capitalists build the bandwagons, and the rest follow.**

In any case, creating this "fear of missing out" (FOMO) and bandwagon effect around Southeast Asia encouraged many global venture capital firms like Sequoia Capital to look at the region and hire talent there to source deals. By 2010, there were a growing number of startups and venture capital firms participating in the region, either set up by global players or returnee entrepreneurs from Ivy League MBAs. However, fundraising activity remained largely centered around early-stage ventures (pre-Series C rounds) with no billion-dollar unicorns emerging yet.

**The best venture capitalists
build the bandwagons and the rest follow.**

The best venture capitalists avoid gravity wells

It would undoubtedly take more than a sales pitch to bring in more global funds into Southeast Asia's ring — the fundamental trifecta of:

1. Internet and smartphone penetration (i.e., technological adoption in general terms)
2. A rising GDP per capita (i.e., rising middle or consumer class in general terms)
3. A mass of entrepreneurial talent to attract more capital into the region and support the growth of the early-stage startups that had just emerged in the ecosystem

Midway through the 20th century, this trifecta was dominated by the rise of the semiconductor and space industries in the US. In China, this trifecta was led by a strong consumer class which rising companies like Alibaba and Tencent could tap into and monetize at the turn of the millennium.

In Southeast Asia, a combination of greater access to the internet, cheaper phones, and a rapidly rising middle class fed into the customer base of up-and-coming early-stage startups. Ultimately, this led to the emergence of unicorns in the region, as investors saw this trifecta coming together, and began pushing companies towards higher and higher valuations.

The region's first unicorn emerged in 2014, when Lazada, the e-commerce company founded by Rocket Internet, was acquired two years later by Alibaba. Following a year later, was a gaming startup from Singapore called Garena (the precursor of Sea Group).

The next two unicorns, Bigo and VNG, were also startups primarily focused on the online internet experience with a video-based social media platform and gaming platform, respectively. Here we start seeing a corollary of the bandwagon effect: **unicorns are vehicles for shaping capital distribution in a market or industry.** For example, it is not far off to presume that investors in VNG saw Garena's success and thought that VNG would be Vietnam's answer to Garena.

Because of this bandwagon effect, unicorns, and any massive fundraising rounds for that matter, effectively become signposts for what investors are looking for. As a result, this pulls capital more towards companies in similar verticals but different markets, or more importantly, companies in the same market but adjacent verticals. Think e-commerce funding laying the groundwork for e-commerce logistics and payments platforms to raise funding of their own, some of them invested in directly by the very e-commerce unicorns that created what we will call a "**gravity well.**"

It is interesting to see how the focus of investors in the region has shifted based on the profile of the companies that became unicorns during these points in time. As we see in Exhibit 1, the nature of the unicorns in Southeast Asia evolved from gaming and social media companies in 2015 to ride-hailing apps (Grab, Gojek), ecommerce marketplaces (Bukalapak, Tokopedia, Lazada, Traveloka), and payments (VNPay, GoPay), to logistics-enabled ecommerce (JD. ID) in 2020. Of course, there are other factors that will influence the investment decision as well.

It's also worth noting from Exhibit 1 that by 2020/2021, only a few of these unicorns had reached an exit event (i.e., when the private investments in these startups are liquidated and returned to investors, presumably at an exponentially higher value) such as going public or getting acquired. In younger ecosystems where the infrastructure is not yet as prevalent and demand from buyers may not be as strong, the path to exit events like IPOs or sizeable buyouts takes longer, and this is something that early-stage investors have to consider. This has resulted in some VCs exiting to growth stage investors in what are called "secondary sales" for certain

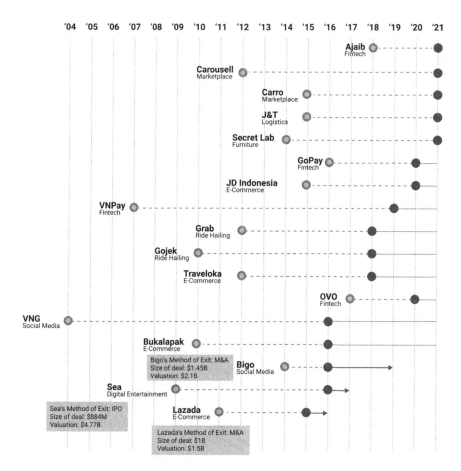

SEA'S PATHWAYS TO EXITS AND UNICORN STATUS FROM 2004-2021

- ○ Incorporation Year
- ● Year unicorn status is achieved
- - - - - Pre-unicorn status
- ——— Post-unicorn status
- ⟶ Time from unicorn status to Exit

Exhibit 1: Timeline of selected Southeast Asia tech startups hitting unicorn status and exiting until October 2021. Notice the industries of these startups and how the business models have become more focused or sophisticated over time. [2][3]

portfolio companies. We discuss these exit options further in Chapter 12.

The bandwagon effect is not all there is. Still, it is certainly a strong macro-indicator of where a market is headed, and possibly a basis for building one's own investment thesis. For the venture capitalist, especially those looking for early-stage deals, spotting these gravity wells can be useful, not to join them, but rather to avoid them entirely and spot where new gravity wells can be made.

Venture Capital is a two-way street; funding is only as good as it is used

Another effect of the unicorns creating gravity wells in the region is that this not only pulled in other startups, but also funds beyond Southeast Asia. As these unicorns raised more and more rounds towards the end of the 2010s, the region saw the likes of Softbank Ventures, Warburg Pincus, and KKR becoming more active and raising funds specifically for this part of the world.

The corporate development arms of Silicon Valley and Hangzhou also started putting larger stakes into these unicorns, like Facebook (now Meta), Paypal, JD, Tencent, and Alibaba. The rounds that came into these unicorns reached such a size that many pundits began wondering how long these unicorns could keep raising while still taking on huge losses.

This brings us to another important aspect of venture capital: **venture capital funding is a two-way street; a commitment, a relationship.** The job of a venture capitalist doesn't end with signing term sheets and wiring money — in fact, some will even say that the real work starts there, ensuring the company uses the cash for profit-making growth and not loss-making growth. Venture capital funding is only as good as it is used. Certainly, some companies have gotten away with venture capital funding subsidizing costs and losses, but at the end of the day, a business must turn a profit to be sustainable and continue providing the value it creates.

This craze around funding Southeast Asia's first generation of tech unicorns hit the brakes of reality with the double-whammy of underwhelming IPOs and IPO attempts by loss-making tech companies in 2019 (most notably by WeWork) and the COVID-19 pandemic. Headlines pushed by unicorns in the region switched focus from "grow, grow, grow" to "grow, grow, and let's also be profitable."

Southeast Asia's golden age

The initial onset of the pandemic in 2020 forced many startups to embrace being lean since fundraising also stalled in the first half of 2020. But what was thought to be the pandemic-driven end of a 10-year bull run in Southeast Asia's private markets turned out to be the beginning of the region's golden age.

For early-stage startups going from seed funding (i.e., the first round of raising private capital) to exit, the influx of capital has multiple sources or underlying factors, which we list below:

- **VC dry powder ferries SEA through COVID:** Venture capital dry powder (money saved up) raised from the fundraising craze in 2017–2019 picked up pace in the latter half of 2020 and provided a critical lifeline for some startups in their portfolios.
- **Bifurcation of major innovation hubs:** Tension between China and the US has also impacted tech companies' internationalization across these two innovation hubs. Chinese tech companies, especially Bytedance, Tencent, and Alibaba, are rethinking traditional expansion plans, which have often involved trying to break through to the US, and are instead doubling down on emerging markets like Southeast Asia where regulation is friendlier and the competition landscape is greener. This movement of companies into Southeast Asia creates greater accessible capital from these tech companies through corporate development offices and corporate venture capital (CVC) funds.
- **Shifts in the investment value chain:** Late-stage players are entering in earlier rounds, creating a more complete investment value chain and pathway to exit for startups in the region. Global investors, including family offices, are placing their bets in the

ring of Southeast Asia in earlier stages like Series A and B rounds. In contrast, the Softbanks and KKRs of the world in the latter part of the 2010s have focused on late stage plays.

- **Public market activity and liquidity:** Increased public market activity coincided with the pandemic's initial onset and supported a flurry of Wall Street tech IPOs in 2020. Special purpose acquisition companies (SPACs) as a public markets vehicle have also found their way into emerging markets like Southeast Asia.

  Sea Group was one of the beneficiaries of the COVID-19 public markets rally, seeing its valuation grow up to US$150 billion over 2020. This drew greater attention from public markets to the region. Then, SPACs targeting Southeast Asia have also found favorable targets in regional unicorns that have been piling on their valuation with subsequent private rounds in the last three to four years.

  The interest of Wall Street has now also renewed motivations for local exchanges like SGX and IDX to also drive more interest among tech companies to list. A good case in point is SGX's recent introduction of the SPAC listing framework in the latter half of 2021, while IDX's adoption of a similar strategy is currently under regulatory review. Even without the SPAC option available in many Southeast Asia markets in 2021, Bukalapak went public through an IPO on the IDX, while Grab and PropertyGuru underwent mergers with SPACs Altimeter and Bridgetown 2 respectively to access public markets in the US.

  As local bourses try to attract more tech companies to the public markets, it is also worth noting that there has been an influx of public market retail investors in Southeast Asia markets, especially Indonesia and Vietnam, over the pandemic, enabled by digital stock brokerage and mutual funds platforms like Ajaib and Finhay.

- **Third-wave corporate innovation driving M&As:** Though public market exit opportunities for startups in Southeast Asia have increased, M&As still dominate the exit landscape in Southeast Asia. Alongside greater interests of more old-line and traditional corporates in investing in startups, there is also a new wave of corporate venture capital with funds and acquisitions coming from homegrown tech startups.

The first wave of corporate innovation saw corporates dipping their feet into the startup pool through low-commitment partnerships. Then the second wave features corporates setting up investment vehicles to have a more direct and strategic influence in the way startups are able to bring value to corporate strategy. The third, new wave is all about startups themselves scaling up to become these massive technology groups and also setting up their own CVC funds to invest in the next generation of startups.

Third-wave corporation innovation through these unicorn CVCs bring in the best of both worlds: the size and scale of a corporation with the understanding and experience of what it takes to grow a startup. The foremost example is Sea Group's US$1 billion venture fund.

- **China's wealth rush into Singapore:** Political instability in Hong Kong and antitrust moves to the likes of Alibaba and Tencent have sped up the rush of Chinese wealth from family offices and high net worth individuals (HNWIs) into Singapore as a place to invest in the global south (Southeast Asia + India).

- **Low-interest rates:** There are multiple ways to slice and dice this. In the short-term, low-interest rates have created a high level of liquidity which allows people, especially the wealthy, to spend more on long-term investments instead of short-term purchases. On the other hand, in the long-term, low-interest rates, especially in Southeast Asia, could lead to higher spending, more monetization sources, and more venture-backable companies.

It is worth noting that along with this influx of capital comes an influx of talent, especially entrepreneurs and engineers, that has opened the floodgates for more startups to emerge and hire technical talent. More professionals are also entering the tech ecosystem, be it as employees of startups, founders, or investors, and some more senior people from corporate backgrounds taking up advisor and C-suite positions with their experience. For example, the entry of big tech companies from the US and China seeking greener pastures in Southeast Asia has seen them hiring more people to build up their headquarters, not just for Southeast Asia, but for the larger East Asia region. This brings more people in the region into the tech ecosystem. Apart from pulling in more talent into tech companies, their expansion has seen former employees also looking into Southeast Asia to build their startups and products.

For the early-stage venture capitalist in Southeast Asia, the fundraising craze towards the end of the 2010s and the ensuing pandemic boom shifted the dynamic of the two-way street. Before the 2010s and early parts of that decade, venture capitalists had more leverage to select which startups they would back, given that there were more early-stage players, no clear winners in most verticals, and unproven models in the region. But as unicorns have emerged and some even went into the public markets like Garena, now Sea Group, the validation from the public markets and late-stage investors has shifted more power to the founders. This is traditionally the case as venture capital is an asset class where the assets still choose the investors at the end of the day.

Early going into 2022, however, this dynamic shifted as valuations in the public tech markets, especially in the US, took a dive, negatively impacting growth stage investor gains and tightening the belts of early-stage investors. This shift came about due to the pandemic as well as global conflicts that came about in 2022, creating a prolonged strain on global supply chains and causing inflation.

Private funding in startups in Southeast Asia were also impacted by the market correction, ultimately giving investors more leverage as demand for capital surpassed supply investors were willing to dole out. Companies with valuations that were significantly marked up in 2021 but unable to keep up with these valuations through their business model or margins alone were put in a precarious position in this market.

The juxtaposition of 2021 and 2022's fundraising environments shows the volatility of this market dynamic between investors and founders. What really enables companies to endure through the changing market climates is having a healthy business model more than a dependence on external funding. The latter is best treated as a vehicle for scale rather than a prerequisite for growth.

Even with the changes in fundraising conditions at the open of the 2020s, a continuing trend is the competitive and relatively saturated venture capital markets in the US and China driving investors to Southeast Asia. This means the competition has stacked even further for venture capitalists in the region. As shown in Exhibit 2, dry powder has accumulated in the region from 2011 to 2021, with closed VC fundraising exceeding VC deployment more consistently towards the end of the decade. It is not enough to simply pitch the region as an investment thesis (i.e., come and invest in Southeast Asia!) or to pitch being a platform for the startups in the region as a value-add.

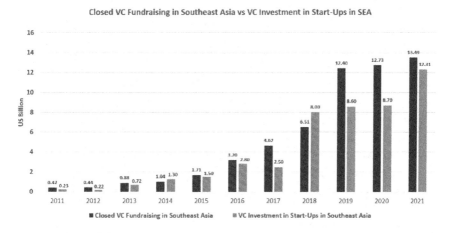

Exhibit 2: Comparing supply and demand for capital in SEA (2010–2020). Specifically closed VC fundraising (from LPs) versus closed VC startup investments per year in Southeast Asia. Data taken from Pitchbook.

This pressure makes it more critical for aspiring venture capitalists to grasp the foundations of investing in and building great companies, and then unlearn what needs to be unlearned to meet the nuances of being a VC in Southeast Asia. That is the first rule of being a venture capitalist in Southeast Asia, and that is something we will continuously come back to throughout the book.

So, What do Venture Capitalists do, Exactly?

Venture capitalists do not just make investments in startups. They do not just build companies. Nor do they just manage assets for a high-risk asset class. Settling on these mechanical definitions limits the potential creativity that could come out of being in venture capital.

In fact, the origins of venture capital do not stem from technology companies or asset management as we know it today. Some will say history's first venture capitalist was Princess Isabella of Spain. She funded Ferdinand Magellan's expedition to circumnavigate the world, which no explorer — at least in the history of the Europeans — had ever been able to do before.

Since then, venture capital has been a catalyst for the emergence of every major global industry, from the oil industry to clean technology, from whaling to alternative proteins, from the gold rush to the digital rush. Some will even say that venture capital made a country like Singapore into what it was today, and that Lee Kuan Yew was one of the greatest venture capitalists of his time.

In an interview, Yinglan explains why Singapore's growth as a country is a source of great learning for venture capitalists:

"[You can] think about venture capital in the context of Mr. Lee Kuan Yew, who founded Singapore as a republic where the GDP per capita was around US$500. And now it's like almost US$60,000. So over 40 years, he made more than a 120 times increase in GDP per capita, with his team of lieutenants.

I find I'm quite fortunate because I get to hear all the stories of the early days of nation-building, how Singapore started from a swamp can be applied, especially when we work with our companies. A lot of companies have had near-death crises and lots of challenges but...similarly, no one expected Singapore to thrive 40 or 50 years ago. It was a swampland with a small population. And in that sense, a lot of our companies are exactly that. They are faced with large incumbents, limited resources, a limited number of people, and [building] products is very rough.

How do they overcome all odds to defeat the large incumbents with more resources? In some sense I'm quite fortunate that a lot of the lessons...are quite instructive to how I think, when a startup asks me, or when a company I'm on the board of, [asks about being] in a space with competition and what [should] they do." [1]

So, what *do* venture capitalists do?

Venture capitalists back those creating value where none previously existed, before anyone else believes in them. This definition of venture capital is not new or groundbreaking per se, but it is important to emphasize because this role, across history, has three implications for markets, economies, and societies that apply even to Southeast Asia.

You're not just investing; you're influencing talent and capital distribution

The first implication is that by backing those creating new value — or as the business world has more recently come to word it, **blue oceans** — talent and capital distribution are shaped by venture capital.

We hinted at the influence of venture capital on capital distribution earlier, discussing how venture capital is a two-way street and how investors had more leverage in Southeast Asia's early days of technology-focused venture capital. However, that dynamic has since then shifted due to increased venture capital activity and more entrepreneurs coming into the fray. Founders follow the money early on in an ecosystem's life cycle; then, as the ecosystem matures, investors start to follow founders.

But capital distribution goes beyond the venture capital industry itself. Family offices, sovereign wealth funds, and other types of investors (even the public markets at times) are readily influenced by the proven successes of venture capitalists because the former recognizes that the latter makes very early, very risky, long-term investments. If these very early, very risky, long-term investments are successful, then it's a sign of a big return coming in, not just for any company but potentially for an entire industry or economy.

So these other investors and funds either *follow on* the investments of these venture capitalists, or *become investors (limited partners) in* their funds. **Southeast Asia's venture capital story is the story of capital distribution shifts catalyzed by venture capitalists. It is a self-fulfilling loop.**

Talent distribution is influenced by venture capital on three levels. First, by investing in businesses, these businesses can create more jobs, which then attracts talent who would have otherwise gone for jobs in other places. Just over the past century, talent has shifted from working in factories to working in sales and distribution offices to working in technology startups. This has been shaped by how "work" has been redefined even in the past two to three decades by venture-backed products and services (e.g. Microsoft, Apple, Zoom, Slack, WeChat, etc.), moving from 9-to-5 offices to flexible and remote arrangements.

Second, they can pull in more, presumably higher-quality talent on a firm-to-firm level, mainly because they can now afford it with fundraising. Depending on how the startup handles its cash and develops its company culture, talent can either stay for the long haul or quickly jump ship, but the point is that talent distribution can be shifted across companies and firms by the decisions made by venture capitalists.

Finally, venture capitalists themselves help source talent for startups. Some early-stage firms even help tech startups hire co-founders and build their first engineering teams. This has long-term ripple effects as these leaders can then hire and direct the kind of organization they are to build. A-tier talent hires A-tier talent, B-tier talent hires C-tier talent, and C-tier talent has difficulty hiring.

Venture capitalists back those creating value where none previously existed, before anyone else believes in them.

Don't just invest, back

If the first implication refers to the impact of backing "those creating new value," the second implication of this definition revolves around the verb: to back.

"To back" carries a heavy weight and responsibility, a long-term commitment that goes beyond investing capital. We hinted at this implication earlier when talking about venture capital as a two-way street — it's a commitment, a relationship. The often repeated line, "I got your back" in action and adventure movies, means that these characters are sticking it out to the bitter end, for better or for worse. The foremost example that comes to mind is Samwise, the hobbit backing Frodo all the way from the Shire to Mordor — and through it all, saving Frodo from downfall many times. Founders will know they have brought in the right investors when these investors support them just as well through the crises as they do through the milestones.

Venture capital is ultimately a service industry — service for the entrepreneurs and companies they back, service for the limited partners who invest in their funds. As such, venture capitalists often support founders in various ways, and most firms in Southeast Asia have institutionalized these operations by forming teams around these specific value-adds:

- **Hiring:** VCs help founders find talent, senior executives, and C-suite often, but in a region like Southeast Asia where hiring tech talent is challenging, most firms in the region extend assistance for these kinds of roles.
- **Legal and Accounting:** VCs help founders set up domiciles, look at term sheet offers from other investors, secure licenses, monitor their financials, and other legal needs of the company.
- **Technology:** VCs help advise founders on tech stack and cybersecurity and even assist in troubleshooting.
- **Product and Strategy:** VCs help advise founders on the direction of product development, go-to-market strategy, market expansion, and overall how to grow the business, often based on an accumulated understanding of what previous closest similar business models have done and what the local market needs (The first rule of venture capital in Southeast Asia).

- **Marketing:** VCs help founders with press releases, gaining and managing exposure to media outlets, investors and talent, and positioning the company through thought leadership.

We refer to these value-adds listed above as **functional value-adds**, as they support specific functions that normally have existing teams within an established company. The issue is that startups, especially those in the early stages, do not necessarily have the people and budget to fill in all these roles, so the VC acts as a multi-purpose agency to ideally offset costs for startups in finding their own agencies. VCs either hire teams of specialists into the firm, or if they are going down a leaner route, they hire a point person who then outsources the capabilities to third parties.

Apart from these functional value-adds, there are two more types of key value-adds. The second is **network-based value-adds**, which involve three types of networks (that we will revisit in the following chapter but for different purposes):

- **Portfolio:** VCs try to link up portfolio founders to create synergies among companies. VCs also align their investment thesis/investment strategy to create a portfolio that can ultimately support each other in their growth.
- **Limited Partners:** It is important to remember that venture capital investors are also financial platforms for other investors (limited partners) to direct their capital towards these tech startups. Limited partners, especially those with strong ties to the global tech ecosystem, like former unicorn founders, can generate useful network effects and provide practical insights for founders, and VCs leverage this potential even in attracting founders to their fund.
- **Industry Connections:** VC investors thrive on growing their professional networks, and one way this network across industries comes into play is when founders need business introductions, be it for a potential hire, advice, or partnerships.

The third type of value-add is around **fundraising value-adds**, basically helping them get the startup from the point from which they invested (in a venture capital firm's case, from seed or Series A) to a liquidity event (e.g., IPO or M&A). So VCs help founders navigate the fundraising environment, from helping them find the right CFOs, who are critical in preparing data rooms that investors request for, to helping them clean and beef up pitch decks depending on the round (e.g., a founder used to pitching with a seed or Series A deck will have to upgrade their deck for later rounds). Another value-add is introducing them to potential follow-on investors and in certain cases, topping off these rounds with their follow-on investment. In Exhibit 3, we summarize these functional, network-based, and fundraising value-adds.

In between these rounds, VCs support founders in managing their cap tables and board meetings and getting to a pre-money valuation where the next round actually increases their valuation (i.e., this is where a lot of the functional value-adds come in). Then as the company nears a liquidity event, the VCs also support the company in getting the right people and partners to facilitate the exit.

Different venture capitalists have varying strengths across these value-adds, and **this mix becomes a key selling point for VC firms.** It's not always necessary to have all these value-adds — it ultimately depends on the needs of the portfolio. What is important to note is

Venture Capital Value Adds

Functional	Network-based	Fundraising
Hiring	Portfolio	Follow-on investments
Product & Strategy	Limited Partners	Exits (IPO/M&A)
Marketing	Industry Connections	
Legal & Accounting		
Technology		

Exhibit 3:   Venture capitalists provide value-add not just to support the growth of their portfolio and compete over attracting companies to join their portfolio, but also because it has concrete financial returns.

that the financial motivation here for venture capitalists is that by providing these value-adds, the business can go beyond a certain valuation faster and more efficiently. Creating this margin will enable the VC to recognize DPI (distributions to paid-in capital) or ROI (return-on-investment) that they can then return to their limited partners and then profit from as a firm.

There are two considerations to note regarding value-adds. The first is that the degree to which venture capitalists will offer specific value-adds over others depends on several factors apart from the VC's capabilities as mentioned earlier:

- Their ownership in the company (if the VC owns less, they are less likely to provide value-add),
- The company's performance (if the company is likely to win, the more they are likely to double down), and
- The stage of growth of the company (in general — though it also depends on the need, the functional value-adds decrease as the company grows).

The second consideration for value-adds, which will be discussed in latter chapters, will be the reality that venture capitalists cannot service all their startups 100% of the time. The laws of physics make this impossible. It is a skill developed by the best VCs to be able to strategize time and value-add allocation towards their portfolio, in the same way that they calculate follow-on dollar allocations within their funds.

This reality makes it more than likely that some founders will receive more of the value-add from multiple investors, as investors want to double down on founders and companies that prove themselves to be leading in their verticals and markets, and where they have significant, if not majority, outside shareholder ownership.

Be early to increase your odds and be more effective

The third implication of the definition focuses on the "before anyone else believes in them" part. Because venture capitalists increase their odds of success by investing in those creating value that previously did not exist, it is important to invest early. The later investors jump into a blue ocean, the less likely that they will be first or have the luxury of finding the winners in that blue ocean. The fact that there is increasing competition in a market like Southeast Asia, makes being early in a vertical or industry even tougher.

Being early to an industry or market does not only increase the odds of success for venture capitalists, but it also enables these investors to be more effective in creating the talent and capital distribution as well as backing companies in the space.

Being early enables investors to be more effective in talent and capital distribution because they will have a better grasp of how the industry or market evolves. Then it also enables venture capitalists to more effectively back the companies they fund because founders are more likely to trust those who believed in them first and stayed with them through thick and thin.

What Makes Southeast Asia so Attractive to Venture Capitalists?

So we've breezed through a brief retelling of how venture capital evolved in Southeast Asia, and defined what venture capitalists do: back those creating value where none previously existed, before anyone else believes in them. So, what makes Southeast Asia so special? Why is it so important to recognize and understand that Southeast Asia is not Silicon Valley as a venture capitalist? There are three main characteristics of Southeast Asia as a market that have made it attractive to venture capitalists.

Perks of being an emerging market

The first is Southeast Asia's growth potential as an emerging market. One might wonder why a region with markets significantly smaller than the US or China, apart from Indonesia, would be able to nest technology companies that raise at massive valuations. It's less about absolute values that venture capitalists are interested in, and more about the trajectories of where internet adoption, digitalization, and consumer spending could go in Southeast Asia's economies.

These continually superseded expectations of growth compensate for the lack of global expansion of many of the region's billion-dollar companies. For a startup in Southeast Asia, the true market is the region. Staying local puts a low ceiling on multiples, while going globally forces the company to compete in a presumably tougher environment — of course, either of these options can still work depending on the business model and industry, but in general going regional is always part of the plan. That said, there is Indonesia, the only market in Southeast Asia where companies can afford to simply focus on a singular market given its size.

The combination of a rising consumer class and increasing smartphone and internet penetration has always been a card to play when pitching the potential of a company in the region, and for good reason. It's usually these two factors that influence a technology ecosystem's growth from the demand side of the market and raise the value for selling digital products and services at scale. In China, it was primarily the rising consumer class that propelled the likes of Alibaba, Bytedance, or Tencent to lead the market there, and why the dominant tech companies in the country were built on social media and consumer services. Meanwhile in the US, it was primarily the adoption of digital and internet technologies that drove the ecosystem, so the kind of tech companies that came to dominate Silicon Valley had their origins in computers, semiconductors, search engine algorithms, and operating software.

In Southeast Asia, it's a combination of a rising consumer class plus increasing tech adoption — but the technological adoption is more centered around smartphones, rather than desktop or laptop computers. This has enabled tech startups in the region to rethink existing applications for mobile-first interfaces. The rate of mobile internet adoption has been speeding up in Southeast Asia markets like Indonesia, Singapore, and Vietnam almost at pace with neighboring China within the 2010–2020, pointing towards a larger opportunity in the former markets where there have been more blue oceans (or less competition) over the same period.

The interest in Southeast Asia's growth potential also stems from its nature as an emerging market, which also means that the kind of problems being solved in the region are also different from those in more mature markets. Looking at the unicorns in the region, it's easy to observe that tech companies emerging from the region are mainly tackling mass market and livelihood needs — from more efficient marketplaces and logistics, to transitioning from Cash-on-Delivery to online payments, to improving MSME financing and supply chains.

Apart from catering to more livelihood and mass-market needs, there's also the consideration of affordability to cost-effectively reach scale, though pricing strategy may not always be the right go-to-market. This could easily mean thin margins, especially for marketplace models, but the companies trade-off margins for scale in the long-run — scale that with the right strategy could enable getting into adjacent services with higher margins.

Localization ain't a challenge — it's an advantage!

The second characteristic of Southeast Asia that makes it attractive is the diversity of the region, and that it is not as monolithic in regulation and culture as the US, China, or even India. This diversity sets up a barrier for global competitors who want to enter the market, as we wrote on *Insignia Business Review* in 2021:

> "One go-to example is Uber, which incidentally realized relatively huge returns from the SPAC merger of its former regional competitor Grab in the past month. Uber's approach of selling an "exclusive, chauffeur service" in the region was foreign to a middle class who were well accustomed to commuting and taking taxis." [4]

This opened up the market for a player like Grab that brought ride-hailing to taxi services. Indonesia's Go-jek took it a step further and tapped into the fact that many in Indonesia commuted or rode two-wheeled vehicles (ojeks) over four-wheeled ones (taxis).

Alibaba has also found it challenging to penetrate the region, specifically through Lazada (which was a foreign player incubated by Rocket Internet), with the numerous leadership changes needed to be made, and the tough competition by local player Shopee, formed by gaming unicorn Sea Group, as we wrote on *Insignia Business Review* in 2020:

> "The political, economic and cultural differences of the various Southeast Asian markets make it difficult for a one-size-fits-all strategy, as Alibaba has been accustomed to in China. While there are similarities between the two regions that stretch back in history, these are ultimately two very different animals that Alibaba is dealing with. Success in China can build up the resources to enter Southeast Asia but does not ensure success.
>
> Even within Southeast Asia, the differences across countries make it difficult for local players to expand in the region. Apart from navigating the differences in space, there's also the differences in time. Southeast Asia is also maturing and growing on its own learning curve as an ecosystem at the same time that Alibaba is getting a hold of how to win in the region. It's like trying to land a plane on a runway that is also moving and changing in shape.
>
> That said, their hands-on approach (compared to other China tech majors like Tencent) has enabled them to be nimbler and more flexible…Whether or not this responsiveness will result in the right answers for the region remains to be seen.
>
> It's also worth noting that Alibaba's strengths in terms of rapid expansion and in-house technology translate differently in Southeast Asia, where rapid expansion is easily checked by market nuances and cross-border challenges and in-house tech can be difficult to implement locally in a market where tech talent remains challenging to come by." [5]

This also makes regional competition less straightforward. Blue oceans in Southeast Asia don't become red as quickly because of multiple markets — you could have a payments company in Indonesia then a similar company in Vietnam that doesn't necessarily compete.

Top 10 Most Visited E-commerce Websites in Southeast Asia
Total average visits obtained by each platform in 2020

Shopee — 281,385,626
Lazada — 137,154,967
tokopedia — 88,889,000
bukalapak — 35,728,425
thegioididong — 28,650,650
TIKI — 22,491,175
blibli — 19,253,900
Sendo — 14,769,700
— 14,348,450
— 7,282,700

Exhibit 4:   Lazada was an early entry into Southeast Asia's ecommerce scene but the rise of Shopee and a whole host of other competitors has made the landscape tougher for Alibaba's ecommerce arm in the region. Data taken from iPrice Group (2021). [6]

As we see in Exhibit 4, although Lazada entered early into Southeast Asia's ecommerce sector and was able to capitalize on that, many other players have emerged to taking on specific markets, like Tokopedia in Indonesia or Tiki in Vietnam.

The same can be said for various segments — there's ecommerce mainly targeting urban areas in Indonesia, then ecommerce models more suited to 2nd-tier, 3rd-tier and rural areas in the same country that doesn't necessarily compete.

The localization challenge that many foreign players face and the abundance of subsegments and markets in the region present opportunities for local players to build a moat or an advantage out of their ability to localize — and this is very attractive to venture capitalists.

There are several levels of localization that venture capitalists can consider:

1. regulatory (e.g., licenses, public-private partnerships, patents, government contracts),

2. socio-cultural (e.g. community-based agent network, consumer behavior, spending habits), and,
3. physical (e.g. physical assets like warehouses, production, supply chains).

When not being early can be a good thing

The third characteristic is that Southeast Asia is not quite early in the game of digitalization. It's in a good position to benefit from learnings of and talent from more mature ecosystems, especially China, given how the market was previously in a similar situation as Southeast Asia is now in terms of its digital adoption. As it is often said in panel discussions, **"Southeast Asia is China ten years ago, but the pace of growth is going faster."**

We see this learning happen not just in terms of founders retrofitting business models from mature markets to meet local needs, but also in terms of the founders and talent themselves and where they come from. Returnees — those who studied or worked for some time in other regions and cities, from the likes of Silicon Valley or Brazil before returning to Southeast Asia — often populate the list of founders of unicorns and fast-growing startups, and for good reason. The education and experience they gain elsewhere make their perspective more holistic. But going back to the first rule, that is not enough. **Southeast Asia is its own region with its own nuances that need to be understood.**

Three Best Practices

1. Invest early. Avoid the bandwagons and gravity wells, unless you started it.
2. As a venture capitalist, it's important to figure out your value-add, not just on a firm level but also on an individual level. How can you create value for your portfolio companies?
3. It's valuable for venture capitalists to help their founders embrace Rule #1, whether that means connections or better understanding the nuances of a local market or industry.

Chapter 2

Rule #2: If You Think You are Aiming Big, You Need to Go Bigger

How do Venture Capitalists Win and Make (A LOT) of Money?

Venture capital is a high-risk game, where investors cannot say in all certainty whether or not the founders they invest in will turn out to build companies that will make 100x return on investment. So how do venture capitalists work the odds and win?

It's important to understand the primary motivation of a venture capitalist, and that is **to grow the money they manage by as high of a multiple as possible**. This is separate from the kind of impact they have on the larger startup ecosystem and economy, which we discussed in the previous chapter.

Venture capitalists and venture capital firms are judged by this ability to grow their funds and hit returns that are ideally above other asset classes or the S&P500 and the public markets through their DPI (distribution to paid-in-capital or return on investment) and fund multiples. Industry analysts also look at the **vintage year of funds**, which is the year when the first investment from the fund is made, to gauge how well it performed later on, as the market environment in a particular year could affect the valuation at which funds are investing.

Venture capitalists make money primarily through earning **carried interest. Exhibit 1 illustrates the math behind this venture capital business model above, and we explain this further below.**

Before getting to carried interest, it is also important to discuss the concept of management fees. Although technically management fees is money paid to the venture capitalists for running the

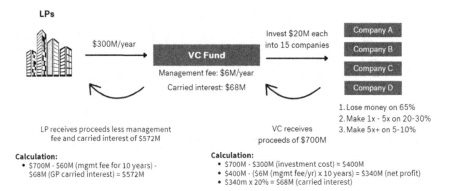

Exhibit 1:   How VC funds get money and make money.

fund, it is not money "made" in the same sense as how carried interest is generated through investments.

Management fees are typically a percentage of the money that limited partners put in, with the industry standard being around 2% of the total fund (some can get up to 3%). Limited partners are the investors in a venture capital fund, and in this respect, venture capitalists are essentially offering their fund management services to these limited partners when they put together a fund. So this fee covers all operational expenses of the firm to deliver these fund management services, unaffected by the performance of any individual fund. This fee accumulates as venture capitalists raise more funds, so two funds worth US$100 million each would accumulate US$4 million in management fees given 2%.

On the other hand, carried interest is tied directly to the performance of the fund and the companies this fund is invested in. One can think of carried interest as profit-sharing between the limited partners and the firm. This is traditionally 20% of the money made on top of the fund.

Assuming a US$100 million fund gets an overall US$240 million return (2.4x return), the original US$100 million is returned to the limited partners or investors in the fund, and the US$140 million made on top of that fund is split between the limited partners and the firm 80–20. So US$28 million goes to the fund managers or venture capital firms. The percentages for both are already set as the venture capital firm fundraises. And then that US$28 million is split among the employees in the firm depending on the individual carry agreements set within the firm (e.g., the one who led the deal will get a substantial carry out of the firm's total carried interest, for example).

While management fees still have to be deducted for operating costs (which is the fee's purpose in any case), carried interests are almost entirely profit, so the venture capital firm's activities are much more focused on the latter than the former, and the use of the management fees are ideally put to increase the chances of getting a significant carry.

Investments are "called" upon by the general partners or VC firm when the investment is about to be made. This method allows limited partners to avoid losing money from the inflation that comes from keeping the entire committed capital idle with the VC firm. Apart from these "capital calls", general partners can also take their management fees yearly at the agreed-upon percentage of the committed capital. In some cases, this rate is adjusted over time as limited partners deem their fees to no longer be as needed as before, earlier in the life of the fund when the VCs spend the most time sourcing and growing deals for the fund.

It is important to note that the funds have a lifespan, which means a period of time after which limited partners expect returns to come in from the investments. For a venture capital fund, this is usually five to seven years. In certain markets, creating liquidity events to see returns through secondary sales (i.e., selling ownership of the company to other investors), listing in the public markets, or M&A can take a longer time than others.

This is especially the case for emerging markets like Southeast Asia, and why M&As dominate the exit landscape — it is easier to gear a startup towards merging or getting acquired and making money out of that than getting a startup to a point where it will make massive returns on the public markets.

This means that the budgeted size of a venture capital fund should match the investment appetite and capabilities of the fund manager. If a fund is too small to make follow-ons, the investors will be stuck making first check seed investments that eventually get diluted as more investors come in on later rounds. If it is too big, then there's also the pressure of exhausting the fund and ensuring that all the investments make some return and that among them, there will be that one fund-making investment.

In general, however, VC funds will want to account not just for the initial investment but all follow-on rounds to support the growth of the company — because growth leads to a higher valuation and a higher likelihood of making substantial returns. Venture capital firms will also want to raise more than one fund, usually with two purposes in mind: (1) to diversify the portfolio (some funds will have completely different investment theses and mandates) and (2) to make more room to double down on winning investments.

This business model of venture capital firms as a fund manager in a high-risk, high-return asset class incentivizes the second rule of venture capital in Southeast Asia: **Never settle. If you think you're aiming big, you need to go bigger.**

This rule applies not just to Southeast Asia or just to venture capitalists. Even founders need to continuously think of the next level of growth even as they achieve milestones they have set previously. **The idea behind this rule is that because of the risk of failure on the part of the fund to make significant, above-market returns, venture capitalists cannot afford to cast small nets and make small bets.**

In this chapter, we cover the key principles of venture capital that enable investors in this asset class to make money, how venture capitalists decide where to invest the money of their limited partners, and how venture capital firms are generally structured and operate to make these potential fund making investments.

Principle 1: Venture capital is a zero-sum game

The first principle is that venture capital is a zero-sum game. This means that in venture capital, investing in one company means that the investors are declaring the company in question as a *de facto* winner of the space. **It becomes a conflict of interest and breach of trust to invest in a competitor.**

This seems quite obvious but in Southeast Asia, it is more complicated because of what we mentioned in the previous chapter about competition in the region being less straightforward. So if you're managing a fund investing in multiple countries, then you have that space to invest in similar companies that are in different countries.

The presumption is that these companies will never cross paths while you are an investor in them (in some cases, once a clear winner emerges, the investor may opt to exit the other players even if they are in other markets to double down) or that these companies will eventually end up having different growth trajectories or focus on different aspects of the vertical.

Another implication of venture capital being a zero-sum game is that intuitively, **the more competitors raise, the harder it will be to prop up the company against them.** Conversely, the more your company raises vis-a-vis its competitors, and the larger this gap in funding becomes, the more likely your company will be the winner in the space. But the end results are not always clear-cut. This David vs Goliath scenario does not always result in the smaller player readily bowing out to the players with the larger war chest. **More than the funding, it boils down to the value customers find in the products and services being offered by the companies.**

The funding primarily provides greater room for the more well-resourced players to adjust their strategy and double down on their lead, but it is still possible for larger players — because of their size — to miss things that smaller players can tap into and use to stay in the playing field and potentially win in other ways.

This lack of clarity or slow pace for the market to declare its winners is prominent in Southeast Asia, especially in markets where the regionally dominant players are usually *not* local players. We saw this in Vietnam for example in the delivery space, where both Grab and Gojek (initially GoViet) came into the country as the "Goliaths" competing against smaller, local players, but it was not a clear victory.

The very same difficulties that we mentioned in the previous chapter that Uber and Alibaba experienced on a regional level could also be experienced by regional players on a country level.

What this means for venture capitalists is that it becomes more important to form a well-informed thesis on what it takes to win a specific vertical or market before even investing. Forming a thoughtful thesis is like mapping out where one is most likely to find winners in an industry or market. Once the investor has committed, it is important to go bigger on backing them especially when they have the potential to win the space, because nothing is certain until the results speak for themselves.

Principle 2: It's all about the fund returners

The second principle is that it doesn't matter how many startups you back as a venture capitalist. **What matters is how many of these companies succeeded** — how many startups among those you backed resulted in an exit that returned 100x or more than the amount that was initially invested into the company.

Given a fund invested in 100 companies, for all these companies to result in fund-making returns each, or basically 100x the amount of the fund all in all, is an unlikely if not impossible scenario. It is more possible, though still not likely, to get a normal distribution where you have ten to thirty companies returning the amounts greater than what was invested in them while the majority returning at cost. It is much more likely that among those 100 companies, there is less than a 10% chance of getting a company that will return the investment and then some (say through a secondary sale), and even less chance of getting a company that will return the investment at an amount that recuperates the entire fund. These probabilities boil down to the reality that the chances of failure or slow, underperforming growth are extremely high for a tech startup. This reality in the world of venture capital has been commonly visualized in the form of a steep curve or a pie with a small slice representing the fund returners as shown in Exhibit 2.

What investors are interested in is not the average performance of all these 100 companies, but the performance of those few (often single digit) companies that do perform exponentially better than expected and grow to a size that enables the investor to recoup the entire fund's amount from that single investment. **It's all about investing in potential fund makers.**

What this means for venture capitalists is that while investing in a lot of companies does not necessarily equate to success, it increases the chance of striking gold. Of course, the assumption here is that each investment is being made with the rationale that this company could be that rare fund maker. Casting a big net also doesn't just refer to the quantity of investments, it also refers to the breadth of where the investors are looking for these investments.

VC Fund Return on Investments

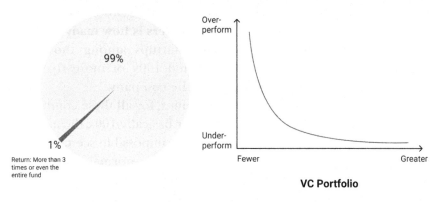

Exhibit 2:   Pie graph and curve for fund makers.

This is also why funds of a certain size are usually sector and market-agnostic. It also means that it is important to be able to double down or continue investing in the winners — these calls are made by tracking certain metrics that indicate whether the firm should add more to their initial investment in a future round of fundraising.

In Southeast Asia, where there are relatively fewer companies but opportunities abound, some venture capitalists don't wait for the apple to drop. Instead of casting a net, they genetically engineer the fish themselves, incubating companies by bringing together potential co-founders and supporting them literally from day zero. Other funds have also positioned themselves as accelerators or incubators to take advantage of the talent influx into the region to support the launch of ventures pre-founding team and pre-idea.

Another caveat to the probabilities of success drawn out for illustrative purposes in this book is that they can change when it comes to the success of a company. A company that was unlikely to become a fund maker could turn its fortune 180 degrees with a product pivot that eventually clicked for a more massive market, for example. The kind of backing that the investor provides throughout this relationship can have a significant impact on whether or not these changes in fortune will happen.

Principle 3: It's bad to lose, and even worse to miss a win

The third principle is that the winning misses weigh more heavily on investors than the losses. A commonly asked question in one-on-one interviews with venture capitalists is, "What is one company that you regret passing on?" The venture capital firm Bessemer Venture Partners even went so far as to promote the companies they believe were big misses on their part. "Honoring the companies we missed," writes the headline of the page listing the likes of Airbnb, Apple, Atlassian, and eBay, and for each company they detail how they met the founders, delayed or didn't do a follow-up, and how these companies wound up doubling or tripling their valuation shortly after.

But for most venture capital firms, while they don't display their misses for the world to see, they do internalize these misses through weekly meetings where they review these companies and how to avoid making these mistakes from a process and best practices point-of-view. In certain cases, upon review, what may seem as winning misses on face value were actually not misses because they did not really fit the fund's investment thesis or there were red flags that the firm could not have accepted at the time and they had no choice but to pass. **Being prescient of the reality that there are companies that one misses is important and making time to study these misses sharpens venture capital intuition.**

The previous principle — that venture capitalists focus on finding fund makers — is the reason why this is a widely accepted best practice in the industry. Every company that becomes a fund maker for another fund is essentially a massive opportunity cost on the part of the firm that could have followed up or pursued the deal but didn't at the time for whatever reason.

At the same time, because of the first principle — that venture capital is a zero-sum game — the cost of winning misses weighs even further. For example, a VC firm backed company A but the competitor company B ended up becoming the winner in the space, and a fund maker for its investors. This means company A could still perform well but it is likely that it may take longer to surpass company B's performance and the likelihood of it being a fund maker for the VC firm may not be as strong. It's important to note that this isn't the former company's fault that the investors missed this win).

Of course, even if investors place a premium on paying attention to winning misses, it doesn't mean there's no value in also learning from the false positives. It's just that it's easier to overlook winning misses and keep finding companies in the same way without realizing that the net that was cast should have been focused elsewhere, or the method of finding companies to invest in had significant gaps. While losses often result from actions of the company itself, **the roots of winning misses often have something to do with how the venture capital firm operates,** which also impacts how the firm ends up picking companies that turn into losses.

In Southeast Asia, where the competition is tighter with fewer players and many vertical and market winners have yet to be decided, regional VC firms won't be able to come up with a list as comprehensive as that of Bessemer's, or most Silicon Valley firms. Because the costs of misses aren't as clear yet, it is an opportunity for investors to continue doubling down on the companies that have potential even if they don't have the biggest war chests and are the Davids in the industry.

Principle 4: What do your founders say about you?

The fourth principle is that when it comes to venture capital, the assets pick the investors. Although we've covered this concept in the previous chapter, what this means in terms of how venture capitalists work the odds and win is that **they need to be able to sell themselves as the ones who can make these companies the fund makers,** as opposed to companies selling their equity (although this does happen when a startup seeks to get acquired, oftentimes to stay liquid).

From the perspective of an entrepreneur, inasmuch as venture capital can have an outsized impact on the industries and economies they pour cash into, venture capital funding isn't always the best type of funding for every type of business, as we wrote in *Navigating ASEANnovation*:

> "And not all companies are suited to take every kind of fuel. Venture capital in particular is like jet fuel that propels companies into space at high speeds of thousands of kilometers per hour. In the tank of the wrong business model, the company could explode. At the same time, venture fuel is not the only fuel out there, though it is the preferred fuel of choice for startups simply because startups aim to grow fast."

Thus, seeking venture capital is often done out of a proactive decision to fuel growth rather than out of desperation and lack of options. Founders are also cautious about parting with ownership in the company, especially to a partner that is presumably also preoccupied with other ventures and may not have aligned interests. **While venture capital's business models rely on deal making, startups don't entirely rely on deals to thrive. With that in mind, it's the companies that have the leverage to choose their investors.**

This means that building the right kind of brand to attract companies that fit the fund's investment thesis and reputation to earn the trust of founders is crucial to a venture capitalist's operation. VCs build their brand and reputation both on a firm level and an individual level, with these two being inseparable. The actions associated with the firm influence a VC's brand on an individual level, while the individual actions of a VC accumulate and shape an opinion on the firm's brand.

While there are many strategies to build a brand on these two levels, the most basic way a venture capitalist builds trust and reputation is through how they form and handle relationships with their founders. Founders will often do (or at least are often advised to do) due diligence on investors even before taking a first call or sending out a cold email. Founders talk to other founders, and they find out what it's like to work with certain investors, or how they were treated in communication during the due diligence process. **These informal conversations can have a more significant impact than any amount of structured marketing strategy.**

We mentioned in the previous chapter that venture capital is a two-way street, and this dynamic also has a role to play in shaping the odds of success for a venture capitalist. If a founder has a lot of good things to say about you, then that is likely to convince other founders they know to talk to you as well. On the other hand, if that founder is an influential person and successful in building their venture, it is likely that they also know other influential and successful people.

This dynamic in venture capital — where assets pick the investors only raises the risk — actually opens up an opportunity for investors to build network effects through the relationships they build and the kind of backing and support they provide to their founders. As a venture capitalist, are you able to list and share the numbers of at least ten founders who can say good things about you?

Principle 5: Invest in companies, back people

The fifth principle is that **venture capitalists invest in companies, but back people.** Although technically and legally, VCs put cash in companies, they build relationships with people — the founders, whose ideas and capabilities they believe in will create value where none hitherto existed (alluding to our definition of what VCs do in the previous chapter). It's important to realize that products and business can pivot, and it's ultimately the people leading these companies who will call the shots that will determine whether or not that company will be a fund maker.

There's one practice that the best venture capitalists do, and that is to be honest and straightforward. By doing so, venture capitalists can add valuable perspectives to how their founders think. Another term for it is to have radical candor.

This radical candor sometimes happens even before founders realize they can be founders, and the partners in a firm convince applicants to become co-founders of ventures rather than join their investment team. It can also happen as founders pitch their ideas pre-product, where the investor runs the founders through multiple ideas and points out which ones are more likely to work more than others. Of course it happens after the deal, as the founders and investors catch up in short calls or in board meetings, and investors tell these founders to get real with how they're measuring growth or competing in the market.

Effective radical candor for the venture capitalist stems from the ability to build up the right connections and expertise to commit to the advice and insights they impart to their founders. VCs don't want to misinform or mislead founders, that only puts them in a bad light and affects them long-term as we discussed in the previous principle. Because venture capitalists are not running the show, **being able to influence the direction of a company ultimately boils down to how good the relationship is with their founders.**

How do VCs Decide Where to Invest?

What are you investing in?

Now that we know what it takes for VCs to succeed, and how to get started from a legal and technical standpoint, it's time to figure out what exactly you plan on investing in. In other words, the **investment thesis:** a research-backed and logical articulation or conceptualization of what kinds of companies an investment firm or venture capitalist believes are worth putting money in. An investment thesis can range in depth from a fund thesis down to a sector (e.g., fintech) and sub-sector (e.g., digital banking) thesis. Having a thoughtful and well-articulated investment thesis is important not just to direct the fund's approach to investing in founders and companies but also to raise money from investors in the fund, or limited partners.

While most regional VCs in Southeast Asia will briefly say that they're [insert headquarter city here]-based funds focused on investing in startups in Southeast Asia, an investment thesis must go deeper than geography. VCs will have different ways of forming their theses, but there are some underlying factors that make an effective investment strategy.

Factor 1: Markets

A farmer working on a small farmland is limited by the amount of crops he can grow on that land. A more fertile and well-irrigated farmland would yield a better harvest. Apart from size and land quality, harvest yield is also impacted by the type of crops grown on the farmland. For example, a hectare of land used to produce strawberries can yield more revenue for the farmer compared to a hectare of land used to produce corn.

Similarly, founders can build large companies if the addressable market is large enough and the market environment is fertile (e.g., for early/nascent markets, this means there is potential for demand to be created). The same idea applies to how venture capitalists consider markets when backing founders.

In this case, planting crops in a more fertile and well-irrigated land refers to investing in a big market typically represented by the total number of addressable users and customers or by the dollar value of total transactions relevant to the market in question.

The motivation to find companies in big markets stems from the second principle mentioned earlier in this chapter, that finding fund makers is paramount. **In order to find fund makers, investors need to be able to find companies in industries where there is space to reach a valuation that *can* return the fund.**

When it comes to tech startups, there are two ways to approach big markets — (1) markets that exist and have massive potential for digitalization, and (2) markets that are not big yet or do not exist yet but are made massive through digitalization.

For example, introducing a new way to transact cars or property (i.e. online and aggregated versus offline and fragmented, for example) or reinventing the way millions of SMEs have packages delivered across an archipelago sees big markets as these industries already exist but are still ripe for disruption and digitalization. These markets are usually very traditional and fraught with inefficiencies.

Then there are markets like ecommerce (eBay and Amazon), ride-hailing (Uber), and flexible short-term rentals (Airbnb) that created new markets and industries that at some point in time did not exist or were thought to be impossible to grow to such an enormous size. These created markets do not just digitalize existing players, but potentially disrupt and replace them by positioning new assets and infrastructure as attractive, entirely new alternatives. Ecommerce began to replace retail shops, ride-hailing began to replace taxis, and short-term rentals began to replace cheap hotels. These big markets usually have to deal with a lot of regulatory white space.

One example in Southeast Asia of a market-creating company is Gojek. As Yinglan shared on a panel hosted by the media publication *DealstreetAsia* in November 2020:

> "When a market is just starting to develop, it's not obvious that it will be big. In the early days of Gojek, nobody really imagined that the two-wheeler gojeks could be expanded to foods, groceries, parcels...so I think the imagination needs to be there."

In this case, the key is to expand into high-margin, large adjacencies, creating a reservoir that not only captures but retains users over a long period of time.

Big markets aren't always obviously defined, nor is size the only indicator of a big market. In the previous chapter, we mentioned Southeast Asia benefitting from being "late" to the game as an emerging market, and we see this aspect of the market being used by venture capitalists to think about which nascent industries can become big markets. Comparables in other countries, especially those that have performed successfully on the public markets, serve as guides for investors to spot not only where these big markets can appear, but what conditions and strategies are needed to create a big market.

This is where the often used "**emerging market thesis**" comes into play, where you have slides comparing the growth of a sector in the US or China, and even India or Brazil, juxtaposed to the potential growth of the same industry in Southeast Asia, with the main message being that Southeast Asia's market is only five to ten years behind.

Another way that a market's size can be assessed is through its neighborhood — the adjacencies that companies in the market can potentially go to, potentially expanding its valuation beyond the multiples of its initial vertical or industry. A marketplace company selling cars, property, or even logistics assets like trucks can go into payments, insurance, and financing, effectively creating an ecosystem that extends the transaction value per customer beyond buying and selling products on the marketplace.

In certain cases, like ecommerce, where the margins tend to be thin especially in a region like Southeast Asia where affordable pricing is a pull for customers, these adjacencies can be an avenue to expand overall margins of the business and eventually reach profitability. Examples are ride-hailing companies Grab and Gojek, which eventually found greater margins in their delivery businesses and other added services than their core ride-hailing offering, which are listed in Exhibit 3.

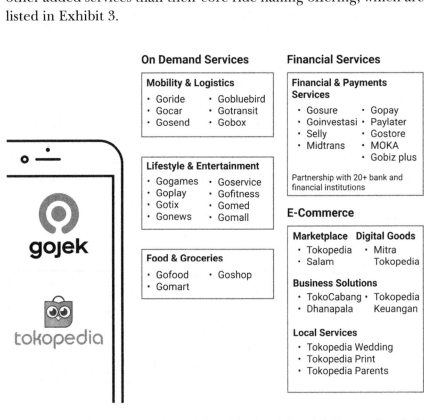

Exhibit 3:   A merger between good "neighborhoods" can shake up the whole country, as in the case of Gojek-Tokopedia. Taken from TechCrunch. [1]

Factor 2: Founders

Going back to the principles of what enables venture capitalists to win, backing people and building relationships with founders is key. At the same time, venture capitalists need to be able to develop an intuition for what makes a founder capable of building a billion-dollar company, as we write in *Navigating ASEANnovation* (2020):

> "Apart from looking at the market and waves of innovation, Yinglan also pays close attention to the founder. **When asked what kind of founders he looks for to invest in, Yinglan always distills his answer into a single word: "unstoppable."**
>
> "Unstoppable" is best captured in the age-old fable of the Turtle and the Hare. The eager hare starts the race ahead, but the persistent turtle wins in the end. Unstoppable founders are neither hare nor turtle. Instead, they translate the early-stage eagerness into long-term persistence.
>
> Unstoppable founders are sustained by an obsession that keeps them on track. It is not an obsession that clouds judgment, but clarifies and reflects in their work ethic and business decisions. If you had gone to Singapore's Blk71 a few years back, you would have seen the founders of Carousell hard at work, and I daresay that has played a role in where they are today.
>
> We back founders and teams who will always choose to be the company that has the greatest impact in the market and have the mettle to commit to that choice.
>
> The race to have the greatest impact in the market is shaped by a vision the founders have for the region's future, five, 10, and even 20 years down the road. Southeast Asia has been through several waves of innovation over the past decade, from marketplaces to enablers to more vertical-specific technology platforms. There are more to come, and the founders Yinglan looks for are already riding the incoming waves."

VCs have used various ways to describe the founder's persistence and stubbornness in pursuit of building their companies. "Unstoppable" is just one way to encapsulate the idea that it is important for VCs to back people who can see through the execution of their vision, and put in the hours to make things happen.

Having this "unstoppable" mindset is also important because it ties in with the idea that pivots can happen, and in many cases, need to happen for the survival of the company. We saw this in the initial onset of the pandemic, when many companies began to refocus their businesses from B2B to B2C to meet the needs of displaced customers, speed up product development to catch the demand for digitalization, or began to develop pandemic-proof solutions like contactless transactions.

But being bold and unstoppable is not enough. One can bulldoze through the friction of building a company that either digitalizes an entrenched industry or creates a new industry that disrupts the status quo, or one can reduce the friction. That's with a lubricant we're going to call "**Founder-Market Fit**", as Yinglan explains in *Navigating ASEANnovation* (2020):

> "One of the more critical things we look for is a founder-market fit — a market that is on a great trajectory for growth and unstoppable founders equipped and hungry to build a fast-growing business in that market.
>
> We've invested in Sayurbox, an agritech cofounded by Amanda Susanti, a former farm owner who became a founder to solve inefficiencies in the fresh produce supply chain.
>
> We've also invested in logistics startups like Janio and Shipper with years of ecommerce logistics experience and connections in their founding team. That said, the founder-market fit isn't just about having experience or expertise. Counterintuitively, a better fit to tackle problems in the market can be found by having a fish-out-of-water perspective. Sometimes the founders can have a compelling, nonobvious view on what the market needs or more importantly, what it can be in the future, that garners our support. (pp 160–161)" [2]

Having this founder-market fit essentially adds on to that localization advantage mentioned in the previous chapter because the nuances of the industry vary from market to market.

This advantage from the view of investors makes the company more attractive.

Another reason founder-market fit is important goes back once again to the idea of pivots. **A founder able to immerse themselves in a specific market can anticipate trends or think of more ways than one to approach a problem.** For example, backing a founder who used to work for Amazon or Bytedance (TikTok) makes them fit to build a platform supporting ecommerce sellers or social media creators.

While the kind of founder you invest in may not be as immediately consequential to forming a fund or building an investment thesis, **it is important to develop an understanding of the kind of founder you would want to invest in** as well as an intuition to spot them amidst the crowd. It also helps to look at how founders of comparables in a certain industry have handled their businesses and infer the kind of experience that would be needed based on that. Seeing good results from this intuition helps other founders build confidence in your ability as a venture capitalist.

Factor 3: Technology (and its application)

The third factor to consider in developing an investment thesis is product or technology. Given Southeast Asia's emerging market growth potential riding on rising internet penetration, regional funds will tend to focus on consumer-focused technology: apps that bring traditionally repetitive, offline services online and automate or aggregate platforms and marketplaces that connect supply and demand more efficiently and then spin out into capturing entire customer journeys around the products being sold on the platform. In *Navigating ASEANnovation* (2020), the value of investing in platform technology is explained further.

> "In a fragmented region like Southeast Asia, where local industries have long-standing inefficiencies, platform companies are best positioned to bridge these gaps digitally and create impact while remaining asset-light and agile.

This focus on platform companies originates from his time spent leading Sequoia Capital investments in Asia, including Tokopedia, Gojek, Carousell, Appier, Pinkoi, and 99.co.

On the surface level, platform companies optimize matching between demand and supply. But through data-driven growth on top of a solid user base, these platform companies have the capacity to create entire ecosystems of products and services, and this is the part that gets investors truly excited. Gojek for example initially began connecting people to ojeks for ride-hailing, but that has since evolved to a whole gamut of services from food delivery to even video-on-demand.

Being able to create and monetize an ecosystem does not only result in scale but can also lead to sustainability for the business. That platform-to-ecosystem growth trajectory, driven by unstoppable founders and A-teams, makes platform companies enduring, like Alibaba, Netflix, and Airbnb." p. 158 [2]

That said, not all venture capitalists in the region are focused on consumer technology. Some have devoted their funds to more deep tech solutions, which is still nascent on its own in Southeast Asia, with talent and clientele largely concentrated in Singapore. Though we are already seeing the intersection of many deep tech companies with consumer platforms.

An example is WIZ.AI's conversational AI technology being used to power the customer service needs of Carro's used car marketplace. Then there are other funds that are also specifically focused on biotech, which has drawn appeal for investors in recent years with the likes of Andreesen Horowitz raising separate biotech funds, but this strong interest has largely been confined to developed markets. More recently, there are funds with a specific interest in blockchain or decentralized ledger technology, and just like biotech, it has attracted greater interest in developed markets. Unlike biotech, it can scale and create ripple effects much faster in emerging markets.

The idea of considering this factor also extends to how the technology is applied in the market. In the case of the platform company thesis described earlier, the idea of a "platform" does not just refer to mobile-first applications and marketplace website applications where you have users connecting over certain services or commodities, but also that using this technology enables companies to reach a massive amount of people in a short period of time, which is the kind of growth potential that venture capitalists want to invest in.

Ultimately this third factor — product or technology — is not just the product or technology per se, but also a unique insight into how this product or technology can be applied in the market.

What's your appetite and secret sauce?

Being able to define the kind of market, founders, and technology you want to invest in as a venture capitalist is key to formulating a strong investment thesis. These factors also influence how much a fund can raise from potential limited partners and the kind of interest a fund will receive.

A smaller market or more niche kind of technology in an emerging market will likely result in a smaller fund, but a more generalist approach will tend to raise more. Generally, as a venture capitalist aiming for massive returns and early investments with a long gestation period (around seven years), you want to have a big enough war chest that will support casting a big net and following through with the winners in your portfolio.

Deciding on the exact definitions of these factors (market, founders, technology) and how they translate into fund size, fund structure, and limited partner composition boils down to investor appetite and expertise. Investor appetites can vary. There are those looking to put smaller, less than US$100K checks in companies very, very early — pre-product, pre-revenue — as this enables them to take a "spray-and-pray" approach to getting these fund makers, investing in as many as 100 companies in a few years. The limited partner base of these funds tends to also be small check individuals, high net worth individuals, and fewer institutional funds.

The downside is that ownership in these companies will easily dilute and because these funds are smaller, there's not much follow-on that can be done in later rounds. Then there are other investors that find their sweet spot in the Series A range of US$1 to 2 million for startups, because it not only puts them in a position to be the largest outside shareholder in the company and first check in, but also enables them to raise enough money to bring in follow-on dollars for the winners in their portfolio. That said, these larger, Series A funds will invest in fewer startups per year.

But apart from investor appetite, there's also investor expertise. It's important as a venture capitalist to know what value-add you can deliver to founders in terms of understanding markets, supporting them as founders, and helping them in the technology space they are in. Even within a firm with a set fund structure and investment thesis, partners and associates form teams to focus on specific verticals and technologies.

This expertise, accumulated through experience and connections over time, will set your investment thesis apart from many others that are looking into a similar region like Southeast Asia, where, as we've mentioned in the previous chapter, competition in venture capital is thickening.

Show your solutions!

In primary school, math teachers often tell us the importance of showing solutions as they show the thinking behind the answer we end up with. In the same way it is important to develop and present the thinking behind an investment thesis, and there are many ways to do so, considering all the factors we talked about previously.

Industry and market maps

A framework that brings these ideas on what defines a big market together is a market map. A market map usually consists of a table with the rows representing various business models (B2C, C2C, B2B), and the columns representing various parts of the value chain in that industry. The intersections of these rows and columns then translate into specific value propositions. For example, the intersection between B2C and mobile healthcare could be mental health applications.

That said, market maps do not have to be illustrated with the table as described above. One can easily find various illustrations of markets in thought leadership articles and opinion pieces on Medium, Substack, or WordPress blogs, as venture capitalists will often use simplified versions of these maps to assert their expertise in an industry and thus a valuable partner for potential portfolio companies, as seen in Exhibit 4.

When it comes to building a deck for fundraising to limited partners, however, the market maps have to be much more comprehensive and specific, versus when they are being used for blog posts and thought leadership. It is also important to consider the point-of-view when constructing these market maps as different POVs can translate into different value propositions. In these market maps, dollar values can also be ascribed to these value propositions and areas for new business opportunities.

Plotting a market map with comparables from other markets and competitors in the region in question is useful in spotting where the white spaces or untapped value propositions are, or in other words, where new companies with high-growth potential can be found.

Focusing on the key numbers

It's important to understand in a given market what are the numbers that matter, or the numbers that reflect the specific inefficiencies and pain points stakeholders experience in that industry. For healthcare it could be the gap in terms of care providers and patients. In education it could be the gap between teachers and students, or the cost of enrolling students into tuition schools.

Presenting these key numbers is important in establishing that there is a compelling reason and space (i.e., addressable market to convert from status quo to new solutions) for companies to come into these markets. Knowing the numbers that matter also points

Backing the Bold

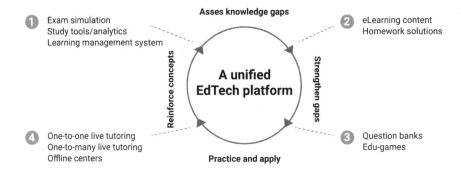

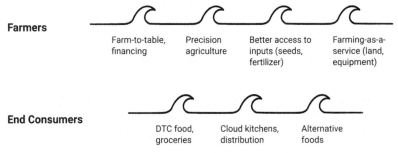

Exhibit 4: Various types of market maps, with varying levels of complexity (T–B: agritech from the point-of-view of farmers and end-consumers, edtech from the point-of-view of students, and ecommerce logistics from the point-of-view of traditional logistics). Taken from *Insignia Business Review*. [3][4][5]

the venture capitalist towards the right places to look. If you're looking to invest in mobile app solutions, then platforms like AppAnnie that aggregate metrics on the performance of these apps are useful.

The top 10 list

Another practice venture capitalists do when it comes to developing an idea for what companies to target in a market is to list the top ten existing players — either in the target vertical or the vertical that will potentially be disrupted by this new market — and reach out to these existing players and scope their own challenges and assessment of the market.

Scoping the environment does not only give insight into what kind of go-to-market strategy or business model will succeed in the market, but it also arms the venture capitalist with insight that becomes value-adding for the founders.

In Exhibit 5, the classic CBInsights graph illustrating how fintechs have evolved from unbundling and innovating individual value propositions is an example of an industry visualization to identify key existing players, especially from the perspective of an investor looking into what the next wave of fintechs will be focusing on after "unbundling the bank."

Ultimately the idea behind using all these various methods is to define precisely where value creation will occur, because that is after all, what a venture capitalist seeks. These frameworks then become parts of how the venture capitalist's present and defend their investment thesis, especially as they raise funds from limited partners.

Given all the considerations for coming up with an investment thesis discussed thus far, it is important to note four important ideas.

The first is that investment theses change over time. This is obvious with the nature of venture capital in the 21st century focusing nearly entirely on the internet and digital technology, and the rapid pace of technological change in these areas. This pace is even faster in emerging markets.

The second is that multiple investment theses can be developed at various levels of a fund. There can be a fund-level thesis that

Exhibit 5: Not exactly a top 10 list, but a useful combination of market map and listing comparables or even incumbents in an industry ripe for disruption. Taken from *Navigating ASEANnovation*, which referenced this from cbinsights.com. [6]

would justify investing in a specific geography, like Southeast Asia, for example. Then if the fund is sector agnostic, there would also be multiple sector-specific theses and within those sectors, sub-sector specific theses. The primary reason for this is because the way that companies capitalize on market opportunities within specific geographies, sectors, and sub-sectors will be unique and it is important for the venture capitalist to have a firm grasp of these nuances to guide their sourcing of companies from these areas.

The third idea is that investment theses are not magic doors to Narnia. They do not directly lead to finding deals. An investment thesis is akin to a hypothesis in a science experiment — it is informed by past research, fundamental laws of science, and is a benchmark for gauging the results of the experiment, but it is not the result of the experiment (in science, results are often described on the basis that the hypotheses are rejected). As such, it is important to sourcing investments, but not definitive. This is why investors will often have several levels of scope to their investment thesis accounting for various possibilities, or even different theses in separate sectors.

The final idea is that while investors want to go big and as a result end up having to understand the complexities of markets and industries, investment theses should be easy to explain and communicate. Of course, this is not to discount the details and thought process behind the thesis, but when it comes to branding the firm and attracting potential deals, investors will often come up with sharp but insightful one-liners for people to know what kind of companies they are looking for.

Perhaps one of the most famous of these one-liner distilled investment theses is that of Andreesen Horowitz's early on in their first few funds — "Software is eating the world." It is broad enough to cast a net for a wide range of investments, and the goal is not to explain the thesis in detail — of course you do not want competitors to find out what you are looking for — but to ensure that people quickly associate the firm with what companies they invest in.

How are Venture Capital Firms Structured and Operated?

What's the shape of your funnel?

Armed with an investment thesis, venture capitalists can then embark on the deal flow process, which encompasses the entire process of finding and investing in companies. We will go into each of these steps in the chapters that follow, but the important idea to take note of at this point is to pay attention to your deal flow funnel, more specifically, to its shape.

There are four major steps in the deal flow process: (1) Sourcing (finding companies to invest in), (2) Due Diligence (evaluating whether or not these companies fit the investment thesis), (3) Investment Committee (presenting these potential investments for approval by partners in a firm), and (4) Closing (where term sheets are sent, negotiated on if ever, all needed legal documents are signed, and money is wired).

Because venture capitalists want to cast a big net to work the odds of finding the rare fund maker, the sourcing section of the funnel should ideally be bigger than the rest. The Due Diligence and Investment Committee sections should ideally filter out some of these companies from sourcing and create a feedback loop to improve Sourcing, and by Closing only the best-fit companies sign the term sheets.

Some funds have a martini glass-shaped funnel (V-shaped), while others have a more margarita-shaped funnel (flatter at the top). Due Diligence filters more in the latter shape than the former. Then there are other shapes that are like wine glasses where not many companies are filtered up until the end.

Understanding the shape of your deal flow funnel is key to improving processes and filters, and checking on the funnel shape regularly is a good exercise. Apart from shape, there's also the duration or time spent on each section. Time spent on Closing can often take longer especially when there are co-investors involved, but the shape of the funnel based on time should ideally be wider in the middle — more time spent on Due Diligence.

Different shapes and sizes, all tying back to the investment thesis

When it comes to how a venture capital firm operates post-investment, firms have approached value-add for founders in different ways. One of the more prominent comparisons has been that between Andreesen Horowitz and Benchmark.

Andreesen Horowitz took an agency model, employing many people with various expertise to tackle different value-adds and exploding into a massive company that goes beyond investments — much of which we glossed over in the previous chapter, and we will dive deeper in future chapters. The firm has even begun creating its own media agency to own the thought leadership it does for itself and its portfolio. This agency model is attractive for Southeast Asia venture capital firms primarily because it reduces the added costs of navigating different markets in the region.

Then there's the Benchmark approach where they only hired senior, experienced investment partners with specific industry expertise that served as their value-add to founders. They operated with a very lean team, which worked well in Europe.

But regardless of how complex or lean the structure of the organization is, which usually is dependent on the value-add strategy of the fund, venture capital firms will have a set hierarchy. Career venture capitalists will have oftentimes worked their way up this hierarchy.

- Analyst — Fresh undergraduate hires with a few years of experience in consulting or startups will often start in the investment team as analysts, working on industry analysis and research, and support with sourcing and some light portfolio management.
- Associate — Typically after leading a deal, analysts will go up the ladder as associates then senior associates, where they will be given bigger responsibilities in terms of closing deals and portfolio management.
- Principals — Principals are usually promoted or brought in (with several years of prior venture capital and investment expe-

rience) to take on a greater role in sourcing and closing new
deals.

- Partner — Partners and General Partners will often take the lead
  on specific verticals or even specific funds, while Managing
  Partners can be likened to the CEOs or COOs of the firm.

The standards for promotion will vary from firm to firm, but are
usually based on the deals these employees can bring into the firm.
The size of the firm also affects the way this hierarchy works on an
interpersonal level as well. More people mean it is more likely teams
are easily siloed depending on focus and hierarchy, but firms will
also want to keep things as flat as possible with various forms of communication and team building.

Apart from approaching value-adds in different ways and con-
cretizing the typical venture capital firm hierarchy, venture capital
firms also vary in terms of how they invest. As we've mentioned
before, there are venture capital firms that have outfitted themselves
as venture builders or incubators to have more control over the
companies they eventually invest in. There are firms that focus on
smaller checks and are okay being minority investors, but they invest
in a hundred or more startups in a year or two. Then there are firms
that invest larger checks but are more strategic and prioritize being
the first check and largest outside shareholder in the companies
they invest in.

These just cover the institutional venture capital firms. There
are also corporate venture capital firms whose investment thesis has
some level of relation to their corporation or conglomerate funding
them.

It's important to note that an investment thesis, while it sets the
foundation for a fund, also evolves and changes along with the market. If you were a fund in Southeast Asia that started in the 2010s,
the thesis would have likely be very generalized or focused on internet apps, but as the firm raises new funds over time, these new funds
could have an "updated" mandate that aligns with what the investors
see in the market at this point. It thus follows that it is possible for a

firm to have multiple funds with different limited partners in each fund.

Three Best Practices

1. Schedule time every month to check your misses and sharpen your investment approach.
2. An investment thesis can be general but still comprehensive. It's important to cover all angles from the market to technology, business models and founders.
3. Schedule time to regularly check your deal flow funnel.

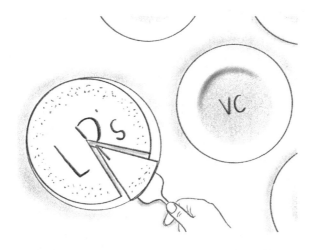

Chapter 3

Rule #3: Diversify, Diversify, Diversify

The Understated Relationship Between LPs and GPs

The goal of any venture capitalist throughout the life of a fund is to generate returns for their own investors — their limited partners (LPs). As we illustrated in Chapter Two, LPs put in money for the general partners or VCs to manage, which then ideally is returned to them and then some, split between the GPs and the LPs.

This relationship between GPs and LPs is often understated in its impact on tech ecosystems. **The LP base of a fund can influence**

the venture capitalist's investment strategy and thesis, ticket sizes, and even how hands-on they might be in terms of driving exits in their portfolio as time goes on.

LPs can also potentially provide value-add to the VCs they fund at various points in the investment funnel and even in portfolio management, from sourcing or venture building ideas to directly participating in follow-on rounds. All of this creates supply and demand shifts between VCs looking for startups to invest in and startups looking for VCs to invest in them.

As we will discuss further in this chapter, these various possibilities within the relationship between LPs and GPs, as well as an increasingly diversified competitive landscape with more funds coming out every quarter (especially in Southeast Asia), means that both LPs and GPs are doing the proverbial investment advice: diversify, diversify, diversify — that is in terms of their relationships with each other.

The LP perspective: Diversification to venture capital

While the impact of LPs on the fundraising market can be understated, most LPs have traditionally put a relatively small amount (around 10–20%) of the money they own or manage into venture capital. The obvious reason is a simple one: venture capital is a high risk, high reward asset class.

This is especially applicable for more institutional LPs like endowment funds, sovereign wealth funds, pension funds, or family offices which already have a set, historically shaped strategy or mandate in terms of their fund allocation across different asset classes (e.g. real estate, bonds, stock markets, etc.).

Some types of LPs like high-net worth individuals or even conglomerates could potentially invest more than institutionals, but compared to their wealth or holdings it may still be a small amount (i.e. an amount they can afford to make no money on). LPs could also choose to commit capital to more than one VC fund to diversify their risk in the asset class — for example, investing in funds that focus on different industries.

However, allocating only a minor percentage to venture capital is not a rule of thumb. In the last decade, allocating more into alternative asset classes like VC has become increasingly commonplace. Yale's endowment fund under David Swensen's management has been the poster boy for institutional LPs to devote more to venture capital, and more broadly, to devote more to equities and hedge funds (as opposed to bonds). Just zooming into the eight years from 2013 to 2021, Yale's allocation to venture capital kept climbing from 13.7% to 23.5%. Over the past three decades since David Swensen took the reins, Yale's endowment fund has secured over 12% average annual gains thanks to this strategy.

Many foundations and endowment funds in the US have also been found to be following suit with this aggressive investment strategy into "real" (e.g. commodities, direct infrastructure investments) and "alternative" assets (under which venture capital falls), with percentage allocation in these asset classes going from under 10% to over 50% over the past two decades.

But one could argue realistically that this strategy is easier said than done. Yale's fund began doubling down on venture capital at a critical juncture in the venture capital landscape of the US. They reaped the benefits of going in early, and Swensen also has been attributed to having the critical ability to find fund managers (VCs included) who could outperform in these alternative asset classes. Yale's most notable return (and only one disclosed) was their US$2.7 million investment in LinkedIn which produced US$84.4 million in gains upon exit.

Apart from the alternative investment trend driven by Yale illustrated in Exhibit 1, venture capital as an asset class has also proven itself to be persistently outperforming the public market. In a 2020 study from the National Bureau of Economic Research, analysis of data from thousands of institutional LPs (pension funds, endowments, and foundations) showed that VC funds (in the US) launched between 2009 and 2017 generated returns (net of fees) that outperformed public market equivalents S&P 500 and Russell 2000. The results of this study are shown in Exhibit 2.

Yale's 2016 Target Allocation

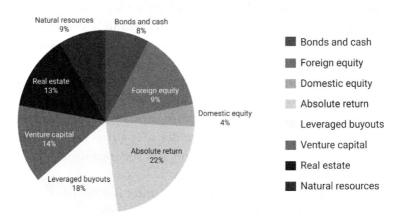

Yale Endowment's Asset Allocation

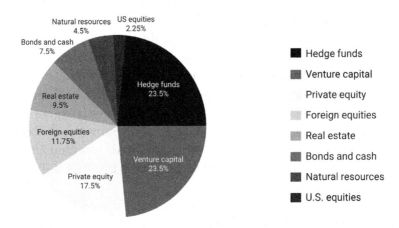

Exhibit 1: Comparing Yale's Fund allocation as targeted in 2016 (top) [1] compared to coverage in the Financial Times in 2021 (bottom). [2]

This sustains a trend that had been previously observed pre-2000s. These post-2000 funds studied are also likely to drive higher returns given the cutoff date of the study at mid-2020, which doesn't account for any IPO or SPAC exits set to occur afterwards. Another interesting insight was that half of VC funds in the study with

Venture Has Outperformed the Public Markets Over Many Periods

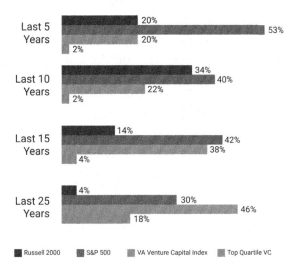

Exhibit 2: VC performance vs public market equivalents (S&P500, Russell 2000, VA Venture Capital Index) across intervals of time. Note that VC performance increases as measured over longer periods, pointing to the long-term nature of returns from this asset class. [3]

institutional LPs outperformed their public market equivalents, which makes a case for greater diversification across venture capital funds from an LP standpoint.

It's worth noting, however, that these numbers mentioned so far were largely driven by market tailwinds in North America and Europe. For good reason — Southeast Asia's ecosystem itself is not yet developed (critical mass of funds in the region thus far are still into their first half of their fund life or the investing phase) or well-documented enough to produce the same depth of literature.

Even then, the Yale model and VC asset class performance versus Public Market Equivalents (PMEs) in the past two decades proved that diversifying into or even doubling down on venture capital can be beneficial for portfolio returns — in other words, Rule 3 — diversify, diversify, diversify! This means it is not out of this world to believe that institutional LPs trying to follow the Yale model would find it reasonable to invest in venture capital in markets that still have a lot more space for early players and high demand for LP capital, say, like Southeast Asia.

Over the latter half of the 2010s, the market fundamentals in Southeast Asia have been lining up with the tailwinds that enabled the Yale model to succeed, at least when it comes to the venture capital asset class — lower interest rates, validation from the public markets, bull run in the global private markets, massive untapped consumer market, rising entrepreneurial class, more potential fund managers to invest in — all market factors we have pointed out in Chapter 1 to explain what has made Southeast Asia such an attractive destination for investors at the turn of the 2010–2020 decade.

The interest is so much so that there are also institutional investors, especially family offices, that are no longer confining themselves to investing in fund managers in the region and instead participating directly in early fundraising rounds of startups. In 2021, the interest showed no sign of slowing down, with fund closes in the first quarter of the year at US$694 million, well above the quarterly average since the first quarter of 2018, as shown in Exhibit 3.

Final closes by five Southeast Asian funds worth $694 million in Q1 2021

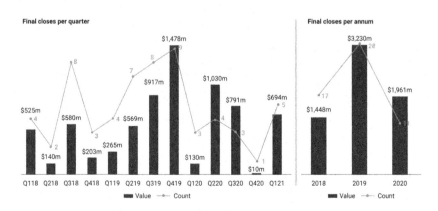

Exhibit 3: A review of VC funds raised in Southeast Asia by Dealstreet Asia [4] from Q1 2018 to Q1 2021 shows a dip due to the pandemic but a general progression in activity around fundraising.

Former Willett Advisors Head of Global Venture Capital, Sherry Lin, who was former head of venture capital at Willett Advisors and Mousse Partners, shares on a panel at SuperReturn China 2021 about how some LPs are preferring to invest in more early-stage plays than pure growth plays in Southeast Asia, as we document on *Insignia Business Review* (2021):

> "Global investors are placing their bets in the ring of Southeast Asia in earlier stages, like Series A and B rounds, whereas the Softbank's and KKR's of the world in the latter part of the 2010s have focused on late-stage plays.
>
> One example mentioned by Sherry Lin was Accel Partners coming into Xendit's Series B, another was Valar Capital investing in Syfe's Series A. And the same trend of favoring early-stage investments is also becoming more popular among LPs and family offices, over the approach of entering late-stage at a point when valuations have ballooned.
>
> Sherry adds, "[There was certainly] the Softbank effect four or five years ago, [but since then] we have had a more wary view of growth…We have shifted more towards the early stage and growing with the early stage because they create that funnel or net for LP investors like us, and they have that special seat at that later growth stage. We've backed away from just pure growth players." [5]

This trend of typically late-stage investors extending their play to direct and indirect investments in early-stage companies will better link up the value chain of early-stage and late-stage investors in the region, creating a more complete pathway for startups to go from seed to exit.

It is a great time to be an LP allocating capital into venture capital in Southeast Asia, especially for LPs based in more saturated fund management markets like North America, Europe, and China. That said, **it is also important to note that many LP bases in Southeast Asia continue to be dominated by conglomerates and "old guard" family money, especially the venture funds set up specifically by these conglomerates or families** — different from Corporate Venture Capital (CVCs) since the funds association with the conglomerate is purely financial. Markets like Thailand and the

Philippines have a long history of intergenerational corporations investing into innovation and driving the tech ecosystem of the country, and GPs raising capital in these countries are likely to get money from these sources.

While new funds in Southeast Asia have been popping up every year over the past decade, the case we've been building in this book that Southeast Asia is a green pasture for LPs looking to double down on venture capital may give the false impression that simply taking a lazy Noah's Ark approach ("build it and they will come") to fundraising will work. While it has certainly become easier in the 2020s to raise a fund than it was ten years ago, especially from the more sizeable LP funds outside of the region, as Southeast Asia is becoming less of a question mark, it is because of increasing clarity on what works and what doesn't in the region that LPs may become more particular in terms of choosing which fund managers to back.

It's also important to note that while we've been talking about venture capital as an asset class from the LP perspective, **LPs ultimately back people (i.e. fund managers) in the same way that VCs will back people (i.e. founders)**, as we write on *Insignia Business Review* (2019):

> "LP interest is similarly focused on finding these groundbreaking ventures that will not only result in high magnitudes of returns, but also drive long-term impact across the board. That ultimately means finding the right decision-makers, both VCs and founders, who will be steering the fleet and navigating the uncharted." [6]

The GP perspective: Democratization of venture capital

Who are these people that LPs invest in? Now that we have a little bit of history in terms of the relationship between venture capital as an asset class and LPs, it's also important to look at the relationship from the GP's point of view. After all, it's a two-way street.

As we've mentioned in Chapter 1, venture capital has a long history, dating as far back as the 1600s in the Age of Exploration, but the various forms of funds that we know today only really began emerging in the 1960s through the 1980s. **Initially venture capital firms were primarily focused on financial value-add and financial returns, but the likes of Matrix Partners and Sequoia Capital emerged to become full-stack platforms and brands for their portfolio, recognizing the need for various aspects of support by early-stage companies.**

Post the dotcom crash, internet and software-focused venture capital began to take root in other markets outside North America and Europe, led by founders and investors who went through the crash and wanted to use their experience to build a more sustainable ecosystem in their localities. Monashees, Brazil's first VC firm, is an example of this, with the founding partners Eric Acher and Fabio Igel finding an opportunity in 2005 to build Brazil's and subsequently Latin America's startup ecosystem amidst the tech nuclear winter, post the dotcom crash.

In the late 2000s and early 2010s, some firms already based in more mature markets began to expand internationally to get early into geographies where they were seeing new opportunities emerge, while early firms in other markets also began exploring in the other direction as they raised more capital from LPs. It is important to note that the internationalization and movement of VCs into emerging markets also coincide with the globalization of the product distributions of Silicon Valley and China's tech companies (i.e. Alibaba, Facebook (now Meta), Apple's iPhone). VCs would be hard pressed to prove market potential to LPs without the presence of some level of tech adoption and infrastructure.

This "geographical democratization" of venture capital in the 2000s was also coupled with "value chain democratization" as the industry began to entertain smaller ticket sizes (less than $1M) to formalize seed and pre-seed funding. This value chain democratization arguably incentivized more startups to form even earlier — pre-product and pre-revenue, as investors became more open to these kinds of investments. This also created demand for programs that could catalyze the formation of founding teams and finding product-market fit, teeing them up to seed and Series A investors. This was then filled by the likes of 500 Startups and Y Combinator.

Towards the end of the 2010s, this "value chain democratization" of venture capital evolved into "platformization", as opportunities emerged even for professionals to become startup investors without necessarily fundraising through angel syndicates, crowdfunding platforms, or rolling funds. The democratization has become so much so that it was tenable for an early 20-something to raise a fund if they have the right background or experience aligned with their investment thesis (e.g., a successful influencer or content creator looking to invest in the creator economy, or a podcaster to raise a fund by virtue of their highly valuable networks). That said, there is still a lot of work to be done to make venture capital more inclusive across demographics and circumstances, such as enabling women to start funds in markets where they would normally be discriminated against.

From this brief retelling of the evolution of venture capital we can see that there are more options for aspiring investors to start a small fund early without a heavy CV (value chain democratization), be part of a firm without having to fly over to Silicon Valley (geographical democratization), or participate in a network of other investors and invest a portion of their savings into startups and ventures they believe in (platformization).

The history and evolution of venture capital — from the GP standpoint — implies diversification as well in LPs — Rule 3! Funds in emerging markets like Latin America or Southeast Asia would also get more local LPs from family offices of conglomerates to sovereign wealth funds, and the rise of more seed funds also opened opportunities for more individuals to be LPs and participate in a venture capital fund. Platformization blurs the line between LPs and GPs entirely, with crowdfunding and rolling funds coming out of pocket, but the difference is the participation is scaled digitally.

The optionality in investing in startups is an important consideration for the aspiring venture capitalist before even deciding to raise a fund, much less start a firm. Perhaps there may be more practical avenues from which to invest and deliver value effectively to startups given one's experience and willingness to commit to building out a very institutionalized platform for a portfolio of investments — we discuss this a bit more in Chapter Thirteen. However, it is worth emphasizing that **one does not have to be a GP to invest or substantially participate in the startup investment opportunities offered by a market.** In some instances, some investors have accumulated enough wealth to be their own LPs and still have enough energy to be a GP or an all-in-one VC firm as well, but that really depends on the person.

Suppose one is already confident in venturing and starting a fund or raising another one. Here are some important considerations for a GP on starting a fund, framed as a checklist that increases the likelihood of LPs in general investing into a fund manager:

- **Opportunity / Investment Thesis:** It is important to have a good sense of where one wants to invest, in the same way that VCs would expect a founder to have clarity on what kind of company they want to build long term. This is ultimately what any GP raising a fund will sell to their LPs to raise capital. It is also important to consider the urgency of an investment thesis and how long it will take for companies in a market or sector to mature, because this will affect the deployment of capital throughout the life of the fund, which is typically five to seven years, plus three for any extensions.
- **Secret Sauce:** Just as it is for VCs investing in startups, LPs are likely to invest in GPs who have an unfair advantage over their peers. This could be network, value-add, investment approach, or even the thesis itself (e.g. imagine being the first VC firm in the market). This consideration can be so strong that it could easily override the need for any prior experience in investing, depending on the LPs that the first-time GP approaches.
- **Track Record:** LPs are more likely to invest in fund managers with a track record, in the same way that startups are more likely to raise capital from investors with a track record as well. It seems like this leads to a chicken-and-egg problem, but this track record can be built by either working at already existing and

reputable VC firms with a sizable portfolio, angel investing, or working in more generalist investment firms (not necessarily venture capital). A GP that has sourced and led investments as opposed to simply riding the bandwagon is also more likely to win the confidence of an investor.

A side note here is that in recent years there has been an increase in popularity around the idea of creating **operator VC firms** — or firms with ex-founders, especially when VC firms expanded from being primarily financial value-add driven to diversifying into other value-adds. There are multiple advantages to either committing capital to or raising capital from an operator VC, ranging from the empathy they have that builds trust and relationships faster to the technical or strategic expertise they could bring to a startup's board of directors. This means that track record could also refer to having scaled and exited one or more companies, and not just investing in a portfolio of them.

- **Reputation and Networks Generation:** This goes hand in hand with the track record of the GP. LPs will want to invest in GPs with the ability to create bandwagons, as we described in Chapter 1 — whether that means pulling in other LPs into the fund, attracting startups and founders to raise capital from them, or even bringing together an all-star team to manage the fund and portfolio.
- **Regulatory Regime:** The regulatory regime the fund is following in its set up could limit the kinds of LPs a fund will attract.
- **Fund Life:** While the typical fund life is around seven years, emerging markets will tend to have longer fund lives to account for how long it takes for companies to reach a valuable exit position. In more developed markets where there are more corporate buyers or buyout firms, say like South Korea, returns can sometimes be expected by LPs within five years. Depending on the market, it's important to consider how the fund life will impact a GP's ability to fundraise.
- **Fees:** LPs will also consider management fees when deciding to invest. This is because fees are oftentimes committed earlier

than any capital calls. However, this may not be at the top of their checklist.

- **Fund Size and Ticket Size:** Fund size (i.e. expected amount of capital to be called from LPs over the life of the fund, including fees) and ticket size (i.e. how much one expects to put in individual investments) are tied to the investment thesis and capabilities of the GP. If there's an untapped opportunity in pre-product, pre-revenue stage venture in a particular market that could be bridged with expertise from more mature markets, that would be justification for an operator VC to create a smaller fund (<US$50 million) with less than US$500K ticket size for seed and pre-seed investments into a portfolio of companies.

The fund size for a specific market in Southeast Asia would also be smaller than a more regional or global play. The fund size and ticket size also affect the kinds of LPs who would be willing to invest. A smaller, seed stage focused fund would likely attract more individual rather than institutional LPs. Institutional LPs would typically invest across the board as much as possible, in seed funds all the way to growth funds as well, depending on the available capital.

Just as LPs will try to diversify their allocation in equities and other asset classes, GPs will also want to diversify their LP base in a way that proves valuable to their portfolio companies at various stages of growth. For example, having multinational corporations in the LP base could be useful in brokering critical business partnerships and opening doors into new markets. Unicorn founders in the LP base would be invaluable in knowledge and insight transfer to portfolio founders.

In many ways, GPs raising funds is not so different from how startups would raise funds from investors. GPs also want LPs they can work with throughout the life of the fund. At the same time, GPs also need to be able to stand out and prove that they have the ability to "de-risk" the asset class throughout the life of the fund.

The trend of democratization in venture capital we've covered earlier in the chapter has led to a proliferation of funds that makes

it important for GPs to clearly identify this "X factor" early on in fundraising, be it through the thesis or value-add. Even if Southeast Asia's ecosystem is still relatively early at the turn of the 2020s and a critical mass of the funds in the region are still halfway through their fund life, more and more funds are coming in and out of the region.

GP Fundraising Considerations, Tactics, and Processes

In examining the relationship between LPs and GPs from both perspectives — How have LPs viewed venture capital as an asset class? How has the evolution of venture capital impacted LPs? — we observe that diversification is the underlying narrative. With diversification there comes greater optionality. And with greater optionality, the pressure for GPs to make the optimal choices (conversely the risk in making the wrong choices increases) in terms of forming a quality LP base increases.

Considerations: Supply, demand, competitive landscape

In embarking on the fundraising process, GPs can strategize and mitigate risks in fundraising by considering (1) market fundamentals (demand), (2) market sentiments (peers), and (3) LP context (supply):

1. **Market Fundamentals:** Venture capital has generally been a bull market for the most part of this 21st century (which also contributes to this diversification trend), so the supply of capital and demand for it continues to be on the up-and-up. The supply and demand dynamic will slightly differ across markets; however, it is important to be prescient of where the market could be heading in the next ten years (a good ceiling on a fund life). Some indicators to look at are:
    a. **The investments and market drivers for these investments:** The quality of the companies and the socio-economic fundamentals of the market that enable these companies to thrive

are important factors to consider. These could even be key in convincing LPs to invest in a particular market, especially one that they are not so familiar with.

b. **Competitive landscape:** A more saturated market means greater supply than demand, so LPs might be investing more into later stage VC funds or even moving out of that market to greener pasture. A less mature market may be ripe for LPs to invest in earlier funds, though more market education and proven understanding of localization challenges would be more important criteria in these markets.

c. **Interest rates:** Higher interest rates might discourage LPs like banks or pension funds to allocate capital to venture capital — this might not be the case for non-generalist or non-"financial" LPs like conglomerates, family offices, ex-founders, or HNWIs. The reason for this is that the more traditional LPs would expect to already get satisfactory returns from less risky investments. That said, higher interest rates could also encourage founders to raise venture capital, as opposed to debt (i.e. borrowing from the bank). The relationships between lending interest rates, demand for capital from startups to VC funds (VC demand) and supply of capital coming from LPs into VC funds (VC fundraising), are illustrated in Exhibit 4, based on a 2017 published study by C. Bellavitis (University of Auckland) and N. Matanova (Pennsylvania State University).

d. **Public Markets and Buyout Markets:** Exit paths are important considerations and points of conviction for GPs to get the buy-in of LPs.

2. **Market Sentiments:** It's very useful to get a feel of the market by talking to as many GPs *in the same target market and growth stage* as possible to decide whether or not to embark on this journey and get practical tips from those who have already gone through all the work. An example of a useful insight from surveying the markets would be to discover what kinds of LPs would be the most efficient to raise from (i.e., how to not waste time) given

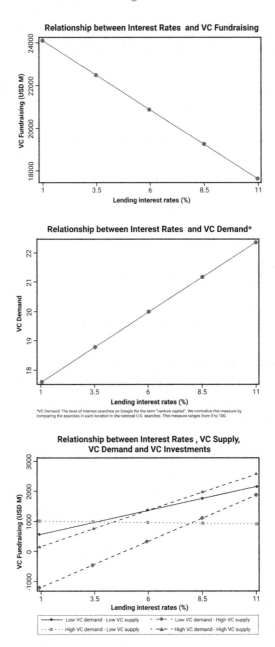

Exhibit 4:   The Economics of Interest Rates, VC fundraising, and VC demand. Taken from a 2017 published study by C. Bellavitis (University of Auckland) and N. Matanova (Pennsylvania State University). [7]

the market and growth stage the fund is focused on. Family offices, individuals, and corporations may be lower hanging fruit compared to institutional LPs in a market with old money but not so strong financial systems, or for a seed stage fund with a 250K check size. This insight is similar to how early-stage startups would raise more from angels and seed VCs/accelerators than institutional VCs.

3. **LP Context:** LPs of all shapes and sizes will want to put money into a fund that invests in startups for various reasons, which could be:

   a. **Financial**: (1) to diversify their portfolio into high risk, high return asset class (as most institutional LPs have been shifting their strategy), (2) to make money (a HNWI or family offices looking to ride the Southeast Asia gold rush), (3) to preserve wealth.

   b. **Signaling:** (4) to get a boost in professional track record with a good investment, (5) for reputation-building.

   c. **Growth**: (6) to get a foot in a market or industry, (7) to build their network of fellow investors and founders, etc.

   These motivations will influence an LP's outlook on the checklist of considerations for GPs we discussed previously — for example, how much minimum experience from the fund manager are they willing to take the risk on? What ticket sizes or fund sizes are they willing to participate in? It's important for GPs to be able to assess these motivations from initial calls and meetings and factor these into consideration when deciding whether or not to take their money. Misaligned expectations could lead to burned bridges, and in an industry where relationships and trust are everything, it may make it harder for the GP to raise a new fund the second time around.

   Apart from motivations, context also includes the investment background of the LP — any decisions they have made in the past that were either mired in controversy or questionable, and how the past or even current positioning and brand of the LP could influence the brand of the GP or even constrain its investment funnel and limit the pipeline of follow-on investors.

The key takeaway from this is that to mitigate risks around LP context, it's important to do due diligence and background checks on potential LPs before even considering taking their money.

Fundraising tactics: Speed, patterns, relationships-building

Apart from looking at demand, supply, and the competitive landscape, we also share some tactics and mindsets that can come in handy to make the fundraising experience as effective and efficient as possible. It's worth noting that most of these tactics are applicable also for founders fundraising from VCs as well.

(1) Optimize Time, but Maximize Outreach

Speed is key, especially in a hot market. GPs typically take 1.5 years to close a first fund, so smaller, earlier stage funds working with more flexible LPs should aim to close faster. There's also the decision point here whether to forgo money for time to close a first fund, and then revisit the pipeline to raise a second fund later on, and doing this could be beneficial in a market where demand is high and the GPs are planning to make light investments across a diverse portfolio.

The fundraising timeline of a GP influences the kinds of LPs the fund will be able to work with — institutional LPs typically have a longer turnaround time than individual LPs. Another option could also be to close the fund in tranches, though this could be risky especially if market conditions suddenly change before the fund could make its final close.

At the same time, while optimizing for time, maximizing outreach is also useful. It doesn't mean accepting money, but simply having built up a record of meetings and initial touchpoints to choose from, and if nothing comes out of it at first, perhaps revisit when raising a subsequent fund and have a more substantial track record or reputation. As the saying goes, "you miss 100% of the shots you don't take." It's better to have tested the waters than to presume that there's no opportunity beneath the currents.

Ultimately, fundraising is a sales process, and it helps to treat it like one to be more efficient, especially in terms of documenting the fundraising funnel and keeping track of the LP pipeline.

(2) Time-Machine Thinking and the Importance of Patterns

One of the key traits of a great venture capitalist is the ability to spot patterns across market, innovation, and time. Patterns are also a useful mental model with which to communicate an investment thesis, because it ties up new phenomena or observations to existing or established precedents that LPs are already familiar with. Using patterns does not necessarily mean looking for opportunities that are *similar or repeating* but sometimes pattern recognition also kicks in when spotting *breaks* in the pattern or disruption.

A classic example of pattern recognition used in GP fundraising, especially in Southeast Asia, is "time-machine thinking", which we've touched on in the previous chapters as well. Investors are more likely to appreciate that "Southeast Asia is five to seven years behind China" rather than "Southeast Asia will be a so-and-so tech ecosystem in the next five to seven years." Having seen how China's VC ecosystem has been rewarded by the likes of Alibaba, Tencent, JD, and their peers, LPs could easily connect the dots across market fundamentals and better project how things will turn out.

That said, GPs could then set up this mindset to dig deeper into specific industries, where perhaps this five-to-seven-year gap may not be applicable especially as the gap between the two markets is closer and the learning curve for Southeast Asia is becoming faster (e.g. social commerce or edtech) because the market drivers are so alike.

(3) Pitch Deck Iterations

A typical GP pitch deck will have slides on the following:

- Investment Thesis (what is the GP's outlook on their target market or industries?)
- History (if it's not the first time the GP or firm is raising a fund)
- Operating Model (how will the fund manage its portfolio?)

- Investment Scope and Strategy (where exactly will the GPs invest?)
- People and Partners (or any Secret Sauce the GPs have)
- Track Record

Because of the importance of diversification and maximizing outreach, pitch decks will have to be adjusted to the nature of the LP and their context. GPs, just like the founders they invest in, will have to go through several iterations on their deck as they go through the pipeline of LPs. The discussions with the LPs themselves will influence how the pitch deck will be iterated.

(4) Leverage network effects, relationship building, branding

Generating leads is one of the more challenging parts of fundraising, and GPs will have had different techniques to do this. One can split possible strategies into push and pull. First time GPs will often have to do a lot of "push" strategies like sending out cold emails or tapping into their network for introductions and referrals, whereas more experienced GPs have a brand and existing relationships that magnetize new LPs towards them if they are raising a new fund or "pull".

The first principle here is that fundraising is relationship building, and that goes beyond developing 1:1 relationships. A tactic could also be to host gatherings where potential LPs could meet each other, get a sense of their potential peers in a fund, and convince them to invest.

(5) Don't celebrate until money is in the bank

Shots don't count until they pass through the net. Even if they hit the ring, it could still bounce off. It seems intuitive enough, but in the heat of fundraising, it can be easy to overcompensate and misevaluate one's performance.

Setting up the fund

Having covered some overarching considerations and practical tactics for fundraising, we move into the technicalities of setting up a venture capital fund. For any financial jurisdiction, a fund manager looking to set up a venture capital fund should already have a well-documented (1) business plan and (2) investment thesis. **At the same time, the manager has to do some research into the requirements to set up a venture capital fund in their jurisdiction. The regulatory regimes for investors can influence LPs proclivity to invest in a certain fund or not.**

It is important for fund managers to do enough research into the licenses and partners involved in setting up a VC firm in a specific jurisdiction. It's also worth repeating that starting a VC firm is not the only way to be a venture capitalist or even invest in tech startups. It is not uncommon for first-time fund managers to have experience as a limited partner or institutional LP (e.g. hedge fund or family office).

The Ever-Changing Relationship Between LPs and GPs

Beyond the capital calls

Once the fund is closed and the GP begins to deploy capital, LPs would still be involved with the fund throughout its life. LPs usually do not transfer all the money they commit to a fund in one go, to protect against cost inflation. That means GPs will have to communicate with their LPs often for capital calls whenever they need to make an investment.

Apart from capital calls, LPs can also provide value-add to the firm and portfolio in various ways. The first big category of value-add from LPs is **knowledge transfer**. This ranges from ideas for how to further develop the investment thesis, which could even translate into concrete venture building on the part of the venture capitalist, or insights for portfolio companies on how to scale their company. Of course, some LPs are more equipped with this ability to transfer knowledge than others — this makes it important to align the LP's contexts and abilities with the investment thesis of the fund and the potential profile of companies the fund will invest in.

In *Insignia Business Review* (2019), we share a concrete example from Insignia Ventures Partners of how this knowledge transfer can lead to investments and venture building and it ties into the "time-machine thinking" we brought up earlier in the chapter:

> "Having seen or perhaps even participated in the miracles of Silicon Valley and Hangzhou, LPs can translate lessons from past cycles into great businesses in emerging markets.
>
> At Insignia, conversations with our partners, 20% of whom come from 55 tech unicorns across Asia, Europe, and the US, don't only cover capital allocation. Instead, it's all about what fast-growing technology businesses can be built in Southeast Asia. Interestingly, 80% of our ideas for growing the portfolio come from 20% of our capital base. This exchange of ideas brings to the table what our ecosystem partners have seen and experienced as a starting point to navigate innovation in emerging markets.
>
> This shift in conversation between LPs and VCs from investing capital to building ventures makes it clearer what value the LPs can bring to the portfolio and enables them to become more pivotal in the portfolio's growth. For example, one of our partners comes from the board of a well-established logistics company in China. He provided the wisdom that helped incubate two very fast-growing logistics companies in our portfolio.
>
> In Southeast Asia, the right talent and capital continues to elude many founders, in spite of the widening of options and increasing flow of both into the region. This is not unique to the region, and many LPs familiar with this narrative can step in and provide clarity and a broader perspective to decision-making.
>
> For some markets in the region as well, the digital infrastructure reflects that of China's several years ago, and the presence of seasoned China founders and investors as LPs provides relatively close case studies of how innovators capitalized on infrastructure gaps to bring the market to where it is today. This relationship [between LPs and GPs] is not about replicating proven models, but rather, equipping companies in the portfolio to deal with market uncertainties and industry challenges." [6]

The second type of value-add is **follow-on funding.** Some LPs might want to directly participate in fundraising rounds for specific portfolio companies in later rounds once the company has proven its PMF or gained significant traction, or is proving to be a category leader in the space.

The third common type of value-add is **network effects and partnerships**. This is often the case for more global investment firms that have multinationals in their LP base who can leverage network effects and potential partnerships to help portfolio companies break into new markets and go global.

The main idea here is not to underestimate the value of a strong and diversified LP base, which ties into Rule #3: diversify, diversify, and diversify. With the democratization of venture capital, there are more ways for LPs and GPs to interact beyond simply being conduits for capital or financial fiduciaries, especially at the micro-VC or seed funding segment of the industry.

Three Best Practices

1. It's very useful to get a feel of the market by talking to as many GPs in the same target market and growth stage as possible to decide whether or not to embark on this journey and get practical tips from those who have already gone through all the work.
2. Optimize time but maximize outreach. Treat fundraising like a sales process.
3. Do not underestimate the value of a strong and diversified LP base.

Chapter 4

Rule #4: Finding the Next Billion-Dollar Company Starts with Asking the Right Questions

Where do You Find the Deals?

The fourth rule to venture capital in Southeast Asia is that **finding the next billion-dollar company begins with asking the right questions**. Venture capital is an industry built on questions (i.e., testing probabilities) — is this the founder to invest in? Does this company have the potential to become the rare fund-making investment? Will this company create massive employment and economic growth in the region? In Chapter 2, we covered key considerations and frameworks to formulate an investment thesis. You can think of this crucial step as laying the constraints and context from which to start asking questions. **This process of asking questions and searching for answers is what the industry calls "sourcing."**

Technically, sourcing refers to the part of the deal flow process where investors go out and search for potential investment opportunities. In this chapter, we'll cover important considerations in sourcing, which ties in with Chapter 2's venture capital principles and investment thesis formulation — how to develop a sourcing strategy, and best practices when it comes to actually meeting the founders and entrepreneurs whom venture capitalists could potentially back.

Back to basics (aka investment thesis)

In sourcing, as with many things in life, it's important to take a step back so that the first step forward doesn't result in several steps back. In this case, taking a step back means ensuring that the investment thesis is a "North Star" for the sourcing process.

When it came to the investment thesis, we emphasized in the previous chapter, the trifecta of a big market with adjacencies, unstoppable founders with a good industry/market fit, and technology/product. These three factors apply to a market-wide investment thesis, but when it comes to deciding investment in specific companies, there are two additional factors to consider: product-market fit and the "X" factor, listed in Exhibit 1.

Factor 4: Product-market fit (and traction, if applicable)

Product-Market Fit is one of the most frequently used jargon in startup and venture capital circles. The reason is that achieving product-market fit is such a critical stage in the growth of a startup, as it opens more doors to investors. Because financing rounds (and

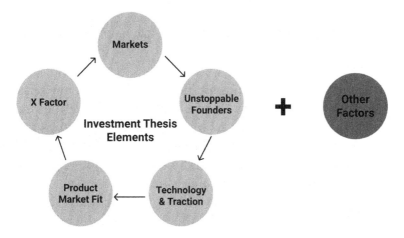

Exhibit 1:   List of investment thesis elements + other factors.

company valuation) are incumbent upon the growth targets hit by the company (e.g. how much of the market have they captured, how much of a user base do they have, how much revenue are they bringing in), **product-market fit will continue to play a role in every subsequent round of fundraising.**

For example, company A could come up with a social networking website that many people come to use regularly and then raise their seed round with the traction gained from that first product-market fit. But to justify raising more money to expand their team and market reach, they need to build their user base and strengthen engagement on their app. So company A also builds their app for mobile and introduces a messenger app separate from the application itself to increase user retention. By finding product-market fit for these new features and add-on services, they can reach significant growth that attracts investors. In this way product-market fit and fundraising are inherently tied to each other. Y Combinator's Michael Seibel puts it succinctly in an article published on the *Y Combinator Advice* blog in 2018:

"The hardest conversation I have to have with a founder is when they've spent their 1-to-2-million-dollar angel round but haven't found product-market fit. Unfortunately, I have to ask them a very unforgiving question: why does your company deserve more money?" [1]

A startup should not fundraise because they have not reached product-market fit and think that fundraising will solve their problems in this area — because it will not. The best startups attract quality money and quality investors *because* they have shown that they can turn cash into valuable products and provide value to people's lives, less the other way around.

The reason this is attractive for investors is because it shows that the business already has customers who find the products or services offered by the business to be valuable, worth signing up for, or even worth paying for. If the company is already monetizing their product or service and getting a steady revenue stream by the time investors conduct due diligence, this sets up a baseline for investors from which to predict future growth and the potential value of a company.

In simplistic terms, investors obtain the valuation of a company based on a multiple (typically depending on the business model or industry of the company) and multiplying it to the key growth metric of the company: revenue. But even if the company is still pre-revenue, having a significant ("significant" would depend on the vertical the startup is in) number of users on board the startup's app or software also provides a baseline for investors to project and even compare to the closest similar businesses or even competitors in other markets with similar environments.

Essentially, the idea behind product-market fit as a deciding factor for investing in a startup is to invest in companies that have found validation in the market and are capable of growth on top of this validation.

In general, product-market fit refers less to any specific numbers that are hit, because this can vary from business to business, but rather refers to the product or service that the startup introduces that actually breaks out in the market, acquires customers, and opens up revenue streams for the company.

From the investor perspective, spotting (that first) product-market fit in an early-stage startup can be as simple as sizing up a user base (or even potential user base for a pre-product company), or better yet, a paying customer base. But even then, that is surface level — the true product-market fit understanding comes with finding out from the business model and product of the company, the makeup of this user base versus what kind of users the product is supposed to attract and why this particular user base was attracted to sign up for or use the product. It is also important to validate if this product-market fit as illustrated or shown by the company is justified by physical documentation (signed contracts vs verbal contracts), but more on that in Chapter 5.

Aside from growth metrics, here are some examples of how companies would show growth specific to their business model:

- Pre-product companies, regardless of business model or vertical, would typically use a waitlist
- SaaS companies would have subscriptions or even contracts for larger companies
- Companies with apps would have monthly active users or daily active users
- Marketplaces would have transactions / basket size
- Fintech platforms would have transactions
- Lending companies would have their loan book size (disbursements) and repayment rates
- Some companies would also use big name users or clients (i.e., all the great logos on the pitch deck) to illustrate some level of product-market fit or traction

When the business has already found product-market fit and made considerable traction, it becomes more attractive to investors, especially institutional investors (as opposed to individual angels), because it fits better into the level of due diligence that goes into investments on a firm level.

Even then, product-market fit and the growth that comes out of striking this gold mine should have a sustainable foundation — this is a key question that investors need to find the answer to through conversations with the founder and due diligence. There's also the possibility of finding "fake" traction if customers come in for reasons like discounts but end up not staying long when the discounts dry up.

That said, given the volatility and disadvantaged situation start-ups typically find themselves in as they enter the market, generating "fake" traction to speed up that initial growth can reap rewards *if* (a big if) there is follow-through with the business model, as demonstrated by the likes of Paypal and Reddit. [2]

A basic and possibly extreme example is how first customers will always typically be acquired through personal networks, which does not necessarily mean genuine love for the product. But if this initial traction can create network effects to pull in more customers down the road, then it may be worth doing. The important thing for the venture capitalist here to understand and talk about with the founder is the driving force of the product-market fit, and how will this need to evolve as the company grows.

On the other end of the spectrum, there are edtech companies, for example, that got subsidized by the Indonesian government amidst the pandemic to take in unemployed people for reskilling. But because the unemployed users did not find value in the platform (i.e., the platform did not get them a job, nor did the skills they gained got them employed), they ended up not using the platform once it was no longer subsidized. That does not mean the edtech company should reject subsidies entirely, but they should consider taking on this "fake traction" and adjust their product to create real product-market fit from the new influx of users.

That said, there are two caveats to note regarding product-market fit and traction as factors for investment decisions. The first is that this process of finding product-market fit and growing on top of it is not a one-time affair. As businesses grow, they have to break through new ceilings of growth, release new offerings to continually engage their customers or update certain products to meet new pain points. **As the company grows, the risk of finding product-market fit increases and stakes become higher.**

Vietnam micro-investment app Finhay's CEO Huy Nghiem paints this picture from his experience, as shared in a Clubhouse session in 2021, also published on the On Call with Insignia podcast:

> "We are on track to find a third PMF and I think it's getting harder and harder compared to the first and the second ones. For example, for the first one we can fail, and it's no problem at all. But at the scale that we are on right now, if we fail our third PMF, then it's really hard to get back on our feet because we're going to lose momentum and not to mention that branding will be damaged.
>
> For example, we are working on a digital bank solution. And typically, if let's say this is our first PMF, that it might take us three months to launch the product and we are okay if there are still bugs, but now it's really hard for us to have trouble because we're dealing with [financial services] and we try to minimize all the bugs and all the mistakes that we don't want to deal with, so it costs us more time to actually launch the product. So it means we have to be more careful." [3]

At the same time, the stakes for investors increase as well. It becomes more important to keep an eye on how the company continues to achieve further product-market fit and traction, so the same scrutiny that goes into the sourcing and due diligence pre-investment should also go into continuous due diligence and portfolio management as the company grows.

The second caveat is that investors can choose to invest in companies pre-product and pre-revenue. A lot of relatively smaller funds do this with a smaller ticket size, decreasing the risk per investment while getting that first check or seed investment in 100+ companies. Some larger funds do this if one of the other three factors we discussed (or even the last one we will mention) compensates for the lack of product or revenue.

Even then, the larger funds will still put in a check smaller than their usual, with the offer of doubling down in a follow-on round if the product the founder eventually releases will see significant traction. This is usually the case for founders who graduate from leadership or venture building positions in regional unicorns or global tech companies, or seasoned founders looking to start the next venture. There are also some cases of investments where the investors support the founders in building out that initial product-market fit and only then put in the money.

Factor 5: The "X" factor

People refer to this "X" factor in many other ways — unfair advantage, secret sauce, competitive edge, or defensive moat. Essentially the "X factor" refers to any asset the business has, tangible or otherwise, that could put it ahead of the pack or enable it to compete with goliaths in the industry. Here are some common types of "X" factors:

Strong Engineering Team: This could be a critical advantage, not just because of the talent per se, but also because this pedigree of talent is more likely to attract other engineers who are just as good. Having engineering talent on the founding team, especially in CEO and COO roles, tends to make the company more product-driven, primarily because the strength and DNA of the company will come from technological expertise. That is not to say that engineering-only founding teams are superior in general; there are certainly pros and cons, but the pros can be a substantial moat against competitors especially if these competitors do not have engineering teams that are as strong.

In the example below from a mini-case study in *Insignia Business Review* published in 2021, we discuss how the tech background of Appier's founding team led them to building a core strength in AI expertise which allowed them to diversify their product offerings and scale as an AI solutions company.

"In much of Appier's press throughout its nine-year history, CEO Chih Han Yu's decade-long background as an AI and robotics researcher at Harvard and Stanford is often mentioned, and for good reason. What has made Appier what it is today is less any single product, market, or person, and more the AI expertise that Chih and his co-founders brought to the company — the DNA of Appier.

Although Appier initially found its footing as a scalable tech company with CrossX, a cross-platform advertising engine, it wasn't always focused on marketing technology, nor was this the limit of the company's repertoire. CEO Chih Han Yu and CTO Joe Su originally came together to develop games, but the publishers they pitched to were more interested in AI after learning about their backgrounds, and how their skill set could help them with their advertising.

While this experience brought Chih Han and Joe to what we'll call founder-market fit (i.e., discovering that founders are best suited to solve a certain market problem), getting to CrossX as it launched in 2014 was not easy either. It took Appier eight unsuccessful product iterations before they finally found product-market fit with CrossX, as COO and co-founder Winnie Lee shares in an article in Digitimes. This strengthened their resolve that their expertise in AI was the way to go moving forward...As their suite of products and value propositions grew throughout the years and reached different types of companies across the globe, one thing remained constant and a foundation for their growth: Appier's AI expertise.

There's a certain stability and longevity that investing in AI expertise brought to the company than investing in say only an AI-driven marketing product or in a certain market like the US or Taiwan would have brought. And this combination of people who knew the technology deeply and people who could market and communicate it to a mass audience ultimately shaped the DNA of Appier and the people they subsequently brought into the team." [4]

Proprietary Technology or Patents: Startups will want to keep core products and services built on top of proprietary technology, not only because it will be more cost-efficient to manage and grow, but because the kind of efficiency or user experience delivered by this technology is what draws customers in. This also ties in with the previous factor where having a strong engineering team can result in proprietary technology that has a competitive advantage. With more deep tech startups, patents are also important advantages because they do not only signify regulatory safety, but also help secure key contracts and clients.

"Been There, Done That" Founders: Founders who have successfully built ventures in the same space, even in different markets, have a certain maturity in their mindset towards company building which was developed through experience. This makes them more suited to repeating that success.

Of course, there are two biases or illusions at play here: hot hand and the reverse of Rule #1. Prior successes have little to no effect on their performance in their next venture, and if this success was achieved in another market, they will likely have to unlearn a lot to execute a similar model in a new country. Even then, there are some verticals, especially in financial services where standardization is part of the industry, where certain models that have worked in other emerging markets like South America or even Eastern Europe would also be playable in Southeast Asia.

In the example below from the *On Call with Insignia Ventures* podcast in 2020, Greg Krasnov, the CEO of Tonik, the Philippines' first neobank, shares his past experience building banks in Europe and fintech ventures in Southeast Asia.

"And before I came to Asia, I worked in private equity in Europe, where a big chunk of my work was focused on emerging Europe and within that, consumer lending and retail finance was a very big theme that we invested in and made money on. Then I became a founder of one of the first consumer finance banks in Ukraine, and we built that into a top-three player in consumer finance with retail deposits.

So the movie of consumer finance is something that I've been watching and playing now for close to 20 years. And I think Southeast Asia is super attractive from the point of view of the scale of the opportunity, as well as the underlying demographics and the strength of the demand for retail, digital financial services. We have a very young population that is very digitally native. This population is demanding solutions for both deposits and loans that are digital to the core, that save them time.

Nobody really wants to ever have to go to a bank branch again. And the size of the market is huge. In the Philippines alone, we're talking a hundred million population, a US$140 billion retail deposit market, and the potential of the consumer lending market to become a hundred billion-dollar asset class. So a very, very exciting opportunity. That's what ultimately drove me to launch Tonik." [5]

License to Get Ahead of the Pack: In a region like Southeast Asia, where each country has its own approach to regulating technology and innovation, licenses are a key defensive moat for a startup, especially if these licenses are obtained before any head-to-head competitors emerge in the market with the same business model. This license battle has heated up in Southeast Asia recently in the digital banking race. Apart from acquiring licenses, another tactic for more established fintech companies has been to use the cash raised from funding rounds to acquire existing banks with the necessary licenses.

Distribution Network: When it comes to Southeast Asia, where an offline-to-online approach is often employed to drive digital services adoption, especially in rural areas, building distribution early on as a foundation for the company can be an advantage with long-term benefits.

Having a network as a go-to-market strategy sets up future products or features introduced by the business to quickly leverage on network effects for adoption. It also provides the startups with a deep level of localization and trust with customers, down to the community level, that foreign competitors would find very difficult to compete with.

We see this distribution network strategy employed to great success across verticals in Southeast Asia, and typically in Indonesia, where the archipelagic nature of the country forces startups seeking to capture the entire market to use distribution networks. Payfazz, in financial services, leveraged an agent network to act as "mobile app bank branches" to drive adoption. Shipper built an agent network to enable their ecommerce logistics network to reach smaller communities across Indonesia. Super tapped into a network of community leaders to facilitate group buying of FMCGs through the company's marketplace.

Will the app or product not be sufficient enough to generate distribution?

The answer is that the nature of adoption for many digital services, especially in rural areas, tends to require a level of trust that only an offline, physical network can deliver. If you are thinking that this will only cost more for the company, **the approach to building a distribution network is not to build it from scratch, but to use what is already there.** Payfazz, Shipper, and Super all tapped into *existing* networks and relationships and simply introduced a new activity or transactions that the people in these networks could benefit from.

For the venture capitalist, these "X" factors may not be apparent when first discovering these startups or meeting these founders. What will be apparent will likely be the performance or growth of the company, but it is important as an investor to find what these underlying factors are, not just to make sense of their growth at the moment of discovery, but also to predict and defend what will be their fundamental drivers for long-term growth.

Apart from considering these factors (to recap: Market, Founder, Technology, Product-Market Fit, and the "X" Factor) as they relate to the investment thesis, it is also important to continually refer to the frameworks we introduced in the previous chapter. Industry maps to map out comparables in other markets, key industry metrics to visualize blue ocean opportunities, and top 10 lists to consider industry incumbents in the same market — all these, and potentially any other frameworks that you may have found or formulated yourself, will come into play when sourcing.

It's important to have the investment thesis as a guide all the way through because when these sourced deals are presented to the investment committee — one can think of them as a "Council of Elders" that makes the final call for any investment to go through and close — these deals ultimately have to be defended according to the investment thesis, not just of the individual investor, which is usually industry or vertical-specific, but also of the entire firm.

Stick to principles

Apart from using the investment thesis as a foundation, there are a number of considerations when sourcing that stem from the venture

capital principles discussed in Chapter 2. We cover one consideration for each of these five principles, listed in Exhibit 2.

Principles & Considerations

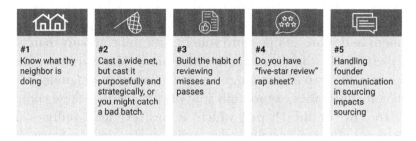

#1	#2	#3	#4	#5
Know what thy neighbor is doing	Cast a wide net, but cast it purposefully and strategically, or you might catch a bad batch.	Build the habit of reviewing misses and passes	Do you have "five-star review" rap sheet?	Handling founder communication in sourcing impacts sourcing

Exhibit 2:   When in doubt, stick to principles.

Know what thy neighbor is doing

The first is to be attentive to what the rest of the industry in your
region is looking at. Venture capital can be quite tight-knit, especially in Southeast Asia, where the population of investors are still
relatively small compared to China and the US — but hopefully
after many of you have read this book, there will have been more
firms and investors in the region.

So considering the first principle, where we discussed the zero-
sum game nature of investing in a company, it means that it is
important to stay ahead of your peers, or as we put it in Chapter 1,
build the bandwagon that others follow. It can also be useful to follow what your peers are looking at, and look for potential competitors
if you believe that the companies they are backing will not win the
space.

Cast a wide net, but cast it purposefully and strategically, or you might catch a bad batch

The second is something we've mentioned in Chapter 2, which is to
cast a wide net to increase the odds of finding investments that make
above average returns, if not return the entire fund.

This doesn't mean talking to every single founder that you meet or taking all the calls that land in your inbox. It means shooting all the shots that are relevant to your investment thesis and checking the boxes in terms of the factors we discussed previously. It is also important to consider the concept that venture capital is a two-way street, and that you will be spending more time on portfolio management and value-add post-investment with the company than you will spend evaluating them for an investment. Many investors have fallen into the trap of investing in an area they are not familiar with or in companies they cannot fully support just because these companies are "in" or the "hype", which at the very least reduces the investment into a pure capital transaction, and at the very worst, can backfire if the business turns out to be a shell or fraud.

Build the habit of reviewing misses and passes.

The third, which we've also briefly noted in Chapter 2, is to spend time reviewing the misses. Apart from the misses, it is also worth taking a look at the companies that could be worth revisiting or monitoring, because as we've mentioned several times before, companies and ideas change. It could be the case that at the time they were discovered, they did not meet the criteria, but with feedback they may have pivoted or adjusted course and that happens to check the boxes they weren't able to before. Having a list of these missed and passed companies worth monitoring, and scheduling regular sessions to review them enhances the net you cast as an investor.

Do you have a "five-star review" rap sheet?

The fourth principle in Chapter 2 is that venture capital is an asset class where the assets pick the investors. This means that venture capitalists are hard-pressed to be differentiated in terms of value-add, whether this means their industry expertise, professional networks, or even the portfolio they have (i.e., sometimes founders choose certain investors because of the community they have in their portfolio — this is especially the case for accelerator-type investors like Y Combinator).

With greater competition for deals, it can be advantageous for your good reputation, positioning, and competitive advantage as an investor, to precede you when meeting with founders. Venture capitalists do this by brand building, and this could involve various activities, from creating thought leadership content (e.g., media features or interviews, social media presence, etc.), to engaging in events. But a lot of brand building happens beyond those activities that one would consider to be brand building, from how the investor manages their portfolio to even how they handle founder communication throughout the deal flow process.

So the important idea here is that more often than not, **non-sourcing activities can be leveraged to help with sourcing**. Responsible founders also do due diligence on potential investors, and they will talk to fellow founders. So from an investor standpoint, a good litmus test is to check if you have at least ten founders whom you are sure will say good things about you to others or give you five-star reviews. That said, it is important to note that good investors accept the reality that it is impossible and impractical to spend the same amount of time with every portfolio company, so it is important to learn how to be strategic with your time allocation for each portfolio company.

Non-sourcing activities can be leveraged to help with sourcing.

Handling founder communication impacts sourcing.

One of the common memes about venture capitalists is the "Let me know how I can be helpful" response VCs often send to founders after passing on them, as shown in Exhibit 3. This has become a meme primarily because VCs are likely unable to commit any help unless it's a startup they are interested in monitoring or revisiting.

While there are only so many hours in a day, it is important for venture capitalists to be strategic with relationship building and to

Exhibit 3:   The infamous "Let me know how I can be helpful" meme from Twitter meme account @vcstarterkit. [6]

be as candid and transparent to founders even when sourcing. Because of the nature of the venture capital industry, how an investor handles the founder's experience throughout the sourcing process directly impacts their sourcing capabilities.

What is your sourcing edge?

A key takeaway from these considerations or best practices is that sourcing strategies are unique to every venture capitalist. It is important to know your sourcing edge. This will define how wide you cast your net, how you look at misses, and how you engage with founders. You can look at this edge as "information asymmetry" between the venture capitalist and the market (or the bandwagon), enabling the former to access investment opportunities before the latter. This edge can come from an ability to understand underlying business models in a particular industry due to relevant background or deep research, or a proprietary network that enables access to private information. This edge also develops and matures over time the more founders you meet, in the same way that your investment thesis would become more sophisticated with more investing experience, so it is important to exercise this muscle as much as you can.

It's also important to note that sourcing techniques and channels need to be applied differently depending on the stage of the companies you are sourcing. For example, a later-stage company will have more traction data available online, or it will be more accessible to the market, versus an early-stage startup in stealth mode.

Given all this, it is important to be thoughtful about the process and communication involved, and we'll cover some best practices further in the chapter.

Network sourcing

Now that we've covered reviewing the investment thesis and implications of VC principles in sourcing, it's time to get into where venture capitalists find deals. In general, there are three main sources: (1) networks, (2) data / research, and (3) inbound. Under networks, there are four types to tap into — (1) the investment value chain, (2) founders, (3) LPs, and (4) industry.

Investment value chain

When it comes to the investment value chain, venture capital firms with different sweet spots often team up to feed deals in follow-on rounds. That is why a VC firm with a Series A sweet spot (US\$1 to 2 million in ticket size) will find it useful to connect with a VC firm with seed-stage sweet spot (US\$250K to 500K ticket size) as the latter's portfolio will likely be looking for investors like the former. Most venture capital firms are in the Series A to Series B sweet spot, although they do invest in seed and pre-seed companies as well, especially those that aim to get that first check in and maintain that majority shareholder position as the company grows. As a venture capitalist, it is useful to identify the firms, accelerators, incubators, and angels that will be helpful to build relationships with and check in with for any deal referrals.

For venture capitalists, it is not just going downstream for deal referrals that is useful. It can also be useful to build networks upstream with late-stage private equity investors for example, to find out what kind of companies they are willing to buy or exit. This adds more depth to the investment thesis, and informs sourcing in a "reverse engineering" manner, where investors find companies to invest in early on because they have an idea of what businesses are likely to get sold at a good price or arrive at a profitable liquidity event later on.

Following the value chain is not just confined to the main players, as intermediaries — from IPO lawyers to accountants handling deals — are also often a useful source of deal flow, given the founders and companies they interact with through their jobs. The dynamic works similarly for these intermediaries operating in more late-stage financing, where they have a better idea of what makes a great exit scenario.

Portfolio founders

When it comes to founders, there are three types of founders from which deals can be sourced: (1) portfolio founders, (2) passed founders, and (3) the mafia.

Portfolio founders can be good sources for deals, because they are in a better position to "sell" the investor to the company, and presumably have networks more relevant to the investment thesis. After all, great founders know fellow great founders. It is this thinking that led Sequoia Capital to start their scout program, which set off a trend in the industry to start scout programs to expand the sourcing capabilities of venture capitalists, especially for earlier stage deals that partners could not afford to spend as much time on. Sequoia's scout program combined the sourcing agility of an angel investor with the network effects and branding of a global VC firm. [7]

While not all firms have the bandwidth to manage a scout program, partners could kick off these scout program-inspired engagements informally or on a person-to-person basis. But regardless of the method, **the idea is that portfolio founders, with their background and career experience, are likely to know founders of the same calibre.**

Passed Founders

As we mentioned earlier in the chapter, there is value in revisiting passed startup investments and maintaining relationships with founders whom the investors decide are worth spending time on.

Unicorn and Tech Mafias

Finally, the third kind of founder is what we call the "mafia", and these are the leadership or executive alumni of regional unicorns or top tech companies who have access to emerging trends or industries and are looking to start their own ventures. This idea of looking into "mafias" to find great founders is rooted in the idea that the top talent with potential for becoming founders congregate in certain organizations, and this strategy extends beyond tech companies and unicorns to looking into the alumni of global venture capital firms or even universities and MBA programs.

A famous example in Southeast Asia is that of the founders of Grab (Anthony Tan) and Gojek (Nadiem Makarim) who were both Harvard Business School alumni, and even Brad Gerstner of Altimeter which eventually entered into the SPAC deal with Grab, was also an alumnus from the same school.

Limited partners

Apart from fellow investors and founders, venture capitalists often work closely with their limited partners to source deals. LPs, especially those who have networks in the tech ecosystem, refer deals to VCs. But the collaboration goes beyond that. LPs also advise on developing the investment thesis, and even share ideas for what might work in the region with the experiences they have had in other markets.

At a venture capital firm like Insignia, where the LP base has a considerable number of tech unicorn founders, these ideas can be very useful and create more synergies for LPs and the GPs in the firm, as written on *Insignia Business Review* in 2019.

> "At Insignia, conversations with our partners, 20% of whom come from 55 tech unicorns across Asia, Europe, and the US, don't only cover capital allocation. Instead, it's all about what fast-growing technology businesses can be built in Southeast Asia. Interestingly, 80% of our ideas for growing the portfolio come from 20% of our capital base. This exchange of ideas brings to the table what our ecosystem partners have seen and experienced as a starting point to navigate innovation in emerging markets." [8]

Industry players (Incumbents and comparables)

Apart from the immediate proximity of their fund (portfolio founders, limited partners, passed founders) and the tech ecosystem (other investors), venture capitalists also deep dive into the networks of the industry covered by their investment thesis.

Usually there will be teams of VCs focused on specific sectors, if not funds, and networking within the industry of focus is essential. In Chapter 2 we talked about listing the top players in the industry and keeping an eye on them. This could also involve networking with the higher-ups in these companies, getting their thoughts in the industry and potentially clues into any up-and-coming players in the field. It is unlikely that industry players will directly field competitors into your view, but conversations with them could lead you on the right path to finding a good company in the industry. This could be in terms of the insights into what will make a startup successful in the space, sharpening the investment thesis.

When it comes to sourcing from networks it is important to note that these are highly qualitative and bear certain risks. It does not follow with certainty that if these founders come highly recommended from portfolio founders and LPs, or if they come from top tier organizations like tech unicorns, Ivy League, or accelerators like Y Combinator or Techstars, that the founder will be successful with the venture you discover them working on. This is where other sourcing strategies and due diligence come into play.

Data or research-driven sourcing

Another way to source for deals is through data. Recently, data application in the industry is deepening as more tools aggregating relevant market data and performance indicators become available and more sophisticated.

We've categorized the types of sources of data where investors dig for sourcing into three: (1) third-party sources, (2) third-party platforms, and (3) in-house platforms.

(1) Third-party sources

Third-party non-aggregators basically involve doing research on sites and resources that are not built specifically to aggregate and analyze data around the industry or startup ecosystems. In a word, "Googling". This can range from setting up Google Trends Alerts for keywords from media articles relevant to the vertical where you are searching for startups to signing up for newsletters and following hashtags or joining groups on social media platforms. These sites are just named "sources" because you need to set up the triggers and filters to make the information they have useful.

(2) Third-party platforms

On the other hand, there are other sites and tools that are built precisely to track industry metrics and company or product performance, like Tracxn and AppAnnie. They typically require a budget to use regularly, but can be useful if the VC firm maximizes it. Compared to non-aggregators, they require less work in terms of filtering and search because these capabilities can be automated using the features of the platform.

(3) In-house platforms

Some venture capitalists find it more practical to hire an engineering team to build in-house data aggregators. These in-house platforms can crawl both previously mentioned third-party sites and other sources to provide deeper analysis tailor-fit to the investment thesis and due diligence performed by the firm. Not all venture capital firms can afford to set up these platforms, and so third-party providers suffice. However, the benefits of having an in-house platform can outweigh the costs, as long as the firm maximizes its usage.

The idea is to have a comprehensive coverage of all data sources, and zero in on specific types of indicators that make a company or founder worth talking to. We list a few of these common flags as questions below:

- Are they getting significant daily active users (DAU) & monthly active users (MAU) growth on their app?
- Are they hiring?
- Did they close a contract / secure a license?
- Is this ex-(insert unicorn name here) executive leaving?
- What are they planning to do next?

Pull sourcing

Apart from using networks and data sources for sourcing, there's a third general method of sourcing that we'll call the "**Noah's Ark**" method. In other words, **build and they will come**, which is also known as pull sourcing. Pull sourcing raises your credibility when you do more "push" sourcing or directly seek out communication with founders or companies. As we mentioned earlier in the chapter, venture capitalists ideally want five-star reviews and positive recognition to precede them. It also creates a filter in terms of inbound leads.

The core of pull sourcing is creating this brand that people connect you to and associate you with as you source companies. This brand should reflect (not reveal) your investment thesis and the way you deal with founders IRL (in real life), as the internet lingo goes. **An effective pull sourcing strategy attracts the right founders to your inbound line of deals while also acting as a lubricant when making introductions to founders you want to go after.**

This brand is built on a mix of activities, which depend on the investor. Some investors prefer penning thoughts like Paul Graham, and set up blogs to share insights on an industry or best practices from their experience. Others like Garry Tan from Initialized Capital have gone full Youtube guru with vlogs sharing juicy experiences, missed opportunities, and learnings as an investor. Other investors prefer to appear on stage, speaking on panels or fireside chats at conferences.

Ideally, as an investor you'd want to have a good mix of all of these. But the key idea here is to go "minimax", or "minimum effort, maximum output." As venture capitalists are not professional content creators or influencers, it is not ideal to spend too much time building thought leadership or attending events, taking away precious hours that could be spent on sourcing, due diligence or portfolio management. There's also the option of building one's own outlet, in the same way that Andreesen Horowitz has, and that takes time and a professional team to manage and grow but it can be useful to scale support for thought leadership on a firm level.

When it comes to Southeast Asia, it can be quite competitive to get space in the best outlets. So it is important to identify the best outlets — media publications, social media / content creation platforms, conferences, types of activity — that will bring in maximum impact while also requiring the least effort.

Especially for investors who are just starting to learn about the industry or market they are focusing on, it is important to seek out conversations with incumbents or investors more familiar in the space. Building this holistic view of the industry will come into play especially when having that first call with a founder.

Investment thesis and sourcing strategies

Every investor has their own sourcing strategy and routine, and the idea is to find the best mix of these sourcing methods (networks, data/research, pull sourcing) and match it to the key elements of the investment thesis (market, founder, technology, product &

traction, X factor) we covered earlier, outlined in the sourcing strategies map in Exhibit 4 below.

For example, investing in the D2C market in Indonesia may require a lot of crawling on Instagram, where many Indonesians set up the digital storefronts of their brands (as opposed to a separate website). On the other hand, investing in SaaS solutions may require more trips to a platform like ProductHunt where engineers and developers test out their initial prototypes. Focusing on the healthcare market in Vietnam may require conversations with local hospitals, doctors, and leading healthcare providers in the country.

As an early-stage venture capitalist, **one way to look at the sourcing strategy is thinking about your investment thesis from the perspective of the founder** — *what kind of pain points are worth tackling in the sector and what would be the best way to tackle these pain points* — **and then combine that view with the perspective of a limited partners in your fund** — *can this company have a massive but still realistic valuation five to seven years down the line, enough to produce an exit with above (public) market returns at least?* After all, venture capitalists are a bridge connecting the capital of these limited partners to the companies of these founders. Answering these questions will

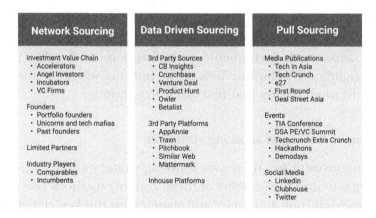

Exhibit 4:   Sourcing Strategies Map with examples for each category commonly used by investors in Southeast Asia in 2021.

inform which networks and sources, and even what kind of thought leadership you should be focusing on.

Sourcing strategies, just like investment theses (the two are inseparable), can change over time. While being able to adjust one's sourcing strategy to a changing investment thesis is important, it is also just as important to concretize this strategy as a routine. Creating this routine and making habits out of best practices in sourcing opens one's ability to be opportunistic in chasing deals and spotting the best ones, especially when one isn't necessarily sourcing at that point in time. In the same way that founders are always fundraising even when they are not fundraising, venture capitalists should always be sourcing even when they are not sourcing.

Working with lack of data in early-stage startups

Given the various strategies available to investors to be able to source companies, it is thus a corollary of the VC principle to cast wide nets that this does not just apply to companies per se but also to the sourcing strategies. For example, an investor cannot afford to always be data-driven in sourcing and evaluating companies, especially when looking for early-stage startups to invest in.

More often than not, it will be through networks and referrals that more of the convertible and quality deal flow will come in. Data is more available in later rounds and will play a greater role in deciding whether to do follow-on rounds or not, but usually when making that first investment in a company, the investor has to consider other factors — many of which we have talked about in Chapter 2.

The lack of data in early-stage VC investments means it is important to develop a greater skill in attracting quality founders and the networks to get referred to these quality founders (note that we use the word founders instead of companies as well given how early and open to change these businesses are). However, it also doesn't mean that data is out of the equation.

It is also possible for venture capitalists to explore deals that are not necessarily within their expertise or even investment thesis purely because they see that the data (usually traction) is impressive enough to invest in. Perhaps, this investment could also open a whole new thesis or insight into the market as well.

Data also plays a role in shaping more macro views of what specific networks or connections to make and how to judge companies when the relevant data is not available for a specific company. This is why Rule #4 is important — because the investment thesis and considerations for what companies to invest in (founder, market, technology, product & traction, X factor, and even investor value-add) ultimately form the underlying foundation for the variety of approaches a venture capitalist can take to sourcing.

How to Make the Most of Initial Correspondence with a Founder?

Asking the right questions gets you to the right place and mindset to find great founders and companies to begin conversations with. **The first call with a founder is a crucial one, not just for determining how the investor evaluates the founder, but also how the founder evaluates the investor** — again, venture capital is a two-way street. As we mentioned earlier in the chapter, it is important to create a positive experience for the founder, as this experience repeated over time for many founders becomes a part of one's branding and reputation in the larger ecosystem.

On a first date, both people on the date are usually sizing each other up — and the final question is always, "Will there be a second date?" The same happens in a first call with a founder. The investor already has information about the founder and the company that they try to dig deeper into or confirm via the call, to decide ultimately whether or not to push for the deal to go into due diligence; the founder also has information about the investor and the firm and they try to figure out whether getting funding from this investor will indeed be worth it.

Not all calls are equal. Some investors will end up spending more time on a call with a founder, depending on their initial impression from the research and referrals that came out of sourcing. Some calls are not as cold as others. If the investor already knows the founder from a previous connection, this could change the dynamic of the conversation, and even the line of questioning.

That said, there are still some best practices worth following when it comes to making the most out of that first call, where, as a venture capitalist, you want to achieve two things. First is to come up with the conviction on whether to continue the conversation and pursue this deal to due diligence, or not push them through the deal flow funnel but still keep tabs with them. Or, completely pass on these deals because of red flags and misalignments with the investment thesis — but this should be rare if not non-existent in practice because the sourcing strategy should already be using the investment thesis to filter out this type of outcome, and every call an investor should be taking should involve some level of presumptive conviction on the investor's part. The second thing to achieve with the first call is to build trust and confidence in the founder when it comes to your capabilities as an investor, regardless of your position in the firm, be it analyst, associate, or partner.

Venture capitalists want to put themselves in a position such that they want to learn more about the company, but already know enough about the space that they can also share useful insights. If the founder leaves the first call gaining something useful, whether or not the deal pulls through, it is a good start to a relationship that could have positive ripple effects down the road.

With these objectives in mind, here are some best practices for handling the first / intro calls:

- **A lot of the work happens before the call** and learning as much about the company beforehand will not only help prepare for the call, but also inform a decision on whether or not to take on the call in the first place. Learning about the company does not just involve research and data collection, but also tapping into networks to get reference checks, not just from fellow founders, but also from former colleagues or even employees.
- **With this pre-call work in hand, it follows that the questions asked should not be surface-level, "Google-able" information,** unless you are looking for confirmation on certain data points.

Questions should ideally also open up the conversation to allow you to share insights and also get the founder really thinking about aspects of the business they may have overlooked. Being able to spot this comes down to practice.

- **Bring up cases of similar companies or comparables as reference,** and even leverage any past experience working in the sector to provide succinct, useful insights for the founder. Bringing up relevant examples shows you understand their business model and what it will take for their company to grow.
- **Get ready for quick maths.** There will be a lot of numbers thrown around in these calls, and it is important to stay on top of these numbers and computations and sense whether or not the founders are actually making sense with the numbers they are sharing given their business model.
- **Take control of the conversation without dominating it.** This comes down to asking the right questions, spending more time listening than speaking, and knowing when (exhaust all the important questions) and how to end the conversation.
- **Position yourself and the VC firm as a way to reach the next stages of growth.** Knowing what the founders need and any gaps in their business allows you to find opportunities to value-add as an investor and effectively sell your end of a potential partnership.
- **Don't play all the cards in the first call.** It's important to assess how urgent a deal is, and the likelihood of getting a second call based on your research even before founders come on the first call. This allows you to set up your pitch and insights in a way that won't overwhelm them or seem sales-y.
- **Keep it short and sweet.** Calls vary in length, but in general you do not want to spend too much time, especially if you have already formed a sense of whether or not you would want a second call and more information from the founders.
- **Be clear about what happens next.** Avoid making any commitments that cannot be followed through. It is also likely that while the first call can already leave a solid impression, there may be

further information needed to really create a good argument for whether or not to pursue this deal. So investors need to be able to quickly come up with next steps towards the end of the call and follow through on these, or if there are no next steps, then sending a conclusive email afterwards. A track record of leaving founders hanging can reflect badly on an investor.

- **If you are working in a VC firm, utilize question/interview templates** (or introduce one) to standardize the information collected from these conversations with founders, not just the first calls.

A lot of these practices apply not just to venture capital, but even to other types of business conversations, from hiring interviews to sales pitches. The reason is that this first call is really a two-way sales pitch at its core, albeit a sales pitch that is not (and should not) be overt but communicated through an exchange of insight and information.

Some key questions to ask

Despite questions varying from company to company, vertical to vertical, and market to market, here are five common threads that are important to cover because they are questions that probe into whether or not the founder has clarity on their business and whether or not the investor is in the right position to be of value. This list presumes the basic details and understanding of the business are covered.

- **Who are your customers? Why are they your customers?** Knowing your customer is one of the most important, but easily overlooked aspects of the business, especially when a lot of the focus for early-stage startups are on how awesome the product is. This question is a stone that hits many birds. The conversation can lead to discussions on market size, underlying growth drivers of the business, customer lifetime value, and user experience.

- **How much does it cost to acquire a single customer and how much revenue can a single customer bring into the business?** This question is basically around unit economics and drills down into how challenging or easy it would be to monetize the business model. It paints a picture from a "unit" perspective of what the business's profit and loss statements would look like, and also sets up a baseline, along with the size of the total addressable market, for a quick valuation estimate (market size x unit revenue x vertical/industry multiple).

- **With these competitors in the market, what makes your company different?** This question illustrates your knowledge and understanding as an investor of the business model. At the same time, it forces the founder to share their "X" factor. This is especially applicable in verticals that are already populated with players that either have already a similar business model in the same market and greater traction, a similar business model in a different market but has the potential of expanding to the same market, or the resources to build out a competitor or acquire a company to build out capabilities in the same area.

Payfazz CEO, Hendra Kwik, shares his experience answering this question on the On Call with Insignia Ventures podcast in 2021.

"This David versus Goliath scenario always happens, especially for us. I remember when I pitched Payfazz to [Yinglan] four years ago, [he] also asked the same question. "Hey, you guys are small. There are some other players who are actually backed by large unicorns and decacorns. How are you going to survive?" And with this same mentality, but over the course of three years with a relentless focus on execution, we actually managed to secure market leadership, and that's also the case that I believe applies today.

It's like the digital bank playbook that we see today. It's a deja vu of the things that we discussed three years ago. Of course, I always believe that focus and localization are key. The fact that our name itself — Fazz Financial — implies that we are a company that focuses solely on fintech will give us a better focus compared to other unicorns that maybe have other bigger businesses that actually make them decacorns, like e-commerce or ride-hailing, so maybe their focus will not be 100% on fintech or banking.

So that's what I foresee in the future, that the guys who have a laser focus on one field and have a very localized approach, especially in the rural areas, [will win]. You may be in the same country, Indonesia, but rural Indonesia will have its own localization. So that rural localization and that laser focus on fintech, especially for the unbanked, I think is our key to be able to defend in our David versus Goliath scenario that we always face." [9]

- **What are the biggest risks at this point to your business?** Investors should already have a good sense of potential risks prior to the call, and the idea behind asking this is to get a sense of how the founder views the business, figure out if there's anything that was not covered in the initial sourcing process, and even have a quick discussion on how to mitigate risks, which can be an opportunity for the investor to share some industry learnings and comparables.

- **What are your goals for the next 18 to 24 months?** This question sets up the founder to illustrate what the bigger picture is, and typically for investors, the bigger the vision and aspirations, the better. A good follow-up is to discuss the high-level strategies to get to these goals. This question is also a way for founders to explain and defend where potential funding will go from the round they are raising. Knowing this allocation allows the investor to segue into potential synergies with the VC firm and its portfolio.

- **Why are you fit to solve this problem?** This question primarily targets founder-market fit, but it also highlights one of the principles of venture capital: that investors ultimately are putting their money in people, not just businesses. This question also fleshes out the potential execution risks of the founding team and what gaps that need to be filled in terms of talent or expertise.

Even though the first call should ideally strengthen or weaken conviction, it is likely that not all the important information can be gathered from a first call. That said, these questions and best practices can be applied to subsequent discussions with the founders leading up to a decision by the firm to sign the required NDAs and get into the due diligence process.

How do Venture Capitalists get Investments Through the IC?

Depending on how the first call goes, investors will collate their notes and prior research into a one-pager and present this to the investment committee (IC). The IC primarily helps the fund filter deals and finalizes deal selection after due diligence and deal negotiation has concluded. From the venture capitalist's point-of-view, the process is like a pitch from a third-person perspective, where the investors paint a concise but informative picture of the company for the IC to make a constructive decision on whether or not to push these deals down the deal flow funnel.

Founders are also sometimes invited to pitch in these IC meetings so members of the IC get a firsthand view of what the investor has experienced. Here are some key tips when it comes to presenting ICs in your firm:

Know how ICs work in your firm. The dynamics of an IC meeting can vary from firm to firm and it's important to have a good understanding of how they work for your specific VC firm. This will influence (1) how you can introduce deals, (2) how to format your presentation, and (3) how often you get to practice pitching deals. There are meetings within VC firms such as pipeline reviews where the investment team gives updates amongst each other on the start-ups within the deal flow process, but does not necessarily finalize any decision on whether to invest or not. Soft pitching can be done in these meetings to get feedback that can better prepare you for an actual IC presentation. IC meetings around a single investment are also likely to happen more than once, especially in larger investments or rounds where the investor is leading, as illustrated in Exhibit 5. This also impacts how much will be expected from

The Funnel Perspective:
Where IC Meetings Are Likely to Happen

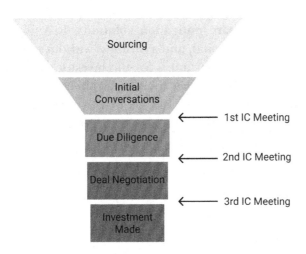

Exhibit 5: IC meetings typically happen in iterations throughout the deal flow process for a specific company, and the exact flow or regularity can differ from firm to firm.

each succeeding IC meeting as deeper due diligence will progressively be required.

Know the deal inside and out. From investment thesis formulation to the sourcing process and the initial correspondence with the founder, the investor should have enough information and insights into the business and industry to be able to articulate their conviction for a deal.

Prepare the founder. It is important to work closely with the founder when preparing for IC pitches (only if this is applicable to your firm's operating procedure) and be aware of the messaging, important aspects to highlight in a product demonstration if there will be one, and how to make the pitch as clear and clean as possible.

Check your maths. Avoid any miscalculations that can set back decision-making and avoid making any assumptions that could be questioned down the line. Given that analysis of a deal should be high quality, fact-based, and quantitative, double-checking and triple-checking information and calculations is always a good practice.

Raise risks and prepare mitigation solutions. Risk is unavoidable especially in venture capital, and a business without risk is not worth investing in. What is important is for the investor to be prescient of these risks and be able to cover them in IC pitches, alongside potential ways to address these risks as part of potential portfolio management. These risks could also turn into indicators or litmus tests for the firm to monitor the company and then revisit when these risks are resolved.

Have your own opinion. There's the perspective of the founder, there's the analysis from research, and then there's your own opinion as an investor. Having the third is key to demonstrating your conviction in and ownership of a deal, and also shows that you have a good idea of how to follow through on portfolio management and support the company in scaling should the firm invest.

It is important to note that IC presentations do not just happen with first-check deals. They continue to happen even when follow-on deals for portfolio companies are assessed, because as we've mentioned time and time again, companies change. The answers to the questions we listed earlier in the chapter will change from when the company raises a seed round to when they raise their Series A, B, and so forth.

Presentations to IC are usually accompanied by one-pagers, which summarize the salient points about the potential investment, and usually contain the following details:

1. **Product / Service**
   a. What pain points is it solving?
   b. What is the value proposition of the product / service?
   c. What differentiates it from status quo or competitors' products?
2. **Business Overview:** What does the business do?
3. **Market**

a. How big is the market (using relevant metrics to size up the market)?

b. Market sizing through Total Addressable Market (i.e., TAM, total market size for a product), Serviceable Addressable Market (i.e., SAM, subset of TAM that can be acquired by a company with this business model), and Serviceable Obtainable Market (i.e., SOM, subset of SAM that can be realistically captured by this specific company / market share) of the company

c. What are the relevant market segments — potential early-adopters, different market segments — within the company's industry/vertical?

4. **Team**
   a. Backgrounds of C-suite and founding team
   b. How many full-time employees?

5. **Metrics** (obtained during due diligence process):
   a. Actual Revenue, Margin, and Profit over past 3 financial years
   b. Quarterly breakdown of monthly revenue, margin, and profit for year of reporting

6. **Business Model / Pricing** (obtained and better understood through due diligence)
   a. How does the business make money?
   b. Unit Economics

7. **Shareholders:** Existing investors, shares owned by the founders, employees option pool

8. **Deal Terms:** Post-money valuation, Pre-Money valuation, Amount to be invested, Ownership

The one-pager is updated as the company goes through the deal flow funnel and more information is made available to the investors. Given how many deals investors go through, one-pagers are a concise way to help ICs make decisions quickly with the right questions, which goes back to Rule #4. Knowing the right questions gets deals assessed faster, without forsaking scope or accuracy. Exhibit 6 is a sample of a one-pager on a biotech company.

Here is an example of a 1-Pager that has been filled:

Company: [Company Name]
Description: Digital biomarkers to accelerate clinical trials in neurobiology

On the scale of 1-5, with the lowest rating is 1 and the highest is 5

US $1B potential	5 - USD 10m projected revenue from clinical trials (B2B) with a total addressable market of $XXbn
Team	5 - Management team has a collective experience of 40+ years in healthcare, life science, and software engineering. CTO and CEO have exited businesses in the past
Traction	3 - is dependent on B2B model until 2023 (transition to B2B2C)
Financial health	4 - Low burn rate with multiple deals in the pipeline

Summary

Digital biomarkers to accelerate clinical trials in neuroscience. Accelerating patient-led neurological research using digital biomarkers

Pain points

1. High drug development cost (USD 1.3 billion) per drug and 13.8% probability of success of drugs entering phase 1 to getting FDA approval
2. Insufficient information for clinicians to treat successfully monitor patients outside of the clinic, 50% of mental health patients do not follow through with their treatments

Value proposition

1. Reduce readmission rates and clinic visits caused by better patient outcomes
2. Accelerate companies' approval processes and identifying suitable clinical trials

Differentiating factor

1. Patented technology
2. Built with robust technology
3. Validated by clinicians through clinical trials with <75% successful predictive rate

Team

1. Co-founder/CEO: Over 15 years of experience, roles have ranged from co-founding a digital startup to managing global strategic developments including strategy design, business case creation and execution, and consumer experience
2. CO-founder/CTO: Over 14 years experience in software engineering and IT solution architecture, former IT professional in MOH, Accenture and Infosys

Traction

	Gross Revenue	Gross Margin	Gross Profit
FY 2018 Actual	----	----	
FY 2019 Actual	27k SGD		-10.5k SGD
FY 2020 Actual	100k SGD		-49.4k SGD
FY 2021 Actual	173k SGD		

Market

USD $68B global market for diagnosed clinical population and clinical trials

Business model

B2B - 50-100k SGD for clinical trials projects; 200-500k SGD for biopharma clinical trial projects.
B2B2C – TBD

Current shareholders

Techstars, startmate, co-founders

Terms

To raise 2.2M USD at 11M USD valuation (pre-money valuation)

Exhibit 6: A one-pager sample from the Insignia Ventures Academy in 2021. [10]

Three Best Practices

1. Come up with your own sourcing strategy tailored to your investment thesis. Certain channels and contacts apply better to a specific vertical or market.
2. Spotting the right signals and reaching out at the right moment can better lubricate initial communication with a founder. Push strategies with "brand" recognition from pull strategies (thought leadership) is an ideal mix.
3. Win investments in IC with conviction, which should be backed by a deep understanding of the ins and outs of the company.

Chapter 5

Rule #5: Always Have a Fresh Approach to Due Diligence

How do VCs Analyze Companies?

It's quite clear from our coverage in the previous chapters that venture capitalists operate in a very high-risk environment. For every company that hits the headlines breaking the unicorn valuation or successfully debuting in the public markets, there are nine others that are never heard of again after their massive seed round or others that turn out to be unsustainable companies with no real business models (only products with no monetization).

This is why even during the sourcing process, venture capitalists are already doing some level of due diligence or DD every step of the way — from researching the company and its products to making those initial calls with the founder, which we covered in the previous chapter. This due diligence continues even beyond the deal being finalized and money being wired.

Arguably, due diligence is even more important once the company becomes part of the portfolio, as the outcome of the company now becomes tied to the reputation and brand of the venture capital firm/s that have invested in them. That leads us to rule #5 of venture capital in Southeast Asia: **always have a fresh approach to due diligence.**

Rethinking first impressions and revisiting assumptions are key. This is because due diligence is an important risk management tool for venture capitalists to get the fullest possible picture of the business and the people running them before investing. Due diligence is also part of fulfilling their role as responsible fiduciaries or fund managers for their limited partners.

But apart from managing risks and fulfilling responsibilities as fund managers, due diligence also enables venture capitalists to appraise and address any issues pre-investment (i.e. sometimes even delaying an investment before a certain requirement is met) and strategize how to approach managing this particular company as part of their portfolio.

It's easy to get comfortable with a company or potential investment especially if it has successfully done the rounds in investment committee meetings, if the deal was sourced through a trusted referral, or if the founder is someone the investors personally know. This fresh approach also applies to conducting due diligence as part of portfolio management. It is easy to take the word of the CEO or founding team that the business is doing well, but part of that commitment to supporting the growth of the company is to be able to exercise vigilance (i.e., spotting the fires before the matches are lit), and candor (i.e., communicating these harsh realities to leadership).

The official due diligence process for venture capital deals typically involves four main activities: (1) securing data rooms from the company, (2) analyzing the company, (3) valuing the deal and (4) finalizing terms of the deal. We discuss three of these in this chapter, and the fourth in the next.

Data rooms

The due diligence process often begins with a non-disclosure agreement between the investor and the founder to ensure no information will be shared by the company to external parties in the process of vetting the company. Signing the NDA is a signal from the investor that they have a serious interest in the company. After the NDA has been signed, the information expected from the company is sent over in what is called a "data room", or a set of files that contains everything the investor will need to know about the company. A data room generally contains the following:

- Investment deck (with the company profile and founding history)
- Documentation of past financing rounds, cap table, and investment agreements
- Market research (market sizing, analysis of landscape)
- Past financial records and growth metrics
- Detailed business model projections
- Legal documentation (key licenses, employee and founder agreements)
- Documentation of tech stack, patents, etc.
- Documentation of organizational structure, and bios of key employees and founders
- Audited financial statements

A data room is essentially the blueprint of the company's operational and financial health. From the company's perspective, with this depth of scrutiny, they will want to present the information that will put them in a good position during the due diligence process. It's important for venture capitalists to be prescient of the reality that in this process they are the tourists and not the tour guide. From the list above, there are some non-negotiable aspects of the business:

1. **Investment Deck.** This is basically a summary of the whole data room, and is like the brochure tourists are given when entering a complex museum — not always used, but a handy reference and easily the first thing that investors will go through.
2. **Key Growth Factors and Metrics.** It's important that the factors that are crucial to the growth of the company are verifiable from documentation. This can range from past records of growth metrics like gross transaction value or GTV (for financial services platforms) or gross merchandise value or GMV (for marketplaces), proprietary technology, written contracts (i.e., ensure that these are written contracts not agreed upon orally), intellectual property, and patents.
3. **Product Roadmap.** It is important to dig deep into the minutiae of the product as it relates to the customer base of the company, for example — why do customers stay on the app if the founders claim high cohort retention?
4. **Financials.** A best practice for financials is to list down all the assumptions behind computations. If assumptions are not listed, be sure to include this discussion in the next conversation with the founders.
5. **Competitive Landscape.** The best startups do not hide competition or the risks that come with the market, instead they acknowledge the presence of these obstacles and offer solutions to manage or mitigate these risks.

A common denominator for all these non-negotiables in a data room is that these aspects help explain the growth (or lack thereof) that a potential investment will or will not claim to have. Once this data is sent over to the investor, venture capitalists will often schedule catch-up calls with the founder to go over follow-up questions with regards to the data room. The ideal situation is for the conversation to go beyond the information that the data room can already provide.

A quick section on pitch decks

We will be covering more on pitch decks in the fundraising chapter, but here are some general things to look out for when studying pitch decks sent in by founders:

1. **Setup — how does it fit in with the investment thesis?** The "Setup" is the first few slides of a pitch deck which detail the industry pain points or market opportunities, the solution to address these pain points or tap into these market opportunities, and the business model to generate revenue from the solution.

   From the investor's perspective, it is a useful step to juxtapose this to the investment thesis, and if this company's proposition resonates or perhaps even builds on top of the hypothesis the investor initially came up with.

2. **Landscape — is it big and realistic?** The "Landscape" covers the slides where the startup usually discusses market sizing (e.g., one way of showing market size is TAM-SAM-SOM: total addressable market, serviceable available market, serviceable obtainable market), comparable comparisons, and competitive landscape (e.g., usually displayed with the x-y graph showing the company as superior in two key characteristics versus competitors).

   Rule #2 comes into play here — "if you think you're aiming big, you need to go bigger." It's important to figure out whether the company is missing out on anything in terms of how they view the market, especially when it comes to competitors and comparables.

3. **Growth — does it check out?** The "Growth" section breaks down traction according to revenue streams (i.e., which lines of

business/product segments are actually driving growth?), how the company achieves profit (e.g., topline metrics like GMV to bottomline like contribution margins), and unit economics or much money the company makes from every user (e.g., including metrics from average order value, customer acquisition cost, and payback period, shown on a waterfall chart).

Apart from these quantitative descriptions of growth, "growth" slides also include the company's vision and the "logos" slide where they include their leadership team, partners, and existing investors. As an investor, it is important to make sure the math checks out, that the growth is realistic vis-a-vis the market landscape as well as the company's business model, and the credentials in these slides check out as well after reference calls.

It's important to note the pitch deck will not answer all the questions an investor has about the company. More importantly, a quick study of the deck should lead to a better line of questioning for the investor (i.e., Rule #4) to understand the key drivers of the company's growth, the bigger picture the company is aiming for, and issues or risks need to be addressed as the company grows.

Also, **pitch decks evolve as the company grows — the depth of information increases as founders pitch in each subsequent round**. This does not just refer to metrics which will obviously expand to include subsequent years, but also the degree to which the company understands the market, their customers, and their competition. This depth of understanding should match the capital that is being asked.

Getting the bigger picture: References and product checks

We separate the different analyses that investors do for companies into two: (1) qualitative and (2) quantitative. **Qualitative analysis covers the people and product aspects of the company.** It can be loaded with bias, but **the idea is to get as holistic of a picture of the company as possible, gathering views from various perspectives.**

When it comes to people, investors typically run various types of reference checks on the company:

1. **Founder checks.** Investors verify the background of the founders through conversations with co-founders of prior startups they founded or with employers / employees at companies they worked for or even investors in prior ventures they built.

2. **Customer checks.** Investors usually ask the company for a list of top customers to talk to about their experience using the products and services of the company. At the same time, they also try to reach out to other customers not on this list for comparison. One strategy investors use would be to act as a mystery customer and try out the product or service without the company knowing, to see things from the customer's point-of view.

3. **Employee checks.** Investors will also try to get the perspective of employees on the company and ensure that employee agreements cover all the necessary protections and are up to industry standards.

   These employee checks can extend to people who are also contributing to the company but not necessarily direct employees of the company, like contract workers. Apart from legalities around employment, employee checks are also done with closer study of the organization to get a gauge on culture and what kind of leaders the founders or C-suite are in the company. Especially for a startup that does not have much traction, culture can be a defining indicator for future growth.

   Investors could also use job portals like Glassdoor where employees leave reviews on the company to gauge how employees view the company with the veil of anonymity. Social media platforms with unofficial company pages or employee communities could also be sources for a perspective on the company.

4. **Investor checks.** Investors will also reach out to existing investors of the company, apart from those who've introduced the company to them if that was the case, to get a fuller picture of the company's cap table.

Product testing

Product testing is done to assess the products and services of the company firsthand. Product testing, especially for early-stage companies, can potentially make or break the result of a due diligence process. Some deals have been closed primarily because of just how good the product is.

Product testing is preferably done by the investor leading the deal, but in some cases this is not possible for products developed only for a certain demographic. In this case it's the investor's responsibility to get feedback from product testers, be it from people in the firm or people in their network who have tried the product or are willing to try it out.

There are no standard rubrics for product testing that are applicable across industries, and so this is where a combination of experience and deep understanding of the kinds of products and technology used in the industry come into play. In some seed or angel investor deals, product testing is often the domino that kicks off the investment process for a company, and in other cases, the final domino that drops to seal the deal.

Social media and online presence

Social media and online presence of the founders, employees, customers, and the company are also critical tools for investors to get a bigger picture of the company and its growth potential, simply by looking at what is happening beyond the company's operations itself, gain a deeper understanding of the kind of attention or audience a company attracts. For example, investors would also check founders' social media and online presence, just as any employer would for their employees.

Too much activity unrelated to the company might be a red flag indicating that the founder is not spending too much time on their company, or if they are found to have multiple engagements, then lack of focus will be a risk. Investors can also go through the followers of a company's social media accounts, especially if social media is a critical part of the company's go-to-market strategy and growth. Of course, online presence is becoming much more relevant in a world that is becoming more adaptable to contactless engagements, so investors are also becoming more reliant on online presence as an initial screening tool for filtering founders and companies as well — do they even exist? What are their credentials? Who are their connections?

Breaking down growth: Unit economics

The key question for quantitative analysis of companies in the due diligence process is to figure out **whether the company is actually making money off its product and services.** Growth in users is one thing, but proving sustainable revenue and profitability is another matter entirely, and that is where the concept of unit economics comes in. Basically, a company wants to prove that it has positive unit economics, or that if it currently has negative unit economics or no unit economics at all (pre-revenue company) then it has a path to eventually achieving positive unit economics.

In Chapter 1, we discussed the ballooning of valuations around unicorns, in Southeast Asia and abroad, regardless of whether or not they were profitable. And although valuations should be justified by sustainable growth and not cash burning, we realize later in this chapter that valuations are not tied to whether or not the present growth is sustainable, as long as investors agree that this growth will eventually turn into massive returns when these unicorns exit in the public markets.

But this thinking has largely shifted after 2019 due to tech IPOs that underperformed — and the poster boy for this was WeWork — and investor sentiment has even swung in the opposite direction as the pandemic struck in 2020, with investors preferring companies that can prove profitability *and* scale.

For venture capitalists, **unit economics is the key to figuring out whether the traction pitched by a startup aligns with its business model.** The "unit" in unit economics varies from business to business.

For a B2C company, it could refer to the profitability of paid features on a gaming app, or an order made on a marketplace app, or even the profitability of an account-holding user for a digital bank.

For a B2B company, it could refer to the sales rep efficiency or profitability of an enterprise client. Generally, however, unit economics uses the customer as the unit, and compares the money spent by the business on that customer (i.e., usually to acquire that customer, but a more complex computation would also account for costs to retain the customer as well), versus the money the customer puts into the business.

Figuring out unit economics generally involves considering several key metrics and ratios that answer certain questions about how the startup makes money (or loses it):

1. **Growth metrics** — how much money is going into the business? How much of the market have they captured?
2. **Churn Rate** — how many customers are they losing on a regular basis? How long is the business able to retain customers? How much growth does the company need to achieve to compensate for this loss?
3. **Lifetime Value (LTV) vs Customer Acquisition Cost (CAC)** — are they earning more money from customers than they are spending to acquire them?
4. **Cash Burn** — how much is the company spending (not just CAC)? Does their business model enable them to reach profitability?

Growth metrics

Growth metrics is generally tied to the revenue generated by the business, which depends on the business model. More critically, growth metrics can show much more than whether sales are improving or falling off. Depending on the business model, here are some of the most common and important metrics that you should consider as an investor.

1. Active users

Active users are the people who interact with the product, website, or application in a given time frame. Startups usually track the number of daily active users (DAU) and monthly active users (MAU). This metric basically shows how many people are engaging with the product on a regular basis as a gauge of product stickiness. **It's expected that the founder should be able to define what "active" means to their growth goals.**

When Facebook (now Meta) hit a billion active users in a day, every writer covering tech rushed to write about it. But according to their stock prospectus, you do not need to be anywhere near the platform to be considered as a "user". All a "user" had to do was to interact through third-party integrations.

The total revenue from active users is simply computed by the average revenue each DAU/MAU brings in over the relevant time period (day or month) and multiplied by the corresponding length of time one wants to measure for (a month, quarter, or year). It is important for investors to consider what constitutes revenue in the engagement of an active user — are they even paying for anything on the platform (paid or freemium applications) or is revenue coming from other sources like ads?

2. DAU to MAU ratio

The ratio of DAU to MAU is a snapshot of user engagement. It looks at the proportion of monthly active users that are engaging with the product in a single day. **It basically measures product stickiness — that is, how often people engage with it.**

For example, if a company has 200 unique active users on an average day and has 600 unique active users in a month, their DAU-to-MAU ratio would be 1:3, meaning that one out of three monthly active users come back to the product on a daily basis.

$$\text{DAU to MAU Ratio} = \frac{\text{Average daily active users}}{\text{Monthly active users}}$$

3. ARR (Annual Recurring Revenue) Growth Rate

Annual Recurring Revenue (ARR) shows how much recurring revenue the company can expect to get, based on yearly subscriptions. ARR is also the annualized version of monthly recurring revenue (MRR) representing revenue in the calendar year. This growth metric is often used to measure percentage growth in SaaS companies.

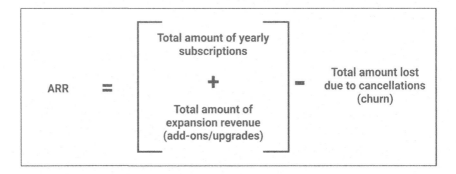

4. GMV (Gross Merchandise Value)

Gross Merchandise Value (GMV) is a metric that measures total sales over a certain period of time. Marketplaces will generally express growth in GMV, as they are dependent on how many products or services are bought on the platform. **Apart from GMV, it is also important to consider the average basket size, or how much a customer will purchase in total per transaction**, to get a more granular view of the engagement of customers and better understand what customers are truly spending their money on in the platform (and even which suppliers are more crucial to the business than others, for example).

$$GMV = \text{Sales price of goods} \times \text{Number of goods sold}$$

5. GTV (Gross Transaction Value)

Gross Transaction Value (GTV) is a metric that is usually used by marketplaces where multiple sellers transact. Financial services companies may also measure growth with their GTV, or the total value of transactions made using the service within a certain period. GTV is computed by multiplying the average transaction value made by a customer on the platform with the total number of customers over a certain period and the take rate or percentage of the transaction that the platform charges as fees or commission.

$$\text{GTV} = \frac{\text{Number of}}{\text{transactions}} \times \frac{\text{Average order value}}{\text{per transaction}} \times \text{Take rate}$$

Growth metrics are important for obvious reasons, but the real scrutiny of the business goes into how the investor breaks down these metrics and questions where each dollar comes from exactly. Common mistakes around measuring growth often involve accumulating different types of revenue into one measurement — for example, putting together one-time fees into recurring revenue when it is not recurring.

For companies with multiple products or revenue streams, investors will want to view a breakdown and figure out which ones are the growth drivers (where is majority of the revenue coming from?), as this will also be critical to valuing the company.

6. Growth Rate

Growth rate is an important metric to consider as well regardless of the business model, in order to get an idea of the pace of the business vis-a-vis the market or its competitors. **Growth rate is simply the change in the relevant growth metric (ARR, GMV, GTV, Revenue) over a certain period.** It can be compared to the cash burn (how much cash the company spends) and investors can check whether the burn of the company is actually converting into growth.

Churn Rate

Nothing lasts forever, and that includes a customer's lifetime. **Churn rate is a measurement of revenue lost from a set group of customers (called a cohort) over a certain time period over the average revenue accumulated over that same time period.** It can be computed over a monthly period by measuring the percentage change in users or customers from the beginning to the end of the month. For example, if there are 500 users at the beginning of the month, and by the end of that same month only 450 out of those 500 users are still using the application, then the churn rate is 10%.

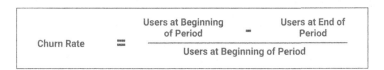

Given that churn rate measures how many customers or users (and hence revenue) is lost over a certain period, it is important not to conflate losses that came from one set of customers or users with another in a previous month. Hence it is important to analyze churn from a cohort perspective, as illustrated in Exhibit 1 below. A cohort refers to a specific group of users or customers that came in a specific time period (say the month of January, or Monday, or 2019),

App Launched ┊ % Active users after app launches ------->

Cohort	Users	Month 0	Month 1	Month 2	Month 3	Month 4
Jan 25	1,098	100%	33.90%	23.50%	18 **Retention over**	
Feb 25	1,358	100%	31.10%	18.60%	14 **User lifetime**	
Mar 25	1,257	100%	27.20%	19.60%	14.50%	
Apr 25	1,587	100%	26.60%	17.90%		
May 25	1,758	**Retention over product lifetime**				
All users	7,058	100%	29.00%	19.90%	15.83%	15.95%

Exhibit 1:   Sample cohort analysis. Note that each row from left to right describes retention for a cohort (a group of users), hence referring to retention over a user's lifetime, while the columns show how retention changes from cohort to cohort over time, as the product presumably changes as well. [1]

considered separately from other groups of users or customers that come in other time periods.

Churn rate will differ across users depending on when they first use the product or service, for a variety of reasons, from the user experience to product feature updates to the seasonality of the business. A business that had a 20% churn rate for cohort 1 might implement new features to better retain the next cohort and the churn rate for future cohorts might decrease after one month, while the churn rate for the first cohort would also decrease after two months with the new features introduced.

Churn also varies from business to business. B2B SaaS businesses would typically have lower month-on-month churn than B2C marketplaces for example. That said, the costs of churn for a SaaS business are also higher for individual customers than marketplaces. For example, a huge contract with an MNC for a SaaS company that isn't extended after five months would impact that company, and they would expect to spend more on sales to recuperate the loss with a similarly large contract or more smaller contracts.

This is why investors also look at **customer concentration risk** in relation to cohorts and churn rate. If the majority of the revenue is only coming from a specific cohort of customers or even market segment, then there's the risk of losing a lot of the business if these customers leave.

Ultimately investors want to invest in a business that can balance growth and churn rates, because this means the business has the ability to retain customers long enough to create a significant margin from costs, which is positive unit economics. When it comes to balancing growth and churn, there is the **Rule of 4 which states that the growth rate-to-churn rate ratio should be four or higher. This means that the higher the churn rate, the higher the growth rate needed by the business to maintain this ratio.** So marketplaces that typically have high churn rate will tend to spend more to increase their growth metrics, regardless of how much it is costing to acquire new customers.

LTV vs CAC

These concepts of measuring growth and calculating for the lifetime of a customer come together in comparing customer lifetime value (LTV) to customer acquisition cost (CAC). Conceptually, **CAC is the total cost used by the business to generate revenue, usually sales and marketing costs, divided by the number of acquired customers. Conceptually, LTV is the revenue, but not profit, that could be generated per user, multiplied by the total length of their lifespan in this business.**

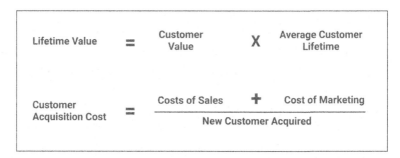

Intuitively, **a business would want to have LTV > CAC, and the rule of thumb is that the ratio of LTV to CAC is at least three — Rule of 3**. In competitive landscapes where customers are expensive and do not easily switch between competitors, having a high LTV to CAC ratio with a customer base relatively smaller to competitors may even be a sign that the business is not investing enough into acquiring customers.

On the other hand, having a low LTV to CAC ratio would make investors question the scalability and sustainability of the company's business model. **The idea of comparing CAC and LTV is that the optimal equilibrium is where CAC that is spent to reach a growing customer base, across use cases and markets, is eventually recuperated by LTV of customers retained by the business, and the margin between the two generates profit which is then used to make CAC and other costs more productive.**

The "cost" in CAC varies depending on the type of business. In B2C businesses, the cost usually involves ad spend on social media, while B2B SaaS businesses would involve more spend on sales agents and software. There is also the nuance of considering fixed and variable costs.

CAC will also tend to vary on the acquisition channels if the business is using more than one, and this is usually the case. An organic user would cost less than one obtained via ads; the former just being covered by potentially server and product costs, while the latter also covered by ad spend. This is why it is important to consider CAC for each acquisition channel rather than plainly using an aggregated value.

On the other hand, the "lifetime" in LTV also depends on the industry and business. LTV can also be derived from the same cohort analysis used to determine churn rate by getting the inverse over a period of time.

Just as with a high churn rate being offset by an even higher growth rate, there are costs associated with low LTV to CAC ratios that can be offset with a fast payback period on the CAC. The shorter the payback period, the more room the company has to reinvest margins into growing the business.

Cash burn and cash flow

Having high cash burn at a certain point in time doesn't automatically mean that the business is irresponsibly spending money. Investors need to take into account a breakdown of where the cash is being spent, and whether it is actually contributing to positive unit economics and sustainable growth.

If it is being spent on acquiring customers that have a long CAC payback period or are not really bringing significant revenue into the business, then there is a higher risk for the business to crash once there is no more cash to burn. If the business is burning cash while having a lot of outstanding accounts receivables or NPLs (non-performing loans, or loans where scheduled payments have not been made, usually 90 to 180 days after disbursement), then that is a red flag for the investor. In general, a scalable startup should be able to manage their cash burn and keep their cash flow healthy.

Managing cash burn does not mean not spending and only keeping money in the bank, although ideally a business should have a good 12 — 18 months runway on average. Cash should still be spent strategically, and costs incurred where there are viable returns to be made, though this is easier said than done for startups, especially in a hot fundraising environment.

For venture-backed startups, the amount of cash poured into the business outside of the revenue made by the business can easily incentivize spending if there is no financial discipline. And with the pressure to reach certain pre-investment valuations so that future financing rounds or potentially even exits grow the company post-investment, it is also easy to forsake maintaining positive unit economics and profitability and just burn VC money on rapid growth.

EBITDA-positive cash flow

The concept of "EBITDA-positive cash flow" is important to consider in analyzing unit economics, although not directly tied to a study of revenues and costs on a customer or "unit" level. **The goal of achieving positive unit economics is to create EBITDA (earnings before interest, taxes, depreciation, and amortization) positive cash flow** — margins that eventually go back into growing the business even further.

If churn has the rule of 4 and LTV to CAC has the rule of 3, EBITDA has the **rule of 40**, where the EBITDA margin as a percentage of revenue plus annual growth rate should be at least 40 percent. This rule captures the balance of profitability and growth in order to reach high revenue multiples. So startups with no immediate profitability have to pull in topline growth of 40% or higher, while a business with larger margins would have more room to grow.

Even if incentives for venture-backed businesses easily lend themselves to forsaking profitability for growth it is still possible for a company to scale rapidly while still aiming for positive unit economics and EBITDA-positive cash flow. Of course, the challenge of doing so varies in complexity depending on the market and competitive landscape — in a landscape where leaders are leading because of subsidies and discounts (i.e. high CAC) the pressure is higher to follow the bandwagon.

But there are other ways to acquire customers and scale the business more strategically than burning cash — in Southeast Asia, that could mean leveraging a strong distribution network (i.e. referrals, FOMO, integrating it into regular interactions, B2B2C), capturing as much of the life cycle of a customer as possible through adjacencies, and tapping into network effects of local partners through investments or M&A. **And venture capitalists can have a significant influence in supporting a startup's search for this balance of scale and profitability.**

On the On Call with Insignia Ventures podcast in 2021, Carro CEO Aaron Tan boils down their company achieving EBITDA-positive cash flow in three years to financial discipline in a commerce landscape riddled with cash burning businesses.

"The third thing I would say is also financial discipline. We have purposely stuck towards the idea of being EBITDA positive and EBITDA neutral. Half the time, whenever investors look at my books, they'll say, "Hey, how come you are EBITDA neutral or EBITDA positive, whereas your competition in other markets is doing far off that? Why are they burning so much money?"

It has more to do with discipline, with the idea of, "Hey, it's important to look up product-market fit before you even try to expand beyond too much, because trying to spend money or burning VC money is very irresponsible. And then at the same time, you probably will end up subsidizing the market too much. And you will stay irrelevant in that sense."

If I look back, one of the many best strategic decisions I have made — I still remember sometimes three years ago, four years ago, one of the earliest investors asked me, "Aaron, it's good that you are EBITDA positive on certain months, but do you really need to be EBITDA positive?" I said, "Yes." And, voila, three years later, we definitely made the right call.

The company has been EBITDA positive for last year and this year. So it is a testament to the fact that we are really running a business here. We're not just running any other tech business. We actually have a path to making money and that has been super critical and actually very positive for us as we're trying to fundraise in this particular environment." [2]

Break down the blended and empty numbers

Digging into the unit economics of a business through growth metrics, churn rate, LTV vs CAC, and cash flow is all about breaking down numbers. **In the qualitative analysis of the company, the idea is to create an aggregate picture of the people's relationships with leadership, the company, and the product, while in the quantitative analysis, the goal is to break down numbers and see where growth is really coming from, why customers are churning at certain points in time, how LTV > CAC can be achieved, and how the startup is managing its cash flows.**

It is important for venture capitalists to be particular with two types of numbers that can easily appear in the process of running due diligence and need to be broken down — (1) blended and (2) empty numbers. Blended numbers often result from mixing or duplicating segments (i.e., cohorts, channels) in the growth metrics that we covered.

On the other hand, **empty numbers refer to any growth that is presented as existing when it has not actually materialized yet —** from verbal agreements counted as recurring revenue or accounts receivables counted as monthly revenue.

Cross-checking numbers requires a trained eye

One of the reasons an investor will want to invest in a market and business model they are familiar with is because they would intuitively be able to gauge how realistic or reliable the numbers of a company are.

For (an extreme) example, pitching for north of 15x multiple on revenue on a brick-and-mortar coffee chain that just started in the last year with several thousand dollars' worth of revenue would not be realistic to the trained eye. Apart from initial judgments, tools like Tracxn with relevant industry data could provide some industry benchmarks for investors.

Tech Due Diligence is not just about tech

Apart from the business due diligence, investors ideally run tech due diligence as well, given that most, if not all, venture capital investments involve a digital technology or engineering component that is core to the business if not an important moat. The level to which tech due diligence is done also depends on how core the technology is to the business model and value proposition of the company.

It also depends on the capabilities of the venture capital firm to run this due diligence, as a venture capital firm could have an operating tech partner who would be better suited to picking apart the ins and outs of how the company has structured its technology. That said, tech due diligence does not just involve evaluating tech stacks and products. It also involves evaluating people and processes. Here are some of the key questions to answer in running tech due diligence:

- How is the team distributed?
- Is the workflow cost-efficient but still effective?
- What systems, tools, and processes are they using to develop their products?
- How secure is the data and proprietary technology or IP that the team has? Do they have an engineer in the team with cybersecurity expertise? If not, what tools do they use to protect their systems?
- How relevant / updated are their tech infrastructure and tools?
- How fast can the team operate and iterate?

Due Diligence is a team effort

Although venture capitalists within a firm will focus on sourcing deals in their area of expertise or vertical's investment thesis, the due diligence process will often call for an entire team effort, some-times involving even limited partners or portfolio founders. This is more apparent in regions like Southeast Asia, and during periods when cross-border travel is constrained and most communication with founders is done via Zoom and other online platforms.

For example, a commerce investor in Singapore could get referred to a founder in the Philippines for a potential deal from a portfolio founder. And so the investor will set up some calls with the founder. Data rooms and other relevant documents can be sent via Dropbox or Google Drive. But if the founder's venture involves a lot of physical or offline products then this commerce investor will work with the portfolio founder that referred the deal and a fellow inves-tor colleague working from the Philippines will get feedback around the products and on-the-ground operations.

Say many of the founders in the company undergoing due dili-gence were previously working at a unicorn whose founder and former CEO is a part of the limited partners' base, the commerce investor would then ask for the assistance of the managing partners to get in touch with the limited partner and get some reference checks. Then the operating partner with engineering expertise would support in running tech diligence, while the finance team of the firm would support in running audits.

This is another reason why venture capital firms will want to put together a multi-functional, diverse team of investment and opera-tional partners. Apart from supporting the growth of the portfolio, this confluence of skills and expertise also helps in running an effec-tive and holistic due diligence. In certain cases where firms do not have these capabilities, they will at times outsource some aspects of the due diligence process like financial audits.

Due Diligence is just as much about the unseen and intangible

Another consideration, knowing all these various tools to evalu-ate the growth and potential of a company as an investment, is to realize that especially for early-stage startups, the due diligence process will not be as complex or filled with data simply because there is less to run due diligence on.

Sometimes there will be no product to product test, no growth metrics to scrutinize, or no app to evaluate with cohort analysis. This is often the case for seed, pre-seed, and angel rounds or even venture-building initiatives where the investors have to rely on more unseen or intangible signals and factors which we have discussed in previous chapters: the character of the founders themselves, how viable their idea is given what the investor knows about the market, and what value-add the investors can provide to build the company, to name a few.

This is where experience and expertise come in to reduce the risk posed by the unseen and intangible factors dominating the evaluation of the company. It is important to note that even deals without revenue or product can become great. Investors should not just develop an eye for this but also ensure that whatever idea the founder is proposing or working on is aligned to what the investor is well-acquainted with. This alignment in expertise does not just allow investors to defend this deal to an IC for example but also explore ways to support the founder in turning the idea into a great company.

That said, even with many early-stage deals lacking data and certain signals associated with a more robust due diligence process, there are other deals that venture capitalists make that are purely because of data, even if it is outside the realm of their expertise. Usually when VCs make these investments, they do not go for the first ticket or lead a round (larger percentage ownership versus other outside shareholders/investors), until they have a better grasp of the space or have the conviction to put in more effort to be hands-on with the company.

Due Diligence should always be done with a fresh perspective

It is good practice for investors to continually run due diligence checks with their portfolio, and not just when they are participating in a follow-on round. Due diligence becomes part of building a strong relationship with a portfolio founder. It shows that as an investor, you are paying attention to the company and are open to supporting them with what they need.

The level of due diligence will not be as comprehensive as it was pre-investment. Instead, the various aspects of due diligence will be done in varying levels of regularity. A financial report, for example, would be requested on a quarterly basis, where the investor would do certain checks before monthly or quarterly board meetings, and the firm might require audits for certain portfolio companies on a yearly basis.

The idea of doing due diligence as part of portfolio management is ultimately tied to the business model of venture capital. Venture capital funds have a target rate of return, and to get those returns, these companies have to grow to a certain valuation from which the investors could then exit their investment through a variety of methods, from secondary sales (selling their ownership to other investors) or an acquisition buyout or IPO. But to figure out what it takes to support these companies to get to this valuation, due diligence is needed. **The best due diligence is done with a fresh perspective, free from the bias of these companies being part of the portfolio.**

How do VCs Value Companies?

Alongside running the due diligence process, venture capitalists will also already be continually calculating and adjusting the valuation assessment of the company. This includes negotiating with the founder, to eventually arrive at a price for the round that gives the ownership that the investor is happy with, without diluting the founder's ownership or messing up their financing round.

To get a better understanding of how venture capitalists value companies, it is important to go back to the principles of venture capital which we discussed back in Chapter 2. The business model of venture capital is built on the idea of increasing carried interest. Carried interest is generated by increasing the overall valuation of portfolio companies by the time they exit, from their valuation when the investor first puts in money. And the valuations (pre-money and post-money) calculated for the deal are inherently tied to this domino effect.

Valuation Principles for Startups

Valuing venture backed startups involves evaluating the company's intrinsic value today and its option value tomorrow (i.e., potential exit value). That means involving comparables. Which billion-dollar company can this start-up be for its market? Can it even replace this company five to ten years down the line? The timeline to exit varies on the market (more mature markets produce exits faster), but in this case, we want to use the typical lifetime of a fund.

Investors will generally look at the public market, venture-backed comparables, or comparables that have gone into highly valued M&A deals as the best-case scenarios to base potential exits on. If insufficient comparables have exited the space, then the most valued comparable would be a benchmark. So a simplistic method to get the valuation of the company — often used in casual conversations and initial calls with founders — would be to get the valuation of an ideal comparable.

A more detailed valuation would consider multiple exit scenarios and assign probabilities to each of these scenarios, as illustrated in Exhibit 2. Typically, this would include the worst case of being shut down and the best case of being an IPO. Then the probabilities of these scenarios would be multiplied to the cash-on-cash or dollar-on-dollar return of each of these exit scenarios then the products would be summed up to get an expected exit multiple. Then the CoC return is how much the company is expected to grow relative to its startup valuation.

Despite exits often being the point of reference for VCs in terms of valuing early-stage startups, there are various factors in determining the right exit multiple, exit options, and comparables. We list some of them below:

- **Experience:** Founders with more experience at venture building and exiting companies will have a higher chance of getting a

Early-Stage Startup A

Exit Scenarios	Probability	COC Return Multiple	ROI
Close shop	60%	0	0
Secondary sales to PE	20%	10x	2x
M&A with global player	19%	20x	3.8x
IPO	1%	100x	1x
Total			6.8x

Exhibit 2:   Arbitrary example of computing for expected returns-based exit scenarios.

successful exit, hence the likelihood of them running the company to the ground is usually judged as low.

- **Big Market = Big Comparables:** A bigger market will likely have comparables that have higher multiples. In some cases, the comparable could also be an incumbent/traditional player that the startup threatens to replace. These incumbent players will tend to be in a large market already especially if the investor is already running due diligence.

- **Traction:** Initial traction means there is more data from which to base a favorable valuation. Even positive qualitative analysis (great customer reviews, publicity) could contribute to greater likelihood of valuable exits. For companies that have already raised previous financing rounds, comparing their post-money valuation vis-a-vis their progress since that round will be a crucial gauge for investors to project future performance.

- **Recurring Revenue:** Recurring revenue opportunities make it easier for investors to project future values, which ties into the valuation methods we discussed later in the chapter.

- **Hot investment:** A "hot" investment may not be the biggest factor for the cautious venture capitalist. Still, it could speed up the process and push more of the negotiating power to the founder especially if the investor has already evaluated the company to be worth investing in by their fund's standards.

Valuation methods for early-stage startups

Working backward from exit scenarios with comparables as benchmarks is at the core of the venture capital method of valuing companies. But when it comes down to the methods themselves, there are several that venture capitalists use, usually in conjunction with each other, and depending on the information available to the company.

The most used valuation methods for businesses like Discounted Cash Flow (DCF) are limited when valuing early-stage startups mainly because of the lack of positive cash flows or good comparable companies. With this in mind, Harvard Business School's Bill Sahlman developed the **Venture Capital Method**, which we summarized below [3].

The Venture Capital Method requires figuring out the following numbers first:

1. **The amount needed by the company for its round of financing.** This is typically taken from what the founders ask for, combined with an analysis of their projected use of funds.
2. **Timing of the exit.** This is based on relative exit timelines in the same region, the performance of comparables (i.e., how long did it take comparable A to reach a certain revenue level?), and the company's past performance if available.
3. **Startup financial forecasts (revenue and profit).** This will be based on the financials submitted in the due diligence process, or comparables if data is unavailable. Forecasts are made until the target exit year as determined by the venture capital firm.
4. **The earnings multiple of comparables that have also exited in the public markets.** This could also be replaced with a weighted probability average from various exit scenarios considered. Multiples vary largely depending on the industry and vertical,

especially how much physical assets and risk is associated with the business. A software company with a fully distributed team and cloud-based servers would have a more justifiable high valuation (say 10x) than a third wave coffee company.

5. **The venture capital fund's desired rate of return.** It is usually higher than the rate of return of public investors to account for increased risk. This rate is also affected by the company's capitalization table.

In computing, the comparable's earnings multiple is multiplied to either the company's net income or revenue at the expected time of exit. The resulting product is the exit value. Then the next step is to discount this value by the number of years it will take to exit, using the fund's desired rate of return. The standard discounted cash flow formula taught in Finance 101 classes will suffice for this: exit value $/$ $(1 + \text{rate of return})^{(\text{years to exit})}$. The result of this Discounted Cash Flow equation is the post-money valuation, or the company's valuation after the round of financing.

To get the pre-money valuation of the company, or the valuation before the investment, the intended amount of investment is subtracted from the post-money valuation. The ownership with that amount of investment is then obtained by dividing the post-money valuation by the investment amount. With this formula, investors will likely adjust or negotiate their price from the post-money valuation.

There are also other valuation methods used for companies that are pre-revenue like the **scorecard** and **checklist** methods, which attribute dollar values to ratings given by the investor to the company across several criteria. But even in this case, investors will also still use closest possible comparables to estimate the exit valuation of the company and then use DCF formulas to calculate the present value of the company (post-money valuation), in a sort of shortcut to the venture capital method.

The three key numbers for the venture capitalist to get out of these valuation methods are the (1) pre-money valuation, (2) post-money valuation, and (3) ownership. Of course, these days with these set formulas and tools like Equidam (or sometimes the firm will build their own in-house tools for calculation), venture capitalists no longer need to work the exact math with pen-and-paper. Given how often VCs negotiate valuation and send out term sheets, there are also generally accepted ranges of valuation for each stage of financing.

Depending on the region, these ranges could shift higher or lower (i.e., more mature, competitive markets are pricier). The idea in covering the Venture Capital Method is to show how the valuation principles of using comparables and working backwards from the exit scenarios play into concrete calculations of valuations.

The computation of valuation is the critical groundwork to lay down for a discussion on the investment terms, because the valuation directly influences ownership, as we have shown, of the investor and dilution of the founder's ownership of the company. It is also tied to the investment amount that the venture capitalist will commit in that round. This investment amount is the key variable that will adjust, especially as more investors join the round.

Finally, valuation is also tied to exit scenarios, as we have discussed. **Exit scenarios are often shaped depending on the kind of influence investors have on the company.** Ownership, investment amounts, and the level of influence investors have on the company are covered and set into writing through deal negotiations, term sheets, and legal documents, which we cover in the next chapter.

Valuations are dynamic

There are some important considerations when it comes to evaluating valuations. First, typical valuations within a market or geography will vary depending on the activity in that market or geography. Valuations are ultimately prices, and from economics, we know that prices can get a premium or discount depending on the shifting supply and demand of a good — the good, in this case, is the company. Generally, prices are higher in a more crowded, mature market than in more emerging markets — perhaps another reason buyers (VCs) are attracted to emerging markets. At the same time, some sellers (founders) will want to raise from Silicon Valley VCs.

It is also why certain accelerators like YC can be valuable for startups from emerging markets because they connect founders to investors accustomed to higher prices. That said, if the founder fills their cap tables with investors who overvalue their company at an early round and try to raise in a market where investors are more conservative, they may have a harder time raising.

Just as in any market, valuation market standards are dynamic, and investors need to adjust their evaluation of companies given the scenarios. For example, a crisis would result in down rounds for some companies, raising at a lower valuation than the previous round. The reason founders would accept this price would be to get access to cash and liquidity.

So even if valuations are often based on comparables in other markets, it is crucial to recognize that the speed at which companies can meet exit valuations will vary depending on the market. Valuations ultimately also need to be justified by growth (projections and time to exit), as we see in the VC method.

Valuing early-stage startups based on growth drivers and market size

But what happens when you are looking to invest in a company with no data, no traction, or even no product? Here, market sizing is used alongside the traction of comparables to fill in potential projections for how fast and big the company in question can go. This requires a deep understanding of the business model. Qualitative factors are also judged based on comparables, in the sense that investors would have an idea of what kind of founder it would take to execute a certain business model.

For unfamiliar business models, investors would also take a look at the potential drivers of growth (i.e., this is why a good question to ask is — what exactly will drive growth and make money for the company?). This is based on what they glean from due diligence and conversations with the founder, which they use as a measuring rod to project growth.

Why (and how) VCs will continue to invest even in rising valuations

In Chapter 1, we saw how valuations of companies (unicorns in particular) rapidly grew as investors continued to pile on financing round after financing round, even if the companies were burning just as much cash and not seeing profitability.

For investors, continuing to invest in companies as the valuation keeps rising and when the bottom line doesn't prove itself doesn't make sense at first glance. **Valuation is essentially the estimated price of a company (if it were to be bought entirely). As the valuation increases, the more costly it becomes to enter the round and ownership in the company**. And the more costly the round, the riskier the investment — using the first principle of venture capital (zero-sum game) we discussed in Chapter 2. A dollar spent on one company cannot be spent on another competitor or portfolio company. So if a large percentage of the fund is concentrated on one company, investors will be more pressured to ensure that that company becomes the fundmaker.

These rising valuations became the case for many unicorns that continued raising private mega-rounds towards the late 2010s. The reason investors continued to pile on is because they eventually expected that the valuations raised by these unicorns will translate to the public markets and the returns on that will be many times higher than what they initially invested. This was regardless of whether or not the businesses are profitable.

The returns on IPOs have also been continuously increasing in the public markets over the 2010s until 2021. Even with the slowdown in 2019, the split in performance between Wall Street (public markets) and Main Street (economy) over 2020 highlighted the potential returns even further even amidst a crisis where valuations were generally expected to drop. Tech companies particularly benefited from this strength of the public markets, with many successful IPOs on Wall Street in the latter half of 2020, including Airbnb and Doordash.

And it goes both ways. Public market rallies can boost buying power of growth stage investors and optimism of early-stage investors as well, creating markups for startups, especially ones in hotly contested sectors. At the same time, as we discussed in Chapter 1, public market slumps can also shift the dynamic or leverage between investors and startups, where investors become more conservative with prices (i.e. ownership) and allocation of capital. This can adversely impact companies that raised on significantly above-market prices and are unable to justify an increasing price with actual growth.

As we discussed earlier, exit multiples at IPOs are often used as benchmarks or even directly in the computation of valuations of early-stage startups. With high-performing returns on IPOs, it is easy to presume that early-stage investors can easily see multiples across tech companies rising. Thus, the high valuations that have ferried unicorns to the public markets do not just affect the companies, but also the larger ecosystem of venture-backed startups. While the costs and risks seem high, the cost and risk of *missing out* on high returns is even higher. Furthermore, investors can dilute this risk on any single company by investing in a whole net of them across various verticals with different multiples.

Even with rising valuations across the market that have also spilled into Southeast Asia, it is still important for investors to ensure that valuations are justifiable — and this is where valuation ties into the process of due diligence and the principles of finding suitable comparables and exit multiples. In the post-WeWork IPO flop era, as we covered in Chapter 1, investors have also shifted their preferences towards scalable companies that can also clear a path to profitability, if they're not already profitable. So even when it comes to valuing startups, just as it is with due diligence, rule #5 of revisiting assumptions and opinions still applies.

Three Best Practices

1. Beware of the blended and empty numbers in running due diligence. Ensure that numbers tie to what the business actually does in reality.
2. It is important to find the right comparable to base exit values to ensure valuations are realistic and justifiable.
3. It is a good practice to set SOPs in place to run due diligence with your portfolio.

Chapter 6

Rule #6: Don't Just Invest, Build Companies

Say you found a great company to invest in. It fits your investment thesis, displays compelling growth, has a seasoned founder, checks out all the other boxes in due diligence, has strong exit potential, and the investment committee seems sold to boot. How do you close the investment?

That's where Rule #6 comes in. While technically this chapter *is* about closing investments, the best venture capitalists will not be shortsighted on closing investments. Instead, they'll focus their attention on the best interest of the company. **VCs don't just invest; they build companies.** The idea behind this is simple. For a venture capitalist to be able to truly follow through on their conviction in a company, and "prove" to their limited partners that this company has the potential to be a fundmaker (or have at least a positive exit trajectory), the company needs to be in a good position coming out of the investment.

To ensure that the venture capital fund maximizes upside and minimizes downside from participating in the growth of the company, the venture capitalist will also want to be in a position coming out of the investment where they can effectively support the company (to become that fundmaker), be it through follow-on rounds, influence on the board of the company, or visibility on the health of the company.

All these conditions for both the founder and the VC coming out of the investment are determined during the closing process, which often begins with investors handing out term sheets and finalizing the valuation and investment amount with the founder.

These two values determine how much the investors will own in the company post-money, and how much the ownership of the founder and other pre-existing stakeholders in the company will be diluted by, unless the ownership of some prior investors are non-dilutive (i.e. the percentage ownership regardless of the valuation of the company is unchanged as the company raises more financing rounds).

The risk-reward dynamic is highly skewed for the founder, even more so than for the venture capitalists or the VC's limited partners. Considering that this is their only venture, they are incentivized to hold on to the majority of the company to reap as much of the rewards as possible once it hits the target valuation and achieves a certain exit scenario. In contrast, VCs are only incentivized to be *at most* the majority *outside* shareholders of the company.

Overtaking the founder in terms of ownership would make the founder less motivated to run the company and result in all sorts of complications — though it is possible that for other reasons, a founder will step back in terms of responsibility and become sort of a "chairman", still retaining majority ownership, while the board hires a CEO to handle day-to-day operations.

VC investment risk in any particular company is also diluted by investments in a portfolio, which we discussed in Chapter 2. So VCs will factor in the existence of other portfolio companies in gauging how much to commit to a company, whereas founders only have that one company — if it fails, it fails and they have to start anew. But if it succeeds, they are likely to be the biggest winners, especially if they handled their capitalization table well. And if the founder succeeds in building their company, their investors win as well. This *long-term* win-win scenario is what a venture capitalist wants to set the tone for with the closing of an investment.

So the question is, how does a venture capitalist create this win-win scenario that contributes to building a great company while maximizing upside for the VC firm?

Know Thy Value

As we mentioned in previous chapters, venture capital is a service industry. VC firms primarily differ in terms of the people (venture capitalists) and their expertise, experience, unique investing, and company building approaches. So even before founders have their first conversation with an investor, they would ideally have done reference checks and research to figure out how a potential investor could be valuable to their company.

The founder's evaluation of an investor's value-add throughout the investment process will impact how much investment amount and investor ownership a founder is willing to accept once the term sheets come onto the table. In simple terms, the more valuable an investor, the more of the company a founder will be willing to give. This value goes beyond the check size, of course.

That is why investors that have been able to lead investments or make first checks into market winners or comparables are generally more attractive to founders. **Investments generate more investments, and setting up that flywheel effect is critical for investors.** For the venture capitalist, the best way to build this trust even before meeting the founder, is through portfolio companies.

But what if the venture capitalist has not had any investment experience before? Typically, career VCs would be active in portfolio management even if they are not in charge of closing the investment so that the founders in the portfolio would know them, and this serves as "brand equity" for the analyst or associate when they go out and source companies to invest in. The firm's brand will also precede them and help grow the individual investor's brand as well.

When it comes to venture capital firms communicating value to founders, it is important to go beyond the firm's brand and leverage the firm in its entirety and the power of having various expertise and backgrounds working together to support a portfolio company. We brought up the value of working as a team in due diligence, which applies to pitching value to founders as well. In some cases, the VC that sourced a company will pass this investment to a colleague with whom the founder will find greater value in collaborating. As we have mentioned in previous chapters, this value could also extend beyond the firm itself, and even to the portfolio and limited partners. This is also another effect of following a thesis-driven approach, where the potential synergies between portfolio companies are clearer. For example, having logistics and payments startups in the portfolio could be valuable for a D2C brand.

However, the angel investor will typically rely on other engagements with founders beyond investing, like consulting on growth or helping with hires (i.e., paying-it-forward). They will also try to invest as early as possible in companies that do not have pre-existing investors and are going through their first round of investing. This gives the investor more room to adjust their value-add to the company's needs, as the company will have a lot more needs at an earlier point in its life cycle. **Knowing one's value as an investor and ensuring that the founder understands this value is critical to ensuring that both the VC firm and the startup come out of closing in great shape.**

Apart from one's value-add, it is also essential for the investor to consider at what point they are investing in the company. From the sourcing and due diligence process, the circumstances and situation of the company, the risks it faces at this particular stage of growth, and the potential growth drivers should be clear to the investor. This understanding of what the company needs and whether this aligns with the founder is critical to creating that win-win situation out of an investment round.

Sometimes an investor will advance on value-add before investing by either helping the founding team secure a senior executive on their C-suite or pairing a CTO with a seasoned CEO or supporting them to launch. In other cases, the investor will also set some goals for the company to hit before an investment is reconsidered, but that does not necessarily mean that an investment will be made if the startup hits these goals.

This alignment on what the investor can bring to the table and what the company needs is rooted in Rule #6, where the goal is to ultimately build a great company long-term and not just close an investment.

Know Thy Instruments

Apart from aligning on value, it is also important for the venture capitalist to understand what financial instruments to use when investing in a company. First, the instruments determine the kind of legal documents involved. Second, the instruments also determine the ownership and dilution that comes with that specific investment round.

Here are some of the instruments that venture capitalists and other startup investors will use:

Equity

This is the vanilla instrument that VCs will use to invest in a company, basically the **transaction of ownership in a company for cash encapsulated in a Shareholders' Agreement (SHA)**. For most equity investments, venture capitalists will want to acquire preferred stock in the company as opposed to common stock. Acquiring preferred stock goes beyond the simple "X% of the company for Y dollars" transaction. It enables certain privileges when the company exits or if the company liquidates — more on that later.

Convertible Notes (CN)

The execution of an SHA can take some time, so for pre-seed and seed stage companies that are looking for quick cash, they will likely use a convertible note instead. In this case, **convertible notes are structured as debt with a special provision that allows the principal and accrued interest to convert into an equity investment at a later date.**

This debt structure allows the company to get access to cash faster and with less legal fees. The debt fund is not only able to finance the company faster through this structure, but they also benefit from accrued interest converting into the same shares as that of the original investment upon maturity. Where the company is being sought after by many investors, CNs are useful for venture capitalists to get ahead of the pack and grab a slice of the pie before it is too late.

Here are some considerations unique to convertible notes:

a) **Interest**: Just like any other debt investment, while the convertible note has not yet converted, the investment accrues interest over time, usually 4% to 8%.

b) **Maturity Date**: By this date, usually twelve months from the date of issuance, CNs are due and payable to investors if they have not converted to equity. Most conversions happen when a subsequent equity investment exceeds a certain threshold (i.e., qualified financing). In the event that qualified financing does not occur before the maturity date, there are also provisions for automatic conversion upon maturity.

c) **Conversion Provisions**: This covers provisions offered to investors for making qualified financing before the maturity date, including the right to convert notes into stock issued in the qualified financing round.

d) **Conversion Discount**: When the CN converts during a qualified financing, investors will often get a discount on the price per share of that equity round. If the price is a dollar per share, and then discount is 20% (a common discount rate), then the principal and accrued interest will convert to shares at 80 cents per share.

e) **Valuation Cap**: This is a ceiling on the conversion price for CN holders, regardless of the price per share in the qualified financing round or next round of equity financing. This also applies to automatic conversions that occur at the maturity date.

From the investors' perspective, the use of convertible notes is hinged upon the idea that this is a tee-up to a larger financing round down the road, ideally before the maturity date. Sometimes, this larger financing round is already seen coming from a mile away and a VC will swoop in with some CNs to quickly get a foot in the door — this is just one of many strategies VCs will employ to pursue a company they want to support.

Conceptually, CNs can also help bring in more investors in the qualified financing round via signalling, and the investors who initially invested through convertible notes could choose to add on more equity in this next round as well. That said, CNs could also impact the company conversely if the CNs take up too much of the valuation cap set.

CNs provide companies a quick line of cash, which can be extremely useful for a startup that, for example, has just experienced massive traction with their products and needs the cash to expand their operations and team to meet the increasing demand and growth (if they manage to prove that the company can handle this growth, then it also makes a stronger case for a future investment round).

That said, CNs can also be tricky, because spending time on raising CNs diverts founder attention from growing the business towards the next round of fundraising. If the company can afford it, the founding team will likely hire a sort of corp dev-type professional to support them in fundraising so they can focus on company building.

Simple Agreement for Future Equity (SAFEs)

If CNs are debt investments that eventually convert into equity, SAFEs bring together the speed of CNs without the debt aspect. First developed by Y Combinator, **SAFEs are a *cash* investment in the company that converts into shares in the next round of financing**. Apart from the lack of accrued interest and maturity, SAFEs also convert similarly to equity investment, with investors preferring discounted and/or valuation-capped conversion. Similar to CNs, SAFEs, also work best for early-stage startups in need of quick cash and getting ready to raise a subsequent round of financing in the next twelve months.

Traditional debt

Debt is often not used as a financial instrument by investors into early-stage startups for the obvious reason that it is risky to presume that the company can make payments. But this can be a useful instrument for more established companies with assets to leverage, companies that have recurring revenues like SaaS or subscription businesses, or companies whose business models are inherently tied to the movement of cash and require heavy amounts of cash without massively diluting the other shareholders, like lending companies or companies that acquire other businesses.

With the initial impact of the pandemic on businesses in 2020, debt financing became an important source of liquidity for some companies that could show profitability and had high quality assets as collateral. Successfully raising debt financing avoids the potential for entering into a downround, or a financing round where the company is valued lower than its previous round, and also builds positive signalling from the confidence of banks to back the company. As Ernest Chew explains on the *On Call with Insignia Ventures* podcast in 2021:

"Debt financing is actually a very important source of liquidity plus a cheaper form of capital than equity. We had a lot of assets going into the lockdown, whether in the form of financing receivables or vehicles that can be asset-backed. We didn't want a "gun to our head" and suddenly be forced then to fundraise at unattractive valuation at, frankly, the wrong time.

From a signalling perspective, the ability for a start-up to secure close to S$150m debt financing facility really demonstrates strong conviction from banks who are generally very conservative backing startups.

So in a nutshell, I think that it's important to think about that. But my advice in raising debt is that it's important to have high quality assets as collateral and think about being profitable, amongst other factors as well." [1]

Of course, in contrast to equity, debt does not come with ownership interest in the company, but in the event of a liquidation scenario (i.e. company shuts down), debt holders are paid in full first before equity holders, so from this point of view, the downside is less risky for debt financiers. Primarily because the transaction does not involve taking ownership in the company, documentation to structure a debt financing round is also a lot simpler and less expensive compared to that for equity.

Because debt is non-dilutive, it can be used by certain business models to fund specific initiatives like serving as acquisition cash or lending principal. One example is Rainforest's US$30 million debt facility raised for its seed round, as covered on TechCrunch.

"Rainforest announced today that it has raised seed funding of $36 million led by Nordstar with participation from Insignia Venture Partners.

This includes equity financing of $6.5 million and a $30 million debt facility from an undisclosed American debt fund. Co-founder and chief executive officer J. J. Chai, who previously held senior roles at Carousell and Airbnb, told TechCrunch that Rainforest raised debt financing (like many other ecommerce aggregators) because it is non-dilutive and will be used to acquire about eight to 12 brands sold through Amazon's B2B service Fulfilled By Amazon (FBA)." [2]

While venture capitalists will not use debt financing as an instrument — there is no ownership in the company and returns are based on accrued interest only, which does not do the VC business model any favors. It is still important for VCs to understand how debt can play into a financing round, as investors will work with other financiers especially as the company grows. Debt financing or demonstrating the company can attract investors who favor more stable targets can be leveraged to bring in other equity investors onto the table in subsequent rounds.

Venture debt

Venture debt initially arose from funds questioning the idea behind early-stage startups being too risky for debt. While the failure rate of startups is still high, some firms like Equitec and Western Technology Investment argued that most failures only occur after a certain period of around three to four years. They then pioneered debt investments to account for this — repayable over three years and with warrants to purchase preferred stock. Warrants are securities that enable, but do not require, the investor to purchase preferred stock before its expiration.

Even if the startup does not have the assets, quality cash flow, and business model that more traditional debt financing can accommodate, there is a way to access debt. It is also less costly because there is no ownership involved apart from the warrants, which is in the single digit percentages.

It is also important to note that unlike convertible notes, venture debt does not convert into equity, though it is often used in tandem with equity financing. The argument is that venture debt lengthens the runway of a startup for founders to maximize valuation in their next financing round while minimizing the dilution that would have applied if the round was raised prior to utilizing venture debt. The types of venture debt also depend on which assets are tied to the financing, whether it's physical equipment (equipment financing) or general company assets (growth capital).

If not structured and utilized properly, venture debt can actually reduce that flexibility that it would otherwise have afforded the company, and actually make it harder to raise equity in a subsequent round, as shown in Exhibit 1 below.

It is important to note that while venture debt opens "doors" for startups that wouldn't be there through traditional debt financing or even convertible notes, the venture debt **should supplement rather than burden the growth** of the company. Venture debt can be a burden for the company if the cash flow of the company is weak, or if the debt payments exceed more than 20% of the company's expenses, discouraging future equity investors. It could also just be a burden if it is not useful or practical, as it is for companies with highly stable revenues.

Valuation Curve

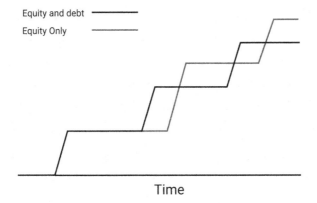

Equity and debt ————
Equity Only ————

Time

Exhibit 1: Venture debt can make it easier for companies to raise at a higher valuation while reducing dilution if the round had been raised earlier. Taken from a Kauffman Fellows' Journal blogpost in 2012 by Patrick Gordan.[3]

The various forms of financing instruments for startups all have their roots in either equity or debt, and have simply evolved, as in the case of SAFEs coming from convertible notes, or venture debt from traditional debt financing, to accommodate the riskier segment of early-stage startups.

For the investor, these available tools can be mixed and matched to meet the needs of the company. For example, if a US$2 million investment is too much to commit in an initial round, the investor could couple 1.5 million in equity and 500 in debt for that round.

It is thus important to understand how they stack up against each other in terms of:

1. **Ownership in the company (and corresponding dilution for the founders)**: how much stake does the investor have in the company?
2. **Voting rights**: how much influence does the investor have in the company?
3. **Repayment**: how will this instrument impact the cash flow of the company?
4. **Dividends (as in the case of equity) or Interest (convertible or not)**: how much is the firm /fund making out of the initial investment?

The venture capitalist will have to be prescient of the company's prior financing rounds if any, and in what shape or form they took place. They also have to be aware of other investors coming in alongside them through other arrangements and how this will impact the company and their position in the company as well. The type of instruments to be used and how they are used in tandem are also tied into the value we discussed earlier. Certain instruments restrict the value an investor can provide and make returns from long-term (i.e., equity vs debt), and other instruments are needed by a company to meet certain business objectives (e.g., acquiring assets). Both sides of the table therefore need to be aligned on how the funding will be used, so that if the financing round proceeds, all parties come out of the investment with potential for long-term upside. Exhibit 2 below summarizes the preceding discussion on the typical investment instruments startups tap into or consider to raise external funding.

	Equity	Convertible Note	SAFEs	Traditional Debt	Venture Debt
Ownership	Yes	Upon conversion	Upon conversion	No (non-dilutive)	Warrants can be used to purchase preferred stock
Voting Rights	Yes	Upon conversion	Upon conversion	No	No
Repayments	Until sale of shares/company (exit or liquidation)	On maturity if not converted to equity	No maturity date	Depends on terms	3 to 4 years typically
Dividends or Interest	Dividends at exit	Interest converted to equity; dividends at exit	No interest	Interest	Interest
For VCs	The typical instrument VCs will use; results in cleaner cap tables though relatively longer process	For VCs to move fast and get in a hot startup ahead of the pack	For VCs to move fast and get in a hot startup ahead of the pack	Not used	Not used
For Startups	Assess to VC money	Pre-seed, seed stage, or in urgent need of cash with presumption of raising qualified financing	Pre-seed, seed stage, or in urgent need of cash with presumption of raising qualified financing	For asset backed, positive cash flow companies looking for non-dilutive financing	For startups looking for debt but do not necessarily qualify under traditional debt standards

Exhibit 2:   How various instruments stack up against each other. VCs will want to invest with equity or CNs, especially for first checks into companies and early-stage startups. It is still important for VCs to be aware of other financing instruments a founder will open up their fundraise to in various scenarios.

Know Thy Term Sheets

Apart from the value exchange and financial instruments, the third element to consider in creating that long-term win-win scenario is the concretization of these two things and their implications for the investors and the company in the term sheet. While there are market standards and a general consensus to the terms that apply for various stages of investment and financing rounds, it is still important to understand the underlying benefits and costs of the terms involved in an investment.

When term sheets are given by a venture capitalist to a founder, they signify that the VC firm (not just the individual investor) is serious in investing, and that investing in the company has been approved by the investment committee. But term sheets are not final and are also non-binding. They are preliminary documents whose terms are ultimately finalized in the shareholders agreement (SHA) and share subscription agreement (SSA), which are both legally binding.

The key difference between the SHA and SSA is that the latter covers terms and conditions for *new* subscribers to acquire the shares in the company — SSAs help to distinguish between financing rounds. Term sheets are also not a guarantee that the investor will wire money at the end of the day or that the founder will push through with bringing the investor into the financing round.

Term sheets are a blueprint of the relationship between the investor and the company, primarily covering two areas: (1) ownership, or the terms and conditions to which an investor or group of investors will subscribe for shares in the company, and (2) rights, or the ongoing rights and obligations of investors, founders, and the company in relation to the investment.

As we just mentioned, term sheets, and even the legally-binding SHAs and SSAs, are generally standardized in terms of what terms are included or expected in the document. In Singapore, the Singapore Venture Capital and Private Equity Association (SVCA) — there are various VCA-type organizations in different countries — put together the Venture Capital Investment Model Agreements (VIMA) kit to provide venture capitalists with a set of standardized documents for seed and early-stage investments. [4]

The VIMA kit has the Venture Capital Lexicon, which is a useful glossary of terms relevant to both founders and investors, a Series A term sheet, both long form and short form (which we will discuss more later in the chapter), a Series A SSA, and a Series A SHA. VIMA also includes the NDA, which we discussed in Chapter 5, that is usually entered into by the investor and the company prior to running due diligence, and a CARE agreement, which is some sort of convertible note similar to YC's SAFE. SVCA explains the following caveats to using the documents on the VIMA kit:

> "For the Term Sheet, Subscription Agreement, and the Share-holders' Agreement, the following assumptions were used during the drafting process: 1) Investors are making a significant minority investment in a growth stage company incorporated in Singapore, 2) the investment instrument is Series A preference shares, 3) the documents are governed by Singapore law with Singapore being the forum for any dispute resolution."

Given these caveats, it is important to consider the nuances of each market, especially for the VC closing an investment for a company based in other jurisdictions — this is one reason why most regional venture capital firms, which are based in Singapore, will want to have companies they invest in to have a domicile set up in Singapore as well.

In Indonesia, for example, SHA and SSA need to be filled out in Bahasa and English. The process of closing a round can get more complicated with more investors involved in the round coming from different countries, especially bigger firms. That said, the more investments are done in various scenarios, the faster they can be closed over time as investors learn how to speed up processes and become familiar with working with one another, which is in the case in Southeast Asia where most of the big investors are familiar faces.

But regardless of the country or jurisdiction, ensuring term sheets create a win-win scenario for both the company and the fund is all about minimizing downside while maximizing upside. So while there are many terms to go over in the legal documents, it is important for a venture capitalist to be able to zoom into the terms that ensure maximum upside of the fund and the company and also protect the fund from downside risk.

There are also two types of term sheets: (1) the long-form and (2) short-form. As their names suggest, the long-form term sheet is more comprehensive, while the short-form is usually 2–3 pages, which is built for speed to secure an investment.

Ownership (and dilution, liquidation) terms

Before delving into the terms that directly impact the ownership and dilution of the investors and founders in the round, it is important to emphasize the relationship between valuation, fundraising, and dilution.

To review: Founders fundraise primarily to grow their companies at a rate that would otherwise be impossible with the current resources they have. On the other hand, investors invest in companies under the presumption that the valuation increase will generate returns that ideally return the entire fund. Investors can only realize these returns by owning shares of the company, which means the founders will have to dilute their ownership of that company (100% at the start).

Founders accept this dilution knowing that the growth that comes from productively using the cash they raised will ultimately raise the valuation of their company by several multiples of its initial value, raising the dollar value of their ownership in the company, even if the percentage value is diminished over time with more investors coming in. This is also the same conclusion that early-stage investors come to as they see more growth-stage and late-stage investors come into the company's capitalization table.

If fundraising is the platform through which dilution is accepted or company ownership is exchanged for cash, valuation is the agreed value between the founder and investor at which this exchange is made. It is also the point at which the founders and the investors are looking to grow towards future financing rounds and ultimately an exit event. This means that creating that win-win scenario we mentioned earlier for the fund and the founder is all about **finding that valuation at which both the founder and the investor are willing to exchange cash for dilution and shell out cash for ownership of the company, respectively.**

But for the venture capitalist this valuation during the investment round is ultimately hinged on an expectation of what the valuation *should* be over the next few years. Thus, the terms in the term sheet stipulate an investor's desire to reconcile this fund goal to reach this valuation with what the founders want in order to take away from the company when it reaches that same valuation. In other words, what are the founders and investors walking away with at the end of the day?

For all the terms we discuss in this section of the term sheet, it is important to note this dynamic, along with a few more key ideas. First, as we mentioned earlier in the chapter, founders will want to hold on to as much of their company as possible because the odds are highly stacked against them. Assuming investors take around 20% equity at each round from seed to Series A, founders will have 80% post-seed and 64% post-Series A, and this not yet accounting for an employee stock options pool (ESOP). Second, an ideal fundraise should give the company a runway of up to 12 to 18 months.

But not all companies will ascribe to this, for both positive and negative reasons. A good reason would be that they are growing so fast that they need the cash to supplement their expansion to stay on top of this growth, while a bad reason would be that their burn is too high so they need to raise money earlier, even if target metrics were not hit to justify a pre-money valuation they would ideally raise at. Third, in a round with more than one investor, usually the lead investor, or the investor with the highest stake in that round will dictate the valuation (or price) which other investors will then tag-along to.

With this relationship between valuation, fundraising, and dilution established, we move on to the important terms VCs should consider in term sheets when it comes to optimizing for ownership.

Pro rata rights

As a venture capitalist, we covered in Chapter 2 why it is important to double down on the winners. Especially if your fund's goal is to become the majority *outside* shareholder in a company, being able to double down and invest more money in a potential fund maker is crucial. Otherwise, other investors will come in and reduce the potential for greater returns (even if your position is non-dilutive).

This is where pro rata rights come in. **Pro rata allows investors to purchase more shares in future equity financing rounds, primarily to maintain their ownership in the company.** However, to protect against overdiluting the founders, these rights are typically afforded only to investors that purchase a certain amount of stock and are bona fide investors. These rights also do not apply to ESOP, equity issued in acquisitions, or "equity kickers" issued to lenders, landlords, or equipment lessors.

Pro rata only allows for investors to maintain its ownership in subsequent financing rounds, so a 20% equity investor, with pro rata rights, would be able to acquire 20% of shares of preferred stock issued in a subsequent financing round. This would be a different value obviously because the price of the next round is different as well, so the math is not as simple as 20 plus 20. That means other investors looking to really swing the upside in their favor will request for super pro rata rights, which extend the ability to join in a subsequent round beyond their pro rata share (say instead of 20% in the next round, they acquire up to 50%). That said, if the price of the subsequent round is too expensive (i.e., the valuation balloons), the existing investors with pro rata rights may not have enough dry powder to follow-on. Hence, venture capitalists will try to keep the initial investment as low as possible, while still getting the maximum ownership possible, and allot more funds to exercise pro rata.

Of course, this is great and all for the investor, but the company should also be strategic with whom they would give super pro rata, or even just pro rata rights to — is this investor valuable enough to justify giving them more ownership of the company? This is why investors will also try to drum up enough support for the company (e.g., helping them with product development, senior leadership hires, or pulling in co-investors for their next financing round) to justify requesting for pro rata or super pro rata rights.

From a portfolio management perspective, venture capitalists in prior rounds would also help founders, especially the less experienced ones, to better manage their capitalization table (or distribution of ownership in the company) so that certain rights offered to new investors don't bite back later on.

While pro rata rights *allow* investors to top up their investment to maintain their ownership or in the case of super pro rata, exceed this ownership, there are also rights that have emerged more recently in the venture capital space, especially in investment rounds for more capital-intensive companies, that *require* investors to top up their investment in future financing rounds on a pro rata basis or more in order to enjoy full certain rights like anti-dilution, board seats, and pro rata itself.

R&D-dependent startups are more likely to ask for these provisions in their term sheets considering the level of long-term investment they need to reach a sizable valuation and compete with incumbents.

The North America Venture Capital Association (NVCA) describes pay-to-play as follows:

"[Pay-to-Play:
[Unless the holders of [__]% of the Series A elect otherwise,] on any subsequent [down] round all [Major] Investors are required to purchase their pro rata share of the securities set aside by the Board for purchase by the [Major] Investors. All shares of Series A Preferred of any [Major] Investor failing to do so will automatically [lose anti-dilution rights] [lose right to participate in future rounds] [convert to Common Stock and lose the right to a Board seat if applicable].]" [5]

Liquidation preference and preferred stock

If pro rata maximizes upside, liquidation preference protects the venture capitalist against downside. In the event of a sale of the company or other liquidation event (not all of which is bad news by the way), preferred stock investors are entitled to receive an amount of money, expressed as a multiple of the original invested capital, usually 1x of the original investment.

Venture capitalists will usually make sure to acquire preferred shares or stock because of this liquidation preference (priority in getting paid dividends). Preferred stock also has the additional upside of being able to convert to common stock. In an IPO, investors could also choose not to liquidate their holdings entirely but also convert part of their preferred stock into common stock.

Then there are also two types of preferred stock: (1) participating and (2) non-participating. Participating preferred enables preferred shareholders to get that liquidation preference and then some remaining proceeds are split between the preferred and common stockholders according to corresponding ownership.

For example, as shown in Exhibit 3 below, a VC invests $2 million into an $8 million pre-money valuation company for its Series A round, giving them 20% preferred shares in the company with a liquidation preference of 1x. Before the company could raise another round, it gets sold for $20 million. With participating preferred stock, the VC with 1x liquidation preference gets 2 million back, and then 18 million gets split 20–80 to the preferred shareholders. All in all the VC gets 5.6 million, while the founders and common shareholders get 14.4 million. If the VC's preferred shares were *non-participating*, then the proceeds would just be split 20–80 straight away with the VC getting 4 million and the founder and common shareholders getting 16 million. Fortunately, the company gets sold 2x its post-money valuation in its Series A, but in some cases the sale price could be lower as well.

Participating vs Non-Participating Preferred

	Participating Preferred	Non- Participating Preferred
Series A investment (($8m pre-money valuation)	$2M	
% of preferred shares in the company	20%	
Price of company at sale	$20M	
Calculation of amount VC gets back	$2M + (20% x $18M) = $5.6M	20% x $20M = $4M

Exhibit 3: Sample liquidation event for Participating vs. Non-Participating Preferred.

The liquidation preference pushed for by an investor can also go beyond 1x during a cold investment climate or a downturn or if the business is particularly risky. 1.5x to 3x liquidation preferences were more common during the first few years following the dotcom crash, SARS, and the 2008 economic recession.

Anti-dilution protection

Apart from liquidation preference and participating preferred stock used by investors to minimize downside risk, VCs will also typically include anti-dilution terms to protect against their ownership losing value as more investors join the party in future financing rounds. Essentially, **anti-dilution keeps a VC's ownership in the company intact**.

To illustrate dilution, we can consider this scenario, also shown in Exhibit 4 below:

1. VC invests 2 million into 10 million post-money, owning 20% of the company
2. Say in the span of 12 months the company grows to become 60 million pre-money in the next round and raises 40 million. Assuming the VC did not do any follow-on convertible notes or

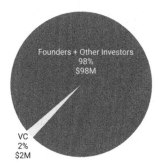

Ownership After VC Invests

Founders + Other Investors
80%
$8M

VC
20%
$2M

Ownership After Subsequent Financing Rounds

Founders + Other Investors
98%
$98M

VC
2%
$2M

Exhibit 4: Demonstrating investor dilution in subsequent rounds if they do not follow-on, using arbitrary numbers (extreme case).

participate in the next round, that initial 2 million at 20% is now just a mere 2%.

Apart from more financing rounds diluting an investor's original position, a potential manifestation of downside risk to protect against would be a downround where the company sells shares to investors at a lower valuation in subsequent rounds.

It's also important to note that not all equity issuances are often covered by anti-dilution. Incentive equity for employees, equity issued in acquisitions and equity issued with bank financing and leases will typically be exempt and agreed to by investors.

The two common types of anti-dilution dictate how the conversion price of the preferred shares owned by the VC are adjusted given the new conversion price in the subsequent round:

1. **Weighted average**: Reduces the conversion price of the preferred stock held by earlier investors if lower-priced stock is sold by the company. So the more of the company that is sold to investors, the lower the price of these shares sold, and the greater the adjustment to the preferred stock owned earlier.
2. **Full ratchet**: This is less used than weighted average because founders will want to avoid this, because the conversion price of the existing preferred is automatically matched to the price of the new shares, no matter how many shares are issued.

Stock options

In a simplified cap table, there are usually three types of shares involved — the (1) common stock held by the founder/s, the (2) preferred stock held by the venture capitalists, and then there's the (3) employee stock options pool (ESOP).

Venture capitalists will usually want founders to have a reasonable amount of the company allotted to ESOP for equity grants, typically 10 to 20%, and this percentage dilutes as the company grows bigger and bigger. The preferred stock terms that a VC will request also gives room for the company to issue these common stock options. These equity grants are used to attract and retain key employees, senior executives, and valuable advisors and board members.

VCs will want this option pool to be expressed as part of the pre-money valuation or already part of the picture before the investment comes in, so ESOP does not dilute the ownership of the investor. But then this means that ESOP and any increase in this allocation then dilutes the founder/s. So founders will then try to set budgets for ESOP, if there is an increase needed in future financing rounds to accommodate more hires.

Future option grants are also expected to be subject to a vesting (i.e., tranched or paid in periods) schedule: usually four-year schedule, with one year of employment required before vesting for 25%, then monthly vesting with continued employment for the next 36 months. This is so that hires don't dine-and-dash on the shares they are granted.

Vesting of founder stock

Apart from vesting ESOP, investors also want to ensure that founders stick around and are incentivized to grow the company. Though the founder/s own all the stock granted to them by the company, the company also originally reserves the right to forfeit or buy back unvested equity in case the founder steps out of the picture, and a vesting schedule provides the founder with ownership over that period that can no longer be forfeited by the company.

If founders' stock is not already subject to a vesting schedule prior to the financing round, VCs will include in their term sheet that the founders' shares be subject to vesting based on continuous employment and then become earned. Standard vesting is usually monthly vesting over a 48-month period, with the first twelve months of vesting delayed until those months are completed. That said, founders can and will negotiate for better vesting terms to credit time already served in the company and accelerate vesting in the event of termination without cause or a company sale ("double trigger" acceleration).

Before we proceed to the other terms usually found in a term sheet, we revisit the dynamics of valuation, fundraising, and dilution with the concepts we discussed thus far (pro rata, ESOP) in an illustration of a sample capitalization table pre- and post-financing with two investors.

To illustrate the impact of some of these ownership terms in a simplistic scenario, Exhibit 5 shows the pre-and post-investment capitalization tables of a company after it raises its Series A, having already raised a seed round from a single investor.

Term Sheet

Seed Financing Cap Table			
Round size ($): 1 million Pre-money valuation ($): 4 million Post-money valuation ($): 5 million			
Shareholder	**Class**	**Ownership**	**Value ($M)**
Founders	Common share	72%	3.6
ESOP	Common options	8%	0.4
Investor 1	Preferred share	20%	1.0
Total		**100%**	**5.0**

Series A Financing Cap Table			
Round size ($): 3 million Pre-money valuation ($): 7 million Post-money valuation ($): 10 million			
Shareholder	**Class**	**Ownership**	**Value ($M)**
Founders	Common share	50.4%	5.04
ESOP	Common options	5.6%	0.56
Investor 1	Preferred share	14%	1.4
Investor 2	Pro-rata capital	6%	0.6
Investor 3	Preferred share	24%	2.4
Total		**100%**	**10.0**

Exhibit 5:   Pre- and Post-Financing Capitalization Tables for a sample Seed and Series A round with arbitrary values. Assumptions: ESOP dilutes, Investor 1 ownership is dilutive. Computed using Insignia Ventures' Captable Calculator. [6]

Investor rights

This next section of terms covers rights ventures capitalists will ask for (or in some cases be granted by the founders) primarily to maintain a certain level of influence in the company. Again, this ties back to the fund's desire to reach a target valuation that makes favorable returns, and seeking this control de-risks or minimizes downside in terms of reaching this target valuation.

Board seats

For the venture capitalist, board seats are a way to exercise more influence in company building. For founders, board seats are a way to get the best leaders to support their growth. This makes it critical for both founders and VCs to be strategic with the composition of a company's board as it can affect the ability of both parties to create that win-win scenario we've mentioned earlier.

Venture capitalists will want to sit on the boards of companies they want to double down on, while founders will want to fill up their board seats with people that support them or are "on their side." Given this dynamic, VCs should ideally fill up board seats they acquire with the right people for the company and people whom the founders or leadership would benefit from working with.

Acquiring a board seat through an investment round depends on share ownership and how much the investor puts into the company. However, not all VCs will avail of board seats and will simply request for board observer rights. Board observer rights still grant the investor access to board meetings, which means they receive the same level of information afforded to board members. The difference is that because they are only board observers, they can only participate in board meetings in a non-voting capacity. This way the VC can still have deeper visibility into the company's inner workings, but without the rigor of having to participate in the board's exercises. Board scenarios coming out of a financing round would vary from majority of seats being chosen by founders, to an even split between founders and investors and then an extra seat mutually agreed upon.

Apart from being able to influence the direction of a company through voting rights (votes are typically on major company structuring or leadership appointments) and getting access to board member-only information, board seats are also part of building founder-investor fit, which we have discussed in earlier chapters. In *Navigating ASEANnovation*, Yinglan talks about board seats from this founder-investor relationship perspective:

> "I often tell my team that being on the board of a company is earned. It's not a privilege but an opportunity and responsibility to influence the direction of these organizations. The top venture capitalists are those who have been able to grow and position themselves as people who founders would want to have on their board, rather than expecting founders to hand a board seat in an investment."

Apart from installing board members, venture capitalists may also include clauses for more specialized roles, like the inclusion of a finance function to be hired by the investor, which could vary from term sheet to term sheet as the needs of the company vary as well.

Veto rights and protective provisions

After a financing round is completed, even if the venture capitalist leads the round, they would still be minority shareholders in the company. To protect against certain actions by the company that could negatively impact their investment, investors will thus include protective provisions or veto rights in the term sheet. Veto rights generally apply to the following actions:

1. Amendments to company charter or bylaws changing rights of preferred shareholders (VCs specifically acquire preferred stock for the rights that come along with it)
2. Amendments to company charter or bylaws changing the authorized number of shares of preferred or common stock (This impacts VC ownership in the company)

3. Redeeming or acquiring common shares, except from employees, consultants, or other service providers of the company, on terms approved by the board (This impacts conversion price of preferred to common stock)
4. Company sale or liquidation
5. Incurring debt over a certain dollar amount (Overleveraging of debt will bleed into equity of the company)
6. Payment of dividends
7. Increasing the size of the company's board of directors

If the investor has a good relationship with their founder, then veto rights are rarely used, because discussions are held beforehand leading up to board meetings and alignments are already there when decisions have to be made. Likely the most sensitive out of all scenarios where veto rights apply is the right to block a sale of a company, which can backfire on the VC's reputation if the sale from the outset is deemed sensible and the investor is simply overprotective of their holdings.

Information rights

Information rights are not negotiated over as much as other rights, but are critical for the venture capitalist to ensure they are included and abided by post-investment. It ties to the ability of an investor to maximize upside for their fund and the company, and is also another reason why VCs will at least want to be board observers. When it comes to portfolio management, VCs need to work with the latest information that comes from their portfolio to make realistic decisions and projections — annual, quarterly, and monthly financial statements, business plans and budgets.

Rights of first refusal and co-sale

In the event of a sale of stock by the founders, investors will want the opportunity to keep the shares within the existing shareholder base. Enter the right of first refusal, where **founders must offer the**

shares of the company to the investors on the same sale terms, before they can be sold to others. Along with the right of first refusal, investors will also want to participate on a pro rata basis (meaning the same percentage as their ownership) in a sale by the founders of their shares.

The idea behind these rights is to protect investors against shares being offloaded to an "outsider" with no real stake in the company or potentially even a shell company. In the event that a purchase to keep the shares within the cap table is not possible, investors will also want to minimize downside risk by also jumping ship with a commensurate amount of shares in the sale.

Drag-along rights

Drag-along rights ensures that in the event of a sale of the company, if all major constituents want to sell (Board of Directors, holders of majority of the common stock and preferred stock), then all shareholders are required to participate in the sale as well. This prevents roadblocks to acquisitions from smaller shareholders. In later stage investment rounds, drag-along rights could be restructured to allow only VCs to invoke drag-along rights. The key application of these rights is during an acquisition, ensuring that the investment can be closed without delay.

Redemption rights

Redemption rights allow the venture capitalist to cash out their investment (of course the presumption here is that at the time of redemption the company has cash to disburse). The typical redemption provision allows investors to repurchase shares at their original purchase price with payments made over a three-year period in equal installments and can only kick in five years after the investment through a majority vote. The important point here is that redemption rights are rarely triggered but they serve as leverage for VC to protect against downside risk and access liquidity.

Registration rights

While seldom exercised, registration rights require a company to list its shares with the Securities and Exchange Commission (SEC) in the event of an IPO so the investor can sell shares. Registration rights are divided into (1) "demand" rights, which require the listing of its shares, and (2) "piggyback" rights, which gives shareholders the right to hop on the registration of shares a company is filing with the SEC. These rights are not so much of a concern by early-stage startups because these are often renegotiated pre-IPO or by later-stage investors.

Logistics and confidentiality

Apart from rights that impact ownership, dilution, and influence of investors in a company, term sheets must also cover some key confidentiality and logistics clauses to protect the investors. A number of these terms below are also binding provisions, versus the previous terms and most of the term sheet, which are not legally binding.

1. **Exclusivity/No Shop:** To prevent other investors from potentially competing with them on terms, venture capitalists (usually lead investors) will request the founder to enter into a binding provision (note that most clauses in the term sheet are not binding) preventing the company from entering into or negotiating with any other party regarding an investment for a designated period of usually 30 to 45 days.
   For the founders, this is a reasonable request, given the amount of resources investors will be putting in to close the investment. Any inquiries or proposals from third parties are also usually noted as subject to review by the investor as well.
2. **Confidentiality:** Related to the previous clause on exclusivity, investors will also have the founders agree to another binding provision that the existence and terms of the term sheet, as well

as the existence of negotiations with the investors, cannot be disclosed without the investors' consent, except to company directors, officers, and attorneys. This prevents founders from "shopping" the term sheet provided by one investor to other investors as well.

3. **Dispute Resolution:** Disputes between the company and the investors over the term sheet are unlikely, but in the event of this happening, term sheets will also include a clause providing for confidential binding arbitration, versus taking things to court through public litigation.

4. **Confidentiality and Invention Assignment Agreements:** Apart from confidentiality between founders and investors, the term sheets will also provide for the confidentiality of all past, present, and future employees and consultants in a Confidentiality and Invention Assignment Agreement.

   This agreement ensures all IP from employees and consultants are owned by the company and obligates confidentiality from these same parties. If no confidentiality agreements were signed by key ex-employees who developed core technology or IP for the company, then this could be a red flag for investors in due diligence as that essentially reduces the tech or IP moat of the company.

5. **Expenses of the Venture Investors:** The term sheet covers commitments from the company to reimburse out-of-pocket expenses from legal fees to due diligence costs, capped at a specific dollar amount and payable at the closing of the round.

6. **Insurance Obligations:** The term sheet may also include terms that obligate the company to maintain liability insurance for directors and officers to cover litigation with respect to duties performed for the company, life insurance policies for key founders (to provide the company cash in the event a founder passes). This protects the company, shareholders, and company employees in the event of litigation and tragedy

befalling key leadership in the company, so the company can keep operating.

Term sheets are about the future

If you notice, most of the terms in a term sheet revolve around the impact of future eventualities on the investor's ownership and the company's operations. This is where mindset of Rule #6 comes in: as a venture capitalist, when you hand that term sheet to the founder, you are not just doing that to close an investment, but also considering what happens after that particular investment round. Will these terms help the company grow? Will terms help the fund generate returns? Are both the company and investor protected against eventualities that could result in losses for parties involved?

The VC is already beginning to play its role in the company building (portfolio management) process through the term sheet and the terms that a VC firm will prioritize on a term sheet (or place focus on to fight for or ensure are reflected in the SHA and SSA) are those that enable them to do proper portfolio management, and by doing so, maximize upside returns and minimize downside risk.

While there are certain market standards and templates as to what to expect and include in a term sheet, market standards are ultimately dynamic, and the company's unique situation should be considered, as well as the overall market environment.

In Southeast Asia, the dynamic we touched on in Chapter 1 between founders and investors can influence the terms that founders are willing to accept or the terms they will ask even in the first call (X dollars for Y% of the company). The more leverage founders have in a market, the harsher terms can become in terms of giving room to investors.

In Exhibit 6 we summarize the terms discussed in this chapter, categorized according to whether they pertain to the economics of

Term Sheet

Ownership (Economics)
Pro-rata rights
Liquidation preference and preferred stock
Anti-Dilution Protection
Stock Options
Vesting of founder stock

Investor Rights (Control)
Board Seats
Veto Rights and Protective Provisions
Information Rights
Rights of First Refusal and Co-Sale
Drag-Along Rights
Redemption Rights
Registration Rights

Exhibit 6: A summary of important terms discussed in this chapter to take note of as they pertain to Ownership/Economics and Investor Rights/Control.

the investment and how it impacts ownership of the company or rights and control granted to investors as a result of the investment.

Closing Begins at the Beginning

In Chapter 4, we touched on the reality that due diligence has already begun in the first call with the founder. In this chapter, we go even so far as to say that valuation, negotiation, and the **"closing" of the investment already begins in the first call.**

Part of that is certainly the founder already vetting you as a venture capitalist — whether they would want the firm and fund to be a part of their cap table and potentially you on their board. That's why we mentioned earlier in the chapter the value of having that "pull" built through networks, 5-star reviews from founders you've worked with, and potentially even prior success in operating companies as a founder yourself or leading investments in other startups.

Now we bring into the picture other aspects of the investment that are likely to be brought up in that first call, including the valuation and funding amount pushed forth by the founder. It is important to leverage some of the tools we've used in Chapter 5's valuation section to have a deeper understanding behind the founder's proposed valuation before giving your own take on the matter. This valuation then influences the amount of money you would be willing to invest — an overvalued or overpriced company will be riskier in the long run while an undervalued company will find it more difficult to pull in more investors.

Some tips to navigate valuation conversations in that first call:

- Come prepared with various investment scenarios.
- Do not hard-ball investment amounts in the first call. Pitch the fund's sweet spot and fall back on general trends in the similar industry or within the fund's portfolio.
- Do not low-ball, be fact-based in your analysis and feedback of the founder's valuation and ask.
- Pitch yourself as on the side of the founder. Make it clear that you are also helping them build their company — which you should be (Rule #6).

Again, these tips are meant to pay dividends not just in any call in particular, but also create an internalized habit and externalized reputation that also supports the investment funnel. Then as the company goes through the due diligence process, it is also important to work closely with the founders for the company to make it through to IC, as this will also influence the relationship going into closing the round. That said, a strategic venture capitalist, with the number of companies they are filtering through sourcing and due diligence, should be able to size up which companies they should spend more time on than others — whether it's because of the strong potential or conviction held by the investor.

Then when the company passes IC and the term sheets are handed, it is important for the VC to guide the founder through the terms, which means that the investor should know the term sheet back to front. Investors should be able to prioritize negotiables (what are the terms where there is room for negotiation or back-and-forth?) and clearly communicate the valuation, dilution, and investment amount that the fund is willing to walk away with.

Potential roadblocks

On the road to closing an investment round, there are potential roadblocks or challenges along the way the venture capitalist will face, especially when the round involves more than one investor. Say the round has multiple types of investors like strategics or corporates, existing investors following-on, and a couple of angels. It is important to make things as simple, smooth, and fast as possible. To that end:

- Ensure transparency. That means no collusion amongst groups of investors! Liaise with co-investors directly.
- Control the process especially if the founder is not savvy with closing an investment.
- Always align before turning in documents.
- Do not get emotional or biased. Fall back on fighting for the interest of the fund and the company (Rule #6).
- Avoid getting legal counsel involved in the negotiations per se, but you can consult with them to get feedback.
- Important to double check strategics / corporate entering the round — avoid having them as the largest shareholder (might lead to any early acquisition), ensure that board seats are truly valuable if afforded to the strategic, and check the value-adds of the strategic to the company.

These tips are particular to a venture capital firm that wants to lead investment rounds or be a majority shareholder in their investments. The main point here is that **while the venture capitalist wants to create a win-win for their fund and the company, it is also important to remember and consider the preferences of other investors in working with the founders to close an investment round. Founder**

Common Founder and Investor Interests

Common Founder Interests	Common Investor Interests
Finance the business toward growth and revenue goals while keeping a substantial portion of equity, which they'll cash out in the event of an exit.	Get the best return for their investment.
Structure financing so that investors are protected but long-term profit potential is not given away.	Protect their investment through liquidation preferences and special clauses that give them favorable options if the company doesn't achieve the intended result (i.e exit via sale).
Develop investor relationships and get financing within a structure that lets the founder keep control of the business.	Maintain corporate governance protections, such as board seats and voting rights, to stay involved in major decisions.
	Include clauses that keep founders and key team members onboard for as long as they continue to add value to the business.

Exhibit 7: It's important to ensure that the investment fulfills both founder and investor interests.

and investor interests when it comes to investment rounds are juxtaposed in Exhibit 7 above.

If you know where you are as an investor in the cap table (lead, minority, etc.), know the rights that come along with that position, and evaluate this position and these rights to be commensurate with the ownership and aligned with the role of this portfolio in the fund, then you should be on the right track as an investor coming out of the round.

And the more investments you do, the more you interact with the same faces or at least the same firms and funds. Especially in Southeast Asia, where the firms and funds at each stage are pretty familiar with each other, it is likely to be co-investing with another firm more than a few times.

Three Best Practices

1. Be transparent in dealing with the founders and co-investors throughout the process of closing the investment round.
2. Get yourself on the side of (majority of) the founders when it comes to negotiations.
3. Always put the interests of the fund and company first.

Chapter 7

Rule #7: Growth is All About De-risking Failure

Why do Companies Fail?

Most startups fail. These three words are the reason why the venture capital business model exists (and attracts limited partner capital), and to an extent, why this book exists at all. The high failure rate of startups comes with the reality that only a few will succeed to become category leaders and generate outsized returns for investors that managed to invest in them early.

It is worth noting at this point that "failure" as is discussed in this book comes in many forms. It could be failure that comes about due to a recession, dwindling customer demand and forcing shops to close. It could be failure in the form of a pivot that leads to the entrepreneur pursuing a more lucrative business. It could be failure in the form of the business finding no significant growth in customers and the entrepreneurs deciding to spend their time on a more productive venture. It could be failure that comes as a result of founders getting into conflicts with their fellow founders, investors, or board.

While startups often fail early on, as illustrated in Exhibit 1 below, with higher risks due to the lack of either clear traction, a business model that is being sustained (whether by external funding and/or profits is another discussion), or a stable organization, more mature startups with larger war chests from venture capitalists are

Probability of Failure at Each Stage

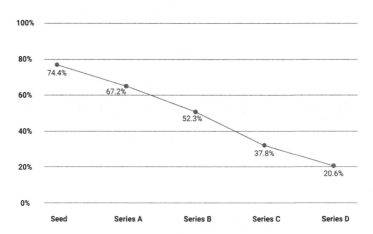

Exhibit 1: Probability of Failure at Each Stage, taken from CAIA. While it doesn't necessarily mean that if a startup does not raise higher rounds that the startup failed, it is an indication of how many startups do get to Series C level valuations and have the potential of becoming billion-dollar companies or fund returners. [1]

not immune to failure. The stakes are even higher for failure as these hypergrowth companies mature.

But while this high failure rate comes with high returns for those who succeed, this high failure rate is also the main enemy of the venture capitalist when it comes to portfolio management. As much as possible, they want their portfolio companies to avoid every possible turn of failure. **"De-risking" that failure becomes the goal with each fundraising round of the venture-backed startup.** This is because, as we have covered in Chapter 6, shareholders in the company, especially the founders and VCs, want each fundraising round to lead up to a higher valuation that could eventually reach a target valuation for a massively profitable liquidation event or exit.

The kind of failures and challenges that plague ventures, some of which are listed in Exhibit 2 below, are not unique to venture-backed startups. For example, finding the right hires are a challenge that many businesses face across various stages of growth. However, for startups the difficulty of these challenges is exacerbated by the pressure of time — the inability to build a team fast enough to keep

Common Reasons for Startup Failure

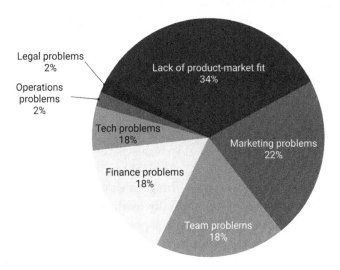

Exhibit 2:   Common Reasons for Startup Failure taken from failory.com. [2]

up with demand for a product could turn PMF into a waste. Competition could easily swoop in with a better hiring approach, get all the best talent, and take advantage of re-creating the PMF that the company lost. In a market like Southeast Asia where startup talent is relatively sparse (especially tech talent) and the landscape is highly competitive, the odds stacked against tech startups in the region are even higher.

Another complication is that there is no hard-fast guide to reduce the risk of failure for startups. We have mental models, tactics, frameworks, which we cover in this chapter, but it is ultimately the unique circumstance and resources available to the company that will factor into the company's decision-making. For the venture capitalist, the goal is to equip founders of their portfolio companies with the best tools and resources to be able to make the right calls for their companies.

Before we present the ways investors "de-risk" failure, it is important to understand possible risks of failure in the context of a startup's growth trajectory. We will use the ideal growth trajectory of a startup, that is to say, what that rare winner will go through to eventually create a high return-liquidity event. A visualization of this trajectory can be found in Exhibit 3. The ideal startup growth trajectory is filled with ups and downs, but it can generally be covered into five areas:

1. Ideation
2. PMF
3. Scaling
4. Becoming Category Leader
5. Exit

The reason why we focus on the growth trajectory to frame risks and challenges that could potentially lead to failure is because it is more practical to focus on internal aspects of the business and what can be controlled at any point in time, rather than wasting time on external factors beyond one's reach. Ultimately focusing on what

Startup Financing Cycle

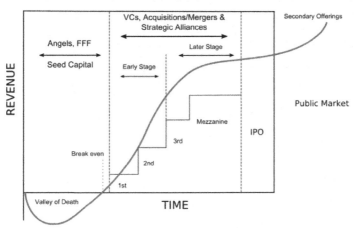

Exhibit 3: Start-Up Nation's Saul Singer on the financing timeline of a startup. Startups are more likely to fail in the ideation stage and as they struggle to find monetization on top of an initial PMF. At the same time, it is still possible however not to break even and continue raising money (which many question). [3]

can be done within the business should be reflected in the kind of external factors it positions itself in. To continue using the example of hiring challenges, putting together a founding team that can attract top talent and create strong employer branding reduces the risks of not being able to hire, even if for example, the market does not have a deep population of talent.

Over the course of this chapter, we will talk about (1) why start-ups fail, (2) how venture capitalists reduce the risk of failure through portfolio management, and (3) what venture capitalists do when it's time to make the call for a startup.

In general, when a startup fails at any of these points in time, it doesn't necessarily lead to the business automatically closing shop or the founders disbanding. This means that "failure" in this chapter does not just mean closing shop or liquidation. **Failure encompasses any risks that materialize and prevent the company from becoming a category leader and creating a substantial exit**. And founders can always pivot from these failures.

The founders of a pre-revenue company could participate in an incubator or accelerator to support a potential pivot while larger companies that have built significant value in the market could get sold by investors to a strategic acquirer (i.e., investors sell their shares and the acquirer closes the transactions by buying off enough shares to reach majority ownership). However these startup failures do have costs, whether it means downsizing in an acquisition or failed IPO resulting in a depressed valuation, or closing shop and having to dilute investments to return to investors.

Ideation

When startups are in the ideation stage or just entering the market, a lot of the risk revolves around the founders themselves, because that's all the company has that is tangible at this point in time. Founder risk at this stage can be defined through these three questions:

1. **Can the founder/s turn their idea into reality?**
This risk is reduced the more past experience these founders have relative to the kind of business they want to build and the market they want to build it in. Of course, this does not mean that it is necessarily a bad investment to put money in first-time founders, especially if they carry with them a certain "X" factor (e.g., technological know-how, corporate or government connections, etc.) that puts them at an advantage compared to more experienced founders.

2. **Do the founders know what they are doing?**
This risk is more difficult to gauge than the first, but from conversations with the founders and how they communicate their ideas, the venture capitalist can assess whether or not the founders have a clear goal for their company beyond simply launching a product. The best founders do not have to make a completely new pitch deck every time they raise money; they already have a clear vision and

story from day one and simply adapt their execution to the changes that growth brings.

3. Can they hire the right people?

People are crucial in building a great company as they are key/important to getting the company through the stages of growth outlined earlier. Great founders have the ability to attract talent.

Apart from innate ability of the founders, a potential source of risk could be co-founder splits, which could emerge from unequal equity splits, life getting in the way, disagreements on the direction of the company, or high-friction in terms of their working styles. The startup world is rife with stories of co-founder breakups, which some will say is also normal. At the same time, the way these risks can be mitigated also tie into the second question we just covered: clarity.

These risks still apply even as the company launches their product and could still emerge to become sources of failure down the road as the company matures, but venture capitalists will want to ensure there are strategies to reduce these risks from overtaking the company even before a product comes to market.

The PMF conundrum

To recap, PMF is achieved when there is (1) high engagement and retention with your product or service, and (2) this high engagement and retention is generated organically. Users have to find value in the company's offerings — that "aha" moment wherein they question where this product has been all their lives. Once that stickiness kicks in, they can't imagine what life was like before that product existed. Take the jargon away and PMF is ultimately about providing value that people are willing to pay for.

When it comes to fundraising, Series A rounds are typically financed on the basis that the startup has found PMF. So these failures are typically associated with startups that do not end up raising their Series A (the startup's claims to PMF do not convince investors enough) or their Series B (the investors are convinced, but the startup fails to build on top of the PMF, or the PMF is not actually organic or substantial enough).

PMF is a (crucial) fundamental aspect for startups such that investors will start to look for it as early as possible. That said, the failures related to PMF could already raise red flags even when the startup is just raising the seed rounds.

We've talked about PMF several times over the past few chapters, from its role in finding great companies to investing until to its role in producing the kind of traction that companies need to achieve a certain valuation. In this chapter, we focus on how finding PMF ties to the possible ways a startup can fail. In the next few pages, we cover some of the types of startup failures related to generating initial product traction.

Organic growth but no follow through

In behavioral economics or psychology, there is the concept of the "hot hand fallacy." It is an illusion where we assume that prior success also means subsequent success as well. It's been observed in sports like basketball, and it is also present in startups, particularly in how venture capitalists evaluate companies.

Venture capitalists, in their search for the billion-dollar company, will often find through their sourcing strategy, companies with stellar numbers and viral applications — but not all that shines is gold. At first glance, it may seem that the company has high organic engagement, but for some reason, it is only temporary.

From the venture capitalist's perspective, it is important to understand what PMF really means given the vertical and business model of the company.

A lot of startups looking to scale quickly will focus on gaining a massive user base first, but this does not necessarily mean that the growth drivers that brought in these users will also be the same growth drivers for monetization. At times this strategy to grow fast is inevitable in a given vertical, like gaming or social apps. Again, the startup needs to be able to have a clear plan on what to do once traction comes rushing in. It is like being a farmer praying for rain but not digging the reservoir to capture rainwater when the rain does come down pouring.

Across verticals, this risk of failure is highest in industries where adoption fluctuates rapidly depending on the season (ecommerce marketplaces) or across products (gaming, social apps).

We discuss some solutions to avoid or reduce the risk of PMF-related failures later in this chapter but generally, when approaching these markets with high fluctuation, startups will tend to take a more flexible pricing model or platform approach to their business model instead of a set subscription-style pricing model or services approach.

Great traction, but it is not organic

Now what happens if traction is not organic? This is a problem many startups face especially in verticals like ecommerce or last-mile logistics where the margins are thin, and competition is largely around pricing. In a price-competitive vertical, startups will either create promotions or spend heavily on advertisements to win over customers, but that does not guarantee that customers are there for the core value proposition of the startup. In a thin-margin vertical, startups easily find themselves in the red, especially if they do not have strong enough distribution to generate baseline growth.

Having traction subsidized by discounts or thin margins is only acceptable if there are plans to later on, top this off with a higher margin service that the existing user base is willing to pay for. If the company will be able to prove that even with the discounts, they are setting up adoption by a massive enough market that would pay back the discounts through other adjacent services, then the subsidies could be justified for a time. Grab and Gojek did this to great effect, moving most of their business from the thin margins of ride-hailing to relatively more profitable food delivery and more recently, financial services. Only if the market is massive enough and the startup has proven itself to be a category leader, would venture capitalists in some cases be willing to fuel this subsidy-driven growth.

If discount-subsidized growth can't be justified, dependence on it will slowly push the startup away from finding true PMF.

No traction at all and failure to pivot

In the first two types of failure, we covered the scenario where there is organic growth but it isn't necessarily built on stable ground (or business model) and does not have any monetization attached. In this third scenario, we consider what happens when the business is not able to find any PMF or traction at all and then fails to move into another direction.

This failure is less tied to the business model or product itself (because these are the variables that are changing) and more tied to the culture of the company and people in the team as they are the elements that need to be activated for the startup to move on and find the right PMF for the business. Perhaps the most famous story of this kind of failure is not that of a startup's, but that of a traditional incumbent — Nokia, as they failed to catch onto innovation that the likes of Apple and Samsung were setting.

Startups are not immune to this risk. Uber in Southeast Asia could be an example for this failure, where they slowly discovered the whole value proposition around paying a premium over taxis for a "chauffeur-type experience" was not as attractive as simply being a better "distributor" of taxis, or even ojeks. They tried a number of service offerings to compete with GrabTaxi and Gojek, but they ultimately could not find space in the market. While it did not run their business to the ground, it dealt a heavy blow to Uber's expansion plans in APAC.

When the market is not the right go-to destination for the company, the founders may pivot to a completely new vertical. For example, the co-founder of social commerce company Super was focusing on building a social media startup which he brought to Y Combinator before spinning out completely into the "ecommerce for rural areas" direction.

But even if the company has a culture and team capable of handling pivots, if finding the right fit in the market takes too long, the external pressures of competition could still prevail.

It is also possible that finding no traction at all is due to bad timing. For example, the startup could be a first mover in the property space, but if the property market is in a downcycle (low demand), then it doesn't matter if the startup is a first mover.

Scaling pains

Once the startup has achieved real growth (or temporary fake growth as part of a clearer long-term strategy) through PMF, then the startup has the foundation it needs to scale. But even as it scales, the challenges continue to compound on each other, and while the risks of failure don't go away, the stakes are higher, with more people involved, employees, investors, and customers.

The challenges and risks that come with scale — what we'll call "scaling pains" — can be divided into 4Ps: Product, People, Processes, and Partners. These challenges and risks we cover typically are encountered by startups after they raise their Series A or find their initial footing in the market, which ultimately have their roots in the company's foundations: leadership, culture, and vision. And the challenges that fall in each of these 4Ps can also be subdivided into "Transition Challenges" or what startups need to overcome or evolve to get to their next stage of growth, and "Market Demands" which cover the risks that come about externally as these startups scale. These delineations are outlined in Exhibit 4 below and discussed further in the following pages.

	Transition Challenges	Market Demands
Product	Finding future product-market fits (S-curves)	Developing moats against new players and incumbents
People	Hiring right leaders to manage processes	Hiring right leaders for expansion
Process	Balancing structure and speed	Crisis management and breathing room
Partners (Investors)	Meet existing investor expectations	Finding new investors

Exhibit 4: Identifying some key challenges (and potential sources of failure if not overcome) that startups face as they scale.

Product

1. **Breaking through the S-curve:** The first PMF is never the last. An ideal growth curve would have an accelerated trajectory that curves sharply up, but unfortunately every product reaches a plateau point where the rate of user growth slows down, as visualized in Exhibit 5 below. This happens for a variety of reasons, from the size of the market to the nature of the product itself. The risk is less about the fact that adoption rates plateau, but rather whether or not the startup does anything to break through this S-curve growth ceiling.

   Consider Facebook (now Meta) for example, and the S-curves they had to go through, from expanding their website to mobile, then creating a messenger app to accompany the core social media app. Netflix moved from DVD rentals to streaming, then from buying media properties to producing their own, then moved to upgrading their algorithms to make it possible to watch on their platform even with relatively poor internet connectivity.

   The idea of breaking through every S-curve and finding a new level of PMF is to open up new market segments that otherwise would not have found the startup's value proposition valuable.

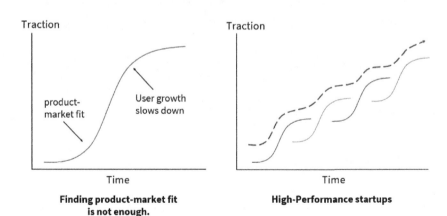

Exhibit 5:   S-curves of growth.

2. **Deepening and widening moats:** Working on moats can help manage the risk that comes with having to deal with tougher competition as the startup scales. This is especially true if the startup is a first mover in the market, where scaling will likely come with competition from both newer players and incumbents, and it is important that the startup has already defined its key differentiating factor and builds on it as it grows. The risk here is that without a clear moat, it could end up becoming a numbers game to compete (i.e., competing on price and market share) and the company could easily be overtaken by competitors.

People

Company Leadership: The demands of growth for a startup also apply to leadership. The kind of leadership roles that are required at scale will often revolve around setting processes (CFOs or COOs) or expanding into new business lines or markets (Country Managers, CEOs for specific business units). The risk here is that without getting these right hires, the company's growth trajectory could stall. Apart from that, other risks associated with process, product, and fundraising can also be mitigated by getting the right leaders on board.

Processes

1. **Balancing Structure and Speed:** Scale is all about balancing speed with structure. The startup needs to grow fast to stay ahead of competition closing in, but at the same time cannot be as scrappy as it was earlier in its lifetime. The risk is that doing one more than the other could put the company in danger.

   For example, an app could continuously build newer and newer features to break through S-curves and capitalize on PMF, but without introducing a more stable structure when it comes to managing engineers and PMs, it could easily become messy and even costly. The processes that come into play will largely revolve around managing an increasingly complex organization with multiple stakeholder commitments and employees, and can apply to technology as well.

More complex frontend applications for example would require a more modular approach to development, as opposed to having a monolithic code base. Alternatively, the startup would have to put processes in place to deal with technical debt (inefficient code written for the sake of speed earlier on). Allowing speed to overtake structure could lead to missing out on valuable growth opportunities presented by the market and create cash burn that hurts the finances of the company in the long run, potentially even forcing the company to raise prematurely.

Finhay co-founder and CEO Huy Nghiem shares on the "On Call with Insignia Ventures" podcast in 2021 how not having processes in place cost them valuable growth opportunities in the pandemic:

> "Back in April when we saw that growth skyrocketed, literally everyone in the company became customer service representatives. And during that time, we didn't have enough tools to serve clients. We didn't have enough admin panels and accessibility to all team members to actually solve cases for the clients. And it turned out to be, even though we had a hundred thousand users come into the app, we lost easily 20–30,000 simply because we couldn't serve them on time. That created a strategy for 2021. We grow in the number of users, but we also need to grow sustainably internally as well by nurturing culture and values." [4]

On the other hand, it is still important to maintain that speed of execution even as the organization grows. Sea Group is one example of being able to do this, with their ability to execute on ideas in weeks even as they became a several billion-dollar businesses in the public markets, as we write on *Insignia Business Review.*

> "As the company grows and even graduates into the public markets, the speed advantage never really goes out of style, especially if it is part of the company's DNA, as it is for Sea.

Sea's fast and exploratory growth has been part of its DNA since day one, and is one of the reasons it has achieved the kind of growth it has since. While some critics have voiced concerns over this speed, Sea's trajectory is not a new narrative for tech companies — this flywheel-ing has also been part of many of its peers' growth stories from China and the Valley.

Of course that doesn't mean that this expansion across markets and verticals doesn't come with its risks and challenges. At the same time, Sea saw the digitalization bus for emerging markets coming from a mile away just when it had gained massive capitalization from its gaming business, and decided it would not miss this ride." [5]

2. **Crisis Management and Breathing Room:** Because of just how much is at stake for startups at scale, and the complexity that comes with growing a company across several markets and business units, it is important for the company as an organization to have processes in place to handle crises, from a PR crisis (SOPs to handle various issues) to an economic crisis (a long enough runway to hedge against a dry fundraising environment).

These crisis management processes are meant to create "breathing room" for the company or insulation against potential external risks beyond the control of the company. While these processes are not necessarily in response to a crisis, they can be fundamental practices, like keeping costs low to reduce the impact of a crisis.

Partners (Investors)

1. **Meeting Investor Expectations and Finding Funding:** From the venture capitalist's perspective, the mitigation of all these previous risks around structure and speed, hiring the right leaders, finding continuous PMF and developing moats — play into the company's development towards north star metrics that would justify a target pre-money valuation. The risk of not meeting these metrics could slow down fundraising in future rounds, though it is not always a hopeless situation, and other angles could be used to sell the story of these companies to new investors.

Across all these focus areas, the risks for failure when it comes to scaling, boil down to two key reasons: (1) the inability of the startup to manage transitioning into a more complex organization (transition challenges) and (2) the inability of the startup to fend off the pressures of the market *in reaction to* the growth of the startup (market demands). These risks, especially those around market demands, carry on even as the startup becomes a category leader. Mitigating these risks early in the startup's growth ultimately pays off when the startup heads towards an exit.

2. **Strategic Investors:** If the founders or VCs do not pay close attention to the control rights strategic investors have, strategic investors could easily pose a challenge to the growth of the company to keep valuations low and position it for an early acquisition.

Category leadership

The reason for a startup to move fast and scale quickly is not just to reach valuations that are attractive to investors. It's all about building a great business, which means becoming the best-in-class and the category leader as much as possible.

Startups at this stage of growth are hardly startups anymore — they have already raised their Series C and are already even preparing to exit in the next year and a half or two years. The startup is also likely a unicorn at this point, especially if it is in a big industry or market. In general, the risks remain the same for the startup even as it has been scaling, but the key difference now is that a lot of the focus will be around keeping the stability and defensibility of the business as it maintains this leadership.

It is also possible that a startup will not have achieved category leadership even if it is already IPO-ready, for example.

But around the Series C and D, and pre-IPO rounds, generally the main difference between the scaling stage is that it becomes more and more important for the company to define what their exit strategy will be. It is even possible that investors would include exit rights in their term sheets in this mid-stage to late-stage rounds to pressure companies to exit within a specific timeline.

Exit

Exits do not always happen when a startup becomes a category leader or regional player. In Southeast Asia, more often than not, M&As will happen right as the startup scales, especially because the scaling pains we just talked about cannot seem to be overcome (i.e., too much competition making it more costly to break through S-curves of growth, inability to stave off a crisis on one's own, or simply no clear path to the public markets).

Even if the startup does exit, it is also not the end of the business growth trajectory as well. Depending on how the M&A is structured, the startup could still be operating as a separate entity with a holding company owning majority, instead of being completely absorbed by the acquirer. For the startup that does go public, it still has to continue facing the same risks it faced when it was scaling, with the added complication of being accountable to public stakeholders.

Essentially, exit events are ultimately fundraising events that involve a kind of conversion wherein some existing investors "exit" their investments and ownership goes to the acquirer or the public markets to be sold to investors. Thus, the risks that come with this stage of a startup's growth trajectory are related to fundraising, and apply to other financing rounds as well:

- **Is the company getting the right investor and investment vehicle?** In the case of the M&A — Is the strategic acquirer really the right fit or are the two entities merging really fit for each other? For the public markets, which exchange would be best and what vehicle should be used (SPAC, IPO, direct listing)? Is the public market environment and timing good for the company to go public? For example, the performance of Sea in the public markets (500% growth in their valuation over 2020) likely helped boost interest among public investors especially on Wall Street.

- **Does the company have the right people?** Getting a company to the public markets often requires having some key leaders in place — CFOs, Corporate Secretary, and a Director of Communications. In fact, in Southeast Asia, a number of the regional giants heading to the public markets — mostly having grown without CFOs for the most part, have all made sure to fill in the role for the business group over the past year.

  Having experienced CFOs (and company leaders in general) also plays into the narrative of the company as it gets sold on the public markets. For M&As on the other hand, it's often less a matter of hiring new leaders to gear up the company for an exit but more of filling in roles for the combined entity.

- **Is the company prepared for the exit?** The risks here lie upon whether the company is in a good position to be acquired (though also a risk for the acquirer) or if the company is ready to handle the rigor of going to the public markets. Preparation here refers to two things: (1) the state of the company as a business organization — finances, organizational structure, internal processes and controls and (2) the plan or strategy of the company in using the capital it will raise from this exit or how it will synergize with the acquirer in an M&A.

We discuss this more in the chapter on exits, but the key idea here is that risks around exits are largely similar to those that start-ups face as they fundraise. One can also account for these considerations in any other financing round, from the investment vehicle and investor itself (as we discussed in Chapter 6) to the preparedness of the company to take on a new wave of capital.

All these risks and challenges faced by startups we have discussed so far across the various stages of growth for companies fall into three main areas: (1) strategy (product, business model), (2) people (organization, hiring, processes), and (3) fundraising (capital, financials). These are the same areas that investors focus on to de-risk potential sources of failure that we have just discussed.

How do Investors De-risk Failure?

Another recurring theme in our discussion of sources of failure is that these risks reappear across various stages of growth, and problems come in all the time. The act of fundraising in itself does not solve these problems — if anything, it adds more complexity to managing the company, as Payfazz's Hendra once put it on the *On Call with Insignia Ventures* podcast in 2021.

> "In the early days, when I raised Payfazz's first ticket from Insignia and the first ticket from YC, I thought that after I have money, problems will be solved, but actually, you will have another problem. Right after Series A, you have another problem. After Series B you think your problems are solved, but actually, you will have another set of struggles and you will realize that actually, it's normal, that you will always find these hardships.
>
> And it will be impossible for you to solve it alone. So that's why I keep mentioning people. You need to leverage people around you. You need to bring a good set of investors who can support you from the investment side, and also be a good board of directors. They can be good people to support you in your decision-making. A good C-level and good team members can be the people to help you execute [on your decisions]. Don't try to do everything alone because that's going to drive you crazy. And maybe a lot of founders try to do everything themselves and that will make them feel really stressed and depressed.
>
> So that's what I want to share with founders: focus on people. In this case, I'm not only talking about the people that you recruit, but also the people on your board and the people that are brought by your investors, because they can influence a lot in your company." [6]

De-risking comes into play with how the company *uses* the capital and how the venture capitalist leverages their presence as shareholders in the company to effectively aid the founders in growing the company.

This whole affair of de-risking an investment as it grows and raises more capital at higher valuations (ideally) is what we call portfolio management. We briefly went through the various areas of portfolio management in Chapter 1 and how they fit into the venture capital firm structure. In the chapters following this one, we will delve deeper into each of these individual areas — building a great team, marketing and market expansion, fundraising and sitting on the boards of companies. But for this chapter, we'll be outlining how portfolio management can effectively reduce the potential for failure in startups.

The first rule of portfolio management is that it is not the job of the investor to run the company. Seems intuitive, but ex-operator investors, especially those in board director positions, are likely to make that mistake. Portfolio management is all about equipping founders with more holistic perspectives, wider networks, and more than enough capital that would have otherwise taken longer to obtain or more time from the founders that could be instead used towards building a billion-dollar company.

Yinglan sums it up in his conversation with Hendra on the "On Call with Insignia Ventures" podcast in 2021, and while it is from a board director's perspective, it also applies to venture capitalists in general.

"It's my job as a board director [not] to run the company for you. And I think a lot of ex-operators make that mistake because they try to operate from the board which is usually a recipe for disaster. I think the right role for us is, "Hey, we can't expect to know what's happening in the, you know, a few hundred people organization like Payfazz. But I think we have a broader vantage point."

So, we can sort of surface things that are happening macro-wise, worthy of consideration to the CEO. Our job is to make you Superman, empower you with some extra superpowers by leveraging our experiences from other domains and other geographies.

Ultimately the decision is still made by you. But I think the beauty is that we may have seen other mistakes or pitfalls in previous companies that may be useful for you to consider. And we try to ask questions that you know best [what] the right answer is.

Hopefully that helps you make a better decision or avoid a pit-fall or pothole. I think that hopefully we've done our job. The other thing that we try to do is that we are essentially a glorified recruiter. I think as you mentioned correctly, you know one of the great things about being a CEO is to surround yourself with good people or great people.

Recruiting takes out a bit of time. We try to share the load by referring you to good candidates or sometimes we help with the recruitment. Sometimes we help with the selling of the candidate. So I think that that is one of the things I spent quite a bit of time on. The third one is of course capital strategy.

If you do your job right, there's only three things you need to do right, one, you need to set a strategy for the company. Two, you attract great people to, you know, do all the jobs. And third is to ensure that the company never runs out of money. So our job is to help you shine in these three areas.

So how do you orchestrate the next fundraise? Some of our companies are going through IPO, M&A, even SPACs. We try to give us some data points, what we are seeing in the industry. So I think that that's our role. And there's no way we can understand what's going on in the company. What we can do is to sort of pick up things we see, and give you some data points so that you can come to the right conclusion yourself. So that's pretty much it." [6]

Here we note the three main areas VCs tend to focus on when it comes to portfolio management: (1) strategy, (2) people and (3) fundraising/capital. But even within these areas the capabilities of VCs vary according to the experience of the investors in the firm, the proclivity to focus on hiring for certain specialists in-house as opposed to having them outsourced, and the fund itself on how much value-add services it can support. So it is important for VCs to set expectations with founders on what the firm can and cannot do in terms of portfolio management, especially if the founders are looking for something specific.

This ability of being able to aid founders in these areas stems from the fact that venture capitalists are not just focused on one company, but an entire portfolio. This brings us to the second rule of portfolio management: **venture capitalists approach portfolio management from a portfolio perspective.** One can think of this as looking at it from the bigger picture and how to create a winning portfolio (scale) as opposed to just focusing on every single company.

Looking at it from a portfolio perspective ties back to the principles of venture capital we discussed in Chapter 2 — the VC is built on finding fund returners. Combined with the reality that not many startups succeed, and investors only have so many hours in a week to spend between sourcing, due diligence, closing investment rounds, and then portfolio management, investors have to be strategic with how they spend their time with each company. There are three key considerations — (1) performance, (2) ownership and (3) urgency:

- **Performance.** For companies that are already performing well, managing their spend and hitting north star metrics, the investors will likely only do a meeting every month, while companies that need more attention will get more time. This will fluctuate of course depending on the urgency.
- **Ownership.** Especially when resources are spread thin, VC firms will focus on companies where they have a larger stake. This larger stake, as we've previously discussed, also reflects the belief in the company becoming that fund returner, so it also makes sense for the VC to double down on potential winners as opposed to companies that have slowed down in their portfolio.
- **Urgency.** Companies that are facing a crisis (e.g., short runway) or are heading up towards their next financing round will need more time fundraising.

This time allocation came into play during the pandemic especially, when firms began categorizing their startups according to levels of need, as Yinglan illustrates on the *On Call with Insignia Ventures* podcast back in April of 2020, during the early onset of the pandemic:

> "What we've done is we've spent the past two weeks doing a stress test on our portfolio. At a high level, you know, I think 75% of our companies have a pretty healthy balance sheet of 12 to 18 months

runway...I think another 10 to 15% have six to 12 months and another like 10% have less than six months.

Those companies we really went down and planned out scenario planning right so assume you know revenue doesn't drop which is unlikely because there's a big demand shock. Assume revenue drops 80% then the worst case assumes revenue drops to zero or 90%. And then come up with what you should do in these kinds of situations. We came up with a lot of defensive measures for people you know, like cutting OPEX or shifting CAPEX payments or stop some of the expenditure and stop the bleeding. Cash is king right now.

And then for the offensive majors, are there new channels that are online? If you have a restaurant for example, can you solve your food delivery online? If you have a cosmetic company, they don't have any offline shops, and you do more of the sales online. And so on and so forth." [7]

The portfolio perspective also involves the venture capitalist finding new ways to scale the value-add that they can do and maximize the time they spend with each company. For example, instead of having to assist the company with their financials or fundraise, the VC might instead connect them with potential head of strategy and CFO.

VC firms might also leverage technology, for example, by creating their own media platforms or hiring platforms, to scale the volume of services they can provide. Then they could also venture-build or source companies that could potentially service their fellow portfolio companies as well. For example, a VC could invest in a HR tech platform to help their portfolio better connect to top talent in the market or invest in a last-mile logistics player to support D2C brands in their portfolio.

But this scaling does not mean removing one-on-ones completely off the table. In fact, the best venture capitalists run alongside their founders. This is rule #3: **portfolio management is about strengthening relationships and building trust.** Investors should aim to be the #1 speed dial on their founders, and a lot of what founders ultimately see as valuable will often stem from the hands-on attention that is given to them and their company.

This relationship-building does not just mean spending time, but what we'll call "get real" time. Venture capitalists have the luxury of having an outside perspective and are less prone to being blinded by bias, and it is important to call a spade a spade, especially when things are not going well. This candor with founders also entails sticking it through with them in the rough times as well as the good.

Portfolio management being part of relationship-building also means that **the effectiveness of a VC in delivering value also depends on how much they know about the company.** There are cases where because the investor fails to keep up with the key metrics of the company, they miss out on situations where the company could be proactive in addressing risks, and those risks escalate into issues that then require more time to support the company.

Sometimes portfolio companies may miss out on sharing information and this is another reason why information rights on term sheets is important, though this does not cover the more intangible risks in the company like those related to leadership, contracts, and personnel. So it is important for portfolio management to enable stronger communication between founders and their investors so that the value-adds are tailored to the company's real needs.

The demands of relationship-building seem to go at odds with approaching portfolio management with a portfolio perspective and doing things at scale. But the reality is that there should be a balance between the two. Every company is unique, but the VC business model also means that VCs can't afford to spread their eggs too thin across all the baskets they invest in.

In order to strike this balance between managing a portfolio of companies and building one-on-one relationships with founders, venture capitalists work as a team, delegating specific value-adds to specialists hired by the firm for this very purpose. Then persons-in-charge (PICs) for each specific company then serve as liaison between the founder and the rest of the team.

These PICs are oftentimes the investor who led the deal, is on their board of directors, or those whom the founders deem best fit to help them with their company. For angel investors, the lack of a team to work with means they rely more on a network to really maximize their value-add. Or they can join a syndicate with other angels, though the syndicate requires less commitment in driving value-add for their portfolio than a more institutional VC firm would.

These "rules" of portfolio management — not running the company, looking at the bigger picture (portfolio perspective), and building relationships and trust — help de-risk an investment by de-risking the investor. Because as we've touched on in the previous section, investors can become a risk for the company especially if they are mishandling their portfolio or leading them down a less than ideal path. By balancing scale and big picture perspective with closer relationship-building, investors can better position themselves to effectively manage their portfolios.

At the end of the day, how effective investors are in portfolio management boils down to getting their portfolio companies from valuation A (pre-money of the round they came in) to valuation B (post-money of the round they exit) at a substantial enough multiple to return the investment and make money for the VCs and the LPs. Every strategy, regardless if it's acting as a "glorified recruiter", advising the founder on expansion, or connecting them to potential lead investors for their next round, should go back to these economics of raising the long-term value of the company.

Below, we discuss the three areas of (1) people, (2) growth/strategy, and (3) fundraising/capital strategy in this context of achieving favorable economics for the fund and de-risking the path towards these valuations.

People: Don't teach them how to fish, get them an expert fisherman

Why teach them to fish when you can get them an expert fisherman? Of course, as we discussed previously, investors don't want to fish for their companies. But at the same time, teaching them how to fish (i.e., handholding) only works in critical junctures (e.g., restructuring financials, cap tables in preparation for fundraising) and cannot be done by the investor all the time.

It is much more efficient for the investor and more valuable long-term for the founder to be introduced to a "fisherman" who can come into the company and not only address the issues at that specific point in time, but also have the bandwidth to lay the groundwork for future risks to be mitigated.

These fishermen will often be senior and leadership hires, so their impact is much more pronounced on the organization. So investors will want to focus more on hires that are in these high-level positions and critical for the company's success. Having these key hires also strengthen investor interest and can even contribute to increasing a lead investor's proposed valuation for a future financing round.

In general, it is much easier to convince other investors to invest when they are convinced by the leadership's ability to execute on plans that will get them to a higher valuation. For the investor that does get these high-value hires into the company, this also serves as incentive for the founder to open up the cap table for the investor to follow-on their investment.

For a startup with multiple investors, it is not uncommon to have a scenario where investors field candidates at the same time. It's key to move fast and identify opportunities so hires are attributed to your firm and not others.

When it comes to finding these key leadership hires, Carro CEO Aaron Tan offers three considerations to make: (1) domain expertise, (2) the fit with other members of the leadership, and (3) hunger. He illustrates this on the *On Call with Insignia Ventures* podcast in 2021 with the head of Carro's multifinance business.

> "...One thing we found that has been amazing is that we have people like Helen, for instance, who is currently still the head of my multi-finance business.
>
> She brings with her a wealth of experience in the depth in the sector. So, the thing when we first got her onboard really was that we thought that, "We need someone really with deep, strong domain expertise." And in this case, we found a friend in Helen because she quite clearly knows her stuff. That's where we can come in and say that "Hey, we can complement her by injecting

tech into the multi-finance business and vice versa. She can complement us by the fact that she can inject her domain expertise into us."

I would also say to a certain extent, age doesn't really matter. At the end of the day, it's really just, it's down to the chemistry between the founders. So I always try to get my other co-founders or other people in the management team to interview other management hires. So the second thing I would say is actually it has a lot to do with chemistry. And you want to make sure that you bring someone on board that your other fellow early co-founders or management team can work with. And that's actually supercritical.

And the third thing really at the end of the day is to bring someone that is hungry. And I always say this, which is, Helen — she's more than 60 years old, but I feel that she can run faster than any of the 30-year-olds or 20 plus years olds in the company. I don't mean it too literally, but that hunger, that passion, that aggression is something that money cannot buy. And it's something that I feel has been critical for us." [8]

The "fishermen" the investor introduces depends on the size of the boat (the company) and the nature of the boat (B2B or B2C). At the earlier stages, the kind of leadership brought in by investors are usually operations-focused or even tech-focused to get the product right. The younger the company is, the less they can spend on leadership roles as well, so investors helping them hire will have to take this into consideration. As the company scales, more leaders are needed to lay down processes, safeguard financials, and expand the business in new markets or revenue streams. The leaders needed by the company will also tend to be more specialized.

Then when it comes to the nature of the boat, companies may also need an entirely new skill set when opening new lines of business, as smart access solutions company igloocompany's CEO Anthony Chow illustrates on the *On Call with Insignia Ventures* podcast in 2020:

"In the first three years of our company, we were very focused on working with distribution partners that have very strong retail reach and after-sales service support for the consumer market, like the individual Airbnb hosts or like the individual home that wants to rent out their house.

But as you go to large-scale enterprise clients, you need a different distribution partner. We need partners that are very strong in the enterprise tender process, you need to have great relationships with system integrators. They have great relationships with the government as far as large MNCs and have sold to these clients before because many of it is all about relationships and also trying to sell them the vision that we are providing them with a solution and also help them grow their business at the same time.

So it was a different style of distributor that we needed to acquire. And so we started acquiring these distributors starting in the second half of this year and going into the early part of this year. And we managed to build up these six to seven great enterprise distribution partners in the past 12 months. And that really helped to accelerate some of our iglooworks deals that we were working on.

The second thing that I really want to highlight is you also need a very strong enterprise sales team within the company. Similarly, before that, we were really working with the retail consumer, SME kind of sales, but as we went into enterprise sales, we started bringing on individuals from the industry that knows how to do enterprise sales to join the company.

So we have brought in leaders from the large enterprise competitors, such as Assa Abloy, which is the largest lock player in the global market, listed on the Swedish stock exchange with over $20 billion in market cap. And the president of Assa Abloy looking after the Asia Pacific joined us to take on our chief commercial officer role.

And he's really building up a great enterprise sales team within the organization. And the past couple of months after you do the sales, you also need to provide a scalable supply chain and after sales service support and to that end, we also brought in a very strong leader in the lock space as well. If you know of the Samsung locks, the Gateman locks, Gateman is really run by this company called Irevo. And the president of the company Irevo just joined us to head up operations for us within the organization.

He's able to help now provide great support for enterprise clients in terms of scalability of the supply chain, which is super important right now, looking at the disruptions that we are facing on the supply chain. And he knows how to navigate the situation.

And so with these kinds of leaders and a couple of others who will join us as well, we built up a foundation to tackle the opportunities that iglooworks has set up to tackle."[9]

The idea of getting expert fishermen or the right senior leadership to help steer the various aspects of building the company has a domino effect on the various risks and challenges we discussed earlier in the chapter. For example, getting the right CFO early on could stave off potential risks in uncontrolled cash burn as the company scales, complications in cap tables as the company raises increasingly complex financing rounds, and risks in preparing the company for an IPO to exit.

Growth/Strategy: Getting real and north stars

When it comes to supporting portfolio companies with strategy and growth, it is all about defining north stars (i.e., What are the numbers the company needs to achieve to reach a certain valuation?) and getting real (i.e., Is it realistic for the company to reach these metrics in its current state? What hard calls need to be made to gear up this company towards these north star metrics?). Getting real also goes back to having that "radical candor" with founders when sharing one's assessment of the company's situation and what needs to be done to hit specific goals.

What these north stars mean really depends on the company's business model (e.g., GMV, GTV, loan book size, MAU/DAU) and the market they are in (e.g., what is an acceptable level of market penetration given the market size?) but these north stars directly impact revenue and thus the valuation of the company.

In order to help portfolio companies reach these north star metrics, we consider once again the growth trajectory we plotted earlier in the chapter: ideation, PMF, scale, category leader, and exit. For each of these stages, there is a focus that investors pay attention to so that the startup can best achieve these north star metrics.

Ideation

It's all about the founding team, as we mentioned earlier in the chapter. Investors coming in this stage of growth will want to ensure that the founding team has all the people needed to hit the ground running with a good product. Apart from that, most of the value-add from the investor will involve easing the founders' go-to-market as they iterate and find their first PMF. This could involve giving them perspective on the market or connecting them with the right market launchers.

PMF

An important foundation for PMF, especially in a fragmented region like Southeast Asia is distribution.

To extend our fishing analogy here, distribution is a net to cost-effectively catch users leveraging network effects, brand, and partnerships, instead of spending heavy marketing or advertising costs acquiring every single user or customer. Distribution can range from creating an agent network (popular in rural Indonesia) to sealing a government partnership or securing a license (digital banks, biotechs), to launching on top of or within a platform with a massive user base (Pinduoduo on WeChat for example).

Focusing on building strong distribution reduces the risks of fake growth by already getting a certain level of buy-in from relevant stakeholders. It also reduces the risks of timing and missing the mark on PMF by creating a sandbox from which startups can speed up their iteration process and build retention quickly once PMF is found. Investors help founders create this distribution by helping open doors that would have otherwise taken months or enabling them to learn from similar models in other markets that they could then adapt to the region.

Scale

Scale is all about creating self-sustaining growth loops. The idea here is to reduce the risk of not being able to go beyond S-curves.

It also reduces the risk of overextending the company's growth (speed over structure) by strengthening the margins of the company and keeping its growth focused (i.e., moving into the right adjacencies).

Moving into the right adjacencies involves enabling the company to learn from its users and growth through data — hence, self-sustaining. One way we have tried to capture this process of creating self-sustaining growth loops is through "The Reservoir Framework" which illustrates five steps that tech startups (platform companies especially) go through in order to become self-sustaining:

1. **Building the Reservoir:** Acquiring users through distribution/ PMF (this is covered in the previous item on PMF).
2. **Capturing the Rain:** The idea here is to focus on retention and lengthening the LTV of each customer so the business is not as dependent on the influx of users. The idea is not to completely disregard new users, but to create a funnel that attracts the right users who are more likely to stay longer than just randomly casting a net for users.
3. **Introducing Use Cases for Water in the Reservoir:** With users retained on the platform, it becomes easier to monetize and expand into adjacencies that still meet the needs of the users and keep them focused on the core value proposition of the platform. Data is a key component here to enable the company to learn from its own traction and move into the right verticals. Ride-hailing companies in Southeast Asia did this step to great effect by moving into a relatively higher margin business (food delivery) that tied in well with their assets and user base.
4. **Expanding the Reservoir:** With a proven template from acquisition to monetization, the business then expands to more market segments or countries to increase revenue. Expansion could also mean increasing price of services or take rate of the platform, but this is less likely in a region like Southeast Asia where value proposition is tied to price and competition is often price-driven.
5. **Connecting to other Reservoirs:** With enough cash, and if the market opportunity presents itself (e.g., intense competition

incentivizing consolidation, or simply the opportunity to incorporate capabilities that would have been more costly to build on one's own), the business can acquire or merge with other "reservoirs." Gojek-Tokopedia is a good example of a merger driven by intense competition driving consolidation and strong synergies between the two players.

The "Reservoir Framework" is visualized in Exhibit 6 below.

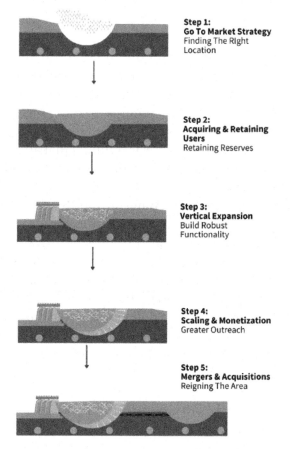

Exhibit 6:   Reservoir Framework for Tech Startups and Platform Companies as described in *Navigating ASEANnovation* (2020). [10] This framework was also discussed in an episode with Insignia Ventures Founding Managing Partner Yinglan Tan on the *On Call with Insignia Ventures* podcast in 2020. [11]

Exit / Category leader

It is important to note that investors should already be constantly iterating exit scenarios for their portfolio, even before the company gets to a point where they may have to exit. Ultimately these exit scenarios inform the investor of how they can help the company throughout the previous stages we have just discussed. In general, when it comes to exits, the main considerations of investors to aid founders are as follows:

1. **Comparables:** What have comparables done? What valuations did they exit at? How were these valuations justified?
2. **Neighborhood:** What is competition doing? Are there potential incumbent/strategic buyers?
3. **Market Data:** What are the opportunities the company can tap into to raise its value and potentially IPO?

Gaining information around these three things are important to effectively advise founders on how to look at life for their company and potential exit paths. These also paint a picture of how to become category leaders as well, though in most cases in Southeast Asia, becoming a clear winner can happen long after exit. Though of course, investors would want to exit when their company becomes a clear winner in the space or pulls off a significant lead.

Capital strategy: Aligning interests

When it comes to supporting portfolio companies for fundraising, the best way to de-risk happens even before the act of fundraising itself. As some would say, **the best companies are "fundraising" even when they are not.** They are constantly growing their companies towards a valuation that will put them in a good position to fundraise. It is best for venture capitalists to also have this similar mindset.

That said, when it comes to supporting a portfolio company through the fundraising process itself, it is about (1) matchmaking, (2) sales, and (3) structuring.

1. **Matchmaking:** Have an iterative list of the ideal investors and strategics for each company. It is always best to aim for the funds that can afford to give more than just money — business synergies, positive signalling, proven track record — and boost the company's valuation (increasing the absolute value of your ownership as well) without making it difficult for new investors to come in the following round.

   This is where knowing where the company is at in its growth and what it can do with a new round of capital is crucial, because this helps to filter the list. Apart from looking at this from the company's perspective, it is also important to maintain good relationships with the funds and investors in this list, even if they are not necessarily looking for a specific company.

2. **Sales: The most effective equity story is the one where investors convince themselves that it is the right decision to invest.** That means it is important to know what investors on the list are looking for and ensure that the companies that are pitched to them align with their expectations so there's a "foot-in-the-door" effect making it easier to convince them this company is the one they have been looking for.

   Of course, the equity story also needs to be grounded in reality, and this ties back to the idea of helping portfolio companies reach their "north star" metrics. A third aspect in driving an effective equity story, apart from aligning with investor interest and achieving north star metrics, is also having a similar view of the world as the target investors. This is where thesis-driven investing comes into play. If you are investing in a lot of health-tech companies, it is important to find investors who also share the same belief in the industry's digitalization prospects.

   This alignment sets up a strong attraction that helps the potential investor to convince themselves that they are on the same boat with you in terms of where their fund is going as well. That said, some funds or firms, because of the signalling and brand they have built, no longer need as much of a thesis alignment, because as soon as investors see that they have put skin in the game, this already draws them in like moths to a flame.

3. **Structure: Investors help their companies raise every round with the next round already in mind.** From an economics perspective, a company doesn't want too low of a raise because it doesn't give enough space for tag-alongs, nor does it want too high of a raise (or valuation) because it makes it more difficult to raise a future round, especially if this is done earlier in the company's life.

From a control perspective, founders want to ensure that proper rights are afforded to investors without infringing on their own capacity to lead their company or board of directors.

Finally, from a logistics perspective, investors will often help founders clean up cap tables and ensure that terms of incoming investors are also in the best interest of the company in the long-term, especially when it comes to strategic investors.

Assisting founders in these three areas reduces the risks of (1) missing out on the right investors, (2) missing out on convincing an interested investor, and (3) missing out on terms and cap table complications that could punish the founders or the company later.

At the End of the Day, There Are Only a Handful of Winners

But try as investors might to practice Rule #7 and de-risk failure, only a few startups will ultimately make considerable returns to the fund, and only a few of those few (one or two) will return the entire fund (if this even materializes for the fund in its deployment lifetime). That's just life. So, what do investors do when the going gets tough and startups fail? How do they hedge against the risk of accumulating failed ventures on their portfolios?

Beginning with the end in mind also applies to portfolio management. While VCs are always on the lookout for fund returners, as the VC works with their portfolio companies, and as these companies grow, it becomes clearer which part of the spectrum the company will fall on, and VCs will correspondingly adjust exit scenarios and work accordingly to achieve these exit scenarios in a way that still returns more than the initial investment. If it's not a fund returner, the fund should still aim to make money on top of the investment. That said, it is hopefully obvious this is not done at the expense of the company.

With IPOs or mergers of equals as the ideal exit scenario, other options for VCs to exit when these two are not as possible anymore include selling their shares to a future lead investor (secondary sale) or helping to position the company for an acquisition that ideally still puts it at a higher valuation than their previous financing round.

But that just covers companies that still perform decently but just don't happen to be growing fast enough or operating in a market large enough to create that fund returner. In other cases of failure where the company closes shop due to a crisis, for example, where clients fail to pay up on accounts receivables or the founder suddenly decides to close shop, the terms of the investment are simply followed, investors recoup as much of the initial investment as possible and write off the investment as a loss. It is important in these cases to have already prepared for these possible scenarios using the terms we discussed in Chapter 6 including liquidation preferences and reserved matters.

But funds obviously want to avoid losses as much as possible, even if they happen all the time in the startup world. This is why they thoughtfully invest in as many companies that fit their criteria early in the fund's lifetime in order to (1) have the time (and follow-on capital) to help build the company towards an ideal exit and (2) if the ideal exit does not pan out, have enough time to also divest before investors approach the part of the fund's life where limited partners begin asking for their money back and more.

Growing a startup is a battle against time for the venture capitalist. And a lot of the risks, challenges, and sources of failure we have discussed in this chapter come from the inability of a startup to win against time and move fast. There's the pressure to help move the company as fast as possible to stay ahead of incumbents and the competition, while at the same time the pressure to exit the company within the fund's lifetime. Hence even with these strategies on finding the right hires, gearing the company towards sustainable growth, and matching them with the right investors, if these are not acted upon fast enough, then the risks will only accumulate for the startup and the investor.

Three Best Practices

1. Avoid giving too much value-add, and where applicable, try to find people who can commit to helping the company and have the specialty to do so for the long-term.
2. Have a dashboard with north star metrics for your portfolio companies to quickly view how they are performing, with notes on action points being taken to achieve specific goals.
3. Have a list of exit scenarios, potential new investors and strategics for each of your portfolio companies that are regularly revisited and updated. Keep in touch with these investors and strategics to get a sense of how their view of the market is evolving and tell them stories of your companies when the opening arises.

Chapter 8

Rule #8: Culture is a Leading Indicator of Startup Success

Challenges of Hiring and Retaining Startup Talent in Southeast Asia

Coming from the previous chapter where we covered the various areas of portfolio management that venture capitalists engage in, we now go into these areas more in-depth, beginning with arguably the

239

most important and yet most challenging of running any business: people.

While hiring and retaining people is a challenge for any business, this challenge is more pronounced for tech startups in their formative years, for six reasons:

1. **Cultural adjustment.** The speed at which the venture-backed startup grows demands an iterative, hypergrowth culture that may be difficult for many to adjust to or keep up with (e.g., the expectations of growth month on month are 30–40%).
2. **Career stability preference.** Second, the risk that comes with getting a startup from zero to one may not be attractive to people looking for stability in their career. Given the size of most startups, where the conventional wisdom is to keep the company as lean as possible, most employees who are not able to find career growth or are not incentivized well enough can easily find themselves looking for their next career move after a year or so of joining.
3. **Costs of hiring and retention.** The top talent that startups would ideally want to have on their team may be too expensive to hire and retain.
4. **Combining industry background and startup preference.** For startups trying to disrupt entrenched or traditional industries, it can be difficult to find people who are both willing to join a startup and also have the relevant industry background.
5. **Competition (or lack thereof).** In a market with an abundance of tech talent, they could be easily taken in by more mature tech companies or MNCs and conglomerates. Conversely, in other markets, there may not even be that much of a population of tech talent to tap into, and some companies might outsource tech teams.
6. **Communication.** Of course, with Southeast Asia being a diverse region with markets having different lingua franca and specific cultural differences (even across regions within countries like Indonesia), this poses a challenge for many startups that inevitably have to go cross-border and hire in markets they are unfamiliar with.

In Southeast Asia, these challenges in hiring and retaining talent for startups are made more complicated by reasons 4 and 5. Most industries in the region that are being disrupted by startups have long been incentivized not to go digital and use the products or services typically offered by startups, with low labor costs making it cheaper to do things manually. The 2020 pandemic has changed the minds of many decision-makers in these industries, but the cost arbitrage remains.

When it comes to competition (or lack thereof), Southeast Asia, as an emerging market that only began to see a critical mass of venture capital and startups come together in the 2010s, has historically had a small population of tech talent and talent interested in founding or working in startups. Combined with reasons 1 and 2 above, conventional wisdom has also deemed a career in startups to be too risky, weakening the incentives to work in a startup. Media, pop culture, and more government and grassroots initiatives have since been turning the tide on this perception. There have also been increasing waves of returnee talent coming from the US and China but the talent pool still remains smaller than more developed markets. But even as greater interest in startups in the region and the continued growth of companies bring more people into the startup space, the competition has also widened over the small pool of talent in Southeast Asia. Early-stage startups find themselves competing against global tech companies or regional unicorns for the best talent.

When it comes to talent, a lot of these challenges in Southeast Asia also go beyond the startup and VC ecosystem itself and are influenced by larger socio-economic factors, like the prevalent organizational culture and work environments, labor costs, and education systems. In the book *Navigating ASEANnovation*, Ridy Lie, partner and head of tech at Insignia Ventures, explains these underlying factors, coming from his own observations as he moved back to Southeast Asia after a decade in Amazon:

"In my judgment, the top talents in the region are every bit as outstanding as their counterparts in Silicon Valley. They are as bright, as hardworking, and as hungry for learning. Unfortunately, there are broader factors that often prevent these top talents from building the best products. These are often embedded deeply into the region's cultures, institutions, and management practices. At the same time, they offer clues as to how things can evolve in future for the region's tech talents.

(1) Southeast Asia's strong culture of hierarchy. In the workplace, employees felt a sense of duty to please their superior. Their sense of community and collectivism leads to camaraderie and teamwork that few Silicon Valley teams can achieve. However, this strength also leads to one crucial weakness: the team's vision is only as good as the vision of the leader. As the company grows, the leader is further removed from customer interactions, and so too will his vision be further removed from what is happening on the ground. Startups in the region will benefit from emphasizing that every employee should place pleasing the customer as a higher mandate than pleasing their superior.

(2) Work arrangements not suited to better performance. Managing tech talents is vastly different from managing employees with clear and measurable objectives. Incentivizing software engineers to meet a managerial deadline will lead to a completed system that works well, but needs to be rewritten in a year. Incentivizing individual accomplishments will lead to a brittle system, like a chain is only as strong as its weakest link. Worst of all, forcing them to work longer will only backfire against long term productivity as quality is compromised. A tech talent needs autonomy to excel at his job. He needs to be given a clear objective, and then given autonomy to execute the objective in his own way, without the need to constantly ask for approvals or produce progress. To illustrate, tech talents are like scouts rather than foot soldiers, exploring unknown terrains and exercising their best judgment on which path to take. And if they find dead ends, they should still be lauded for providing valuable information for the army. Many companies in Southeast Asia fail to develop the environment of trust that is needed for this autonomy, and thus remain pinned with tech mediocrity.

(3) Low labor costs incentivizing manual practices over automation. Labor costs in many regions of Southeast Asia are still relatively low. This leads to a greater inertia to adopt a tech platform that requires significant investment of resources; why move to an automated solution when an army of admins could do the job at an acceptable cost? Take for example the financial eco-system in Indonesia. Top payment channels still include manual bank transfer (through ATM or manned kiosks) and cash payment on delivery to customers. Furthermore, many major banks do not have a programmatic interface, so fintech companies are forced to use a complicated and brittle solution of website scraping and even makeshift hand robots to operate physical security tokens.

(4) Fragmented education systems and hiring market. Lastly, hiring remains a perennial struggle in the region. The relatively few demonstrably strong talents are fiercely sought after by established companies and even global tech companies. For the rest, uneven education quality makes it difficult to find the diamonds in the rough. In general, tech talents are hard to come by, but I can see this changing. The success stories of multiple unicorns in the region are piquing the interest of many young minds. I am seeing more and more people, from Vietnam to Indonesia to Myanmar, choosing tech as their career choice."[1]

In spite of all these challenges, startups still continue to do eve-rything they can to build teams and develop talent. Venture capitalists can play a definitive role in this regard, lowering the bar-riers to connecting with key hires, especially for specialist or leadership roles, and positioning themselves as a third party in dif-fusing conflicts, addressing organizational issues, and providing insight for culture and team development.

What we'll uncover in this chapter is that it is one thing to over-come the challenges to bring in great talents and retain them, and another to really inculcate a company culture that enables this team to really perform and build a great company. What venture capital-ists learn over the course of investing in and supporting various companies in their portfolio is that culture, while in itself intangible, has concrete impact on the different aspects of the business.

This leads us to Rule #8: **Culture is a leading indicator of startup success.** While many people will look to P&Ls, users, growth metrics, and funding raised — these are lagging indicators. Being able to create the environment that empowers people to work together to turn ideas into these results and numbers is what company culture is all about.

This means that it is important for founders to not just pay attention to the money and the business itself, but also to the people who drive this business forward. Everyone in the company has motivations, mindsets, and morals (3Ms) they carry with them that reflect in their work, and especially in a fast-growing startup, these can easily clash or wear out. It is key for leaders to be able to align these 3Ms with the vision and goals of the business, and that is where company culture, as expressed in values, ideal behaviors and work environment, comes in.

For the venture capitalist, paying attention to culture matters because culture is ultimately shaped and finalized by leadership, whether it comes bottom-up or top-down — and VCs back founders. Apart from the role of leadership in developing company culture, culture is also what draws in and keeps employees — a key factor for growth in most startups, and VCs invest in growth. So VCs need to be able to evaluate how leadership forms, scales, and guides their employees as part of an organization in order to properly support them with recruiting and managing people.

How Do Startups Build Great Teams?

Before we get into the specific ways VCs help startups build up their teams, it's important to understand how startups build up their teams. We divide this endeavor into four sections: (1) founding team, (2) scaling the team, (3) building (and managing) a tech team, and the (4) impact of the company culture. For each section, we tackle some strategies and approaches founders can take to bring together and develop talent.

Founding team

Bringing together the right founders and early employees to form a strong founding team is one of the most important and yet least controllable aspects of building a team.

"How do I find the right co-founder?" is a question one will often hear in startup events, usually asked by an eager, aspiring founder. Unfortunately, **the reality is that there is no straight formula to finding the "right" co-founder. It is a personal decision, and highly circumstantial, even when the environments are "engineered" for people to meet.** In fact, one could argue that this variability in how one can meet a potential co-founder is part of the beauty of founding a startup — that the beginnings can come from the most unlikely of places. On a more practical note, the story of a founding team getting together can be an impactful part of the equity story, from raising angel or seed rounds when the focus *is* on the founding team, to when this story is also used to sell the company to investors in the public markets.

While there is no surefire way to pin down the right co-founders, attending programs, events and using platforms that form communities for potential co-founders to meet *can* increase the chances of finding other individual(s) who are more likely to form a founding team.

Apart from communities set up with the specific intention of bringing together potential co-founders, many founding teams come together through university connections (as in the case of Carro, where the founding team were all Carnegie Mellon computer science graduates), company peers (as in the case of Pinhome and other startups formed by unicorn mafia), or long-time friendships or relationships. Below are some examples and origin stories of startup founding teams in Southeast Asia.

- **Hackathons**

  Anthony Chow from igloocompany, shares his founding team's origin story on the "On Call with Insignia Ventures" podcast in 2021.

  "I just graduated from Stanford. I came back to Singapore. I spent about two years working at Singtel. I was in the data science team writing algorithms, analyzing data. But at the same time I was running a small property on the side, trying to manage it because I love to travel using Airbnb and I thought that when I have a spare room...I would just rent it out on Airbnb and make some money from it. And at the same time, I was also doing a lot of hackathons. On weekends, I would join different hackathons and try to do some coding and hopefully win some awards. So there was a particular hackathon that we won, where we proposed an IoT solution to help Airbnb hosts around the world, manage their properties in a much easier fashion and that idea actually stuck with us after the hackathon. And we thought that we could actually scale it up. So we took the idea back over a couple of weekends, we started designing solutions, building it up. And that was kind of the genesis behind starting igloohome. Of course it was a period of a couple of months before we said, let's go all in, but yeah, this is the short gist of it."[2]

- **MBA programs**

  Ajaib co-founder and CPO Yada Piyajomkwan shares on the "On Call with Insignia Ventures" podcast in 2021 how she and CEO Anderson Sumarli got together to start the Indonesian retail investment platform.

  "So Anderson and I met at Stanford during our MBA program and we connected really quickly because we're both from Southeast Asia. We have both worked in consulting in the region, in financial services. I worked on financial inclusion a lot with governments. He worked in fintech a lot with corporates. So we have a lot of shared experiences and passion and we connected really quickly." [3]

- **University Classmates or Serial Entrepreneurs**

  Indonesian money transfer platform Flip CEO Rafi Putra Arriyan shares on the "On Call with Insignia Ventures" podcast in 2020 how he and his classmates in university came together to start their first prototype while still in university.

  "Before building Flip, I'm with my two co-founders, and we're still in college, and before that we made many failed products together. We built things that at first, many people were excited about but as time went on, they don't use anymore. The common things that we see in terms of our failed products — the reason why these products fail, is because we were focused on the solution and not the problem.

So when the idea of Flip arose, the first thing that we did was not build the product itself, but we wanted to validate the problem first. So we wanted to know if interbank transfer fees are something that is a big problem for Indonesians or not. So I started to talk to my friends, but most of them said that they are okay with the fee, because the fee is a common thing.

As long as I remember, since I was in elementary school, the fee is already there in the market. So most Indonesian people already see the fee of interbank transfer as a status quo in Indonesia. But because at that time we were college students and we didn't have that much money and when we did interbank transfer, we saw it as one lost opportunity for a meal, because the fee that we need to pay to the bank was quite equal with the fee we needed to pay for a meal in our canteen in college. So at that time because we really believed that this problem was a big issue in the market, we started to think, "Let's just try to build a very simple solution and share it with the market and see how the market reacts." That's the start of how the Google Form idea came up." [4]

- **Ex-Colleagues (e.g., ex-unicorn mafia)**

  Dayu Dara Permata and Ahmed Aljunied, co-founder of property transaction platform Pinhome, share how they decided to start their company coming from Go-Jek at the end of 2019 on the "On Call with Insignia Ventures" podcast in 2020.

  "So [at the] end of 2019, I found my momentum. Go-Jek was transitioning from a founder-led startup to a successor-led scaleup when Nadiem left in October 2019. And I personally had learned everything about building and scaling a tech company. Also, the five hundred people team that I managed was self-sufficient, I thought. They would function well with or without me. So I spoke to Ahmed about this intention to start my own thing. So Ahmed was the mini-CTO for it, the same services I [was] responsible for…And Ahmed also felt the same way.

So we discussed what sector to focus on, what model to validate, and because we were deeply passionate about property and real estate, we decided that you know, it was going to be our first focus.

And why property? I mean it started from my own pain points. We used to live in a boarding room, eventually managing to save money to buy my first property. And every year [I've] been buying one property. Now I have 10 properties in total big and small, you know, from a US$5,000 piece of land to a few hundred thousand dollars landed house. And my dream is for all Indonesians to own a home and the vision is to make property more accessible for better livelihood and financial inclusion."[5]

For Ahmed, he viewed his time at Go-Jek, working with Dara, had reached its maturity and he decided it was time to work on something new. "The transition was very natural as Dara mentioned. We had a unique setup in Go-Jek where we ran our businesses like individual startups. So we would present our plans to leadership. We would raise funds for these individual products, which would essentially be our yearly budget. We were very autonomous. So we were free to identify opportunities and pursue them. So with that excellent brand, we were able to grow our teams at a suitable rate to match our growth.

But I eventually reached a point, coincidentally, around the same time as Dara, where our teams had the right leadership and had gained a level of independence that required less of our attention. At the same time, our desire to solve problems at scale was stronger than ever. So it was very natural to identify the next larger challenge ahead of us and apply ourselves to it."[5]

Mental models on putting together a strong founding team in Southeast Asia

There are two-levels to approaching this question of "how to find the right co-founder". There are the spaces and connections to *find* co-founders, but then the next level of the question is — "how do you know they are the *right* one when you do find them?" We list some mental models used to approach building a founding team:

Functions: The 4Hs

This is one of the more well-circulated and well-known recipes for a founding team of a startup, focusing more on the necessary backgrounds that co-founders should have.

The first "H" refers to Hustler, often the CEO or COO and the one in the team who has a sales or business development background. The second "H" refers to Hacker, the CTO or Head of Tech with a tech or engineering background. The third "H" is the Hipster, often the co-founder who leads design, marketing or even product.

The fourth "H" is the "Hunk", and is often not included in conventional retellings of the original 3Hs. But we decided to include this "H" because of reason or challenge #4 we talked about in the previous section: the need for industry expertise, especially in traditional or niche industries.

The "Hunk" is buffed up with all the necessary expertise to navigate the obstacles presented by getting into an industry like financial services, healthcare or edutech or a market like the rural economy.

While these 4Hs are identified as distinct characters, a set of two or three founders or even a solo founder could have all these four relevant backgrounds. That means when looking for co-founders, it is important to have a good understanding of one's relevant backgrounds and who else is needed to complete the "puzzle".

Geography: The pan Southeast Asian team

One way to look at life when it comes to building a team in Southeast Asia is identifying the key strengths each market in the region has to offer in terms of talent and building around that.

One idea (told as a joke) is to set up HQ in Singapore, set up a sales team in Indonesia, hire devs from Vietnam, and put together a customer service and success team from the Philippines. Whether this would really work or not is beside the point. The idea is to cover as much ground in the region through the founding team so that when it comes to scaling, there is already a leader who can focus on each specific market.

When Carro CEO Aaron was deciding on co-founders, he approached university peers who came from different countries in the region. This paid off in enabling them to grow their teams in these other markets early on.

Again, just like the 4Hs, the necessary coverage across geographies could already be present through the background of one or two people. SME neobanking startup Aspire's CEO Andrea Baronchelli's background as part of the founding team in Lazada put him in leadership roles in various markets — all of which Aspire has found itself present in. This also enabled Andrea to bring together early employees across all these markets, as he explains on the "On Call with Insignia Ventures" podcast in 2020.

"So that's really an interesting thing because we find it really helpful to have a distributed team because we need to make sure that we are always trying to be close to our customers and for us it has been working quite well. We started from the beginning as quite a distributed team. Obviously, we have people now working remotely anyway but even in the past, we had a lot of interaction across various jurisdictions. We have a lot of our regional strategies and teams that are taken not from people sitting in Singapore, even if Singapore is our headquarters. And this allows for the company to be not really centered, but it's basically moving as the market is basically evolving."[6]

Even though the mental model is named "Pan Southeast Asia Team", not all startups will need a distributed team across the different markets in the region, depending on the focus of their business. Nevertheless, the same principle still applies. If a startup is focused on offering a product to rural communities in Indonesia, a founding team with background or relationships tied to these communities would have a stronger advantage.

Social commerce platform for rural Indonesia Super's CEO Steven Wongsoredjo explains how they built their team around their focus on rural communities on the "On Call with Insignia Ventures" podcast in 2020.

"We are very fortunate and we have a very unique set of the team. Starting with the co-founding team we are all Indonesians.

Three of us used to study in the US, and we grew up in tier-two cities. We speak the local language. Therefore it gives us an advantage, I would say, to speak with locals to build our marketing field team.

So our marketing field team basically consists of villagers, so we directly hire people from the villages to be able to tell us to identify which organizations we can go after to find these community leaders that are basically people who have 50 to a hundred network across their WhatsApp group or social media, and then they're known in society.

Because social capital is quite important here for Indonesians, so once you gain trust from other people, it is easier actually for you to sell to other people. And other agents consist of typical housewives, who are community leaders. Some of them are mom-and-pop owners." [7]

Geographic fit does not just pertain to the ability to build teams within the market but also navigate it and leverage relationships there, with suppliers, investors, or even regulators.

Market: Deep vs Shallow markets

This mental model evaluates markets as a basis for deciding how to put together a founding team. A "hot" or "deep" market with a lot of talent coming in, like ecommerce or fintech, means that it is better (and easier) to have a flatter organization where you have multiple co-founders or leaders contributing specialist perspectives and skills applicable to that specific vertical. The founders can afford to hire a lot of talent who have backgrounds in the same vertical, and the challenge is to actually sift through the noise and find the talent who will truly contribute to the team.

On the other hand, a "cold" or "shallow" market with not that much talent, say in agritech or even space tech and blockchain tech, may require a founder to build a more "octopus" type of team with one or two founders leading the way while there are more function-specific specialties who may not have industry-relevant background. The presumption is that in a market with a small pool of talent, founders are forced to hire outside of the industry and even though they get the best talent for specific functions, the founders still need to provide direction relevant to the industry.

Aside from influencing the way a founding team might be managed, the depth of a market also affects the way the founding team will balance hiring for tech skill sets and industry experience. **One way to get the best of both worlds is by hiring to build teams, instead of hiring to get the best individuals**. By forming teams that can work together and benefit from having both tech and industry expertise, this reduces the risk posed by not operating in a deep market.

Skill Level: "A" engineers attract "A" engineers

Another way to approach putting together a founding team, especially for a tech startup, is to focus on having the best tech and engineering talent. The principle behind this is that "A" engineers attract "A" engineers, "B" engineers attract "C" engineers, and "C" engineers find it hard to attract anybody.

Bringing together top talent in the founding team sets up the company for more success in scaling the team later on. This could apply not just to engineering but to other types of roles as well. But how do you know they are the best, especially if you are not an engineer yourself? A lot can be gleaned from the background and given the supply-demand dynamics for engineering talent in the region, the bargaining power is still largely in the hands of the engineers and those with high qualifications.

That said, in the pursuit of finding "A" engineers, tech companies within the region will set up teams from other markets where there is a greater concentration of tech talent, forsaking geographic priorities of their business to have the best engineering talent on their teams, whether they be based in the Silicon Valley, Hangzhou, or Bangalore.

Culture: Hypergrowth fit

This mental model focuses on the ability of an individual to work in the unique environment that a startup offers — an environment where execution speed is much faster than most business environments, and the expectations of growth are also much higher.

Often described as "hunger", "grit", "self-motivation", having people with this mindset in the founding team and early on in the life of the company is critical to getting the startup off the ground and reducing the risks that come with building a business fraught with such uncertainty.

Keeping up with the growth of a startup may not be for everyone, which means founders need to be conscious of this ability to adapt as they hire, as Indonesian insurtech marketplace Lifepal CEO and ex-Lazada co-founder Giacomo Ficari explains on the *On Call with Insignia Ventures* podcast in 2021.

"Hypergrowth is not for everyone. And I'm realizing that not everyone has the origin and personality to grow the business or a department by 30–40% every month for years.

Many people like the idea but they actually fail to execute. And this is really hard because lots of times it's the motivation because it's really hard to grow 40% especially in the early days when resources are limited and you need to really be focused. So I've seen people accepting smaller growth because hypergrowth is painful or maybe they are unable or unwilling to grow personally or willing also to find the resources externally.

So to solve this problem I changed my hiring criteria. Before, I was hiring by startup fit. That has always been really important, especially in the early days. Now I started hiring by [evaluating] fast-growing startup fit. And if a person has been part of a startup that grew like 3–5x a year this person probably is comfortable with hypergrowth and thinks that it is even normal. Otherwise, it can be painful for many people, this journey.

Sometimes product-market fit and product iteration take time. And even if you get it, really few companies get product-market fit that really is exponential. Lazada was not really exponential by magic. It was us in the beginning who really pushed the growth and really understood things and executed things and solved problems.

And this is something that doesn't come for free. And it's a lot of stress, right? Because you don't know what the future will look like. You don't know if you're going in the right direction or maybe you have been failing the past six months. So this kind of sense of uncertainty and the fact that you need to push it and it's not automatic makes it really draining.

And I think that uncertainty can be really heavy for many people. On the other hand, I think people who have lived that, actually have this mindset where they actually accept that it is tough. Maybe because their first job was actually in a fast-growing startup, so they don't even know how easy things are in a nice corporation.

And sometimes I meet with people that say, "Oh, you're growing 40% a year. Oh, this is really slow. When my previous company did an IPO, we were growing much more." And then you meet the opposite person, "Oh 40% you are kind of the idol." So you really see different perspectives of what is normal and it's really hard to change how people see normality." [9]

This hypergrowth fit and desire to create impact can be motivated by belief in the vision of the company, as Intellect CEO Theodoric Chew shares on the *On Call with Insignia Ventures* podcast in 2021.

"When we hire, we try to hire quite strongly for culture fit as well right, not just the fact that they are collaborative, but also what the motive is behind when they join a company. Is it for a stepping-stone to the next big career in the next few years, or is it really trying to solve an issue? So again, we've been quite lucky here in the space that we're in, with the attention that we've been getting as well, we get quite a good amount of interest from people that have two things, right?

It's number one either they have a strong case and passion for mental health as a whole. We've got about a good one-third of our team that has strong journeys on their own with their mental wellbeing. They've been through therapy, myself included — I get this quite often that's why I started the company. It's because I've been through therapy, I've had anxiety and I've seen the benefits of it. And I think a lot of people can benefit from it as well. But one thing is we definitely can't expect to find [patients] in every hire we make as well. So the other thing is that we try to find people that have a desire to make an impact in their own way. Be it reaching people to benefit them or just trying to reach a scale that can have some form of impact. Whether it's the health space, whether it's finance, whether it's insurance. I think it's just impacting people in different ways. They don't see it as a job itself, they have deeper [motivation] that drives them to stay the extra hour to kind of do this or wherever they're needed. That's a key piece that I think we have on our side with the space that we're in."[9]

The mental models for forming founding teams and bringing together key early employees are summarized in the table in Exhibit 1 below.

Mental Models	Focus	Questions / Considerations for founding team, early employees
4Hs: Hustler, Hacker, Hipster, Hunk	Functions/ Skill Sets	Which of these skill sets or functions are already present in the current team? Which ones are missing?
The Pan Southeast Asian Team	Geography	What geographies/market segments are important to the business? Are there people in the team who can navigate the business (regulation, relationships) and help grow teams in these geographies?
Deep vs Shallow Markets	Markets	How deep is the depth of talent in the sector? Is it a competitive space for hiring talent?
"A" engineers hire "A" engineers	Skill Levels	How skilled are these people? Will they be able to attract equally or more skilled hires as well?
Hypergrowth	Culture/ Work Ethic	Is the team capable of handling hypergrowth and have the drive to pursue it consistently? What drives or motivates them to be a part of the team?

Exhibit 1: Summary of Mental Models and corresponding considerations.

These mental models can and should be used in conjunction with each other. While each mental model focuses on different aspects (functions, geography, market, skill and drive), the underlying principle for all four of these is to form a founding team that (1) complements each other and (2) can attract the right talent relevant to the business as it scales later on.

Finding **complementary founders is important because the *inability* to gel together and resolve *incongruencies* poses high risk for the startup as it grows.** As we mentioned earlier in the chapter, **founding teams determine the direction teams will scale.** It is best for founders to plan several steps ahead when it comes to the implications of bringing in co-founders or early employees. These mental models can also be revisited as the company scales to see if the company (as a more complex and populated organization) continues in the same direction it did in its formative period.

For the venture capitalist, these mental models can be useful in gauging whether a team is well-suited to tackle an industry or vertical. It is important for VCs, even in sourcing, to already be able to reason why a founding team would be worth investing in or not and can use several of these mental models as it fits with the demands of the market.

Apart from getting into spaces or communities that increase the likelihood of finding potential co-founders and being able to evaluate what kind of founding team would best fit the business, there is also the matter of what it will take to attract the right co-founders and early employees.

Some considerations of what will attract talent:

- Do you offer ESOP (Employee Stock Ownership Plan), benefits, insurance? For ESOP in particular it is important to note that ESOP (typically around 10%–15% at the beginning) is diluted as the startup fundraises and it may be necessary to top-up ESOP especially if the startup is looking to hire more specialized roles or seasoned industry experts as the startup scales or expands into new lines of business. ESOP top-ups impact shareholders, an important consideration when allocating and offering/ spending ESOP.
- What kind of work culture is the company forming? Is it aligned with their work style or values?

- Would they have good chemistry with the rest of the founding team (important to have conversations with other co-founders especially if they are taking a leadership role)?
- Are they able to meet certain work arrangements?

Scaling teams

In the process of turning an idea into reality, iterating until the first product-market fit and launching the product, the founding team's leadership and the approach to hiring employees generally follow similar notes of laying the groundwork to be able to grow the organization in the right direction.

But as the startup acquires more users, opens up new opportunities for growth, or undergoes a critical pivot, the approach to acquiring and retaining talent has to be tailored to deal with an increasingly complex organization and the demands of ensuring people can keep up with growth.

In this section, we cover several scenarios or challenges that startups will face when it comes to developing their teams as their business scales:

Hiring ahead

An important mindset to have when scaling a team is to always think ahead — having foresight on how the company will scale in the next twelve to eighteen months and what gaps need to be filled in terms of roles. Mental health company Intellect CEO Theodoric Chew explains this mindset on the *On Call with Insignia Ventures* podcast in 2021.

"As a founder, I do take a step back and assess what are the biggest gaps in our team right now. What are my ceilings? What are my co-founders' ceilings that we've kind of reached and crossed, right, and I'll give you an example from the start.

For the first twelve months or more, I was the PM, I was the product designer, I did the UI, did the copy and it kind of reached a ceiling. We did pretty well, but until a certain point, I didn't have the bandwidth to do it, so I shouldn't do it. And then there's a lot of gaps that I can't handle myself as well.

So that's one key piece of how we get people that can fill the gaps that myself and my co-founders have, and then, really grow from there as well. So when we hire as well, we try to hire what's the best fit for us and for the next twelve months to eighteen months, rather than thinking of going for the next, like the most senior person. So I think that's something I have to learn the hard way. So those are a few things that we try to do in these two points that you mentioned."[9]

Entering new verticals

As the startup goes from one product to a platform and ecosystem of various products and services, it is highly possible that leadership will find themselves in unfamiliar verticals, and need more specialized leadership to help navigate this new territory. For example, a payments platform expanding into a digital bank will want to have a banking professional familiar with regulation and licenses.

An ecommerce company looking to upgrade their AI capabilities to improve the consumer experience on their platform will want to bring on an AI expert to oversee these initiatives. Bringing in specialists or vertical-specific experts goes beyond leadership — it could also be a matter of creating entirely new teams.

In Chapter 7 we talked about smart access company igloocompany's expansion from B2C to B2B or enterprise solutions, and this required leadership to bring in industry veterans to lead new enterprise sales teams. But the formation of these teams also still starts with having the right specialist leaders.

One can think of it as creating startups with the startup and having mini-CEOs for each business unit. Setting up specializations and the resulting siloes are inevitable, and this makes cross-functional communication all the more important.

Going cross-border / entering new markets

Apart from entering new verticals, Southeast Asia startups are also likely to find themselves entering new markets as they scale.

Similar to entering new verticals, leadership will need to build teams to occupy these new markets.

Ideally, following the mental models we listed earlier in the chapter, if this market expansion was already in the cards early on, they would have already gotten somebody in the team who could then help with expansion at the right time. Regardless, occupying new markets can be approached in three ways.

The first is by having a team from HQ migrate and set up shop in the new market, serving as leadership as they hire local employees. This is practical if the team from HQ is already composed of locals in the target market or if the business does not find the need for localized leadership given the industry they are in. The second is by building the team from the ground up in the new market, hiring a local as head of the country. This is best used in cases where the business only needs a small team in that market or if HQ leadership deems the head of the country to already be aligned enough.

The third is in the middle, where HQ leadership comes in to explore the market for a period of time, while bringing in local employees, after which local employees are promoted to lead the business. This third approach is sort of a "compromise" between the two, still bringing in the benefits of having leadership from HQ being able to align the local team while also having the local team eventually take the lead, knowing the market best. Janio CEO and co-founder Junkai Ng explains on *Insignia Business Review* in 2019 how the third method worked in expanding their team across Southeast Asia.

"There are generally two ways to go about setting up a team in a new market. Either HQ can hire a local as head of country first or send people to do the initial setup.

It is too much to expect that a fresh local team would be able to lead country operations with 100% cultural and [strategic] alignment. They may be able to move faster, but they would operate with their own agendas and SOPs. If not handled carefully, this can have severe consequences down the line.

On the other hand, sending over a team to a new market trades off speed for alignment. The team's acclimatization can weigh heavily on the company's runway. Janio got rid of the trade-off problem and did both approaches.

"What we do now is station folks we trust in Singapore overseas for three to six months and give them a fixed set of agenda to achieve within that period. Once they hit those milestones, we build a secondary local team below them who can inherit those roles. By then the culture has set in and is closely aligned to what Janio represents in Singapore.

Imagine in Southeast Asia you have six or seven offices across the region. If every country office has a different culture, you're screwed. That's something that we are very cautious about," says Junkai Ng.

This approach does not apply to all countries they operate in, however. Given Janio's adaptive approach to cross-border logistics, full-service hubs, or countries with strategic value in terms of import and export, receive more attention in terms of human resource development.

Pure origin markets have less functional requirements and tend to be more commercial heavy than operational. The culture is still there, but it doesn't have to be as strongly ingrained as a full-service team with many moving parts." [10]

Choosing between the three methods is a balance of consistency (i.e., aligning culture, vision, and strategy) and localization (i.e., adapting the culture, vision, and strategy to the local market in concrete tactics). Of course, another option to capture a new market as we will discuss later in the book is to acquire a local company and integrate in such a way that the leadership of that company effectively serves as the "country head".

Going remote-first

Apart from building an organization across borders, it is important to be able to set processes and people to facilitate efficient communication across country teams. These measures were put to the test for distributed teams during the 2020 pandemic, and even those without distributed teams were forced to go "distributed" with lockdown measures. Indonesia money transfer company Flip went fully remote amidst the 2020 pandemic, as CEO Rafi Putra Arriyan shares on the *On Call with Insignia Ventures* podcast in 2020.

"So before we were a traditional company, we worked from the office. Since COVID, we see that we need to do business via remote because going to the office is not an option. At that time we are quite worried about the effectiveness of the way we work if we do it remotely.

But because we don't have any other option, we make mitigation, we start to work out how we could operate via remote, and somehow after an adjustment around one week, we could have quite the same output when we do remote compared to doing work in the office.

Because of that we started to build Flip to become a remote team. When we talk with the team, most of them prefer to work remotely rather than at the office because of many factors that happen in Indonesia right now. And on top of that we also see that employee happiness also increases. They don't need to spend time on the road. They don't need to really face traffic. That is another good impact from COVID in terms of the way we work at Flip." [4]

While this phenomenon is not necessarily tied to scaling, being able to manage a company "remote-first" and distributed is a good sign of being able to sustain cross-border operations. The teams that were already "remote-first" (i.e., adjusted to being distributed) had the advantage amidst the pandemic. Ridy explains what remote-first means on the *On Call with Insignia Ventures* podcast in 2021.

"We have a small team, but we've always adopted the remote-first culture. So that means as a company, we are committed to making it this first-class experience for remote workers. If you are working in different countries, if you're working at your house or in the coffee house, we give you a commitment that you will not be missing anything. All our processes and tools are designed in such a way that more [remote] workers will be able to fully participate." [11]

Going remote-first effectively is a combination of communication practices and communication tools. Practices can include "anchor" meetings to ensure there are periods when the team can align regardless of the preferred work schedules of the people in the team and breaking down large projects into short but quick

sprints so coordination is tighter. Tools include using the likes of
Notion or Lark, many of which ballooned and emerged during the
2020 pandemic.

Although workforces were forced to go distributed due to pandemic lockdowns, not all functions, and not all stages of growth of
a company are suited to remote-first arrangements. Operations
and some types of customer success will need on-the-ground coordination. The younger a company is, especially in the pre-PMF
stage, the more important it is for the team to be able to interact
face-to-face.

Finding tech talent

As operations need greater automation (to keep cash burn low),
the product or ecosystem of products becomes more complex, and
the startup can no longer "scale by doing things that don't
scale" — as the famous Y Combinator advice goes — it becomes
important to expand the tech capabilities of the company. But as
we have mentioned several times already in this chapter, tech talent is a challenge to find in Southeast Asia.

Gojek's approach to filling its engineering needs was to acquire
startups with high calibre engineers, not in Indonesia, but all the
way in India. Gojek's tech backend facilitating the ride-hailing
platform was primarily managed through spreadsheets, and it was
only until Sequoia India invested in Gojek in 2015 that the possibility of acquiring engineering needs in India became tangible for
the Indonesian startup. In the process Gojek acquired three startups: C42 Engineering, CodeIgnition, and LeftShift Technologies.
C42 focused on app development, CodeIgnition on the backend,
and LeftShift on design and mobile app interface. Interestingly,
while Gojek's tech machine was largely based out of India, the
founders gave the Indian teams free reign to develop their own
company culture. [12]

Carro on the other hand, did not just hire from any specific
country, but had formed small tech teams across multiple countries, wherever they could find great engineering talent. They had
engineers in Myanmar, Vietnam, Indonesia, Singapore, Taiwan,

and mainland China. Having learned how to manage engineering teams remotely also helped them transition more easily when the 2020 pandemic hit. Kelvin Chng, Carro co-founder, explains how they came to having a distributed engineering team on the *On Call with Insignia Ventures* podcast in 2021.

"The good thing is we were actually operating in small teams before COVID-19 actually struck. So we actually have a team in Myanmar, a team in Vietnam, a team in Indonesia, a team in Singapore, a team in Taiwan and two guys in Wuhan...Because we have multiple small teams, not by choice, we were actually forced into it. I think you guys would know the hiring of engineers is extremely difficult in the region that we are in. So we actually chose to go where talents are rather than being fixated on a country. So we chose to actually have micro-small teams to specialize or get them to so that we can hire specialized skill sets with each team. And we were very forward in thinking that if we were to operate these small teams, we needed better tooling, better collaboration. So right from the start, right, we actually tried to find tools that will allow multiple small teams to communicate with each other." [11]

Rethinking leadership

A common theme across the scenarios we have covered when it comes to scaling an organization is the importance of leadership. As we discussed in Chapter 7 through various scenarios, the kind of leadership needed will change as the company grows.

In this chapter we share some considerations and aspects of the company or the role that need to be communicated to potential hires for leadership roles as the company goes from startup to scale-up:

- **Culture-Fit.** This goes without saying, and it is important for culture to be communicated as clearly as possible to potential hires — whether through marketing or through speaking with the founders and hiring directors. By this stage of the company's growth, the culture should more or less be set and communicable.

- **Why is there an open position in the first place?** It is important to be clear on why a certain leadership role needs replacement or why a role was created with regards to the changing needs of the company. With this clarity it will be easier to convince the right people that they are needed and can contribute a lot to the company with their background and skill set.
- **What do they gain from this role?** It is a two-way street and the demands of leadership roles are higher than entry-level.
- **Do they gel well with the rest of the leadership team?** While less tangible to measure, chemistry is also important for the individual to be effective in their role and stay in the role longer as well. CEOs will have potential hires that have already been curated through initial interviews and talk to the rest of the leadership team to get the perspective of the rest of management as well.
- **Can they manage hypergrowth?** This goes back to the mental model earlier in the chapter and demonstrates how this ability to adapt remains relevant even as the company matures. Oftentimes, the potential hires for leadership roles as the company scales will have come from more stable or corporate jobs and it's important for them to be willing to adjust.

What does culture mean for startups and how does it impact business?

A recurring key element in forming great startup teams is company culture. As we have mentioned earlier in the article, the importance of culture in driving the growth of a company is often understated primarily because of how hard it is to create benchmarks to quantify this.

There are certainly guides like Netflix's Culture Guide to refer to and similarities that can be drawn from the stories of many founders and employees in startups, but company culture is ultimately specific to the company's people. Nevertheless, we will try to identify some of the "cultural highlights" common across startups and more importantly, tie them to the concrete impact they can have on various aspects of running a company.

What is startup culture: A case study of corporate to startup transition

Start-up culture is best defined by those who have come from more traditional business or corporate cultures and jumped into the world of startups. Ernest Chew shares his experiences on the *On Call with Insignia Ventures* podcast in 2020 joining Carro as CFO in the middle of a pandemic.

> "It had been a great 14–15 years in investment banking. Grueling but a great experience. For many investment bankers, it's a lifetime where burnouts are quite common. I have learnt as much as I could in banking. I've worked at three financial centres across three continents: HK, London, New York. I've worked on landmarks, complicated and cross-border deals worth billions of dollars. I've rebuilt up the Asian team at HSBC. Along the way, I've met incredible and inspirational people.
>
> But I was far from burning out. In fact, I was full of energy, and I wanted the next chapter to be even more exciting. I wanted to meaningfully contribute to building something with strong growth. Something future-proof and tech-related. At the same time, leverages on my strategic, automotive, banking, and capital raising experience. Ideally but not as important was going back to Southeast Asia, where I'm originally from.
>
> When I came across Carro, this reminded me of an advisory mandate for a private equity firm in their acquisition of a Western used car auction business. I watched that business grow 5–6x to a 2 billion British pound business over a decade, despite it being in a mature geography. The opportunity was a perfect match — first, tech and strong secular growth. Second, the role leverages my experience. Third, going back to Southeast Asia, in itself a vibrant region with strong growth markets.
>
> And I had, over the course of my work, dealt with larger start-ups. Also, during my garden period, I read a lot of books about start-ups. I spoke to friends from start-ups. What's the big deal, right? But all I'll say is that nothing could prepare you fully for the startup experience.

Firstly, there's the size. I was part of a giant banking corporation. I was used to dealing with much larger businesses and deals. Start-ups are a lot smaller, in many senses. In one instance, I had coffee with an ex-colleague who is now a country head of banking. When I probed their lending appetite, she asked if I was missing quite a few zeroes — we had a good laugh over coffee, and we remained friends. As a CFO, I would query about the $1000–2000 cost here and there, but back in banking, this is frankly a tiny fraction of travel expenses for bankers!

Second, growth in a startup. In a big MNC, when people talk about growth, attractive growth means double digit % year-on-year growth. A few hundred % growth, it's pretty much unheard of. Given our size, Carro doubling or tripling in revenues is actually quite feasible with the right planning and team.

And now on the third point, speed of communication and decision-making. At big MNCs, decisions take quite a bit of time — plenty of analysis, sometimes quite complex and complicated. Then plenty of discussions with many stakeholders across the globe and across many businesses. Even one senior hire will take weeks if not months.

At Carro, discussions are done with one or a very small group of relevant people. Whilst in the past Blackberries kept me hooked to my work, now we communicate via Whatsapp at Carro. And the responses generally are very quick. We are very nimble. Decisions are made almost instantly. In fact, I've come to learn at Carro that a bad decision is better than no decision at all. Frankly, a complete 180-degree compared to a corporate who tends to want to perfect the plan before deciding on something.

Then the fourth point, it's the culture of experimentation. To innovate, we need to experiment and learn — even a bad decision will give valuable lessons. The fear of standing still at a startup is greater than failure. The great Peter Thiel once asked a contrarian question: "What important truth do very few people agree with you on?" Now, despite the fact that cars have been transacted in a certain way for decades, the truth is there are plenty of pain points for both consumers and dealers. So, we challenge ourselves every day — to make the car purchasing experience better, faster and safer." [13]

From this story we can draw three key common cultural highlights of a startup. The first is that startups generally have less cash than most businesses relative to the kind of growth they want to achieve, thus spending has to be strategic. This 2–3x revenue growth benchmark that Ernest brought up forces venture-backed startups to be resourceful. Even if the startup has raised the most amongst its competitors, it does not make as much of a difference in the early stages of scale, as it would when the startup is more mature.

The second is that decisions are made faster in startups, because teams are often leaner and organizations flatter, and operating in the internet economy, the results of decisions made could easily be observed within a matter of hours. The tight budgets, fast growth and speed in decision-making creates an environment where ownership is incentivized and the team has to work less like a ship and more like a soccer team, where everyone collaborates rather than any one person calling every single shot.

Finally, the third cultural highlight is experimentation. Ernest brought up the value of having to iterate in order to learn in real-time and innovate over short periods of time.

In an emerging market like Southeast Asia, the presence of these cultural highlights — strategic spending to achieve hyper-growth, making fast decisions, and experimentation — in startups are incentivized even further by the inevitable costs of expanding across the region (for a startup that wants to be a billion-dollar company), the lower amount of dry powder relative to developed markets, and the reality that there is still a lot of untapped opportunity in the region.

Of course, these cultural highlights are easier said than done, but when concretely exercised, these aspects of startup culture can reap benefits for various aspects of the business and reduce some of the risks we discussed in the previous chapter. We cite some examples below:

- **Experimentation can keep the company's finances healthy.**
  Important to note here that we are talking about low-cost, targeted, and small-scale experiments. The idea is to reduce the

risk that fake product-market fit poses and the resulting costs
that this would mean for the company, which are presumably
larger than simply testing things out first, as Ernest shares on the
On Call with Insignia Ventures podcast in 2021.

"At Carro, and quite different to large corporate and large
MNCs as I alluded to, experiments or small experiments are very
encouraged. These experiments don't cost a lot of money, but
we can learn and innovate, then a larger, incremental budget to
support the product growth. Essentially the culture we have is
you need to try and learn something out of these small experiments without deploying huge amounts of capital. So the risk of
failures is generally lower." [13]

Obviously how the experiment is run matters, and oftentimes
it involves doing things that don't scale or going on the ground
and engaging directly with target users to avoid incurring engineering and other implementation costs too early.

With low-cost experiments, hard-won capital could be deployed
more efficiently towards resulting products or features that truly
have product-market fit or customers find worth using or even
paying for. This in turn reduces the risk of costly mistakes, as the
leaks and loopholes in product ideas are plugged early on, at a
stage when the costs incurred from these mistakes are low.

And while it seems more prudent to run less experiments, the
power of a tech startup, versus other types of businesses, is that
running more experiments reduces costs in the long run.

- **Ownership develops results-driven marketing DNA.**
We talk about how ownership is a favored trait in startups
because of the need to be strategic with spend (across all aspects
of the business) and the need to make fast decisions (one company's wasted time is another company's treasure, or so it goes).
This ownership is also important when it comes to making a
brand.

On the *On Call with Insignia Ventures* podcast in 2020, Janio
co-founder and head of marketing Nathaniel Yim concretely ties
this concept of shared ownership of a brand to how they can

create content from the involvement of various teams within the company.

"Everybody in the company should be able to help represent the brand and also should be involved in developing the brand...I think that the more common way to be involved with marketing and content would be to provide insights into various aspects of logistics and ecommerce. So for example, our ops team, they facilitate the flows of the physical products. They work with network partners. So they're the most in-tune with what's really happening on the ground when it comes to the operational side of things." [14]

- **Ownership also creates an organization of mini-CEO product managers.**

Apart from owning the brand, it can benefit the product development of a startup to build a culture of ownership, essentially creating an organization of product managers who act like mini-CEOs. This enables the product team to move faster and break through the risk posed by hitting the ceiling of the S-curve we covered in the previous chapter.

On the *On Call with Insignia Ventures* podcast in 2021, Yada Piyajomkwan talks about how she and her team at Ajaib laid the foundations for the retail investment app that eventually became the fourth largest in terms of trade volume on the Indonesian Stock Exchange at the beginning of 2020, six months after they launched their stock brokerage product.

"When we started my team and I were looking through other applications, mobile apps and websites in the market, right. And we're always quite frustrated by how they look and things are difficult to understand compared to apps that you would find in the US, in China or in India.

They have all the right information; it's just shown in a way that's quite difficult for first-timers right, more so to experienced investors. So that's why we invest a lot in our product from the beginning. We talked to a lot of users. We experimented with a lot of ideas and we're reinventing the experience from scratch, from what we think millennials would appreciate, and for you to do something like that, you need to have a very stellar product team because they need to understand what building a product from scratch means.

And I talked to a lot of product people in Indonesia. And I think that a lot of companies here misunderstand the product role, right? So if you look around, there are product managers, product owners, product analysts, product marketing managers, business product managers, technicals, right? That's just not how product roles work in Silicon Valley actually.

And because I have seen what it's like I want to bring that mindset into Indonesia and build a product team that is similar to the ones we see in the Valley. And what that means is that product managers have the mindset of being mini-CEOs. So they would make all the decisions starting from strategy to execution, creativity, design, technicality, everything. So they are the one calling all the shots. And you need a team like that to iterate on a good product because you need speed and a lot of ownership when you're innovating new things." [3]

- **Simplicity manages the risks of organizational and product complexity.**
We didn't mention simplicity as one of the cultural highlights gleaned from the anecdotes we shared, but this ties directly to the speed at which venture-backed startups have to grow. The faster the startup grows, the more difficult it becomes to keep up with the demands of a more complex product and organization. Ensuring that even as the product adds more and more features, the value proposition remains clear to the users is an important part of this.

Lifepal CEO Giacomo Ficari explains on the *On Call with Insignia Ventures* podcast in 2021 how they had to re-simplify their insurance marketplace as they scaled and engaged more agents and consumers:

"I saw also in Lazada when we were growing, we had to kind of go through and re-simplify things over time, because it's so easy for your software or your program to become more complex...Where we saw that is really on how we manage our agents whom we like to say are our customers as well because they use our software. And those are people that don't really have necessarily an insurance background. So if we don't make things simple, you have lots of screw-ups and that translates into a really bad customer experience. Everything on our software for agents is really straightforward and is really a controlled environment where it's really hard to make mistakes." [9]

Why and How do VCs Help Startups with Hiring?

We have tackled the ways startups approach building and scaling teams, as well as the impact of company culture unique to startups on their growth. While we have yet to touch on hiring or building teams from the VC perspective, it is important for the venture capitalist to gain a sense of what makes a successful team and culture from the founders' or leadership's point of view.

With this awareness, a VC becomes more well-equipped to support its portfolio in terms of bringing the right people to the company. To some degree, depending on company leadership, venture capital firms can operate like startups. There are also lessons from startups to be learned for any type of business.

The most important and impactful non-capital value-add

Hiring is arguably the most important non-capital value-add for four reasons. First, bringing people into the company can have long-term, decisive (positive or negative) impact, versus simply pointing them in one direction through a single strategy meeting or helping them with a one-time press release.

Second, we already mentioned earlier in the chapter that for several reasons, finding and retaining talent is a massive challenge especially for startups, and all the more so in Southeast Asia.

Third, hiring the right people (especially if they are sourced through the venture capitalist) can save the VC time on supporting the startup for a specific function (e.g., instead of micromanaging their fundraising strategy, why not bring in someone who is familiar with fundraising and can lead it for the portfolio company?)

Fourth, having a hire brought in by the VC gives that VC some amount of leverage when it comes to requesting for more rights (e.g., pro-rata or super pro rata) down the line or gaining more visibility into the company (i.e., CFO hired by the VC would be more likely to regularly share financial reports).

That said, the idea behind helping a startup hire is not to run the company but the opposite — so that the VC can trust that they can be more hands-off in terms of portfolio management.

The 5Ss advantage of working with VCs for hiring

But what advantages do venture capitalists have as recruiters? We list them in 5Ss — Speed, Scale, Signaling, Sales, and Subtlety:

1. **Speed:** VCs live and breathe professional networks. They can connect candidates to founders as soon as the opportunity or need arises, sometimes just by dropping a WhatsApp, Line or WeChat message.
2. **Scale:** VC firms will often hire an in-house recruiter to manage several hiring pipelines for portfolio companies and/or run their own portal to funnel applications to their portfolio companies and help their portfolio companies, especially the early-stage ones, with employer branding.
3. **Signaling:** Because of the networks that VCs build and their sensitivity to career changes (part of the job/sourcing strategy to be aware of career changes in their professional network), they could leverage these signals and direct candidates ready for a career towards their portfolio companies if they meet the criteria. Signaling also works the other way, where simply having a prominent VC's brand tied to the startup makes it a more attractive place to work for many candidates.

4. **Sales:** There are times when VCs will be in a better position to sell the role to the candidate than the founder (i.e., having a "third" person POV), convincing the candidate to leave a cushy, high-pay job for the grind of a startup. It also helps that with the VC's propensity to view the bigger picture and the long-term (it comes with the job), the pitch can become more convincing. There is also the possibility that having a prior relationship with a candidate means the candidate is likely to trust the VC more than a founder they just met.

5. **Subtlety/Secrecy:** Because VCs have the trust of the founders (ideally), they are also in a better position than, say third-party recruiters, to do more confidential replacements or strategic hiring that founders would not want to be leaked to competition.

These 5Ss capture the main advantages founders would have working with VCs in terms of hiring. But it is important to note that these 5Ss make the following assumptions: (1) the VC *does* have the network and industry connections fit for their portfolio companies and more importantly, can leverage these networks to help their founders, (2) the VC has a reputable brand (not necessarily prominent) or resources to efficiently help their portfolio at scale, and (3) the VC is trusted by the founders they are helping. This means that the founders do see the value in having this particular venture capitalist help them in looking for the best candidates.

The 6Fs of how VCs help startups with hiring and people management

In terms of how VCs help their founders with hiring and people management, we list six roles VCs can play with 6Fs — First round of screening, Final Filter, Fees, Formator, Fire extinguisher, Fisherman:

1. **First round of screening:** Especially if VCs source the candidates, they will often do an initial interview to curate the pipeline and ensure the founder does not waste their time talking to any of

the candidates the VC introduces. This can also be useful for founders who are less experienced in recruiting or companies with no HR or recruiting function yet.

2. **Final filter:** Before leadership finalizes the hire, most key and executive candidates are screened by VCs chosen by the founder or VCs on the board of directors, either as a background check or via a chat with the VC. Passing the VC screening increases the likelihood of converting the candidate into a hire, and the screening can also save time, instead of having to do multiple rounds of interviews.

3. **Fees:** When third-party recruiters are involved, VCs can work with these agencies to secure blanket rates for their portfolio.

4. **Formator:** If the VCs are equipped with the right in-house resources, they could also offer workshops, coaching, or consulting for startups on culture building and leadership.

5. **Fire extinguisher:** In some instances, VCs will step in to resolve internal conflicts, from diffusing politicking to facilitating the removal of underperforming or potentially dangerous people from executive roles. This could translate into taking action in board meetings or spelling out the harsh reality to the founders, especially if bias prevents them from taking action.

6. **Fisherman:** This goes back to the analogy brought up in Chapter 7, where we talked about how VCs will often prefer to hire people who can commit to supporting their portfolio company full-time rather than spending a disproportionate amount of time micromanaging a specific need of the company. The extent of the involvement could range from making the introductions and connections to actually pitching the company and convincing the candidate(s) to work with their portfolio company.

The Gojek example of Sequoia India pointing them towards three Indian startups to be acquired is one scenario. Another is that of Insignia Ventures' founding managing partner Yinglan Tan introducing Phil Opamuratawongse, a venture capitalist fresh from Floodgate, to a potential new venture he could be a part of in Southeast Asia, as Phil shares on the *Alcott Global* podcast in 2020.

"I was fairly new to [Southeast Asia] despite growing up in Bangkok, so I started meeting basically everyone I could shoot an email to entrepreneurs, investors, and everyone else in between across multiple countries. One of the folks I met was Yinglan Tan, the founding partner at Insignia Ventures Partners (a top VC in Singapore), and he said to me, "look, why don't you come sit in my conference room and meet with all the startup founders who walk through the door, so you can get a sense of what problems you could solve in the region." I basically got paid to get up the learning curve and meet with potential business partners! After 45 days of camping out in Yinglan's conference room, I met Budi Handoko (co-founder at Shipper). He was actually someone Yinglan had already backed, and Budi had been building an earlier version of Shipper by himself. While Budi and I were both passionate about the opportunity to streamline fulfillment and shipping, what we both believed to be most important was our great "co-founder fit". [15]

It is important to note that with these 6Fs, VCs will want to focus on helping out with leadership roles and issues around company leadership because the impact of having the right leaders trickles down through to the rest of the organization — thanks to company culture. Regardless of what measures VCs adopt, it is important to **never underestimate the impact of company culture on the success or failure of a startup** — especially considering the difficulty of coming by talent in the region and the need to be creative and flexible when building a strong team.

Three Best Practices

1. Focus on executive hires for portfolio companies where the fund has high ownership.
2. Organize your network to be able to easily find people whom you can introduce to founders if they are looking for specific hires.

3. Do not just liaise with the CEO — work with the rest of the leadership team to get a better sense of company culture and how the company is growing and developing as an organization.

Chapter 9

Rule #9: Scaling is Growing by Doing More with Less

Learning From Patterns

Following the previous chapter's discussion on how venture capitalists help their portfolio companies in building teams and developing culture, we move on to the second main area where VCs do portfolio management: **growth and strategy**. As we have mentioned before, the main reason VCs would want to support their portfolio in this area is to ensure that they can reach the "North Star metrics" that would convince the VC to follow-on or that would indicate that the company has become mature enough to make a valuable exit.

In this area, VCs with operator or founder backgrounds are better positioned to support their portfolio companies because they can empathize with the founders, and have the experience to draw insights from, accompanied with a breadth of understanding around the industry. In general, however, **VCs will reference learnings from companies that have come before and comparables in other markets in order to guide their portfolio companies when it comes to growth.**

In Chapter 7, when we covered the portfolio management for growth, we talked about it in the context of the various stages of growth for startups, but in this chapter, we will only focus on scaling. We focus on this stage — when startups move from finding that initial product-market fit to achieving a billion-dollar valuation or an exit or category leadership — because it is in this stage that venture capitalists are usually putting in the most effort to support the growth of their portfolio companies.

It is also the stage in a company's growth that is arguably the most unique to startups in the sense that the speed at which they are expected to scale is magnitudes greater than expected from other businesses, if these businesses want to scale at all.

The kind of scaling strategies available to a startup are tied to how they positioned the company initially in the market, which makes scalability also a function of how clearly the founders view the company's growth trajectory. Finally, many of the risks and bottlenecks for growth materialize at the scaling stage when startups have to wrestle with defensibility, constant product innovation, and operational sustainability on the ground and in reality.

When it comes to scaling, it's all about optimization, or Rule #9 — how can the company do (exponentially) more with less in order to grow? Startups are already operating with minimal resources (ideally minimizing burn). They are also maneuvering in an environment full of uncertainty and market forces threatening to put them out of commission. That means growth needs to deal with these circumstances while still generating outsized returns. While this may be an immense challenge **because of the many startups that succeeded and failed in the past, patterns of behavior have emerged that founders and venture capitalists can study and improve upon.**

In this chapter, we look at three types of patterns relevant to scaling in Southeast Asia. First are the three overall trajectories tech startups have taken to reach billion-dollar valuations or sizable exits. Second are the methods tech startups will typically use to scale — grow their user base, retain their user base longer, strengthen distribution, and leverage network effects. Third and final are the practical ways that venture capitalists support their portfolio companies in growth.

Three Trajectories for Growth in Southeast Asia

When it comes to growing in Southeast Asia, there are three trajectories that startups can take. In general, these trajectories are defined by two things: Rule #1 and Rule #2. Rule #1 — "Southeast Asia is not Silicon Valley" — speaks to the reality that Southeast Asia's markets have their own nuances that companies need to navigate in order to grow within those markets. This rule applies more to certain industries than others, like banking (Rule #1 more applicable), for example, versus SaaS (Rule #1 less applicable). Rule #1 sets the upper limit on how much certain businesses can grow and the kind of competitive landscapes that form in the region. The depth of localization required to conquer a market correlates with its population (more people, more segments to deal with) and its productivity (higher GDP, generally more of a market to capture).

For example, in the SaaS industry, while most big enterprise customers will look to more mature companies typically found in the West for solutions, there are certain functions or operations like frontline SOPs that are better served with localized solutions. The SaaS provider could also be more focused on targeting smaller businesses to be users of their localized product, knowing that they would not be able to afford or effectively use the foreign alternatives. In the same way that companies from the US would find it difficult to set up shop in Southeast Asia, so would Southeast Asia startups face the same localization challenges entering the US for example.

On the other hand, Rule #2 — "If you think you're aiming big, aim bigger", sets the lower limit on the kind of growth that startups will aspire towards. While aimed at venture capitalists and creating investment thesis and sourcing, this also applies to startups. No startup worth investing in will be content with just a corner shop or a few hundred customers. For startups in Southeast Asia, the expectation is to go for as big a market as possible, given the product-market fit, competitive landscape, and available capital (all controlling factors influenced by Rule #1). A benchmark we'll refer to (and have been referring to in past chapters) is for startups to become billion-dollar companies or unicorns — a benchmark made on the assumption that the VC invested early in the startup and already made an outsized return when the startup reaches a billion-dollar valuation.

For example, a company could aim to become a category leader in Southeast Asia, but once it has achieved that, leadership could then set its sights on exploring other markets. Sea Group is already doing that with the capital they've raised on the public markets, exploring the expansion of Shopee into Latin America. Whether or not the startup *can* actually meet these expectations of going big is another question entirely, and something we will try to address in this chapter, but what is important is that the startups inherently *want* to go big.

With these upper limits set primarily by the circumstances of localization and the lower limits set by the expectations of going big, we can derive three trajectories that Southeast Asian startups will go for to become billion-dollar companies:

Scale across Southeast Asia

The first trajectory is the most obvious, albeit seemingly the most arbitrary (as Southeast Asia is not a united political entity). Given the history of Southeast Asia's tech ecosystem as we discussed in Chapter 1, startups in the region will generally adapt existing solutions in the market and make them suited for Southeast Asian markets — whether that means making the product or service affordable (think ecommerce or even ride-hailing), align with cultural or religious values (think Sharia finance), or the infrastructure in the region (think social commerce). With this line of thought, the intuitive idea is to become the X or Y of Southeast Asia.

But apart from that, there's also the approach to find Southeast Asia specific needs or issues that say individuals or businesses would face only in Southeast Asia. The most obvious example is logistics, given the fragmented nature of the region, and the pain points for MNCs to navigate logistics in the region. Tackling this kind of problem would naturally lend itself towards going regional, right from day one.

Another key reason why startups would want to go regional apart from the "grouping" of Southeast Asian markets as a region or naturally occurring needs or pain points from the region is that individual markets within Southeast Asia simply do not have the volume to contain the market for a potential billion-dollar company, especially for consumer-facing platforms. A business within a market would already be limited by its products and industry with regards to the kind of users it could get from a single country's population, so it makes sense to look at neighboring countries.

A third reason is that in spite of Southeast Asia having a diverse set of countries within the region, there are some key similarities across these markets, especially in urban areas. There are similarities to be found in the cosmopolitan settings of Manila, Ho Chi Minh, Singapore, Kuala Lumpur, Jakarta, and other capital cities that are prime opportunities for scaling innovation. The success of regional unicorns like Sea, Lazada, Grab, Carro, Ajaib, and Appier is a testament to these similarities in consumer preferences and behavior. While there will be differences in the minutiae, the business model and user-experience generally remain the same for the platforms operated by these companies.

Scaling across Indonesia

We mentioned earlier that population and GDP are indicators of a market with deep localization and therefore pose more opportunities for a company to expand further within its borders without having to necessarily go abroad. With more than a billion dollars in GDP and upwards of 270 million people as of 2020, Indonesia is the clear standout in the region to provide this type of depth for startups to scale.

This does not mean that every Indonesian startup is best suited to capturing as much of the Indonesian market as possible. Again, it depends on the industry and target segments as well. A startup with a product suited for urban areas might benefit from actually going cross-border instead of trying to go from urban areas to rural areas where preferences, behavior, and infrastructure can vary wildly across Indonesia. The key benefit of this trajectory is that it allows Indonesian startups to tackle uniquely Indonesian challenges and still afford to focus on their own market, whereas another Southeast Asian country tackling their own local problem might be hard pressed to find enough users or customers to keep growing.

An example here is Flip, which initially began tackling the pain point of the ~6.50 IDR fee that came with bank transfers in Indonesia. They offered a digital service that would eliminate that fee and have since partnered with several local banks. They also expanded into other types of cash transfer use cases, like for businesses (which they then charge a fee for, though still lower than most banks) and remittances or international transfers. Flip might not have been as successful as it had been if they had not come from Indonesia — and the founders might not have observed or discovered this pain point to be a valuable one if they were not from Indonesia themselves.

At the same time, there are also startups that find themselves pivoting to focus on Indonesia seeing the immense potential in the country. There's stock trading platform and Indonesia's first unicorn in the wealth management space Ajaib, which in initial press releases following their Y Combinator graduation, mentioned plans of expanding to Thailand and other Southeast Asian countries, but they have since doubled down on expanding their product offerings from mutual fund investments to a digital stock brokerage and pre-IPO investment products, to bring in more Indonesian millennials into the investing class.

Even in the case of unicorns Gojek, Tokopedia or Bukalapak, Indonesia still has enough room to contain competitors from outside the country and still have more untapped opportunities. In ecommerce alone, most of the major marketplaces have only managed to occupy around 60% of the market in the last ten years up to 2020, opening up more opportunities to support long tail sellers.

Tackling the massive market size of Indonesia is also complicated by the disparities across regions and provinces *within* the country. The market size does boost valuations for startups going down this path, but that does come with the expectation that the funding being put in will go towards navigating the intricacies of the market.

Because Indonesian companies going on this trajectory will also take time to really capture a significant portion of the market in their sector, some of them may also, along the way, explore other markets to potentially boost their capitalization if certain markets provide an easier entry than laboring solely in Indonesia. Gojek did this in Singapore, Vietnam, Thailand, Malaysia, and even the Philippines (if you consider its acquisition of Coins as part of this cross-border growth trajectory), to varying degrees of success. Of course, there was the competition with Grab, but the danger of going for both the first and second trajectories is being spread too thin and only accumulating costs without being able to secure enough market share as compensation. Gojek in the years since pushing for regional expansion, has become more strategic about its regional approach but has also not entirely abandoned balancing the two.

On the other hand, because of how attractive Indonesia is as a market in its own right, many Singapore companies, while headquartered in the city-state, have gone to market in Indonesia or house/have most of their operations in Indonesia. This echoes the pan-Southeast Asia team mental model we brought up in the previous chapter. Then there are also Chinese and Indian founders who purposely move to Indonesia to start their next ventures in the country. Of course companies of this nature are at a disadvantage, especially if the sector requires deep local knowledge and the founders do not have that or any connections to the local market coming in. This weakness could be compensated however with the right co-founders and also having a strong local team.

Scaling globally

One often understated trajectory in Southeast Asia is going global, mainly because the sectors where this is the more sensible trajectory is not where a lot of the regional financing goes into (i.e., ecommerce, fintech, last-mile logistics). Sectors where going global comes more naturally are sectors like gaming or content platforms where there are lower barriers to entry when expanding across markets. The classic example here is Garena (Sea Group's gaming arm), which also helped it with its equity story as it went to the public markets. Then there are sectors like SaaS, deep tech, or even biotech, where going global also makes sense for Southeast Asia companies because customers are more familiar with these solutions. These customers are more likely to be found in markets like the US or Europe because the opportunity costs of not using these solutions are higher and the ability to pay for these solutions is higher as well.

The incentive to go global has also historically come from Singapore-based companies, given the reality that there are a lot of regional MNC headquarters in the country, many of the founders who are in the city-state have a global network or background.

Singapore has traditionally gathered a lot of talent and infrastructure to support the kind of sectors that are more likely to go global first like with deep tech — and these things are key elements to going global from day one.

igloocompany is an example of a company that has gone global from day one. Anthony Chow explains on the *On Call with Insignia Ventures* podcast in 2021 that the thought process behind going global — or gunning for any trajectory in general — should really be based on product-market fit.

> "It's important for every company to be very focused on the market that the product is being built for, the product-market fit, not specifically looking at the geography. The market fit is actually more important than anything.
>
> One example from our history is that when we first started, we wanted to be very focused on the vacation rental market. And in the whole world, the Airbnb market was the biggest in the US and so while we designed the solution, we needed to understand the pain points and the use case for an Airbnb host in the US because that's the most mature market for this kind of home sharing. And so that's where we started.
>
> And in fact, what we did was also to really understand our customers, we lived a day in the shoes of our customers, and by being Airbnb hosts ourselves. So in fact, in the first 12 months, we actually had a property with five rooms renting out on Airbnb and using our own solution so that we know what kind of productivity gains, what kind of benefits and value that our products can bring to our customer and to ourselves. And from there it's easier to then scale up to any other Airbnb hosts.
>
> So I think the important thing is to really understand your customer as well, to actually live a day in the shoes of your customer. And then you look at which geography is the one where you can maximally penetrate that market that you want to go into.
>
> And then I think subsequently, once you've identified which geography that you want to go into where the maximum potential is there, I think it's important to then find strategic partners within the market itself. You will never know the local cultural norms, the local cultural business practices, and also the network and

relationship in the market. And it's very important to find a partner who is strategic to you in their market, not just in terms of a
potential sales network, but also in terms of deployment servicing
the customer. And after that finding good capital within the market is also important as well."[1]

Another reason why going global is understated is because it is
much more difficult to scale this way even if the product-market fit
does align, because the company opens itself to a lot more competition, and because going global naturally implies that early on in the
company's life, the team already has to work on expanding and
navigating a new market (which is likely not the case for the other
two trajectories). Going global is also more likely to lead into an
early acquisition, even before the company reaches a billion-dollar
valuation.

A few caveats to take note of having discussed these trajectories:

The first is that these trajectories are not mutually exclusive.
Companies are more likely to use some combination of these three
in varying orders, especially when different business units are introduced into the company, whether it be going global with one
business then going regional next with another unit (e.g., Sea), or
going for Indonesia for the full suite of services but going regional
with more strategic offerings (e.g., GoJek), or going regional and
then gunning for global aspirations.

**The second is that these trajectories can change as the ecosystem
matures and the countries in the region develop further in terms of
infrastructure and supporting tech companies.** This has been the
trend for the last half of the 2010s, and has served as a mental model
to look at how startups can achieve unicorn valuations in the region
moving into the 2020s. At the same time, it is not an impossible or
even an unlikely future to imagine other countries in the region like
Vietnam and the Philippines being able to support unicorns that
operate purely in those markets. This can be the case as time
goes on.

**Finally, the purpose of these trajectories is to have a mental
model to potentially learn from and aim for as a company in general**

terms (i.e., illustrative and descriptive rather than prescriptive). Ultimately, it should not be the basis for making expansion decisions for a company. For the venture capitalist, these trajectories are important to consider on a sector and subsector level, because as we've seen, a lot of these trajectories are tied to where the company originates (Indonesian companies have more options than Singaporean companies, for example, though one could argue that Singaporean companies could tackle Indonesia as a go-to-market) and the kind of sector and sub-sector the company is in. All these considerations play into the investment thesis of the VC and how they approach advising companies. The discussion on the three trajectories is summarized in Exhibit 1.

Scaling in Southeast Asia

Having illustrated the trajectories startups in Southeast Asia will normally take to become billion-dollar companies, we now dive into the concrete actions startups can take to scale in the region. The assumption in this discussion is that the startup has achieved product-market fit, and now the question for the business is *how* to replicate this PMF across a larger user base, potentially opening up new user segments, tackling new PMFs, and entering new markets.

As we mentioned earlier in the chapter, scaling is an optimization problem — Rule #9. **It's about focusing on the one-to-many, finding the least number of keys that amount to the most doors, generating more revenue for every unit of resource used by the company.** One can also think of scaling as a ratio of output over input, and the idea is to either increase output relative to input, decrease input relative to output, or do both.

An aspect of scaling that is particular to startups is speed. So while larger corporations continue to scale themselves, the difference between these larger companies and leaner startups is that the latter should be able to move faster.

Startups scale for two reasons. First, the reality that startups move fast means competition is always just right around the

Trajectory for tech startups to reach billion dollar valuations	Southeast Asia (typically includes Singapore, Malaysia, thailand, Viernam, Indonesia, Philippines)	Indonesia	Global
Motivation	Opportunity spotting pain point that applies to a lot of Southeast Asian countries Advantage in team, produce or business model that makes it easy to move across markets	Already sufficient market size Business model just focusing on Indonesia	Product or sector too early for Southeast Asia or going regional does not provide enough business
Sectors/Focus of companies that typically take this trajectory	Ecommerce, fintech, ride hailing (sectors with some key commonalities in terms of adoption scross SEA markets SEA-specific problems (SEA logistics)	Most sectors in Indonesia Indonesia-specific problems (e.g. rural Indonesia, cash transfer pain point, etc.)	Sectors where customers are more easily found in more mature markets than Southeast Asia (SaaS, deeptech, biotech)
Challengs on the road to becoming unicorn	Finding/creating network effects to move from one market to the next (e.g. founding team, creating local team, acouisitons, customer networks)	Driving digital adoption given fragmentation and infrastructure issues (especially beyond urban areas) Creating local advantage if HQ or founders from other market (typically Singapore, China, India)	Global competition Having to enter a new market earlier on in the life of the company Finding the right local partners across various markets Avoiding early acquisitions (unless that is the plan of company leadership)
Benefits	Going regional (proving capability of company in 3 to 4 markets) makes the company better positioned to compete with or even beat more local players on homecourt	Potentially more cost-efficient to focus on Indonesia, even without category leadership, localisation can prove to be a sufficient moat to foreign entrants	If succeeds in solidifying position in the market, potentially larger valuation than going regional (still depends on sector) More familiar to global bourses when going public

Exhibit 1:   Three trajectories for growth in Southeast Asia.

corner — whether competition comes in the form of new companies doing things similarly or new technologies or business models that could upset whatever advantage the startup has in the market. Second, scale opens up growth opportunities that may have otherwise taken more years or resources to get to.

Scale is often measured in terms of (1) acquisition (i.e., how fast and efficiently the company can acquire customers) and (2) retention (i.e., how long does a customer use the product and how much value is derived from this usage). Cohort analysis is often an instructive tool to measure how efficient the scaling strategy of a company is, especially on a product level.

For all the emphasis both founders and venture capitalists will put on scaling the company, there are two main risks to scaling for startups.

First, the company may not have the operations, capabilities and processes to handle the rigors of scale. We discussed some of the consequences of not having this pinned down in Chapter 7. Second, because startups are often venture-backed and raise a lot of capital in order to fuel these scaling strategies, burning money without creating any tangible momentum can be dangerous for the startup. It could easily force board directors to vote for taking drastic measures, like changing leadership or even selling off the company to keep the finances afloat. Of course, the startup has to use the money it has raised, but it must be based on results.

In order to reduce these risks, there are two prerequisites, which startups can take before venturing into any scaling strategy. The first is to stay lean and remove waste as the company grows. It is likely that certain practices or resources were necessary at the point of the company's growth but moving forward it could only be dead weight. **Scaling is not just about expanding and adding but also subtracting.** Second, the company should have a rallied team aligned on the mission and vision of the company, and capable of dealing with hypergrowth — which, as we've brought up in the previous chapter, not everyone is comfortable with.

In the next few pages, we tackle seven strategies to scale a tech startup. Just as with the trajectories, these approaches are based on what we've seen in tech startups and companies do to scale, with none of them being mutually exclusive, though some have prerequisites or limiting factors.

Data and the self-learning product/platform

We mentioned in Chapter 7 that **the scaling stage of growth for a startup is all about creating self-evolving products or platforms.** This is tied to the previous point we made about optimization — Self-evolving products or platforms exhaust less resources to pin down the next area of growth or extend the value proposition. This is because the best opportunities are informed by the users themselves and their interactions with the product or platform. Ecommerce and social media platforms have used this to great effect, pushing products based on past searches and purchases, or pushing content based on frequently visited or viewed pages and accounts. Marketplaces can use this strategy given the data that various stakeholders can provide about each other. For example, a marketplace for trucks and shippers would have data from shipper usage that would help narrow down the decision-making process for trucks using the platform, and vice versa.

This strategy of leveraging data to enable a product to be self-learning applies to a whole host of other business models and sectors as well, from SaaS to edtech. For SaaS, for example, the main draw for businesses to outsource certain operations to a SaaS product as opposed to building it themselves is that the company can continually improve the product based on the usage of a multitude of users, ultimately paying dividends for the user-experience of every single company using the product.

The main benefit for users is creating a more personalized experience and more precisely meeting their needs. The more targeted a product or service, the more likely the user can be retained. They can then be engaged further with upselling or cross-selling (if the business model monetizes from users) or enabled to be a driver for further growth through referrals or user-generated marketing (i.e., organic reviews).

If a company uses this strategy, they are able to navigate product development cost-efficiently and create a more targeted user experience, and reduce dependency on market forces for growth. It's impossible to completely become independent from the market. In the Reservoir Framework in Chapter 7, the idea is to have a solid user base (i.e., the reservoir's collected rainwater) as opposed to constantly having to acquire new users (i.e., depending on rainwater for survival) because existing users churn quickly. Growth then becomes more platform-driven, instead of entirely market-driven, as shown in Exhibit 2 below. This advantage is useful in markets where it is costly to acquire new users, and the opportunity cost of losing them to incumbents or competitors is also high.

Finally, another benefit of this strategy is potentially reducing the need to rapidly grow certain parts of the workforce, because the product itself becomes part of the workforce, the sales team in particular.

The biggest risk to this strategy lies with its greatest advantage: the data. Ultimately the data is based on user interactions. However, if these user interactions are not genuine, it could lead the product or platform to point the business in the wrong direction in terms of what to focus on or build next.

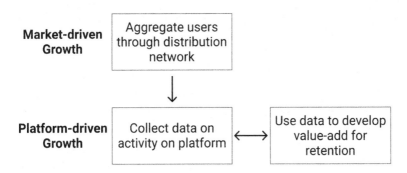

Exhibit 2:   Moving from market-driven growth to platform-driven growth. Taken from *insignia business review*. [2]

Customer life cycle

Another way to think about scaling is to think of the product as potentially becoming a super app and think of the suite of services that should be available to users of the product. How does this differ from the first strategy? Rather than depending on what the product usage data shows, **the idea is to identify the key user of the product and build around the user's entire customer life cycle**. It's an exercise of constantly asking "What would users want to do next on this app?" or "What would users need to do next having made this transaction or done this interaction?" For example, when it comes to marketplaces for cars or properties, a natural way to capture the life cycle would be to cater to the financing needs of users, and then maintenance when they have finally purchased or rented the car or property.

The startup's value proposition is no longer just about transactions, but the entire experience around a product or service. This thinking is also especially useful for K12 edtech platforms, where an idea to scale would be to capture the students' entire learning cycle, from taking in information (i.e., online classes, content) to evaluating their knowledge (i.e., testing, classroom management), as illustrated in Exhibit 3.

The objective is similar to the first though, and that is to strengthen retention and remove the dependency on the market for

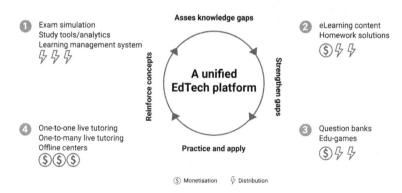

Exhibit 3: Capturing the K12 learning cycle. Taken from *insignia business review* (2020). [3]

growth, maximizing the lifetime value of each customer. Doing this means creating what we'll call a "**hypervertical platform**", a sort of super app built around a specific user experience. Another motivation for this approach would be to move into higher margins adjacencies especially when high distribution businesses (i.e., business models designed for capturing a large user base) typically come with the trade-off of thin margins. This has been the case for ecommerce players going into payments and logistics in order to consolidate the entire customer experience from searching for goods to getting them to their doorstep.

The risk to this strategy is of course the capability of the company to handle managing this entire user experience and costs that could come with taking on these other parts of the customer's life cycle (e.g., they could be asset-heavy like doing last-mile fulfillment for ecommerce). The ability for the company to buy out its neighborhood also depends on whether there are already neighbors. Furthermore, this strategy may not be as practical with neighbors that are already category leaders, unless a solid business case can be made that having that product or feature within the same platform is worth going up against the standalone competitor.

Value chain

The first strategy focuses on scaling on top of product, the second on scaling around the customer's life cycle. This third approach focuses on scaling up or down the value chain in an industry.

The motivation for this approach is to gain network effects in terms of capturing other players in an industry. For example, in trucking, a trucking marketplace might offer value-add services for both the shippers (typically FMCGs) and the truckers that shippers employ to transport goods.

The other potentially stronger motivation is that this approach solves fragmentation in an industry. By aiming to scale across the entire value chain, prices and efficiency are improved for the end-consumer and suppliers on the other end also benefit from better monetization on their own businesses. The best example for this is the farm-to-table business model in agritech, though it also applies to most logistics-type businesses in Southeast Asia, where fragmentation is often the key pain point. Traditionally, logistics and supply chain industries are dotted with middlemen who increase prices of goods as it goes from producer to end-consumer. The farm-to-table business model and many other logistics enablers, by disintermediating these middlemen and consolidating the value chain, reduce these added costs for the end-consumer. They also enable sellers and producers to earn more from their goods because the costs incurred by unsold inventory or inefficient logistics (e.g., paying for multiple providers) are also reduced by a consolidated value chain.

On face value, it does not seem practical to own an entire value chain and scaling across the value chain does not necessarily mean owning assets. It could involve working with existing infrastructure and players in the value chain (e.g., agent networks or using mom-and-pop shops as mini-fulfillment centres), acquiring or investing in smaller players, selling software that consolidates these players (e.g., API for banks and SMEs or API for logistics players), or coming up with a replicable service or business model that all other players in the value chain could use (e.g., supply chain financing).

The risk of this strategy is whether or not the startup *can* come up with a way to approach consolidation in an asset light way, as the costs of doing this physically or offline might be too much for a startup to handle. Another risk is being able to prove that the business model will work for other parts of the value chain as well, in the case of companies trying to bring the same services upstream or downstream.

Super app

The previous approach viewed scaling from the perspective of capturing the value chain of an industry or vertical. This approach, on the other hand, goes horizontal, aiming to capture not necessarily adjacent services, but services that would either (1) keep users within the app or (2) make full use of the company's advantage or assets (this goes back to our whole optimization objective).

It's the super app approach, one that has been pursued vigorously by Southeast Asian unicorns Grab and Gojek, as they expanded from service to service from ride-hailing. The main draw of the super app approach is that it incentivizes an existing, massive user base to stay on the app — because why would you need another one? If the suite of services is set up strategically, then this approach can also maximize the foundation of the company — be it the presence of a social network or a network of riders and drivers. Super apps like WeChat have also unlocked a third capability, which is to be a platform-as-a-service, where other companies can execute their go-to-market strategy or launch through the super app itself. The classic example here is the social commerce pioneer Pinduoduo, which got its start on WeChat.

That said, super apps are not just lifestyle apps. One could also see them incorporating productivity and entertainment services as well. Google's suite of services is an example of this, from Youtube, to Meet, to Maps.

This approach has some prerequisites that startups do not usually have in the early stages of growth. Super apps are built on core products that have gathered a massive and highly engaged user base, and the decision to venture into super app-dom also needs to consider the consumer behavior and preferences of the market. Asian markets have historically shown the tendency to adopt "complete" super apps more than Western markets, given the mobile-first nature of most markets in the region. The most super-app-like products in the West are still compartmentalized within segments like entertainment (Spotify for example is arguably on its way to becoming a super app around audio) or productivity.

The competitive landscape also influences the viability of this strategy, in the same way that we considered competition in the previous strategies. Strong competitors, especially when it comes to user experience, pose a legitimate threat as users could consider having that service in another app simply because their experience is better there. Finally, there's also the concern around cash and the liquidity to fuel this kind of expansion across services.

Because the super app strategy involves bringing in services that are not necessarily adjacencies, the company may not even bother building it in-house but just form a strong corporate development team to find the right acquisitions to build out their capabilities. While B2C super apps get a lot of the media attention, the super app strategy can also apply to enterprise software companies as well, with platforms like Cisco, Adobe, or Bytedance's Lark capturing a lot of business-focused services within one application.

Building (agent) networks

While there may be delineations between the previous strategies we have tackled, this strategy can be applied for any startup, in any sector. It helps more in certain sectors than others, but it is critical for startups to be able to think about how they are building distribution, and one way of doing that is through setting up networks.

It is especially important in Southeast Asia, going back to the common problem of fragmentation across industries and the challenge of driving digital adoption especially in rural areas. Shipper in Indonesia saw that simply providing a software solution for SME sellers to organize their fulfillment was not going to solve the first mile logistics inefficiencies, and introduced an agent network a year later and warehouses a year after that (note that this is also the value chain strategy in action as well) to create this first mile logistics distribution network across Indonesia. For social commerce platform Super, their whole approach to social commerce has been to build this "logistics backbone" with agents, often housewives or community leaders, who facilitate last-mile fulfillment, and Super Centers or warehouses to buy the FMCG and fresh goods they distribute at wholesale.

This strategy also applies to insurtech, where the likes of Lifepal in Indonesia and PolicyBazaar in India, combine online content to generate leads and a network of insurance agents to convert these leads into customers. This network creation works well with O2O business models, serving as the offline aspect to supplement the digital touchpoints, be it a website, online content, or a mobile application.

Payfazz in Indonesia also built their own distribution network of agents, typically *warung* owners, to be facilitators of their financial services through these *warung* owners' smartphones. Payfazz built trust and dependence by helping *warung* owners generate income through transactions (which in turn brings more foot traffic to these *warungs*).

While setting up this network is often done early on in the company's growth, it is foundational for the company to eventually scale, as it creates pathways to distribute new services and an effective template to expand into new areas. Because of the company's reliance on this network, building trust with agents is critical. It's also important to diversify the concentration of revenue across the network so that the business is not dependent on any single set of agents within the network.

As we've seen from the examples, while this strategy of creating distribution early on and doing this through a network can be applied in various ways to many startups, this strategy works best in markets with low infrastructure and high barriers to entry, like rural Indonesia and insurance.

Ecosystem of companies

This strategy for scaling applies best to startups that are already gunning for regional expansion, but do not have enough resources to set up an entirely new business unit from the ground up. The company will typically set up a holding company and through that make strategic acquisitions to expand in multiple markets as well as beef up any capabilities these acquisitions can offer. Apart from acquisitions, some companies also opt to make minority investments instead of acquisitions, especially if the investing company believes the founders are better suited to continue running the company and there is still opportunity to create synergies.

Gojek employed this strategy heavily in its initial regional expansion efforts, though it's not as easy as simply picking a local player in a target market. In a way it's similar to venture capital in the sense that the company wants to avoid spending cash on an acquisition that only weighs down its financials in the end. We write more about the considerations for acquisitions in Chapter 12.

This strategy has been commonplace for unicorns, but even companies with enough capitalization from private financing rounds can employ this approach if there is already enough momentum to explore other markets.

Striking gold

Sometimes the best strategy is to follow the money, even before the money gets there. In a gold rush, one wants to be ahead of the curve, and in this approach, the idea is to invest early in emerging trends to avoid "doing a Nokia or a Blockbuster," as we'll call it. These two companies were successful over a certain period but were easily disrupted because they missed the train to the next gold rush.

And these efforts to catch the wave take time to work. In the case of Netflix, scale came when they struck gold with the show "House of Cards" and reconfigured their streaming algorithms to cater to a wider audience. In Southeast Asia, we see how the ride-hailing unicorns rode the next wave of food delivery and then financial services as companies in these sectors began raking in the money.

This approach is also useful for companies looking for the next S-curve to ride or looking to de-risk the competition of new trends or innovation by pivoting. Of course, the risk here is the speed and capability of the company to adapt, and whether or not the trend or innovation being followed will truly last. When it comes to how enduring an innovation will be, time can only tell. As we've seen with most, the confidence in these trends in consumer behavior or technological innovation can evolve over time, as it has for cashless payments or blockchain-enabled transactions.

Strategy	Basis	Why	How	Risks	Examples
Data and Self-Learning Product/Platform	Product	More cost-efficient product development Higher likelihood of user retention Reduced dependence on new user acquisition Reduce need to expand workforce quickly	Data from user interactions used to strengthen retention and direct product development	Quality of the data	Most sectors
Customer Life Cycle (Hyper-vertical)	User experience	Higher likelihood of user retention, maximize lifetime value of customer Move into higher margin business lines, better monetization after gaining distribution	Capturing entire customer life cycle/ user experience	Costs to consolidate user experiences Competitive landscape	User experiences that are beneficial to be consolidated (lifestyle purchases, edtech, healthtech)
Value Chains (Vertical)	Vertical value chain / industry	Network effects of working Solving fragmentaiton	Setting up infrastructure or acquiring businesses	Infrastructure costs / cost to consolidate	Logistics / farm-to-table agritech Fintech (rebundling of the bank)
Super App	Horizontal integration	Ubiquity of the platform Maximize assets and advantage Product platformization: Companies building on top of superapp	Gather massive, highly retentive user base and move into various offerings	Enough cash? Solid enough user base? Narrow competitive landscape	Lifestyle, entertainment, or productivity apps
Building (Agent) Networks	Distribution/go-to-market	Primarily a key go-to-network strategy that sets up company for success in scaling Low cost method of funneling new products or services	Integrate with existing infrastructure Build agent network (online-to-offline distribution) Partner with other players in the same value chain to share resources	Concentration risk of network (geography-based) Needs high level of trust to work with company	Early-stage startups, especially in markets with low infrastructure, hgih barriers to entry, and O2O business models
Ecosystem of Companies	Competitive landscape	Regional expansion	Acquisitions / minority / investments / creating separate business units	Right acquisition? Product-market fit for new market?	Companies looking to expand regionally
Striking Gold	Trends / innovation / fundraising	Pivots Breaking through S-curve	Pivoting the company to new focus	Long-term vs short-term trend? Too early or too late for tech innovation?	Companies in traditional industry

Exhibit 4:   Summary of strategies startups can use to scale.

All these strategies, as summarized in Exhibit 4 above, are useful for VCs to think about in terms of whether or not it would apply to their portfolio companies and the sectors and markets these companies are in, and potentially point founders in these directions or set these expectations in line with more quantitative "north star metrics". For example, an expansion into financial services might be suggested in a board meeting for an ecommerce company, but the VC will advise to only consider this move once the company has reached a certain GMV or user base. Then when these north star metrics are hit, additional funding might be given in a bridge round to be able to attract more investors and fuel the scaling strategy of the company.

That said, these strategies are also considered and talked about with founders even before making the investment. VCs will want to invest in founders who have clarity in what they want to do with their company and how they expect to see it grow, accounting for potential risks along the way.

How do VCs Help with Scaling?

In Chapter 7, we talked about two important aspects of venture capitalists supporting the growth strategy of their portfolio companies: north star metrics and getting real. North star metrics sets the targets and expectations, at least from the VC perspective, while getting real is the ideal attitude VCs have when dealing with their portfolio, primarily because VCs have the advantage of seeing the bigger picture and are more detached emotionally from the company. **A lot of the work VCs do specific to growth strategy is to shine a light on possibilities and open doors, equipping founders with opportunity. That said, ultimately it is up to the founders to make the final decision,** even if the VC can try to exert some influence to convince founders to take one path over the other.

Below we list down seven ways VCs help companies in scaling — People Placement, Partners-in-Crime, Pushing the Product, Positioning the Company, Portfolio Synergies, Painting the Market, Policing the Metrics:

1. **People Placement**
VCs will often help their portfolio companies by making introductions to the right people to help the company scale at critical junctures — the specifics we've already covered in the previous chapter.

The right people typically fall under three categories: (1) specialist experts (e.g., an AI expert to boost the self-learning capabilities (read: scaling strategy #1 in the previous section) of an ecommerce platform), (2) process superstars (e.g., Group CFO to get the financials, finance and accounting processes, and burn of the company in order and gear them up for valuable acquisitions as they expand regionally), and (3) market entry or business unit leads (e.g., Head of [insert country here] to lead the entry of the company in a new market or vertical).

Helping hire a person for a specific role could make a suggested direction for the company more convincing to leadership. For example, if the VC believes that the company should be building a platform to be more sustainable and attract more users, but the company is not able to do that currently without a CTO, the VC might go ahead and line up some CTOs for leadership to interview and potentially hire, setting the company one step forward in the direction the VCs would prefer them to go.

2. **Partners-in-Crime**

Apart from getting people into the company, VCs will also try to assist their portfolio companies by working with various people in the leadership, not just the CEO. It's important for a venture capitalist to build relationships beyond the CEO and with the other C-suite executives (the CEO's Partners-in-Crime or the company's various Persons-in-Charge if you will). This puts the VC in a prime position to closely advise these leaders on specific areas of the business, if needed. This is especially important during the earlier stage of scaling when the company is getting a hold of operations and processes. VCs will typically help finance and accounting teams with organizing financials and capitalization tables or marketing teams get a more regional reach when announcing company milestones or fundraising rounds. VCs with founder or operator experience could help with business model or technology-related issues, as some VC outfits will also have in-house engineering teams.

Partners-in-Crime also extends to other investors of the startup in the cap table. While VCs on the same cap table will ideally have shared interest in the future of the company, perspectives on the means (how to scale) may vary more than on the ends (north star metrics). This variance across investors on the cap table is what VCs need to manage and deal with.

3. Pushing the Product

VCs will also leverage their networks to make critical introductions for portfolio companies to potential customers (especially for SaaS companies) or partnerships to enter new markets or new verticals. The brand itself of the VC could also serve as a magnet for potential customers to approach portfolio companies or speed the sales cycle even.

4. Positioning the Company

Because VCs will often help their startups raise future rounds of financing, they will also try to ensure that the positioning of the company towards potential follow-on investors aligns with what is really happening on the ground. This is done not for the sake of attracting any specific type of investor, but because the VCs believe this is what will bring the company to a comfortable position from which they can then go out and work on follow-on investors, strategics, or exit scenarios. This positioning involves helping their portfolio companies improve their pitch decks, word their investor outreach, and support press release announcements to attract investors. We write more about this in the next chapter on capital strategy.

5. Portfolio Synergies

VCs will also leverage the synergies with other portfolio companies, and the potential synergies could range from (1) portfolio companies becoming customers, (2) portfolio companies serving as distribution channels, partners in offering repackaged products, or partners in integration, or (3) portfolio companies merging with each other. For example, a social commerce company could work with a payments company with e-money services in the portfolio for customers of the former to pay for goods through the latter.

6. Painting the Market

One of the most common things VCs will do is send their portfolio companies industry analyses, projections based on submitted financial reports and more importantly, sit down with founders and illustrate various scenarios depending on the potential decisions they could make at critical points. This happens often with companies that are unable to manage burn properly or where there seems to be deep misalignment as to the direction of the company, especially between investors and the founders, or even among the founders themselves.

7. Policing the Metrics

Another common thing VCs will (and should do) is to track the metrics of the company. There are information rights in the term sheets that allow this to happen but enforcing this is another issue altogether. VCs will try to make the process of updating them on numbers as easy as possible but will also chase the finance team or founders for the numbers if they fail to submit them on schedule. One can think of this as due diligence happening throughout the course of the investment, and in these "due diligence" processes, the same Rule #5 still applies — due diligence with a fresh perspective. With this information from the company, VCs will also make sure to sit down with the founders on a regular basis (outside of board meetings) and have some kind of office hours to align with the founders on the "north star metrics" and if necessary, give them some "real talk" on the situation of the company, especially in the context of the competitive landscape and other external risk factors.

Exhibit 5 summarizes these seven ways venture capitalists play a role in supporting the scale of their portfolio company.

Value-add for scaling still needs to follow Rule #9

There are two main assumptions we make in sharing these tactics VCs use. The first is that the VC is pointing the company in the right direction. But in reality, there is no 100% assurance that any

VC Value-Add for Scaling	What Happens	How It Helps Portfolio Companies Scale
People Placement	VC hires for: 1. Specialists 2. Process superstars 3. New market / new vertical leads	Unlock new markets, deepen capabilities Potentailly alleviate effort to find right hire
Partners-in-Crime	VC works closely with other C-suite executives and critical teams (e.g. finance) as well as other investors on cap table	Faster coordination to support leadership team and work with other investors on cap table
Pushing the Product	VC makes intros to potential customers or business partners from their network	Could speed up sales cycle or open up growth opportunities that were previously not there or would have been more costly to pursue otherwise
Positioning the Company	VC help founders pitch their company to follow-on investors, strategics, acquirers	Speeds up fundraising process, aligns investor interest with the direction of the company on the ground
Portfolio Synergies	VC links up port co to other port co for potential: 1. Customers 2. Business partners or intergrations 3. M&A	Could speed up sales cycle or open up growth opportunities that were previously not there or would have been more costly to pursue otherwise
Painting the Market	VC prepares briefs and research to advise founders on competitive landscape and potential trajectories and expansion opportunities	Shorten decision making process and exploration of the founder and provide another perspective to make better decisions
Policing the Metrics	VC collects regular reports on company metrics and financials, does office hours with founders	Keeps port co in check as they scale ensuring scaling strategies are efficient and sustainable

Exhibit 5:   Seven ways VCs help their portfolio companies in scaling.

proposed direction would truly work, and VCs are simply there to equip founders with opportunity and potential plans, as we've mentioned earlier. This leads to the second assumption, that founders (or the non-founder CEO in some cases) are also in the end, the ones steering the ship.

A lot of the time of the VC is spent iterating on the various possibilities of where the company can go and proposing a preferred trajectory to take given the interests of the VC firm in mind. This involves monitoring competition, building up a deeper understanding of the industry, and even networking with industry veterans (potentially floating them as advisors for their portfolio as well).

Regardless of how the VC helps the founder to scale, this value-add should still be guided by Rule #9: enabling the company to make exponentially more with less, as opposed to giving the founder more unnecessary work, wasting their time, or setting unrealistic expectations.

Three Best Practices

1. Segment portfolio companies under your purview into different levels of priority and schedule update meetings with founders depending on the level of priority.
2. Don't just work with the CEO. Get to know the rest of the management team and build working relationships with them to easily coordinate any support provided.
3. VCs are not meant to run the company. Avoid crossing the lines in intervention and instead enable change rather than managing it. Any level of support in terms of growth strategy begins from the context of the founder and company.

Chapter 10

Rule #10: Always Be Fundraising

In the previous two chapters, we covered two of the three main aspects of portfolio management for a venture capitalist — people and growth. In this chapter, we cover the third, which is capital strategy.

Capital strategy is the last we discuss because it ultimately takes together the gains made from helping out a portfolio company with the first two. Helping a startup hire a great CFO and equipping them with valuable connections and industry insights will eventually pay dividends in attracting the right investors for the company's next round of funding.

This means that helping portfolio companies with their capital strategy is not just about the fundraising process itself — investor outreach, sending out pitch decks and data rooms for due diligence, negotiating the terms of an investment, and closing the round. It is also about helping them keep checks on how they use the money they raise (i.e., burn), setting them up for another financing round (i.e., bridge round), and ensuring that they are on track to reach their north star metrics — as these metrics play an increasingly greater role in the equity story of the company as it matures.

That leads us to Rule#10: Always be fundraising. While a startup may not always be in the actual process of raising money, every decision made will affect the kind of money a startup will be able to gather the next time they need a capital injection. And when that time comes, there may not be enough time to patch up a company's risks if they have been allowed to fester.

In 2020, this became a very desperate scenario for startups that found their runways shortening by the month amidst a pandemic where investors were also tightening their belts. This challenge was only exacerbated by risks that inflated because of the pandemic like loans that defaulted or accounts receivables that never got to be paid. And unfortunately, new investors would not be keen to put their money into businesses that are already down a slippery slope.

It is important to remember, however, that startups do not exist to fundraise. The focus of the startup should be to build a great business, and growth attracts the money. The most successful startups do not fundraise because the company *needs* the capital, but because the company *can grow exponentially with* it.

With that mindset, these startups are effective with their capital strategy, using fundraising opportunities as catalysts or leverage to get to the next level. Think of it as one of those shortcuts on Super Mario Bros that has enabled speedrunners to quickly get through the various levels of the game and finish the game in a matter of minutes. They could still finish the game regardless, but with these shortcuts, they win much faster — and speed is everything for a tech startup in a rapidly changing market.

For the VC, ensuring that portfolio companies are always looking towards the next level of growth means ensuring that strategic decisions will increase in their value in the fundraising market and open up that "shortcut" to get their valuation boosted and reach a massive enough size to generate a valuable exit if the VC sells their holdings to secondaries, the company gets acquired, or the company goes public. So "always be fundraising" is a mindset that makes the company less dependent and more opportunistic when it comes to *actually* fundraising.

Why do Startups Fundraise from VCs?

Startups will fundraise specifically from venture capital, as opposed to borrowing from banks for three reasons: (1) startups are not in a position to take in traditional forms of capital because they will often fail to meet the requirements and bear intolerable levels of risk especially when they are early-stage, (2) they are aiming to scale in a way that traditional forms of capital may not be suited to help them achieve, (3) the business model of early-stage venture capital as we discussed in the earlier chapters has been designed specifically to meet the pain points (1) and (2), where you have businesses with high uncertainty but are aiming to grow fast in the next twelve to eighteen months and need the capital to fuel and scale their operations.

If one defines startups as simply being small businesses that are starting up, then not all startups are suited for venture capital funding. We write about this on *Navigating ASEANnovation*.

"Startups are often fuelled by venture capital firms. Venture capital investments are often made on the general presumption that the company is well-positioned to multiply the dollars put in by investors.

This belief in the possibility of reaping exponential returns comes from the benchmarks set by tech companies to rapidly scale and massively impact millions of people. By investing an X amount to develop a software program, that X could become 100X or a 1000X if that program becomes a household necessity across the world — and that is a big "if."

And not all companies are suited to take every kind of fuel. Venture capital in particular is like jet fuel that propels companies into space at high speeds of thousands of kilometers per hour. In the tank of the wrong business model, the company could explode.

At the same time, venture fuel is not the only fuel out there, though it is the preferred fuel of choice for startups simply because startups aim to grow fast. Even with venture capital rocket fuel, because of a combination of factors, from the startup's tenuous position itself to changes in the market, only a small percentage of startup investments eventually make it into space and land on the moon. This is not to say that the business inevitably closes shop, but that like a startup "Apollo 13", the moon landing had to be aborted." [1]

As we illustrated in Chapter, 3 venture capital has evolved in such a way that it has catered to increasingly earlier-stage companies, creating vehicles that we discussed in Chapter 6 such as convertible notes or SAFEs to be able to hedge the risk of a company folding before it raises its first institutional round.

As these startups mature, the sources for fundraising widen significantly. They can begin to raise funding from investors reliant on more traditional methods of valuation and more comfortable with proven and projectable growth, sometimes raising debt. Traditional debt can be useful to shore up cash without getting affected by depressed valuations in a bear fundraising market). These startups might also want to raise funds from private equity firms.

Another important reason startups raise venture capital funding, especially as the asset class has evolved over the years, is the expectation from these firms not just to be a stopgap in the lack of funding for the fast-growing startup, but also to be an active

participant in reducing or mitigating the risk that prevents a startup from raising capital from more traditional sources.

This is where portfolio management comes in, and why start-ups will not just raise simply because of the price (valuation) and funding amount they receive. These startups are not just raising capital but also bringing in valuable connections, insights, and relationships.

But even if startups these days raise with the expectations from the investor to help "de-risk" the company's growth, especially in the early stages, **fundraising does not solve the problems of the company.** Instead, fundraising can be a tool to get the right people on board the company (e.g., directly getting board members, ESOP for senior hires, or impressive fundraising news becoming a magnet for more employees) who can help overcome the challenges a company faces as it grows. Hendra Kwik, CEO of Payfazz, shares this mindset shift on the *On Call with Insignia Ventures* podcast in 2021.

"I'm speaking about the startup that maybe just started and is just starting to raise its first Series A capital. That it will always be hard. In the early days, when I raised Payfazz's first ticket from Insignia and the first ticket from YC, I thought that after I have money, problems will be solved, but actually, you will have another problem. Right after Series A, you have another problem. After Series B you think your problems are solved, but actually, you will have another set of struggles and you will realize that actually, it's normal, that you will always find these hardships.

And it will be impossible for you to solve it alone. So that's why I keep mentioning people. You need to leverage people around you. You need to bring a good set of investors who can support you from the investment side, and also be a good board of directors. They can be good people to support you in your decision-making. A good C-level and good team members can be the people to help you execute [on your decisions]. Don't try to do everything alone because that's going to drive you crazy. And maybe a lot of founders try to do everything themselves and that will make them feel really stressed and depressed.

So that's what I want to share with founders: focus on people. In this case, I'm not only talking about the people that you recruit, but also the people on your board and the people that are brought by your investors, because they can influence a lot in your company." [2]

How do Startups Fundraise?

Considerations that impact valuations

From the perspective of the founders, startup fundraising revolves around the exchange of equity for capital and the presence of the investor on their cap table (and board for the lead investor typically), which would ideally be helpful for the company to grow and "gain more equity" to sell to potential investors. But the price at which this transaction happens — valuation — can vary greatly on various factors as we've touched on in Chapter 5 and 6, and these factors are also important considerations for founders before fundraising:

Traction (What is the company's stage of growth?)

A company with revenue will typically raise more than a company with only an MVP to speak of. As we've mentioned earlier, as the company matures, a shift in the money they can raise from close contacts happens. From raising from the proverbial 3Fs — friends, family, fools — to angels to seed funds startups then start to raise from institutional, regional VCs and then global growth funds. This is simply because the latter investors have more money to give with the level of risk they are undertaking.

Goals (Where is the company going and how much does a company need?)

Given the traction the company has, founders should also have a clear view of where the company is going in the next twelve to eighteen months at least and how much the business would need to maximize growth in that period of time. This will inform the founders' decision making on how much to raise for the round, at least on a baseline amount, as well as how much equity they are willing to sell to get that amount. Inherently tied to these goals is also the positioning of the company and how it communicates its business model, value proposition, and even traction (e.g., which comparables and competitors will juxtapose itself to).

Geography (Where is the company raising from?)

By virtue of economics 101, more mature and saturated markets where supply of capital can outpace demand, will tend to have pricier transactions. So some startups from Southeast Asia will choose to raise from investors used to these higher valuations, however if done early could lock out more local investors. More local investors will also tend to enter earlier in the life of the company and set them up for funding rounds with more global investors — we've seen this with Southeast Asia investors setting up their portfolio for rounds with the likes of Softbank and Tiger Global, for example.

But as investors used to higher valuations come into an emerging market where prices have historically been lower, this could prove to be beneficial, at least in the short term, especially for early local investors because their holdings in the company increase as these "pricier" investors put in more money.

Market conditions (Is it a good time to fundraise?)

The overall outlook of investors on a market can easily shift valuations one way or another. In the initial onset of the pandemic in 2020, the fundraising landscape was hit with down rounds and depressed valuations as investors wanted to shore up their spending on new investments and focus dollars on portfolio companies that would need it. In hindsight, one could say that startups could simply avoid fundraising during this period, but many got a knock to their senses realizing they didn't have enough runway left.

Because it is impossible to prepare for these eventualities, this scenario brings back the importance of Rule #10: where the "always be fundraising" mindset in this context means maintaining a healthy runway through both the good times and the bad so the latter will not impact the company as much. Apart from runway, startups that got a "traction boost" from the 2020 pandemic thanks to the industry they were situated in or the business model they operated on could also afford to live on revenues while setting up a "post-pandemic" equity story to bring back confidence to investors. On the *On Call with Insignia Ventures* podcast in 2020, Dianping founder Zhang Tao recalls his experience navigating Dianping through the 2008 economic crisis.

> "So this crisis has both elements of '03 and '08, so always about, you know, a lot of companies kind of [running out of] cash and they will be in trouble.
>
> So we kind of went through that a little bit. We were planning to raise a new round of funding in the next six months before the '08 crisis but obviously we didn't go through the funding; the funding [landscape] dried up. Fortunately, operations were still kind of small. So meaning the burn rate is not that high.
>
> And so we were able to kind of, you know, increase the revenue source and just really push on the cost side. And we actually survived. And it's a blessing in disguise, we actually didn't really need money. So [we] saved a lot [on] dilution and actually the company's healthier because we are going through more revenue and cash quality routes.
>
> So I think, you know, probably all of you guys here have heard it a lot already. I want to emphasize that this is — it's going to be focused on the cash. I think that the environment is changing for the startup; the funding [landscape] is going to be different. We see that it actually started in China a couple of years ago. [There] used to be a lot of funding, a lot of money; the valuation just shot up the roof. And actually, I've been in Singapore for a little over a year and seeing that in the Southeast Asian market; the valuation is just high." [3]

In bull markets or hot periods of fundraising, valuations will generally be high and the opportunity is ripe for startups to fundraise but the risks here are that startups will be under more pressure to live up to their valuations (especially the more mature they become and the more scrutiny they draw, say pre-IPO), and the investors with the "best money" will be more strategic and likely to pile up on a bandwagon for specific players, making the market more averse to #2 or #3 players in the industry.

Industry maturity (How much are comparables or competitors?)

Apart from looking at the overall market, it is also useful to consider how nascent or developed the industry is in the startup's market of focus, vis-a-vis other markets. We discussed in Chapter 6 how venture capitalists will often look at the valuations of unicorn comparables or successful exits in other markets, especially because the dominant approach to investing in Southeast Asia has been to look for how existing playbooks could be implemented or adapted to the region.

A startup in an industry with a billion-dollar comparable is more likely to get a higher valuation than a startup in an industry without any proven models. However, developed markets are not necessarily the best position to be in, especially if the market has a lot of competitors — which could bring down the valuation especially if the heavyweight investors are circling around a single player in the field. Nascent markets could be beneficial for a startup's valuation if the company is a pioneer or early mover, there are successful comparables in other markets, and the startup is showing some early traction as well.

Investor profile (Who are you raising from?)

Another important consideration is also the types of investors that would invest in the company given the previous considerations we've mentioned: (1) traction, (2) geography, (3) market conditions, and (4) industry maturity.

When it comes to traction, the fundraising cycle has generally been segmented into (1) seed — typically the first round of financing a startup receives, historically from angels, family and friends but has since evolved to be more formalized to also have micro-VCs or VCs coming in with convertible notes that kick in upon Series A, (2) Series A — typically the first round of financing where institutional VCs are fully involved with the startup proving product-market fit, (3) Series B — typically the first round where growth or global investment players will come in with traction becoming more significant and the startup already proving scale, and (4) Series C and above — rounds where global heavyweights enter and startup boards will set up the company to go public, unless the startup is acquired or decides to stay private. Strategic investors (or investors with ties to corporates and other institutions) will enter at various stages depending on their fund mandate.

As venture capital has evolved and democratized, there have been more segmentations in the early stages with pre-seed and pre-Series A rounds (usually bridge rounds to get to a more institutional round).

It is important to note that while these labels exist, the benchmark values for how much is raised at each round and at what pre-money valuation has and will continue to change over time, thanks to the considerations we've discussed until this point — for example, the 2010s have seen seed round sizes in the US jump as the profile of seed investors became more diverse from just family and friends to more institutional seed investors (thanks to the diversification of venture capital). Some startups will also raise more than one Series A or Series B round and do an extension especially if they have a market or product launch coming up and need the capital to scale that specific launch.

In Southeast Asia, as the region's startups have gained more interest globally, institutional investors have also become more interested in going earlier, with VCs comfortable with Series A also getting into seed rounds for companies or founders they really like and growth stage players that typically do Series B or C rounds also adjusting to be opportunistic with Series A investments. That said, it is worth noting that a startup *does not* have to raise a seed round if the business model is already fueling growth at a pace well enough to eventually raise a Series A or raise with institutional VCs.

Paying attention to these segments and how they are evolving in the market is less for the founder to decide how much they need, but more for them to align what they need with the types of investors that would be willing to invest. Venture capitalists will usually use these frameworks to differentiate or compete with peers, as well as set boundaries in terms of what they are willing to invest.

Geography will also define investor profile — specifically when it comes to the markets that the startup wants to focus on. A startup focusing on Indonesia is more likely to benefit from raising seed money from an investor based in Indonesia or a regional firm with an Indonesian partner than a global firm or a firm based elsewhere, even if the latter might offer a better price.

Market conditions can also widen or narrow down the pipeline of potential investors. Investors with a lot of dry powder in a cool fundraising landscape would be a potential target for startups needing a bridge round. A hot fundraising landscape would mean a proliferation of investors but then startups, now with more leverage, have to exercise more scrutiny at which investors will truly be beneficial beyond purely a financial standpoint.

Industry maturity also opens doors to get strategic investors who would be valuable in entering new markets or speeding up the process for business contracts. For example, Southeast Asia banks have slowly begun setting up their own investment arms to work with fintechs as the whole trend around open banking and leveraging APIs to extend distribution of banks into consumer journeys has been rising.

An important part in considering the investor profile is not just looking at investors from a firm or fund perspective — but also at the specific investor or partner the startup would end up working with once the investment is made. This could be one of the most understated decision points for startups to choose their investors, amongst what we've discussed so far. It ultimately boils down to relationship building, and partnering with the right people should create valuable, long-term network effects for the company.

For startups raising their first round (seed or Series A), choosing individual investors (angels) over early-stage VCs is also a decision the startup founder has to make. With angels the main risk is the variability in how angels can operate, whereas VCs generally follow industry expectations. On the other hand, VCs may not be as effective or experienced in delivering the right value-add, especially if the VC did not lead the investment. Having a close relationship with a reputable angel might at times be even more valuable.

All these considerations come together in influencing a founder's decision on whether to raise money or not at a particular point in time, and what kinds of investors would be the best to approach in a particular round. **If anything, the main takeaway from this is that due diligence on investors goes both ways, and VCs should be aware that founders also do reference checks and DD on potential investors.**

Process

Say the startup is in a good position to fundraise — how does the process usually go? The length and demands of the process on the startup can vary depending on (1) the size and stage of the round (i.e., there will be deeper due diligence at a later stage and larger round, mainly because there's more to do due diligence on), (2) how many investors are involved (i.e., first round institutional investors can usually close out an investment in two weeks if they are sole and lead investor), as well as (3) the profile of the investors (i.e., angels can write checks off the bat, some early seed investors can close an investment in a day, while strategics can take longer to close).

Regardless, there are common steps and approaches to how the fundraising process evolves, which founders can take to close successfully and efficiently, listed below and visualized in Exhibit 1 that follows:

1. **Kickoff: Action begins before even kicking off.** In the spirit of Rule #10, it's important to start early. Three to six months ahead, plans must be drawn already in terms of going through

Steps From Founder POV

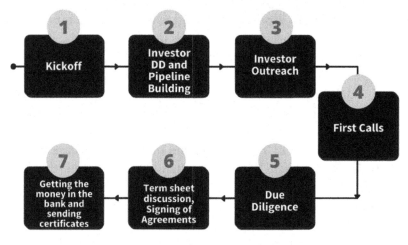

Steps From Investor POV

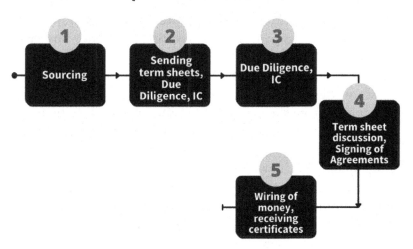

Exhibit 1: Fundraising process from the perspective of the founder versus the VC.

the various considerations we've discussed earlier in the chapter and deciding on which investors to reach out to. Especially for new investors, relationship building can already begin ahead of kicking off the fundraising so that the startup has warm leads. For existing investors, they can already be lining up potential meetings or catching up with their networks to see who would be interested in participating.

2. **Investor DD and Pipeline Building: Scope out investors and run checks.** It's important to consider the firm's funds, portfolio, and the partners or individuals who would potentially be the people the startup will be working with from the fund. Founders will usually ask portfolio founders they are close to about certain investors and get a feel of the working relationship and the value-add.

3. **Investor Outreach: The warmer the better and pulling in investors is always best.** Warm introductions are better than cold outreach, so founders will try to get in touch through second degree connections or referrals rather than just sending out cold emails or tagging investors on Linkedin. What is even better than reaching out at all is drawing investors in through the company's performance in the market (i.e. which investors will typically be tracking through a third-party platform), press releases on company milestones (e.g., product launch), or thought leadership from the founders.

4. **First Calls: Prepare and be brief.** First calls set the tone for the rest of the investment process. We discussed first calls in Chapter 4 from the perspective of the investor. For the founder, it's all about capturing the attention of the VC in a few minutes and making a lasting first impression. VCs see so many potential investments in a day that it can be easy to be passed on without even playing the startup's trump card that could have otherwise changed their mind. Succinctness is therefore rewarded in positioning the startup and getting the VC interested to learn more and schedule a longer call.

5. **Due Diligence (submitting data rooms and follow-up meetings): Don't downplay risk or exaggerate in pitching.** When it comes to positioning the startup, it is still important to be transparent with weaknesses and realistic with growth. At the end of the day, startups want partners not fans or followers in their investors. And even if the founder isn't upfront about these realities,

investors ideally do their best to see whether the financials and operations match the pitch — sifting through the noise is the bread and butter of venture capitalists. Conversely, when investors raise objections, founders can play the "data" card to address any concerns investors may have throughout the due diligence process.

6. **Term sheet discussion and Signing of agreements: Be scrutinous with what is being exchanged in the transaction.** If the investment passes IC, the VC will then get into discussions with the founder regarding the terms of the round, which should have already been raised in the initial calls, specifically the funding amount, valuation, and details of other investors joining the round. Term sheets should also have been sent earlier in the interaction between the founder and investor, after the first few meetings and the investor has decided to proceed with due diligence.

7. **Getting the money in the bank and sending certificates: Don't celebrate until the money is wired!**

Pitch decks

A key component of a startup's outreach and positioning to investors is the pitch deck. We already presented a sample outline in Chapter 5 broadly of what pitch decks should cover, and in this chapter, we revisit some of the key points venture capitalists will look for in startup pitch decks (and pitches in general):

1. **Market:** As Rule #2 goes, investors will be looking at how big the market is. Big is anything upwards of half a billion dollars.
2. **Unfair Advantage:** This is the "X factor" we discussed in Chapter 4. This answers the question, "Why are you as founder/s and not some other person the *best* people to work on this startup?"
3. **Urgency and Timeliness:** This sets up the FOMO effect and answers the question "Why should the investor put in money now and not five years later or five years earlier?" Considerations

including the evolution of the business model or technology as well as market education can be accounted for in this point.

4. **Monetization:** An attractive business model would typically have recurring revenues (or a flexible business model that can adjust to shifting supply and demand if strictly recurring revenues are not possible) as well as a high gross margin.

5. **Moat/Defensibility:** The "unique" here does not necessarily mean one-of-a-kind but refers to the ability of the technology or business model of the business to create a moat or set up defensibility against potential future competitors or incumbents in the space. Examples could be first-move disintermediation, or a data-driven approach to the customer experience or even regulatory advantages.

6. **Pied Piper:** Investors will also try to spot from the founder's pitch and the company deck whether leadership has the ability to attract the best talent from the market and even senior hires down the road.

7. **Chemistry:** Through conversations with the founders and reference checks, investors will also try to gauge chemistry among the founders as well as between themselves and the founders. They are incentivized to invest in a founding team that will stick it out through thick and thin, and work alongside a founder who knows what they are doing.

8. **Movie:** Pitches are just snapshots of the company, but investors are putting money in the movie, so they will try to see if the founder has clarity or conviction with how this movie of their business will play out, at least in the next five years.

With these points in mind, we share another framework (in addition to the one in Chapter 5) for putting together a pitch deck that remains relevant regardless of the stage. The order can be adjusted. The priority is to present these points in such a way that they answer the common questions of investors (the list we just covered) and flow in a cohesive narrative that hooks them in the start and delivers a punch at the end, as outlined in Exhibit 2:

While the general content of the pitch deck stays consistent throughout the life of the company (unless there is a dramatic

Area of Focus	Question to Answer	Considerations/Ways to Illustrate Points on A Slide
Company Purpose	Why does the company exist?	One-liner / Title slide
Problem	What is the pain point in the market the company is addressing?	Customer perspective: customer journey Market perspective: statistics Competitive landscape: comparison of existing value propositions
Solution	What is the value proposition of the company's product/s or service/s?	Lineup of product/s and service/s and how they address each of the pain points identified Customer testimonials Traction and cohort analysis
Why now?	Why now?	Evaluation of technology/infrastructure (e.g. smartphones enable on-demand access to online content) Evolution of business model (e.g. unubundling of the bank) Evolution of market (e.g. consumers moving to marketplace)
Market Potential	How big can this business be?	Comparables: How big are they in their respective markets and how similar are they to the business? Market: TAM-SAM-SOM
Competition / Alternatives	What are potential customers currently using/doing to address these pain points? Who are your competitors?	X-Y graph showing two key metrics and how competition landscape performs on those metrics Checklist of key metrics or value propositions and shows how company ticks off more boxes than competition
Business Model	How does your business make money?	CAC and LTV/Payback Revenues and costs per monetization stream/product
Team	Why are you the best people to build this business	Logos of past experience
Financials (if any)	Is your business making money? When will it make money?	P&L statement
Vision	Where will your business be in the next five years?	Vision statement North star metrics

Exhibit 2: Framework for pitch decks (and Presentations in General) for Fundraising.

pivot), the (1) depth, (2) design, (3) and focus of the pitch deck changes at various stages of growth. We consider these changes using the stages we introduced in Chapter 7 — ideation (pre-seed and seed round), PMF and scaling, as detailed in Exhibit 3 below:

Founders may also find the need to adapt the pitch deck to specific investors, especially for investors whom the founders have

Growth Stage	Fundraising Stage	Narrative for Fundraising	Focus of Pitch
Ideation	Pre-seed, seed	There's a problem that needs solving and we are the best people to solve this problem and this is what we plan to do or what we have built to solve this problem. We need capital to hit the ground running.	Founders: Capability of founders to execute and build a team Market: Pain points, urgency, and potential of growth Product: Development roadmap Traction: Initial customer funnel, early adopters
Product-Market Fit (PMF)	Series A-B	We've addressed a pain point in the market with our value proposition. We've gotten signficant positive response from the market and we need capital to sustain this traction and scale on top of it.	Solution: What value proposition has achieved PMF, Traction, Cohort Analysis: Proof of PMF Market: Pain points solved by achieving PMF, potential of growth Business Model: Ability to attract new customers, monetize and sustain PMF Financials: Targets to achieve in terms of profitability, users, sales in the next 12-18 months with this PMF Team (esp non-founder leadership): Ability to execute on growing on top of PMF
Scaling	Series B and beyond	We've mangaed to grow this business to this size and need the capital to unlock the next phase of our growth.	Solution, Business Model: The next phase of growth of the company Traction: Data-driven, customer-centric strategy for future growth Financials: Capital strategy for long-term expansion Competitive landscape: Defensive strategies Team (especially for new markets or lines of business): Evolution of leadership to meet complex needs of the business

Exhibit 3: How the focus of the pitch changes at various stages of growth.

gleaned from initial conversations and reference checks to be particular with certain aspects of the business over others.

It's also worth creating two sets of pitch decks: a short version that can be used in presenting or introducing the company in investor outreach, and a more comprehensive one that includes the nuts and bolts of the business that can be included in the data room of the company.

Fundraising tactics

Aside from everything we have already covered, we've also outlined some useful fundraising tactics:

1. **Set expectations.** Learn what the founder-investor relationship will involve and set expectations as early as possible. Figure out what the investor can offer as an individual, as well as the firm's value-add.

   Questions like where the fund is in terms of its fund life are often understated but can be useful in gauging whether or not the investor is the right fit for the company long-term.
2. **Tranche the round and leverage PR to attract new investors.** Even before the round is closed, founders can do an announcement after the first tranche to potentially attract new investors — this has to be obviously cleared first by the investors participating in the first tranche.
3. **First check determines the checks that come after.** This is an important mindset to have and makes it all the more important to think long-term even when selecting an investor for that first institutional round.
4. **Treat fundraising like a sales process.** We emphasized this in Chapter 3 when it comes to GP fundraising from LPs. This also applies to startup fundraising. By treating it like a sales process, that means building a pipeline (CRM) and constantly aiming to stay connected and top of mind with the investors in this pipeline. It also means treating the investors as potential customers

and ensuring that the company (through data rooms, pitch decks, customer interviews) is shone in the best possible light (but still factual and realistic). It also involves making the information as easy to unpack as possible.

5. **Always fundraise for the next round.** In the spirit of Rule#10, founders should already discuss expectations with investors for any follow-on and decide on valuation, investment amount, and the investors themselves with the next fundraising round in mind already.

6. **The smaller the pool, the more confidence in the founding team.** When it comes to ESOP, the smaller it is on the cap table, that means the more capable the founding team is of holding its own without having to leverage ESOP to hire senior leadership. Of course, there are certain situations where this is unavoidable, but this is more applicable to earlier stage startups where securing senior executives may not be as necessary.

7. **Get used to no's, but maintain relationships.** Investors will pass more than they say yes — given the nature of the asset class, they will like to "see" more than they "do" investments. That said, be sure to stay on good terms with as many investors in the pipeline as possible, because one never knows when these connections may be revisited in the future. Perhaps the investor may have a change of mind as the company evolves or changes direction.

8. **What got you here won't get you to the next stage.** It's an important mindset to have — that the "rules" and "routines" will always change as the company grows and enables leadership to be more flexible and adaptable when it comes to meeting the changing demands of fundraising.

How do VCs Help Startups with Capital Strategy?

We've spent most of this chapter talking about fundraising from the startup's point of view, for two reasons: (1) we've already covered VC's point of view extensively from sourcing in Chapter 4 through closing investment rounds in Chapter 5, and (2) it's important to know what the experience is like from the founder perspective to best help them when it comes to fundraising.

That said, fundraising is not 100% of capital strategy. When VCs support their portfolio with capital strategy, we discussed in Chapter 7 how it also includes helping founders better structure their capitalization tables for future fundraising rounds, and earlier in the chapter we point out that in order to "be always fundraising", good capital strategy involves using capital efficiently.

So, we break down the three areas mentioned in Chapter 7 further — matchmaking, sales, and structure — and identify the specific areas venture capitalists support their portfolio in capital strategy:

Capital support

(1) **Follow-On (Bridge Rounds):** This idea here is to put skin in the game so others will follow. Existing investors will support their portfolio companies by joining in follow-on rounds to bring in new investors or form a bridge round to tee up the portfolio company towards a formal round with more new investors.

Fundraising proper

(2) **Investor Outreach:** VCs will often leverage their networks in the investment industry to make introductions to the portfolio company as warm as possible. Sometimes, earlier stage VCs will arrange more scalable programs (investor meetups or matching) where portfolio companies can connect with investors at scale.

Other initiatives for VCs will also include helping portfolio companies build their mindshare in the ecosystem to pull in investor interest and keep them top-of-mind (again, going back to the idea of treating fundraising as a sales process).

(3) **CapTable Structuring:** VCs are incentivized to help portfolio companies in cleaning cap tables because this also impacts how

the company raises money in succeeding rounds and consequently what kind of investors they can bring in. With a complex cap table (e.g., a lot of convertible notes) founders can end up giving more than they initially intended.

(4) **Closing Investment Rounds:** VCs, especially if they lead a round with a number of investors, will often help the founders to manage and speed up the closing of an investment round.

Post-investment portfolio management

(5) **Board Decisions:** VCs with board seats will be able to vote on issues related to capital strategy (e.g., selling of shares) which dominate most board decisions.

(6) **Hitting North Star Metrics:** In the spirit of Rule #10, VCs will keep tabs on their portfolio companies and help them stay on track to be in position to maximize their next fundraising round.

(7) **Hiring CFOs or strategic development leads:** VCs will help portfolio companies hire CFOs or strategic development leads to (1) help with fundraising, specifically organizing and communicating company metrics and financials (i.e., data rooms) to investors and answering questions about this information, especially when the company is more mature, and (2) keeping tabs on the capital efficiency of the business.

(8) **Cooling the Burn:** VCs will also keep tabs on *how* the startup spends capital and suggest measures (especially in board meetings) how to keep burn under control.

A pattern throughout all these eight aspects of supporting portfolio companies with capital strategy is that it encompasses all aspects of the company, from leadership to growth strategy, and even to exits as well. And this ties back to Rule #10: Always be fundraising, where fundraising is not just about the process itself but how the company grows and matures over time.

Three Best Practices

1. Always fundraise with the next funding round in mind. Keep tabs on your portfolio companies and air concerns in regular meetings, but keep a healthy distance as well and let the founders come to you for help as much as possible (certain scenarios this may not apply).
2. Regularly revisit and iterate investor pipelines for fundraising.
3. It's always better to get a CFO or strategic development lead than to spend a lot of your time on supporting specific companies with their fundraising. This way you can focus more on the origination and introductions rather than the communication or coordination.

Only select
investors can
come on board

Chapter 11

Rule #11: Building a Strong Board of Directors is about Balance, Not Control

How are Startup Boards Formed?

Having discussed the three areas where VCs support portfolio companies — people, growth strategy, and capital strategy — over the past three chapters, we now move onto an important avenue through which venture capitalists try to support company management in these three areas. This avenue is the board of directors.

Do VCs have to be a board of director or even a board observer to help a portfolio company? No. The presence of a venture capitalist on the board of a startup is less like a door opening up for the VC to help, and more like a sign that the founders or company leadership values the VC enough to bring them on, not just as a shareholder on the cap table, but as a director of the board as well.

Board seats are not given but earned and earning the trust of a founder to be given a board seat through the term sheet begins even before the founder and investor meet in person. The formation of startup boards is inherently tied to the fundraising process, and so the ability of a venture capitalist to land on the board of a startup is also tied to their sourcing strategy and how the VC manages their investment funnel.

Startup boards are typically composed of just the founders, if the startup has not raised any financing round yet. Through successive financing rounds, a startup board will then eventually have more investors and people brought in. Until an IPO or exit, these investors will generally hold preferred shares (as we learned in Chapter 6), which grants them rights to nominate board members. The evolution of a startup board is quite similar to ownership of the startup in the sense that the control of the founder/s dilutes over time, but as we will emphasize throughout this chapter — **Rule #11: A strong board of directors is about balance, and not control.**

Board formation requires balance

The typical members of a company board include more than just the founders coming from the company. Apart from the CEO or founder-CEO, there may be a chairman (oftentimes in the case of startups, former CEO or part of the founding team) set as a distinct person from the CEO. There may also be several directors (management) and executive directors (C-suite) who are remunerated or obligated by contract to sit on the board.

These "employed" board members often come in at a later stage of the company's growth, when the company's organization and governance become more complex that it takes more than a single founder-CEO to represent the company's organizational structure. In the meantime, however, most startup boards will be composed of the founders, VCs or typically lead investors of each funding round, and independent board members.

While startup boards generally introduce more external persons (i.e., not employees) as the company raises more rounds of financing and matures as an organization, there are various recommendations on how to compose an ideal startup board. Union Square Ventures partner Fred Wilson recommends having 2–3 fellow CEOs or peers (who have presumably built their own ventures or are in the process of building successful companies), alongside an influential angel or venture capitalist. Brad Feld, the author of "*Startup Boards: Getting the Most out of Your Board of Directors*," recommends having at least one independent director and a legal counsel on the board. [1]

A common thread around all the different compositions of a startup board is **to have a balance in perspectives across functions as well as across viewpoints on the company. Board members are there to fill in the gaps.** VCs and other outsider board members have the luxury of taking a step back and not being as emotionally attached as the founders would be. Having financial, legal, strategy, and networks (hiring) expertise on a board can also be a huge asset for the company in general, as leadership has immediate access to resources they need to make quick top-level decisions, which is critical for a startup.

With the right choice of board members and a proactive approach to board formation (e.g., already doing due diligence on investors before the first meeting and considering their potential role on the board), startup founders will be able to arm themselves with a "Council of Elders" of sorts capable of accelerating growth even in the short-term.

This demand of balance in perspectives and functions in a startup's board changes as the company grows. We've documented these shifts in the last three chapters as they relate to the kind of talent the company needs, the strategies they employ when scaling, and the demands of fundraising. The impact on startup board formation is no different. Earlier in the life of the company, there may be a need for more expertise around market and product development, and as the startup finds its product-market fit and scales, the focus shifts to guiding the founders on sales, finance, and operational controls. Then as the startup matures in the growth stage, the role of the board may be focused more on key leadership roles who can steer an increasingly complex organization.

Because of how similar board formation can be in terms of hiring company leadership, **it is a good approach for founders and CEOs to develop a startup board the same way they would form their management team — ensuring that there is alignment not only with the skills needed by the company at that particular period in the company's growth, but also their values and team or culture fit.**

Another consideration in board formation is also remuneration, especially for independent directors (not VCs) who are brought in, and this is usually done through small equity stakes, ranging from 0.5% to 2.0%. These stakes have to be considered in the company's cap table in the same way that allocations are made for management or senior hires.

Best practices for startup board formation and development

With this concept of balance and the reality of a rapidly evolving company in mind, we list down some key best practices or crucial ingredients for founder-CEOs (who are often the one in charge of bringing together these boards early on) when it comes to startup board formation. **These best practices revolve around resisting temptations to seek control and diluting the ability for any single director or agenda to take full control, and instead opting for balance and focusing on what the company really needs.**

1. **Due diligence.** As we've mentioned earlier, bringing together a board is best done the same way one would hire company

leadership, and fundraising is also tied to this process. The discipline to consistently check every prospect thoroughly and methodically, whether an investor or independent director, running reference checks and being strategic about what gaps are important for the board to fill for the company. Even when the potential board member has an impressive reputation at the outset, CEOs should still resist the temptation to just take them in because of their halo effect without the proper checks.

2. **Independents.** It can be tempting to stack up the board with people unfailingly on your side (even to the point of bringing in family and friends), but this can work against the founder in terms of attracting VCs in the long run. For the VC as well, it may be tempting to also stack the board with people they can readily influence or control, but the ideal board should also have that independent director separate from the founder's and VC's own.

3. **Tight Ship.** Even for VCs that are board observers, it is important for the CEO to be fully aware of the role these participants have, because they effectively receive the same information and can easily have the same "voice" in board meetings as actual board members (especially if they are influential), despite not having the same voting rights. Tight ship also refers to CEOs paying close attention to the alignments that could potentially form from the people brought onto the board, especially when high-profile personalities are involved.

4. **Strong Chairman.** A board's chair will tend to be a key leverage point for founders or early CEOs, acting as a bridge between the board and management. Oftentimes in startups, this role is filled in by the founder-CEO already. But as the company matures, it may be prudent to offer up the seat to someone more experienced. This does not weaken the ability of the CEO to run the company. In some ways, it frees up the CEO from the politicking that inherently comes with managing the board and enables focus on the company's growth.

A strong chairman has the ability to pull in the right people to the board or management team, guide the CEO, and act as a filter for all the noise that can come in from the board. In other cases, the founder-CEO becomes the chairman and the board hires a new CEO to take that spot, especially if the founder-CEO can no longer handle the rigors of the day-to-day operation but still wants to manage the overall strategy of the company.

5. **Board Exits.** An effective board has members who know when it is time to leave. As we've emphasized earlier, the demands of growth also affect the kind of board of directors needed by the company.

   The period in a company's growth where this shift is most pronounced is a company's entry into the public markets wherein VCs will typically exit the boards of public companies. First, the mindset they have may no longer be relevant for the board of a public company. Second, it is important for the board of a public company to have directors who can fully commit to the company, without being distracted by other portfolio companies to handle, especially as the rigor of governance increases with the maturity and size of the company.

   During this time, boards will also typically introduce sub-committees in order to meet specific knowledge gaps (e.g., medical technology committee to help the company launch a product with FDA approval).

Some of the classic examples of boards becoming unhealthy are the well-documented cases of Theranos and WeWork. Theranos's board was filled with high-profile directors, but none of them had the expertise (or arguably even the incentive — because, going back to tip #2, the directors were all *too* close to the CEO) to conduct proper due diligence on the business.

On the other hand, WeWork saw its founder-CEO leveraging his control and running the company towards a financially unpleasant position as the company was selling its glitzy equity story to public investors (which inevitably creates cognitive dissonance for the IPO investor), to the point that the larger shareholders (Softbank) had to step in and stop the parade.

How do VCs Become Effective and Valuable Board Members?

Board membership for VCs also requires balance

From the perspective of the venture capitalist, one's role as a board member is also to provide balance — one can think of it as being part of a Jedi Council, bringing balance to the Force.

Technically, the mandate of any board of directors (startup or not) is corporate governance. This mandate is exercised through three levers: (1) designation of management rules, processes, and policies, (2) selection of management (especially the CEO) and (3) approval or veto of capital allocation. By exercising this mandate, the VC already introduces balance into the board. The assumption here is that the VC brings in a position or perspective that otherwise would not have been available to company leadership *and* would be extremely useful for the growth of the company.

While providing balance to the board with their own unique perspective, the VC board member also has to balance their dual duties to both the fund and the company. We brought this up in Chapter 6, where the VC fights for the interests of both the fund and the company in closing an investment. This mindset carries over into portfolio management especially if they become board members. In general, these interests are aligned, both parties want to maximize and benefit from the upside of the company's growth.

There are some cases, however, where these interests are not aligned, especially when the VC is looking to exit their investment early to cut losses for the fund while they have a board seat, where duty expects them to keep the invested capital. These types of exits, typically done through trade sales, are often resisted by the common shareholders, but VCs will work around this resistance by sharing these trade sales with the founding team. As we will discuss in the following chapter on exits, VCs will also want to avoid these kinds of exits especially if they are a lead investor or have a board seat, unless this direction is aligned with that of the founders and CEO.

Considerations for VCs to be board members

With these dual interests potentially becoming an issue, founders will try as much as possible to minimize the risk posed by this by ensuring that board members are aligned to the needs of the company as much as possible. Below are some of the key considerations for founders and VCs before taking a board seat in the company:

1. **Lead investor:** Lead investors will typically include a board seat in the term sheet, and that is intuitively tied to the fact that they are the lead investors and believe enough in the company to lead the round and commit to a board seat as well. That said, corporate venture investors and strategics will likely not ask for a seat even if they do lead the round.

2. **Investor Status and Track Record:** Founders will want VCs on their board with a reputable status and track record that is *aligned* (this is key!) with their industry. We discuss more reasons why this is the case later in the chapter as they relate to the value VCs bring to a startup board, but primarily it is to ensure that the company *will* benefit from the background and status of the VC as opposed to the lack thereof.

3. **Investor-Founder Relationship:** A lot more intangible but something that is key to have is a level of chemistry and strong communication between the investor and founder, and this goes beyond industry and expertise alignment. Founders will often depend on their board of directors to be accessible, especially the VCs, through the thick and thin of building a company — a level of commitment that some will argue (or joke) is more demanding than that of a marriage.

4. **Geographic Proximity/Market Familiarity:** We include this consideration not because it is necessary to have board members be physically present, but because it is important to have board members who understand the market as much as the founders do, especially when the company is still in its early stage.

The value-adds of a VC board member

With a venture capitalist on a startup board, we list down some of the key value-adds VCs bring to the table as board members, and in what way exercising these value-adds can VCs become effective as part of startup boards.

Been there, done that

The top VCs to have on a startup board are those who have "been there and done that". That means that they have either backed successful companies in the same space and even sat on their boards, or they had a significant hand in building those companies as operators, whether as founders or executives. This experience does two things. First, it creates a level of empathy that strengthens the ability of the VC to communicate ideas to leadership and increases the trust of leadership in seeking the opinion and perspective of the VC. Second, it gives the VC greater clarity into what a company in the space needs to succeed; it is not just informed by secondhand research but firsthand, on-the-ground failures and successes.

If the VCs on your board do not have that depth of experience, it may also be advisable to bring someone on the board who does have that operator experience. On the other hand, founders also need to be careful about ex-operators on the board who may try to run the company. Again, there needs to be a balance.

Big picture thinking

As we've mentioned earlier in the chapter, VCs come into the board from the perspective of having studied (or even experienced) the market the startup is in. To an extent, they are expected to be the members on the board who can command context, providing a big picture take or benchmarks to guide the company. Because patterns recur so much in startups (which is actually one of the underlying reasons for Rule #1: Southeast Asia is not Silicon Valley), there are a lot founders can learn from businesses that have left "footprints in the sand", from go-to-market and the right executives to hire to market adoption and monetization.

This is where having a VC on the board with either a lot of prior investments in the same space or a global footprint comes in handy. Of course, each startup is unique (Rule#1), but comparing and contrasting with comparables or competitors can prove valuable in making the right business decisions. The best VCs at exercising this value-add will often cite anecdotes or actual case studies from past experiences or investments rather than dropping hypotheticals.

Another dimension of this big picture thinking is not just the depth of the industry but breadth in terms of time, specifically the implications of major business decisions over time. While founders and the executives are busy with the day-to-day operations, the board of directors best operate thinking long-term. The onus may appear to be on the management to show growth to keep the board happy, as in a private company they typically have the largest shareholders. That's true but only because this growth is part of the bigger role of the board in keeping management on track for the long-term.

So the onus is really on the board to ensure that management's decision-making is informed as well by long-term thinking. An acquisition today may temporarily boost a company's transaction volume and customer base, but will the margins be sustainable enough to not just be a burden on the business? They may be already looking for a new country head, but is this even the right market for the business to enter in the first place? These kinds of "first principles" questions are important for startup boards to bring up as management explains their strategies to grow the company.

Branches

The best VC to have on a startup board is one with rich networks. This can be of immense value to startups especially when they are still in the early stage of growth. The impact of these networks can range from hiring to business development, advisors to potential investors. When it comes to exits, VCs will also often be the key mediators for these events, fostering relationships between strategics, as we discussed in Chapter 10, or ensuring that the company is prepared to go to the public markets.

What's important to note here is the timing of these introductions. If there is overexposure to a network when these introductions may not be so useful or the company may not be mature enough to make anything out of these connections, then the VC may have just wasted time. At the same time, VCs will want to slowly get management acquainted with the right people over time and not simply expect these connections to result in transformational initiatives overnight. It's also important for VCs to keep their networks relevant to how the industry is evolving. It's not worth having a network of potential hires if the role they could be great for is no longer relevant to the portfolio company.

Brutal honesty

Radical candor (as termed by Kim Scott) or Radical Transparency (as termed by Ray Dalio) is critical for board members to be effective, and VCs are well-positioned to deliver this kind of feedback given the big picture perspective they carry and their psychological distance from the company. This brutal honesty is a combination of exploring the uncomfortable topics while being constructive and consistent when it comes to communication. All of this should be motivated by the board enabling management to make the best decisions possible.

Because startup founders are always on the grind and have a front-row seat at the roller coaster of running a fast-growing company, it can be easy to misjudge situations or even their own capabilities. The board is there to "normalize" perspectives rather than pile on top of the founders' already skewed perception of themselves and the business. While "normalizing" perspective may seem intangible, this can be one of the most dangerous value-adds *not* to do. Fuelling a leader's skewed view of the world, as we've seen in circumstances even outside of corporate governance and running companies, can lead to some detrimental situations. The board should be able to hold up the mirror to management and break harsh realities to them.

"Best friend" to call / speed dial

A lot of the work of board members goes beyond participating in board meetings. This is especially the case for startups, where changes in the company happen day-to-day while board meetings still happen quarter-to-quarter or month-to-month. This means effective VC board members are responsive and committed to returning messages within a short timeframe, helping to put out fires at a moment's notice — essentially becoming "speed dial" for the founder.

That said, it's not just about speed. It's also about consistency and follow-through. Consistency means that even if this rapid communication is not always pivotal in the moment, these "micro-advice" sessions can provide indirect ammunition for more pivotal decision-making, or accumulate and influence the way the founder or CEO thinks. Most of the time, they can inspire confidence and build assurance in a founder, especially when they are going through unfamiliar territory in the company's growth. Follow-through is also important because this also encourages the founder to think long-term and reduce the risk of similar situations.

Not all VCs, or even board members for that matter, will be able to fill in this role, and each founder will typically have that one or two numbers that become the proverbial "first call". It's the mark of a great VC not just to be that "first call", but also to be that "first call" that founders look back on and say was extremely valuable in growing their company — regardless if it was pivotal in the moment or accumulative in its impact.

Cheerleader vs Judge and jury

With these value-adds that make an effective board member, it can be easy to sway up and down the scale of being too much of a "cheerleader" versus being too much of a "judge and jury". However, either side of this scale is risky. While founders may intuitively want to have a board of cheerleaders, this board runs the risk of being blind to the mistakes management may be making that ultimately pile up and can result in the company's failure. On the other hand, a board that tries to take the steering wheel away from management also runs the risk of driving the business into failure because they may not be well-equipped to actually operate the company or not have the same kind of relationship management has with employees.

Once again, balance is key, and instead of being either, it's far more important to be a "companion" of management, one who can empathize with what company leadership is going through, but also knows when to step in and keep them on the right track. Once again I bring up the example from Chapter 1 with Sam and Frodo in "Lord of the Rings". Sam helped Frodo through all sorts of ups and downs, but also did his best to keep Frodo on the right track — even when Frodo himself was possessed by the Ring. One could argue that Sam would have been a great board member — able to stay close, but also keep distance and not get influenced.

How are Effective Startup Board Meetings Run?

Board meetings play a huge role in influencing the direction of the company. Scheduled in regular intervals every quarter or so, they are an opportunity for management to formally communicate the progress of the company, the issues they would like to be addressed by the board, and to vote on decisions that need to be made as part of the board's mandate. For board members, these meetings are a space to communicate critical ideas and feedback in full view of all other board members and the relevant management executives. As we will emphasize later on, **a lot of what happens in board meetings are the result of what is done outside of the boardroom, but the board meeting per se is the space and time where all this work culminates into concrete decision-making.**

There are multiple mental models and frameworks out there on how to run effective board meetings, from Sequoia Capital's Board Meeting Deck, which really drills into the minute-by-minute flow of the meeting, as well as how management should frame their presentation, to the Board Triangle of True Ventures, which is broader and just pinpoints the three key must-haves in every board meeting discussion. Both are illustrated in Exhibits 1 and 2.

Running an Effective Board Meeting

By Sequoia Capital

1. Big Picture

CEO update, highlights, challenges, discuss company needs

2. Calibration

Funnel metrics, engagement metrics, financial metrics, performance vs. plan

3. Company Building

Org chart, product roadmap, quality, updates from teams: engineering & tech, growth, marketing, business development, operation, quarterly P&L, monthly waterfalls

4. Working Sessions

Topic 1
Deep dive: functional area, large partnership opportunity, business challenge

Topic 2
Deep dive on quarterly company goals, product challenges

5. Closed Session

Formalities, stock option grants, etc

Exhibit 1:   Sequoia Capital's Effective Board Meeting Schedule. [2]

Exhibit 2: True Ventures' Board Triangle. [3]

In general, we can segment each meeting into five parts:

1. **Before the meeting:** Founder-CEOs need to be prepared for these meetings, weeks before they actually even happen. This does not just involve preparing a deck to show the latest progress of the company, but also finalizing the agenda first with the independent and non-executive directors on the board on short individual calls. One can use the "Board Triangle" above as a mental model when framing the agenda. This agenda will inform what should be in the board pack, which should then be sent out to board members ideally three days to a week before the meeting, so that board members can come into the meeting in the right frame of mind. Sending the board deck ahead also reduces the "reporting" time and frees up more time for more constructive discussion. Prior to the meeting, it's also important to plan time allocation for each of the sections of the actual meeting.

2. **Reporting:** During the reporting proper, the Founder-CEOs are expected to kick things off with top-level highlights of the company's growth since the last meeting, as well as one to three strategic issues that need to be discussed during the meeting.

The second part is followed through with more detailed north star metrics (e.g., revenue, sales, engagement, lead generation, or user feedback). Here the founder-CEO may choose to bring in the appropriate person from the management to do the briefing — the CFO, CTO, or VP of Sales, depending on the business model of the company. In many cases, these other C-suite executives may be in a better position to report certain aspects of the company and take questions from the board.

The reporting is concluded with more forward-looking information, which would ideally include a product roadmap for the next 12–18 months, the team composition and roles that need to be filled moving forward, and any business development or operations related partnerships or initiatives that need to be made. It is important to tie this forward-looking section back to the top-level highlights and how the former will build on top of or improve the existing situation of the company.

3. **Working Session:** A deep dive (around 30 mins) session into the strategic issues raised during the reporting, where board members bring in their expertise, suggest networks, and most importantly, provide perspective.

4. **Summary:** To close off the board meeting, the founder-CEO will take the opportunity to express concerns and engage in an unfettered discussion with board members, especially with respect to issues that were not covered in the prior sections. Administrative matters are also wrapped up before the meeting ends.

5. **Post-Mortem:** After each meeting, it is useful to debrief on how the meeting was run, whether it was effective or not in addressing the key issues that leadership wanted to bring up, and iterate on the format to improve the logistics, reporting, and discussions in future meetings.

Regardless of the flow of the meeting, there are some important mindsets to have especially in board meetings of startups.

(1) Enable the founder-CEO to take ownership.

Venture capitalists (and other independent directors and non-executive board members for that matter) do not sit on boards to run the company. It is far more effective for VCs to enable the founder-CEO to take ownership of (1) the issues they are facing and (2) the solutions that come out of the meeting. One could stick to the rule of three when giving key insights at a board meeting and delivering these insights in a way that does not feel imposing but puts the founder in a position to really think about how they should approach a certain problem.

(2) It's less about sharing what you know, and more about asking the right questions.

This is one way to feed insight into the discussion without spoon-feeding answers or making one's presence feel too overbearing. It's better to guide founders to the right questions rather than adamantly pressing them to stick to what one thinks are the "right" answers. Questions can also be more empowering in that they serve as cues for the founder-CEO to take charge and figure out an answer. They are more open-ended, so they engage rather than impose. Instead of thinking about three key insights, maybe think about three key questions to ask in each board meeting.

(3) Make it as easy as possible to have the critical discussions.

Meetings should be set up so that the time to have critical discussions and for the founder-CEO to candidly share their concerns is maximized and prioritized over information that can be disseminated through an email.

(4) Board meetings are only as effective as what happens in between them.

If it's not yet clear, a lot of the value-adds we outlined earlier in the chapter can only be exercised outside of the board meetings. So it is important for both the VCs and the founder-CEOs to have multiple conversations between meetings. This is all the more relevant for startups. Through these conversations, VCs can stay up-to-date on where the company is and provide timely feedback that would otherwise be outdated if they had waited for the next meeting. These 1:1s also enable the founders to be more candid and is a sign of greater trust between the founder and the investor.

Once again, running effective startup board meetings is also about balance, not control — Rule #11. Balancing what happens outside and during meetings, the insights shared with what management shares, and the amount of time to dedicate to updates and focusing issues — all these things are important considerations.

At the end of the day, this balance is not just meant to reduce the risk of going one extreme or the other, but to actually foster a founder-investor relationship or founder-director relationship that maximizes what each brings to the table in building a great company. In an industry where egos can be inevitable (one needs some level of ego to build and believe in crazy ideas), the temptation to slip off-balance can be high, but the ability to manage this balance is what makes for a great venture capitalist, or even founder-CEO, for that matter.

Three Best Practices

1. Enable the founder-CEO to take ownership during meetings.
2. It's less about sharing what you know and more about asking the right questions.
3. Board meetings are only as effective as what happens in between them. Maximize board meeting prep in update meetings with founders and management.

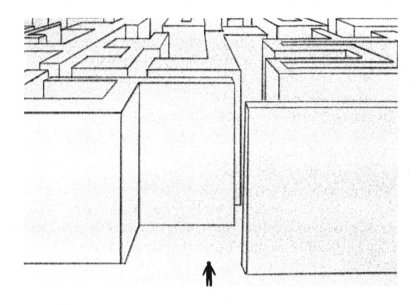

Chapter 12

Rule #12: Finding Exits is an Exercise in Creativity

Beyond the Hype of Exits

In October 2017, Sea Group went public on NASDAQ through a milestone IPO that marked a new chapter in Southeast Asia's tech ecosystem. In the years since, this IPO set a standard for tech start-ups to follow, often referenced as the first in the region. At the same time, it was quite interesting that Sea Group's IPO day was initially covered as "off to a rocky start" and a "roller coaster ride" in tech news publications.

Coming into the public markets, Sea was facing increasing losses with its expansion into ecommerce, a cash-burning, highly competitive space at the time, and payments, a practical but low-margin vertical. Around the same time, Financial Times also reported Sea's possible ejection from one of the company's largest markets, Taiwan, following investigations from Taiwan's Investment Commission on the company's ownership.

Then when shares were finally offered, the stock faced rapid ups and downs within the first few hours, jumping from the initial offer price of 15 dollars per share to 17 then back to 15, before wrapping up the day at around 16 dollars per share.

While it was a rocky start, Sea's life in the public markets turned out to be a critical source of fuel for Sea to dominate the ecommerce race in Southeast Asia and double down on financial services with bank acquisitions and digital banking licenses. They even funded their own corporate venture capital fund, ushering the ecosystem into a new stage of maturity with local unicorns starting their own funds.

Sea's achievement as the world's best performing stock in 2020, catalyzed by pandemic-induced digitalization, is likely even a factor in why more investors began looking at other tech companies in the region to bring to list through special purpose acquisition companies or SPACs. By mid-2021, Sea even began expanding into Latin America in Chile and Colombia, putting their market cap above Softbank's at US$140 billion.

Just a year before Sea Group's public market debut, Lazada, the main competitor of Sea's ecommerce arm Shopee, was acquired by Alibaba in an equally momentous deal for the regional ecosystem, becoming the first exit of a startup in Southeast Asia. The acquisition comes just months after the platform claimed to be the largest in the region, accumulating US$1.3 billion in gross merchandise value (GMV) in 2015 across six markets. Alibaba likely saw the rising ecommerce player to be a unique opportunity to expand and diversify, paying US$500 million for new shares in the company and acquiring a similar amount of shares from existing investors, including British supermarket company Tesco.

In the years that followed, however, Lazada's dominance in the space became increasingly tenuous with Shopee's parent Sea going public and more country-specific players like Blibli and Tokopedia gaining ground in their local markets. Alibaba realized that simply acquiring Lazada would not be enough, and had up to US$3 billion more in the company over the next two years, and appointed new CEOs three times over the next five.

News outlets also reported the long-term challenges of post-acquisition integration, especially when it came to reconciling cultural differences between Lazada and Alibaba. In 2021, a consortium co-led by Alibaba and Hong Kong's Baring Private Equity Asia invested US$400 million into CrownX, the consumer retail arm of Vietnamese conglomerate Masan Group, in an attempt to diversify its ecommerce holdings in the region as the Indonesian landscape stabilized and investors turned to Vietnam.

For all the hype tech ecosystems put around exits, there are three often understated realities around exits demonstrated by Sea's experience in the public markets and Lazada's acquisition by Alibaba.

The first reality is that exits are not the end

Exits are just another practical measure to get to the company's next stage of growth, and do not necessarily determine success or failure of the company.

As we pointed out in the previous chapter, while category leadership is ideal to achieve for investors before exiting (the valuation at exit is higher that way), it is not necessary and often, occurs early in the life of the company, especially M&As. IPOs, botched or not, does not necessarily mean the end of company-building. WeWork continues to run even after its botched IPO in 2019, and in mid-2021, it reported its best sales quarter as workplaces slowly reopened in developed markets. Sea Group used the liquidity gained in the public markets to pull ahead in the ecommerce race and expand aggressively in new services and even continents.

Exits have just received the acclaim they have in startup ecosystems and narratives because (1) venture capitalists invest early into a company's valuation and successful exits typically represent a massive valuation jump from that first ticket, creating massive wealth for the shareholders that placed their stakes early on, and (2) exits generate validation which investors like to use as benchmarks for potential investments in a similar market or vertical (i.e. the whole concept of using comparables).

In reality, exits can either be restructuring and/or fundraising tools for the company to (1) increase their liquidity or lengthen their runway to fuel future initiatives, (2) cost-effectively acquire capabilities or market share that would have otherwise been impractical to do solo or with private funding, and (3) stabilize or deepen the company's defensibility.

Exits are built for the company, and not the other way around

That leads to the second reality that at the end of the day, exits are built for the company, and not the other way around. While we talked about valuing startups based on the potential exit in Chapter 5, and even gauging portfolio management based on exit scenarios, when it comes to the actual execution of an exit, it should be done in consideration of what is best for the company and its stakeholders, not on the presumption that it should be able to achieve a specific exit.

To put it in a more personal context, one could dream to be an astronaut as a kid, but as the kid grows up, they form new experiences that are likely to lead them to other career possibilities. There's also the reality that society makes it difficult, if not near-impossible, for a kid to become an astronaut depending on where they live. The market demand for astronauts is too small versus the number of kids who at one point in their lives dreamed of being an astronaut. Analogous to that, the market demand for tech IPOs is generally far too small versus the number of founders who aim to bring their companies to the public markets, and even the number of investors who want these companies to succeed in this way.

We saw this "reality-upending-expectations" situation materialize in WeWork's IPO, when the expectations of a public market that is suspicious of tech companies unveiled cracks in the company's management and relationship with its investors.

When Coins.ph was acquired by Gojek in 2019, it was likely not what the founders or their early investors had in mind when the company initially started out, but the payments landscape in the Philippines was becoming more competitive amidst the backdrop of the accelerating regional rivalry between Gojek and Grab. The founders had to make a tough decision.

> "We had to make a decision on how we want to continue growing our business, and we felt like ultimately together with Gojek we could build something that is overall bigger and better for our customers," Ron Hose, co-founder and CEO of Coins.ph said in a phone interview with TechCrunch at the time. [1]

One then wonders what could have been if Coins.ph did not take the deal. There are some who have argued since then that Gojek's moves into other markets was premature and nothing was made out of their acquisitions outside of Indonesia. That said, the Gojek acquisition likely provided Coins.ph some form of stability, in the same way that its competitors in the ewallets space were incubated and backed by larger conglomerates. ESOP was also likely paid out as well to early employees, which could have been something that factored in the decision making.

So regardless of what expectations are, exits must be executed with reality in mind. What can the company achieve with this acquisition? How will capital from the public markets fuel the company moving forward? This point seems too intuitive to even mention in writing, but it is easy to lose sight of, especially when the collective narrative places so much emphasis and premium on startups entering into landmark M&As or ringing the bell on Wall Street.

The best exits (the fund returners) take time

The third reality is that the best exits (the fund returners) take time. For one, venture capitalists would want to avoid divesting their positions in their portfolio company too early, unless there's a rare change in mandate or there's a pivot in the investment thesis. The more a portfolio company can grow from the point in time that the VC puts in their first check, the better it is for the returns of the fund. Then the longer the company can last, even if the VC has already exited its investment, the more it will continue to contribute to the VC's brand and strengthen its sourcing funnel. Of course, a VC *can* exit the investment after a few years, but it is likely not a fund-returner.

Apart from the economics of the VC business model incentivizing patience and consistent follow-through, there is also the factor of geography and exit paths available to startups in that market. This factor changes over time as the ecosystem matures, but for the better part of the 2010s, IPOs were a difficult bridge to even arrive at for Southeast Asia startups, let alone crossing that bridge into the public markets. So exits will take time.

Going back to the Sea Group example, it took eight years from founding to IPO, whereas Lazada took four years. M&As typically have a wider range in terms of time to exit and happen earlier. In contrast, going to the public markets take longer to achieve, because the qualifications in most exchanges have conventionally favored stable, mature companies (which arguably fast-growing startups will have a challenging time transitioning into).

That exits take time also means a lot of the work that leads to a substantial exit boils down to (1) continuous and consistent growth and (2) the right investors to help the company do (1).

In the case of Appier, their path to the public markets was a nine-year journey, and a lot of their growth over the past nine years leading up to the Tokyo Stock Exchange owes to the fact that Appier played the long game in a rapidly changing space: artificial intelligence. We describe how Appier played this long game in a mini-case study on *Insignia Business Review*.

"While investing in expertise has made Appier an enduring company, the fact that this expertise was AI also played a huge role in the kind of scale they achieved over this past decade, which has been a hallmark period for AI digitalization, especially in Asia. Perhaps Appier themselves may have had a hand in driving this trend as they expanded rapidly across East and South Asia in their first three years, but regardless of how it came to be, timing played perfectly for the company.

Venture capitalists often talk about big picture technology developments in waves, and usually conclude that the best founders and companies are those that are either making the waves or riding the waves long before they reach the shore. What is less talked about is that sometimes these waves don't crash all in one go, and sometimes you have long waves that come in slowly.

So Appier didn't just make a wave or ride it early on — they continue to ride it and make sure it spreads to as wide of a beachhead as possible. And in this regard, the nature of AI helps immensely, as Appier's growth is not tied to its geography nor centralized around its headquarters in Taipei. The founders shared the view even early on that Appier should become global in reach, not just because of the market potential or the borderless nature of their expertise, but also because the data needs to be big in order to best inform their products.

That said, it is also important to note that making their waves first in the Asia Pacific region, compared to, say, if they had started in the US or Europe, also put them in a better position to be a market leader. In 2019, the US and UK accounted for around half of the US\$121 billion spent on marketing technology, and that opened up a less competitive space in Asia for a company like Appier to dominate. This gave them the space to expand quickly across Asian cities, especially pre-2017 when they were just focused on growing the reach of CrossX (Appier's first and flagship product)." [2]

In order to play this long game, they needed the support of investors at critical junctures. It wasn't easy finding VC money early on, however. Their first institutional investor was Sequoia Capital, and while the VC firm came in around three years after the company was founded, Sequoia also entered and offered critical value-add to help in an important juncture in the life of the company — the same year Appier launched its first product, CrossX. We write about this critical juncture for the company in a mini-case study on *Insignia Business Review* in 2021.

"Over the first two years with only their headquarters in Taiwan, it had been difficult to convince international VC firms to invest in AI startups (at that time it was even more difficult to win over enterprise clients), according to Winnie Lee in this article.

Enter Sequoia Capital. When Appier opened their first branch office in Singapore, the 42-year-old, global VC firm also had its Singapore office in the same building. According to Appier CEO and co-founder Chih-Han Yu in the Tech in Asia article announcing their Series A round, "We weren't thinking about doing any fundraising back then, we were just planning on bootstrapping the company and growing our own revenue." Incidentally, Appier was also Sequoia's first — first Taiwanese startup in its portfolio.

That US$6 million Series A round fuelled Asia expansion and R&D, but more than the capital, Appier was also able to leverage on the connections the global VC firm offered. As Chih adds, "Sequoia impressed us with their global connections and experience building world-class companies. They [introduced] us to partners that would normally take us years to meet."

Over the next three years, Appier raised three successive rounds of funding: US$42.5 million in two rounds of Series B and a US$33 million Series C round. Then towards the end of 2019, right before the pandemic, they closed a US$80 million Series D round. Among their investors include Softbank Group, LINE Corp, Naver Corp, TGVest Capital, and Temasek's Pavilion Capital. Insignia Ventures joined Appier's cap table in their 2019 Series D round. In total, the AI company raised US$186 million dollars and was recognized as one of the two first Taiwanese unicorns in 2020 by the Ministry of National Development Council in Taiwan.

For a Taiwanese tech company that was initially planning to bootstrap and grow purely on revenue, it is remarkable how much and from whom they raised successively after that first round in 2014. Sometimes all it takes is the first check, but what's more important is that there was a founder-investor fit. The VC saw the long-term potential of a company investing in its ability to build AI solutions for a wide array of customers, and Appier saw the potential customers and investors they could bring in partnering with Sequoia." [2]

It was important that Appier chose their first investor not purely because of the capital or the brand, but because the investor understood their business enough to concretely help them — in this case, broker partnerships and deals that would have taken longer to do on their own. **This founder-investor fit we have mentioned in previous chapters also plays a role in enabling that ideal, fund-returning exit scenario to happen.**

Carro CEO Aaron Tan emphasizes this relationship between finding the right investors and startup success on the *On Call with Insignia Ventures* podcast in 2021.

> "It's super important to have the right investors who believe in your vision and your dream and in building the business. Because it's not something that you can do overnight. You need years. And congratulations, you [Yinglan] have an IPO coming up soon [referring to Appier's IPO], but that was also many years in the making. For us, we need to look for like-minded people. Otherwise, life is too short for you to deal with investors who don't understand what you're trying to do and then keep giving you problems and pressure, which is unnecessary...I would say really it's [important to choose] the right investor." [3]

How do VCs Approach Driving Exits for Their Portfolio?

The three realities discussed in the previous section — (1) exits are not the end, (2) exits are ideally designed around the company's existing circumstances, and (3) exits take time — frame the venture capitalist's approach to driving exits for their portfolio, which we list in four points.

358 Backing the Bold

VCs continue to fight for both the interest of their fund and the company in an exit

First, VCs continue to fight for both the interest of their fund and the company in an exit, as they would in any financing round. It is in the best interest of the fund to ensure that even if their investments have divested in a company, the company will continue to endure. It works against the brand and reputation of the VC firm if the companies they back get into exits and go public, but the acquiring or merged entity shuts down or the public market performance of the company is dismal.

Sometimes the VC will opt not to divest their entire investment, perhaps only what needs to be returned to LPs, and continue to keep some shares in a company even as it goes public or gets merged (as the merged entity could then go public as well).

VCs need to look at exits from a fund perspective

Second, VCs need to look at exits from a fund perspective. As we covered in the previous chapter, the venture capitalist's primary motivation to manage their portfolio is for portfolio companies to reach a certain valuation that would be acceptable for the investor to walk away with the corresponding returns. But as much as the investor works to bridge the gap between expectation and reality, market forces and statistics cannot simply be won over, and investors will need to continuously adjust exit scenarios of their portfolio companies over time.

Even if one hopeful exit does not pan out as expected, the war is never fully decided until the fund's life is over. So, as mentioned in the previous chapters, in the same way that VCs should look at portfolio management through the lens of their entire portfolio, VCs should also think about exits from a fund perspective.

In a typical venture capital fund life, the first half is usually allocated for making investments. The capital required to make these investments are not in the bank of the VC firm. Instead, this capital is called from the LPs when it is needed to protect against inflation.

In the second half of a fund's life, typically no further capital calls are allowed and the fund is expected to make returns through the form of exits (or liquidity events).

Given this dynamic between the general partners (VC firm) and limited partners, VCs need to be strategic regarding the companies they focus on in order to exit earlier in the life of the fund. Depending on the performance of the companies and the likelihood of them reaching unicorn or decacorn status halfway through the fund life, VCs may consider divesting and finding pathways to exit that ensure positive returns, even if it doesn't return the fund. Finding this pathway depends on a number of factors:

1. The valuation it should achieve to generate DPI (distributions to paid-in capital) or positive returns on investment.
2. The time it will take to reach this valuation, which then depends on the market itself and the business model. The VC will often refer to comparables and suggest pivots or additions to the business model that would help the company shorten the time it takes to reach the target valuation.
3. The available and accessible exit avenues in the market, given the valuation, vertical, and business model of the company. Which private equity firms would be willing to do a buyout? Is there a regional exchange that would be beneficial for the company to go public on? Are there strategic acquirers willing to take on this company at this price?

In developed markets like the US, companies are usually able to find a viable and positive return exit within five years of founding, and that includes going IPO, with local bourses a lot more accessible. In Southeast Asia, M&As have typically been the way to go for the better part of the 2010s, though in the 2020s, with the massive increase in interest in the region, SPACs and IPO opportunities have opened more, and not just on Wall Street. Local bourses like IDX have also been adapting to make their exchange more friendly to tech startup IPOs. In August 2021, Bukalapak became the first

Indonesian unicorn to list on IDX under the ticker symbol BUKA. Indonesia's Financial Services Authority (OJK) have since also been in the midst of discussion regarding new regulations to make it easier for unicorns and decacorns to list on IDX. In April 2022, GoTo Group also went public on the IDX through an IPO that had been long anticipated by the market.

In Exhibit 1 we see that over the 2010s decade leading up to 2021, pre-exit funding of the top VC-backed exits has largely remained below US$2.5 billion. This points towards the reality that from an investor perspective, exit events are ideally optimized for efficiency or to use the commonly passed around investor adage, "buy low and sell high." Exits also take into consideration not just the potential gains, but also the cost it takes to get there (i.e. capital

45 TOP VC-BACKED EXITS

Based on ratio of exit valuation to total pre-exit funding.

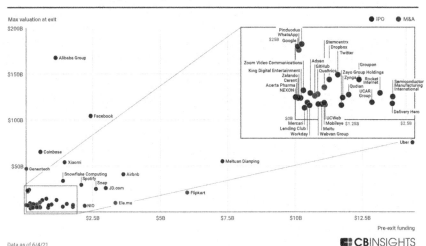

Data as of 6/4/21

CBINSIGHTS

Exhibit 1: 45 top VC-backed exits according to the ratio of exit valuation to total pre-exit funding, as collated by CBInsights. Worth noting here that most of these exits are IPOs (granted they are in mature markets like the US or China), and most of them land in the box within the US$2.5 billion total funding to US$50 billion exit valuation. Those outside of this box are an even 5:5 split between US companies and Chinese companies. It would be also interesting to compare in a graph how long it took to exit and how much the first VC/institutional check was in the company. [4]

injection plus time to get attract follow-on investment and other buyers).

This cost optimization is not necessarily disadvantageous for the VC-backed company; it can also be beneficial, especially when the company is able to grow sustainably beyond the VC funding and the buyers are willing to pay for that premium. Investors will also want to support their portfolio companies in creating that "premium" for exit buyers to cash in on to create sizable gains that exceed the cost of the invetment.

Finding the best exit is all about moving fast and slow

Third, finding the best exit is all about moving fast and slow. In the startup and VC world, speed is rewarded, but this often refers to critical decision-making at key moments in a company's growth, like pivots, finding product-market fit, or closing financing rounds.

VCs and founders are consistently working to move from one milestone to the next and they are also playing the long, slow game of building a company that, as much as possible, stands the test of time. This mindset goes beyond achieving exits; the best exits (i.e., fund-returners) concretely validate (1) valuation growth, (2) progressive and consistent portfolio management, and (3) strong foundation to be an enduring company.

In other words, the road to an ideal exit is all about moving fast (from one stage of growth to the next) but also moving slow (playing the long game). This mindset is tied to the reality that startups fail fast, but succeed slow. The majority of portfolio companies that would be marked as failures, especially for an early-stage investor, happen early in the life of the fund, but the exits (and the best ones as we've mentioned) take time to materialize.

Finding the best exits for portfolio companies is still ultimately an exercise in creativity

Fourth and also the featured rule in this chapter, finding the best exits for portfolio companies is still ultimately an exercise in creativity, even with increasing investor activity in the region and complementary regulatory adjustments to make exits more accessible. **Creativity is important because there is no set formula to generate home-run investments in venture capital.**

Amidst all the processes that come with each of the exit paths for startups, much of the work of the VC goes into the intangible things: building the necessary relationships and selling the company well enough with the right people. VCs also have to make periodic judgment calls on which companies to focus on and which companies to divest or sell, and the right decisions are not set in templates or books like this one. Indeed, there is much to learn from past exits, as we've detailed a number of them already in this chapter, but everything in VC boils down to a case-to-case basis.

So apart from just presenting examples of exits, mostly in Southeast Asia, as well as some abroad, we will also run through the thought process of investors when iterating and pinning down exit scenarios for their portfolio companies and funds. But before that, it is important to understand the various exit options available to startups in Southeast Asia. Do note that we do not cover liquidation in these scenarios.

How can Startups Exit?

Secondary sales

A less documented exit than M&As and IPOs, but still an important form of divestment, is through selling shares. This form of exit is often viewed as an unfavorable one for VCs because the decision to get shares in portfolio companies bought out too early in the life of the fund goes against the goals of the VC business model to always maximize returns on an investment. That means holding on to positions for as long as the company continues to grow.

But as the fund approaches the end of the commitment period (or allocated time that limited partners agree to continue providing capital), VCs will already begin assessing whether their portfolio companies can actually grow significantly further, become unicorns or even fund returners. For positions that are not moving as much, VCs may decide to just divest or set a realistic plan to grow the company up to a target valuation and then divest from there.

Divestments will typically take the form of secondary sales if the company has not reached the point where it is attractive enough for potential acquirers, or the potential acquisitions are also not attractive enough from the founders' and investors' perspective. VCs will sell their shares according to the terms set in the term sheet when these shares were initially purchased.

This generally happens in a subsequent financing round with a new investor coming in to mop up these shares and top up the valuation of the company with additional funding. These shares are often sold to either a private equity firm or a late-stage investor — some examples of these types of investors looking to buy out shares from earlier investors are KKR, Warburg Pincus, Tiger Global or even Softbank.

This happens also from the buy-side perspective for VCs when they come in as lead investors in a Series A round, for example, and essentially buy out the angels that invested in the company back when it was just an idea and a founding team.

The main issue with this form of exit is that it is ultimately a judgment call for a VC and does not impact the company as much, especially if the VC is not a majority outside shareholder (and in this case, the VC is less incentivized to sell their position). It is possible the venture capitalist is selling their shares because of market factors, but then the market's tailwinds post-exit could change, the fortunes of the company turn around, and the VC regrets taking out the investment too early.

It also does not reflect well on an investor if they make a habit out of exiting their investment too early through sales. It's almost like consistently folding in poker and not sticking it out for any round. After all, VC's build their brand on being able to commit and stick through the thick and thin with founders.

On the other hand, if the company itself is not performing well enough and if the VC does not have big enough ownership to justify continuing to try and turn things around, the performance and low ownership could make a case for a sale. Another scenario to make a secondary sale viable is if the entry of a more dominant investor would be beneficial to the company long-term for purposes beyond capital (i.e., better facilitators for the company to exit).

M&A

M&As take up much of Southeast Asia's landscape, and for good reason. In an article by Tech in Asia covering 2006 to 2020, a total of 326 tech startup M&A transactions took place in the region, versus only one to three IPOs from tech companies in the region.

Interestingly, while some of the biggest M&A transactions in the region were facilitated by Chinese (Alibaba acquiring Lazada and JOYY Inc. acquiring BIGO) and American (Intuit acquiring TradeGecko and 8×8 acquiring Wavecell), much of the region's M&A activity revolves around more local acquisitions made by emerging national tech champions, tech incumbents, or even more traditional companies on startups that either aligned with their market expansion plans or beef up their tech capabilities. Exhibit 2 below illustrates the top ten startup acquirers in the region in 2020, and majority of them are fellow VC-backed tech companies as well.

The fact that most tech M&A activity is local reflects in the median disclosed deal value in the region as of 2020 to be around US$6 million. It also comes as no surprise that Gojek is the top acquirer in the region as of 2020, having used M&As as a strategy to expand across business lines in Indonesia and enter other markets as well (which stands in contrast to Grab, which, for the most part, has entered new markets through direct expansion).

From an ecosystem perspective, M&As have dominated Southeast Asia for a number of reasons. First, the reality that Southeast Asia is still emerging has made tech companies in the region a target for companies in more mature markets that have been looking to Southeast Asia to expand, case in point being Alibaba. Though in this regard, many big tech companies from mature markets have largely exercised restraint and have only confined themselves to making significant private investments.

SEA Top Startup Acquirers

Acquirer 🛒	Company 🏢
gojek	mᵁcommerce **LOKÉT** Kartuku mapan midtrans promogo coins.ph **moka**
fave	GROUPON DISDUS.com cutQ FoodTime
yello mobile	pricearea ADPLUS gushcloud COMPUTERLOGY
xurpas	STORM Seer yondu art of click
carousell	WATCH OVER ME C⊕ duriana 7⊙l
REVASIA	SirapLimau MyResipi Resepi.com iMEDIA
migme	LoveByte SOLD.sg hipwee SHOPDECA
iProperty Group Asia's No.1 Online Property Group	thinkproperty.my rumah123.com thinkofliving.com
ifashion group	INVADE DRESSABELLE nose MEGAFASH
foodpanda	City Delivery Food Runner ROOM SERVICE

Exhibit 2: Top acquirers in Southeast Asia by 2020. Companies per acquirer are arranged in chronological order. Data taken from Tech in Asia. [5]

Second, Southeast Asia's diversity and multiple markets provide sufficient motivation for companies in one country to acquire similar companies in another market to become more cost-efficient in expansion. An example here is Carro acquiring MyTukar as it expanded into Malaysia.

Third, from a venture capital perspective, there have not been that many other exit options in the region unless the company reaches a certain size that could have only been achieved by either becoming a Southeast Asia dominating unicorn or Indonesia-dominating unicorn, so unless these two scenarios are possible within the fund's lifetime, selling to acquirers is likely the top option for an exit strategy. This is also complicated by the lengthier exit timelines (i.e., longer it takes for a company to reach a valuable enough exit valuation), as well as the historical lack of infrastructure and liquidity to support local IPOs, though the latter has been changing as well with the likes of IDX adjusting to host its local tech unicorns.

Why do M&As happen?

There are various motivations for M&As, and we can broadly categorize them into three: (1) growth, (2) competition, and (3) synergy.

1. **Growth**

   When it comes to discussions around corporate strategy for innovating products or expanding market share, there are usually three options that come up: "build, buy, or partner." M&A falls into the second option and is exercised when build is not practical and the corporate decides there is enough money in the bank to buy and exercise more control over the acquisition rather than just partnering.

   Then there are different types of growth motivations for M&As. It could be a **strategic acquisition**, which either involves **market expansion** or **capabilities expansion**. Market expansion M&A transactions include the likes of Alibaba-Lazada, Gojek-Coins, or the Carro-MyTukar acquisitions we've previously mentioned in this chapter. These market expansion acquisitions could also be indirect. For example, in 2021, PropertyGuru traded 18% of its business to its competitor in Australia, REA Group, to acquire the latter's business units in Thailand and Malaysia.

Strategic acquisitions could also be capabilities driven, and these usually happen within a market as the acquirer seeks to achieve or solidify market leadership. Shipper in Indonesia acquired warehousing solutions company Pakde and local delivery startup Porter to expand their capabilities in these areas further across the country. Teladoc in the US acquired Livongo to bring in the full capabilities of the former's healthcare provider network and the latter's lifetime chronic disease management program to meet a long-term shift towards more personalized care and treatment in the market.

A more popular example here is the Amazon acquisition of Whole Foods, which brought Amazon's ecommerce business into fresh produce as well. Capabilities could also cover acquisitions for licenses, as in the case of Sea Group acquiring Bank BKE in Indonesia to expand their financial services capabilities in the country or Indonesian retail investment platform Ajaib in acquiring stock brokerage Primasia Sekuritas to launch their app-based stock brokerage service.

Then there are tech deals, where companies acquire the company specifically for patented technology or proprietary software. This happens often with FAMGA (Facebook (now Meta), Microsoft, Google, and Amazon), where they tend to acquire companies that have some core software or technology that could boost one or more of the tech giant's business lines. If the company's value proposition is not centered around proprietary technology, these big tech companies are more likely to invest, then see if it's worth acquiring rather than acquiring straight away.

The third type of acquisition is called an **acqui-hire,** which often has similar motivations to tech deals, but has the added element of hiring the team into the acquiring company along with their technology. It seems the most predatory amongst the three because the acquired company is fully integrated into the acquiring company, whereas in strategic acquisitions and tech deals the acquiring company could spend a few years keeping the acquisition separate, either because the acquired company is already performing well on its own or the acquiring company is figuring out integration. Acqui-hires also happen more often in younger companies and is not necessarily a negative affair as long as the founders that are getting acquired are aware of what the acqui-hire entails.

2. Competition

If you can't beat them, buy them. Players within a market seeking to take out competition will often opt to buy them out if possible instead of burning through the bank to outprice them or fight for market share. Uber was on the receiving end of this twice as it expanded in Asia. First in 2016 when Didi acquired Uber's China business as the latter was facing estimated losses of US$2 billion in a competition to gain market share.

The second was only two years later in 2018 when Grab acquired Uber's Southeast Asia business in exchange for a 27.5% stake in Grab at the time. Interestingly, this stake in Grab enabled Uber to also benefit from the Southeast Asia ride-hailing business's SPAC merger. These transactions are often coined in the media as mergers but the transaction usually involves the homecourt or "winning" company acquiring the "losing" company's business in the market in exchange for cash or a stake in the winning company.

Here we use the word "winning" to connote the company that stays in the market and "losing" for the company that leaves. Once again, worth noting that even the "losing" company does not necessarily lose entering into these kinds of M&A transactions; it is likely more economical and beneficial financially down the line.

3. Synergy

If it's not to expand or to box out the competition, companies will merge with or acquire others to maximize the synergies that could come out of being able to work under one roof (a combined entity). Synergies could mean horizontal integration where offerings from both companies could strengthen the overall experience of customers from either company.

With conventionally low-margin verticals like payment or ecommerce, this could result in potentially increasing margins through cross-selling and up-selling products and services. Synergies could also mean reducing overhead costs and the opportunity cost of having to build up and even compete with the advantage of the other company.

Whether it augments value propositions or reduces the costs of strengthening value propositions, these synergies will vary from company to company, and the discussions around what gains could be made from an M&A transaction heavily influence the purchase price, apart from the size of the companies themselves. Failed M&A deals in this category would typically come from overpricing transactions against the actual synergies that either party would gain.

Compared to the growth-type M&A transactions, those motivated by synergy typically involve mergers rather than acquisitions and the creation of combined entities housing the two companies involved.

These mergers would also vary on how integrated the two companies will be, if it involves integrating entire teams, cost structures, and revenue streams or if it is more of a strategic or positioning type of relationship, where the combined entity and newly defined relationship between the two companies still draws the line between the two but makes it easier to work together across all facets of both businesses.

The most significant synergy-type M&A in Southeast Asia is that of Gojek and Tokopedia (GoTo Group), which had long been speculated by ecosystem observers but only came to fruition in 2021, following the fallout in the talks for another merger, that between Gojek and Grab. Its significance came with its timing, with both companies having already raised massive amounts of private capital over the past three years but still facing heavy competition from Sea Group and Grab within Indonesia.

The fact that both Gojek and Tokopedia are also not within the same vertical but still complement each other (Gojek being more in the services (lifestyle and payments) and last-mile logistics area while Tokopedia is in ecommerce and SME enablement) has also made the merger even more compelling.

The merger also puts GoTo in a better position to list on the public markets with a much larger valuation than both companies' individual valuations combined (north of US$18 billion, as pointed out by GoTo Group CEO Andre Soelistyo in a CNBC interview).[11] This higher valuation entry to the public markets gives both Gojek and Tokopedia the liquidity to strengthen their moats against competitors and better solidify their stronghold in Indonesia.

Synergy-type M&As also happen often with companies that have not reached unicorn status. In the case of Payfazz and Xfers, Indonesian fintech platform Payfazz made a minority investment into Singapore fintech API company Xfers and together they formed a combined entity Fazz Financial Group.

Payfazz had already found Xfers' API to be valuable in facilitating their payments services, and through Fazz Financial Group, would be able to host a single API infrastructure in their ecosystem of financial services, instead of having to build this infrastructure entirely on their own. Xfers being in Singapore also gives Payfazz visibility beyond Indonesia that would have been more costly to acquire on their own.

As for Xfers, co-founder and CEO Tianwei Liu mentions in a TechCrunch article that Xfers' shared goals with Payfazz for financial inclusion was a primary reason for them to join forces. Tianwei adds, "This is also coupled with the fact that last year, the COVID-19 pandemic has driven a significant increase in demand for digital payments and financial services across Indonesian rural areas, creating a huge growth opportunity for us." [6] Fazz Financial Group has since been making minority investments in other fintech startups across the region including Credibook and Modal Rakyat.

So as the examples above demonstrate, these mergers go beyond business and product-level synergies. The combined entity could help strengthen the position of both companies against competition, set them up for a more valuable exit in the public markets, and enable further investments or acquisitions in relevant spaces.

Considerations in the market for acquiring or merging

Regardless of the motivation, be it growth, competition, or synergy, there are some considerations to make when looking at potential acquisitions or mergers. This is especially useful for venture capitalists advising their portfolio companies on acquiring or merging with another company. There are two levels of consideration: the market and the target company.

For the market there are four general points to look at:

1. Size and potential growth of the market
2. Regulatory barriers to entry
3. Competitive landscape
4. Supplier and buyer dynamics

This could be the market the company is already in or the market the company plans to expand into. For the target company, we can classify considerations according to motivation, as illustrated in Exhibit 3:

Regardless of the motivation, the M&A process typically happens along the same lines as a typical fundraising round, except the due diligence is more comprehensive, involving multiple initial calls and meetings, interviews of the entire team and more, and the investor in this case is not only acquiring shares but buying enough shares to have majority ownership in the company. From the VC perspective, these acquisitions can also happen through trade sales, where the VC sells shares to a strategic acquirer, or private equity buyout, where the VC sells shares to a private equity firm. Exhibit 4

Does the target company have...	Growth	Competition	Synergy
Financials	Financially stable or profitable with growing revenues?	Mounting losses and would benefit from getting acquired?	Financially stable or profitable with growing revenus?
Market share / Customer base	Large or growing market share/customer base?	A lot of expenditure going into growing market share/customer base but not much progress? (i.e. stalemate in competition)	Potential for a combined entity's market share/customer base to create a significant lead against competition?
Team	Are they a capable and experienced team?		
Assets	Advantage (e.g. patents, licenses) in the target market/vertical that will make it easier to capture or establish leadership in the market/vertical?	Advantage that they would leave behind after exiting the market?	Cross-selling or up-selling opportunities through repackaging of value propositions?

Exhibit 3: Some considerations for target companies according to the type of acquisition/merger.

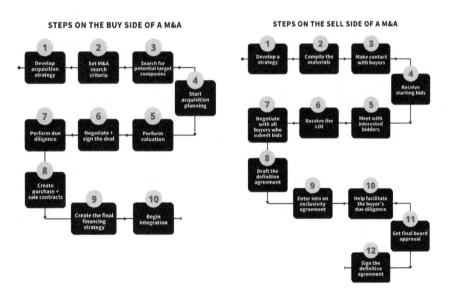

Exhibit 4: Step-by-Step Process for M&A from both the buy side and sell side perspectives. Important to note that these processes can take from months to years depending on the level of communication and intent between the two parties. These negotiations can also fall through if expectations are not met.

illustrates a typical M&A process from both the buyer's and seller's perspective.

The other side of the table: Getting acquired

We've been talking about M&A transactions largely from the point-of-view of the acquirer. However, **acquisitions are a two-way street, just like venture capital investing, and a lot of the problems that arise during and after the M&A process come from not acknowledging this reality.** How does this impact the way that companies being acquired should look at acquisitions?

1. **Don't underestimate investments as a foot-in-the-door.** Strategic acquirers will often test the waters with potential acquisitions through corporate development investments or their corporate venture capital fund if they have one, and while we did warn against giving away too much to strategic investors, it is still important to have them on the cap table to tee-up towards an acquisition when the time is right or when the company decides that is the best direction forward. Selling to strategic investors as potential acquirers may also be easier than having to build familiarity with the company from scratch.

2. **Is it the right time?** It's important to consider timing. Acquisitions may not be the best option when the company is just at the cusp of running a product that could create another S-curve for the company or open up monetization.

3. **Seal it while it's hot.** This basically means not to wait too long to close the acquisition or even find acquirers if that is already the plan for the company. It is better to get acquired while the company is in a good position financially.

4. **Focus on the long-term.** As we've mentioned earlier in the chapter, exits are not the end, and founders of a company getting acquired should think about their company's position post-acquisition, and what's the best way to build on growth as part of a larger entity, regardless of whether the founders will stay on as C-suite execs or leave to start another venture. Concretely this means being clear about the kind of relationship the acquired

company will have with the acquiring company, and what lines will be drawn.

5. **Keep it tight.** Tight communication between the two parties involved in the acquisition is important for strategic alignment.

6. **Manage transparency.** It's important to manage how information is communicated to the rest of the company about being acquired and what this means for everyone involved. It is prudent *not* to disclose information earlier on until the details are ironed out, and even then be specific with regards to the impact of the acquisition on the company.

7. **Culture eats acquisitions for breakfast, too.** Cultural integration is understated in a lot of acquisitions, mainly because it takes some time before the effects of cultural integration (or lack thereof) bubble to the surface. This issue of cultural incongruencies is especially prominent in cross-border acquisitions where the acquiring company is leveraging on the acquired company to learn more about a new market. The way to work around this is to ensure that the right leaders are in place — leaders who know both markets, and that there are clear alignments between the mission of the acquired company and the acquiring company.

When it comes to finding acquirers, we discuss more later in the chapter about frameworks to link this to valuation targets, the company's business model and north star metrics. But in Southeast Asia, the kind of acquirer VCs would want to introduce to their portfolio companies can be narrowed down according to the following considerations:

1. **What would acquirers want from the portfolio company?** You could then segment acquirers according to various value propositions for the acquisition (e.g., growth, competition, synergy). It's also important to consider the acquisition history of prospective buyers identified and see whether it is aligned with their shopping list.

2. **What is the neighborhood of the company?** Here we bring back the concept of the neighborhood, and the idea is to expand the list of potential acquirers from just comparables and competitors to even unconventional but still viable options like local conglomerates or MNCs — not necessarily tech companies but could still provide immense value to the acquired company through other aspects.

3. **What is the size and positioning of the portfolio company relative to the competition?** A regional market leader would be more attractive to cross-border acquisitions, say from the likes of Alibaba or Tencent.

4. **What is the valuation of the company?** This would determine how much it would cost to buyout the majority of the company's ownership, and various acquirers have their own ticket sizes.

5. **What is the cap table of the company?** For more stacked cap tables, there needs to be some level of alignment through board meetings on the viability of an acquisition to be made.

Public markets

The public markets are often considered by venture capitalists as the best buyers of portfolio companies, thanks to the volume of capital especially in Wall Street exchanges and growth potential the company can achieve from the get-go, all while enabling the founders and leadership team to still retain control over the direction of the company.

However, going to the public markets has historically been quite the challenge in Southeast Asia, with the high ceiling for startups to go on global bourses like the New York Stock Exchange, NASDAQ, or the Hong Kong Stock Exchange, the lack of infrastructure and liquidity in the region to support tech startup IPOs, and simply the maturity of the ecosystem in terms of producing companies that could thrive in the public markets. But at the turn of the 2020 decade, there are three key shifts that have pushed the public market accessibility and capabilities of the region forward:

Sea group's 2020 wall street performance

Over 2020 the internet company reached nearly US$100 billion in market cap, zipping past Tesla to become the world's best performing stock that year. This had two implications: (1) greater interest in originating companies from Southeast Asia to list on Wall Street exchanges and (2) greater interest among special purpose acquisition companies or SPACs, which were also coincidentally taking center stage among US tech companies, to find targets in Southeast Asia.

An important lesson from Sea Group's life in the public markets was choosing where to list, especially in terms of geography and exchange. Some of the parameters to consider when finding the right bourse (exchange) include the following:

1. **Liquidity:** What's the trading volume available in the exchange? Will this will be the source of fuel for the company in the public markets?
2. **Regulation:** What kind of regulation will the company be subject to once on the public markets? Does it allow for the kind of business model the company has or are there misalignments?
3. **Strategic Alignment:** Is the exchange located in a geography that is critical for the company's stakeholders — investors, customers, business partners, HQ? Do investors in the exchange know the company well enough to be able to confidently invest?
4. **Equity Story (Pitch to Raise Money):** This ties in with strategic alignment as well. Will the equity story of the company be relevant enough to investors in the exchange?

Sea Group capitalized on their "monopoly" of the Southeast Asia equity story on Wall Street, as we write on *Insignia Business Review* in 2021.

"One of the interesting aspects of Sea's decision to list was its choice of Wall Street over SGX, Hong Kong, or China, somewhere geographically closer to home. And this choice is rooted back in the idea that IPOs should be aligned with what the company wants to achieve from raising capital, and what expectations it can meet by doing so.

When going public, it's all about maximizing exposure to match the scope of the company's ambitions and their capability to capture this scope. Even if Sea's headquarters are in Asia, given their positioning and even market reach as a global company, especially in gaming, it made sense to list on NYSE.

It's also important to note that while NYSE offered a greater volume of fuel for Sea, it came with greater pressure to meet investor demands. And managing these expectations is critical for any company fresh to the public markets.

It's always better to set the bar slightly lower and over perform for the first few quarters to gain the trust of public market investors, than overselling and underperforming. And from an ecosystem perspective, Sea's monopoly of Wall Street when it came to Southeast Asia tech companies also made it a channel for public investors to invest in the region as well." [7]

Once an exchange has been chosen, the path to IPO is no small task. It involves up to a year's worth of S-1 (IPO prospectus or declarations of the company to potential investors) preparation, roadshows to attract initial investors, financial audits, SEC reviews, and investor meetings all before d-day, which is when shares of the company begin to trade. The general path to an IPO, regardless of the exchange, features six steps:

1. **Bakeoff:** The company makes a selection of investment banks. These banks (or underwriters) serve as facilitators of the IPO process, drawing from their past experience of helping hundreds, if not thousands, of companies go public. This selection process is like an audition of banks for the company to decide which one/s they will work with — the lead bank or "Lead Left Underwriter" and other banks or joint book-running managers and co-managers. These banks help with the formal process of selling the IPO shares and publishing quarterly reports to entice prospective investors.

2. **IPO Prep (6 months):** This involves drafting the S-1 document
   or IPO prospectus of the company, which includes all the information about the company a prospective investor would need to
   know to make an informed investment decision — from the
   business overview, detailed historical financials, risks (the most
   interesting part of the S-1!), market sizing, cap table information, past financing, investment banks working with the company,
   and much more.

   The S-1 has to undergo intense legal scrutiny and several
   iterations to ensure nothing is amiss. This is then filed to the
   SEC for review and further iterations before this document is
   made public. Apart from the S-1 itself, the company will also
   have to prepare another set of relevant company information to
   be compiled into a pitch for large, institutional investors for
   their roadshow.

3. **First Public S-1 Filing:** Once the company goes public with its S-1
   filing, timelines formally come into play, meaning the company
   intends to go public in the next three weeks at most. For steps 1
   and 2 there are no hard deadlines. This is important to consider
   especially in times of market volatility. This first public filing
   involves going over final edits with the SEC and filling in details
   to complete their S-1, with these edits filed as S-1 "Amendments".
   One of the most important edits is including a specific price
   range or range of how much money the company aims to raise
   through the IPO.

4. **Second Public S-1 Filing (Roadshow + Initial Price Range):** With
   a proposed price range in their S-1 Amendments, the company
   is now ready to meet and pitch with prospective investors, primarily large institutional investors like hedge funds and mutual
   funds, who typically buy up to 15% of total shares offered in the
   IPO. After these pitches, the investors decide if they will place an
   order in the IPO. It is worth noting that these orders are not
   limited to investors that were met through these pitches.

   Each order specifies the maximum number of shares the firm
   would like to purchase and a limit price (or no limit, if the investors decide). From these pitches it is not uncommon that there

are more orders than shares offered, otherwise known as being "oversubscribed". In these scenarios, given the magnitude of the oversubscription, the company may decide to raise the price range, taking into account advice from investment banks.

5. **Setting IPO Price and Allocations:** Typically eleven days after the roadshow, the company, investment bankers, and board members will gather to decide on the final starting price of the IPO, and allocations to investors. While this process is heavily nuanced, the key to this process is to form a strong investor base, which means combining both long-term and more short-term holders.

6. **Shares trade:** This is IPO day! And worth noting on this day is the expectation of an IPO pop or a sudden boost in price on the first day of trading. This is usually engineered to demonstrate strong new investor interest in the stock.

Exhibit 5 details the typical IPO timeline for a company as we discussed above, alongside an example from Spotify's experience of going to the public markets. Spotify's journey is worth noting because they used a direct listing method, where instead of the company selling part of itself by issuing new stocks (hence, initial public *offering*), the company sells existing stocks owned by the employees and the directors.

Even with this difference, the timeline and steps are still largely the same, with much of the difference having to deal with the economics (for example, different allocation since there is a limit to what the employees and directors own). You can head to the end of this section for a more detailed comparison of IPOs and direct listings.

The SPAC rush in Southeast Asia

Apart from the greater interest in companies from Southeast Asia to list on Wall Street and more global exchanges, another shift at the turn of the decade has been the emergence of SPACs targeting Southeast Asia startups. Special purpose acquisition companies,

ILLUSTRATIVE IPO TIMELINE

SPOTIFY'S PATH TO DIRECT LISTING

Exhibit 5:   A typical IPO timeline and below, Spotify's path to the public markets. While Spotify did this through a direct listing, the steps are still largely the same as going through IPO, with the differences lying more in the economics (allocation of the shares). Taken from Clouded Judgment Substack. [8]

or SPACs have been around for a while, and have traditionally been seen unfavorably due to the underlying mechanism of using blank check companies (which had gained a level of notoriety around the time SPACs were introduced), and the idea of investors potentially being exposed to the risk of fraudulent targets.

That said, SPACs, being a more cost-effective and faster way to get to the public markets, have attracted more and more startups amidst a rise in tech IPOs in the years leading up to 2020. Combined with the increased investor interest in Southeast Asia, more SPACs have been created targeting the region, like Hong Kong tycoon Li Ka Shing's Bridgetown SPAC. On the other side of the table, Grab announced its merger with the Altimeter SPAC in April 2021, and other Southeast Asian unicorns are looking to SPACs as well. Just 8 months after the announcement, the merged entity made its debut in Nasdaq in December 2021, making it the biggest U.S. listing by a Southeast Asian firm.

A SPAC is a blank check company formed for the sole purpose of raising investment capital through an IPO. The IPO then allows investors to invest money towards this company to be used to acquire one or more businesses, at this point unspecified. For putting in capital in the IPO, each investor gets to own a unit (think of it as a package) of shares of common stock in the SPAC and warrants to purchase more stock at a later date. Each unit of securities is almost always US$10. These warrants are an additional incentive to hold on to their position in the SPAC as the SPAC looks for acquisitions and presumably, the value of the SPAC will increase as it acquires companies). After the IPO, this package becomes separable and tradable in the public market. Exhibit 6 below illustrates the dynamic between investors, the SPAC, and the target company.

Meanwhile, the money raised from the IPO is held in a trust and these businesses or targets are required to be identified and found within a time period otherwise the SPAC is required to return the funds raised to investors. If the money in this trust account raised from the IPO is not enough to close an M&A transaction with the target company, the SPAC sponsors or founders have the option to

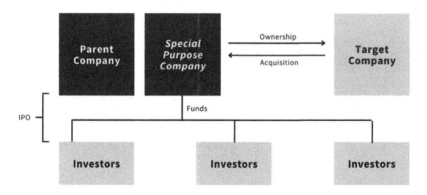

Exhibit 6: The SPAC "ecosystem". Taken from Seeking Alpha. [9]

seek a PIPE (public investment for private equity) deal to raise additional capital. That means they offer private equity investors shares in the SPAC in exchange for additional capital. For example, in Grab's SPAC announcement, Altimeter, the SPAC sponsor, had to raise US$4 billion from PIPE led by US$750 million from the SPAC's funds.

The structure is eerily similar to venture capital in the sense that investors put money into a fund that then looks for other companies to invest into with two key differences: the SPAC is public and the investments are not just investments but M&A transactions. The process by which the SPAC undergoes an M&A transaction with a target company is called the De-SPAC process, named such because it already involves a company publicly trading shares.

The De-SPAC features four stages, also illustrated in Exhibit 7 below:

1. **Bakeoff and SPAC outreach:** Similar to the IPO, where the company looks for investment banks to help facilitate the process. Additionally in this part of the process the company, with the assistance of the investment banks, identifies and sends a letter of intent to a SPAC to merge with.
2. **Due Diligence and PIPE building (Post-Letter of Intent):** Once the company signs a letter of intent with their chosen SPAC, the

ILLUSTRATIVE DE-SPAC TIMELINE

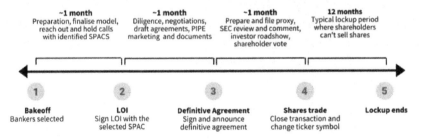

Exhibit 7:   De-SPAC Timeline. Taken from Seeking Alpha. [9]

due diligence process starts (similar to a financing round). At the same time, agreements are drafted, PIPE marketing materials are developed, and pitches are made to potential PIPE investors.

3. **SEC review and shareholder approval (Post-Definitive Agreement):** This involves SEC review and approval of the De-SPAC process. This approval is done through a shareholder vote — because SPAC shares are publicly traded — and the transaction has to get an affirmative vote from 37.5% of public shares (those that are being traded), and 20% sponsor shares (majority of SPAC founder shares).

   Upon approval, the SPAC and the company combines into a publicly traded operating company, with the SPAC funds (raised from the SPAC IPO) and PIPE cash (raised separately) on the combined entity's balance sheet.

4. **Shares trade.** The ticker of the stock gets changed following the M&A transaction and the closing of the business combination is announced.

While SPACs have positioned themselves as a faster and more economic pathway to get to public markets, this is not the only way exchanges have adapted to attract more startups. Exchanges like TSE have set up boards and listings specifically for tech companies and tech startups, with lower fees and profitability requirements to list. SPACs in themselves may not dominate the pathways to the public markets, its rise (or return) to the spotlight in 2020 and 2021 especially in Southeast Asia is tied to a greater, and more serious interest among startups to go public and led to more initiatives among local bourses to host venture-backed tech companies.

Southeast Asian exchanges opening up to attract tech companies

Local bourses in the region like Singapore Stock Exchange (SGX), Stock Exchange of Thailand (SET), and Indonesia Stock Exchange (IDX) have been making moves to attract more tech companies to go public, from opening up to SPACs as in the case of SGX and adjusting qualifications to open up to local tech unicorns as in the case of IDX. These moves by the exchanges could also potentially encourage more investors to participate in tech IPOs.

Another important part of this value chain are other third-parties like digital stock brokerages that help facilitate first-time investors into the public markets. While these efforts are likely not to dissuade Southeast Asia startups from switching from the likes of NYSE and NASDAQ to more local exchanges, especially once these startups have reached a certain valuation, there could be more double listings between more local and global exchanges.

These three shifts — investors from public markets focusing on Southeast Asia (which also pulls in more traditional and institutional investors), the SPAC rush expanding into the region, and Southeast Asia exchanges making adjustments to attract more local tech companies — are important to consider because **these shifts cover the three key elements that are essential for companies to go public: (1) investor interest and liquidity, (2) attractive pathways to go public for venture-backed tech companies, and (3) regulatory support through exchanges.**

Exhibit 8 summarizes the different pathways to the public markets discussed, according to considerations for both the company and its buyers (IPO and public market investors).

Navigating life in the public markets

Going public is one thing, but life in the public markets is another beast altogether. It is important for founders to prepare for this life even before shares trade, and that goes beyond the documentation and pricing. There are three principles to take note of when going public:

1. **The wheels should be fast but the machinery should be robust.** That means that the ideal public tech company should still be able to execute quickly *while* still having robust internal processes and frameworks to handle governance, risk management, financial reporting, and other key areas.

Parameters	IPO	SPAC	Direct Listing
For Startups			
Accessibility for Startups	Low	High	Very low
Capital	Can raise primary capital	Capital raised through SPAC	Cannot raise primary capital
Deal Structure	Rigid	Flexible	Rigid Avoid dilution for existing ivnestors
Lockup Period	Yes	Yes	No
Pricing	First day price pop missed opportunity to raise more capital	Agrees to single price from SPAC No market-driven price discovery--still opportunity for first day price pop	Market-driven price discovery
Speed	6-12 months	4-6 months Faster and simpler than IPO for target company (less financial and business disclosures and regulatory scrutiny)	12-18 months
Process	Established mechanism -- underwriters provide regulatory guidance, pricing advice, sale guarantee, post-issuance pricing support	More straightforward for target company, only dealing with one party	Limited experience/history No post-issuance support
Fees	Higher fees than direct listing	Higher fees than direct listing	Lower fees than IPO or SPAC
For (New) Investors			
Liquidity	Less trading volume, liquidity	More flexibility and liquidity than IPO for investors	More liquidity than IPO
Allocation	Allocation not strictly based on market demand	Allocation not strictly based on market demand	Democratic allocation based on demand
Execution Risk	-	Higher than IPO Uncertainty for investors in SPAC IPO regarding target company and price	Lower than IPO

Exhibit 8: Comparing pathways to the public markets, for startups and new investors.

A single reporting error can send stock plunging, as much as a tweet from Elon Musk can send Tesla stock up and down. These processes and frameworks should already be something the founder considers and sets in place as early as possible, even before they decide if and why they want to go public. At the same time, the company should still be able to innovate and improve its business as it did before life in the public markets. We write on *Insignia Business Review* about how Sea maximized its presence in the public markets.

"In the book *Navigating ASEANnovation,* we talk often about the importance of speed in the early stages of a startup's growth. And as the company grows and even graduates into the public markets, the speed advantage never really goes out of style, especially if it is part of the company's DNA, as it is for Sea. Sea's fast and exploratory growth has been part of its DNA since day one, and is one of the reasons it has achieved the kind of growth it has since. While some critics have voiced concerns over this speed, Sea's trajectory is not a new narrative for tech companies — this flywheel-ing has also been part of many of its peers' growth stories from China and the Valley. Of course, that doesn't mean that this expansion across markets and verticals doesn't come with its risks and challenges. At the same time, Sea saw the digitalization bus for emerging markets coming from a mile away just when it had gained massive capitalization from its gaming business, and decided it would not miss this ride."

2. **Steady hands guide the boat.** This refers to the importance of leadership and consistency, especially in the first few quarters of the company, because this time period is when expectations are set with these new public investors. The equity story should revolve less around short-term price fluctuations and valuation, and more around leadership and the ability of those at the top to get to where they say they are going to go in a consistent manner.

3. **It's still about building a good business, but there's a necessary mindset shift around complexity.** This applies not just to public market exits, but to any kind of exit, and that while startups may obsess with the idea of exits, the core of the matter is that the company should still be able to produce good margins and profitability at the end of the day. While the number of stakeholders may increase and the interactions with stakeholders more

complex than handling a Series A cap table, the demands essentially do not change, though it may require a mindset shift to manage interactions with public investors. It is important to note that having gone through the process of being reviewed by lawyers, investment banks, SEC, and most importantly, the public, means that there is already an attached branding to getting on the public markets that has its advantages in securing business partnerships or driving acquisitions but also comes with its own weight of meeting public investor expectations.

Exhibit 9 summarizes the exit pathways discussed, from secondary sales to M&A and public market offerings.

	Secondary Sales/ Early Divestment	M&A	Public Markets
Motivation	For investor only: to divest and focus more energy on potential unicorns and fund returners	• Head of Strategic Development • CEO • CFO	Solidify market leadership or build more defensibility through access to structurally cheaper liquidity
Mechanisms	Secondary sale in financing round	1. Mergers 2. Strategic acquisitions 3. Acqui-hire 4. Tech acquisitions 5. Trade sales 6. Leveraged buyouts	1. IPO 2. SPAC 3. Direct listing
Considerations / Prerequisites	1. Company performance vis-a-vis overall fund performance and resource allocation 2. Likelihood of becoming unicorn or fund-returner	For target companies: 1. Financials 2. Market share	1. Investor interest and liquidity 2. Attractive pathways to go public or venture-backed tech companies 3. Regulatory support through exchanges
Role of VC	Decision on whether to sell or not and how to reach target valuation to make selling profitable	Finding acquirers and helping company time acquisition	Setting up connections to facilitate process, participating as PIPE investor if SPAC

Exhibit 9:   Summary of Exit Pathways for Startups.

How do VCs Find the Best Exit Strategy?

With these various exit scenarios and strategies, venture capitalists still have to constantly narrow down and identify the best options for the portfolio companies and the fund as these companies grow. As we've reiterated across previous chapters and in earlier sections, the goal is to produce positive returns, or be able to divest an investment in such a way that would not just return the initial capital called from limited partners but also generate carry for the LPs and the firm.

The DPI holy grail

The way funds measure the success of a divestment is through **DPI** or **distributions to paid-in capital**. DPI is the amount of capital returned to investors divided by the fund's capital calls at the valuation date. When it comes to must funds, not just venture capital funds, DPIs increase in value as funds begin to exit their investments. Obviously, VCs want a fund DPI greater than 1. While DPI refers to exited capital, **RVPI** or **residual value to paid-in capital** refers to the fund value that has not yet been realized, computed by dividing the Net Asset Value (NAV) or fair value of the fund over the capital called at the time of valuation. When you add DPI and RVPI, you get the **TVPI** (**total value to paid-in capital**) or the total fair value of the fund over the capital called from limited partners at the valuation date. DPI and RVPI are both divided by the capital called from limited partners at the date of valuation to account for changes in the NAV of the fund and amount of capital called over time.

$$\text{DPI} = \frac{\text{Sum of proceeds to fund LPs}}{\text{LP capital called}}$$

$$\text{RVPI} \quad = \quad \frac{\text{NAV}}{\text{LP capital called}}$$

$$\text{TVPI} \quad = \quad \text{RVPI} + \text{DPI}$$

In a typical fund life, TVPI usually starts out less than one because of management fees, which account for upfront costs paid by limited partners to the firm to run the fund. In most of the early half of a fund's life, TVPI equals RVPI because the firm is busy investing into portfolio companies, and the ratio increases as the investment valuations presumably increase relative to the capital called to make the initial investments (i.e., the portfolio companies grow).

Note that while VCs could brag about their fund's TVPI (3×, 5×), it doesn't necessarily mean the fund is performing. This is because it is possible that the TVPI is still mostly RVPI, and the fund has not exited any investments, meaning the investments are not realized yet. For all we know, the company that contributed to this 3× or 5× TVPI at one point in time suddenly closes shop a year later and that negatively impacts the DPI (and consequently the TVPI at the end of the fund life). TVPI doesn't bring food to the table at the end of the day.

That said, VCs will try to maximize TVPI early in the fund's life, so that resulting DPIs are also high. Maximizing TVPI is all about increasing the valuations of portfolio companies. But as the fund matures, DPI takes precedence. As investments are exited, portions of the fund's value are realized and converted to DPI. DPI continues to rise and RVPI continues to drop as the fund continues to exit more investments, and by the end of a fund's life, TVPI equals DPI, and here DPI reflects the fund's money-on-money multiple (MoM) or investment returns.

The relationship between DPI, RVPI, and TVPI illustrates the dynamics of a fund as it spends most of the fund's early years making as many investments as possible, then before reaching the halfway mark the firm already begins making divestments. The early divestments are usually done with companies that are projected not to be market leaders, unicorns, or decacorns in the long run, and begin to show a slowdown in the growth.

Achieving high fund DPI is no easy task. In a report by Cambridge Associates in 2017, covering US VC funds set up from 1986 to 2015, the median fund returns 1.04 DPI, while the median TVPI is 1.77. [10] This gap between median DPI and TVPI, both of which are lower than what funds would typically advertise, shows that it is one thing to source and invest, another to grow their valuation (raising TVPI), and an entirely different beast to drive exits (turn RVPI into DPI).

The task is arguably more difficult in a region like Southeast Asia, where, for most of the ecosystem's development, the exit avenues have been fewer and exit timelines have taken longer, though this is also changing with increasing global interest in the region.

While certainly a challenge, achieving this DPI holy grail is an accumulation of maximizing the DPI or ROI of each investment into a portfolio company. This means ensuring the money the firm takes out of its ownership in the company at the time of exit is multiples greater than what the firm initially called from limited partners to put in. As illustrated in Exhibit 10, some funds may also get an extension in their fund life, creating more time for the GPs to generate returns and completely divest.

We list some frameworks VCs can use to think about how to concretely coordinate (1) the situation of the company and the market at the time of consideration (exits are based on reality, not expectations, as we have mentioned earlier in this chapter), (2) the corresponding potential exit scenarios, and (3) concrete steps both on the part of the investor and the company to achieve the ideal exit

TYPICAL LIFE OF A VENTURE FUND

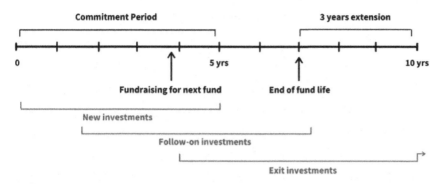

Exhibit 10: Typical VC fund life. In some funds, there could be an extension granted for the fund to completely divest, as agreed upon by the limited partners.

scenario and target valuation and account for other possibilities as well.

Framework 1: Learning from comparables

The idea behind this first framework is to leverage the knowledge of a comparable company in order to assess how the company can go from valuation A to valuation B. This framework involves going through the following key questions:

1. **What does the company have?** Consider their assets, their "X-factor" or competitive advantage, and what kind of business model they are currently operating.
2. **Where is the company going?** Note down their future plans, if pivots are involved or market expansion.
3. **Study an ideal comparable.** An SME payments or financial services company might look to Stripe, but there's also StoneCo in Brazil. For emerging markets like Southeast Asia, while it might be easy to look at developed markets, it is important to also consider comparables in similar developing markets or markets that have similar industry conditions to make a precise assessment of

where the portfolio company can go. In studying this comparable, one can ask:

   a. What is their current valuation? How did they grow to such a valuation?
   b. What revenue stream or value proposition contributed to their growth the most?
   c. Were there external market factors that influenced this growth trajectory?
   d. How did the company exit?

4. **Given the current valuation of the company and the firm's ownership in the company, set a target valuation with an industry multiple.** This requires some research and looking at the multiples at which comparables are trading.

5. **Consider the business strategy the company should take to reach the target valuation with the findings from the comparable study as reference.** Structure this strategy in a step-by-step process.

6. **When the company reaches the target valuation, list the potential exit options for the company in order of likelihood.**

   a. Which stock exchanges can they list on?
   b. Which companies would be willing to acquire them?

7. **If the company does not reach this target valuation, what are the other exit scenarios to consider?**

The principle behind this framework is to walk in the footsteps of the comparables — tapping into the wisdom of Rule #1 in Chapter 1. But even if a company does follow a comparable company's playbook to the T (and goes without saying, also adapting the strategy to the local environment), the market may not be as mature enough or big enough to enable the same kind of growth as the comparable.

The most important thing is that the target valuation still produces returns to the initial investment. So say the comparable is US$20 billion in the public markets and the portfolio company's target 10× valuation is only US$600 million — this is okay with the assumption that the firm entered at a US$60 million valuation with 10% ownership (assuming the portfolio company does reach US$600 million in valuation eventually).

Framework 2: Looking from the buyer's perspective

This second framework focuses on acquisitions, with the presumption that the portfolio company in question is set to be acquired. This framework studies the buyers' point-of-view in a specific vertical or industry in an effort to align with the interests of acquirers and find the right one for the portfolio company. This is similar to the same principle we introduced in Chapter 7 where VCs align with potential follow-on investors to pitch to the right companies.

The first step is not to assess the buyers but to establish the positioning of the company. What is their value proposition? This value proposition determines the types of buyers to look at. For example, an SME financial services company might be valuable to a retail conglomerate but not a real estate company for acquisition. Once the company's positioning is established, buyers can then be assessed through three questions:

1. **What are buyers buying?** This covers what specific assets or advantages are being acquired by the buyer. It could be the brand, the distribution, tech infrastructure, or users owned by the portfolio company. This is important to identify what are the selling points. It is also useful to reference similar acquisitions in the space that were made to acquire similar assets or advantages.
2. **Why are buyers buying?** This is an important question because it contextualizes #1. Knowing *what* buyers are buying, the motivation becomes clearer. Motivations could be internal for the buyer, like beefing up the business or expanding into the market, or it could be opportunistic and external, having looked at the industry and seeing impressive metrics relative to the industry standards.
3. **Who are our buyers?** Having considered the objectives and motivations of potential buyers through their lens, VCs can then narrow down the options to specific companies that need these

objectives or have these motivations. Buyers can be neatly classi-
fied into local and foreign buyers.

This framework is visualized in Exhibit 11.

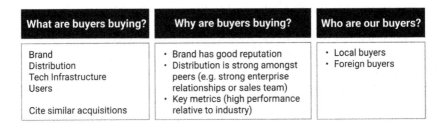

What are buyers buying?	Why are buyers buying?	Who are our buyers?
Brand Distribution Tech Infrastructure Users Cite similar acquisitions	• Brand has good reputation • Distribution is strong amongst peers (e.g. strong enterprise relationships or sales team) • Key metrics (high performance relative to industry)	• Local buyers • Foreign buyers

Exhibit 11:   Sample Buyers Framework.

Framework 3: Identifying prerequisites

The third framework is the most straightforward, and focuses
primarily on identifying the prerequisites for each potential exit
scenario a portfolio company can have at a certain point in time.
While it is similar to the first in that the idea is to come up with concrete strategies for the company and the VC, it differs in that it
doesn't necessarily consider a target valuation or a comparable, but
just directly asks — *what does this company need to exit in this way?*

As the definition suggests, exit scenarios are first listed down. It
can be arbitrary or listed according to possibility. A percentage
could be attached to each scenario as perceived by the investor to
align with the rest of the firm and even the company in terms of
expectations for each exit scenario.

Given these exit scenarios, potential targets are identified. For
going public, the list would include specific bourses or exchanges
where the company could list, as well as the method of listing. For
M&As, the list would have acquirers, buyers or companies to merge
with. For secondary or trade sales, the list would have PE firms or
other investors.

The final piece of this framework is of course the prerequisites.
The prerequisites could include a target valuation for each exit
scenario, but the most important point to make is to figure out what

steps the company needs to take to be in a good position to reach these exit scenarios. An important point to keep in mind regarding listing prerequisites is that they should be made not just with the portfolio companies' situation at the time of consideration, but also with the interests of the targets in mind, especially if acquiring companies are involved.

This framework is visualized in Exhibit 12.

Exit Scenarios	Targets	Prerequisites for Port Co
IPO SPAC	TSE, HKSE, SGX Bridgetown, Altimeter	Become category leader (B2B or B2C) with minimum annual revenue
Acquisition for capabilities	Tencent, Alibaba, Amazon, Go-To, Sea Group (horizontal tech giants) Local conglomerates	Traction in space that acquirers are looking at
Acquisition for market expansion	Comparables, competitors in other markets Companies up or down the value chain (suppliers/distributors) Industry incumbents	Strong distribution and specialities to be attractive to acquirers

Exhibit 12: Sample Prerequisites Framework.

Framework 4: Assessing forked roads

This framework is designed specifically for companies at a crossroads, and when their investors are considering exit scenarios depending on which direction they take. It's a prerequisite framework but in reverse, where the company's potential outcomes are taken into consideration first before the exit scenarios and targets.

The goal of this framework is to not only assess exit scenarios, but to also help a company decide on which direction to take, or convince them to go one way or another, especially if the case makes sense from an exit-perspective. There can be more than one outcome to consider depending on the business, but oftentimes the fork in the road involves two options the company needs to mull over.

While the example in Exhibit 13 only illustrates exit targets, the framework can also include potential DPI for each exit target, as well as specific companies to reach out to for each exit scenario.

Outcome #1	Exit Targets
Status quo/Agency approach	• PE buyout • Secondary buyout (later-stage investor) • Acquisition within the same industry
Outcome #2	Exit Targets
Technology platform	• Acquisition by traditional company looking to digitalise • IPO/direct-listing

Exhibit 13:   Sample Forked Road Framework.

Turning Exit strategy into execution: The DPI Hit List

The frameworks above are not mutually exclusive; they can be used in conjunction with one another, and can be developed with more specificity (including specific north star metrics) to better aid the venture capitalist in coordinating portfolio value-add with an exit strategy.

An important step after figuring out exit scenarios, targets, and steps to take is to actually build and maintain the relationships required to see through an exit strategy.

That means coming up with a "DPI Hit List," or a list of companies and relevant people to reach out to, according to the exit scenarios and targets that were identified through the frameworks in this chapter. The key point here in creating this hitlist is to identify specific people who can facilitate relationship building between the portfolio company and exit targets, effectively translating strategy into execution. And obviously, the VC would want to optimize for time spent in managing each portfolio company as well. A sample format for this list is illustrated in Exhibit 14.

This execution is not always about hard-selling the portfolio company or getting right into the M&A and IPO process. Oftentimes

Exit Option	Companies	People to Contact	Status
Conglomerate Buyout	• Conglomerate 1 • Conglomerate 2	• Head of Strategic Development • CEO • CFO	• Emailed • Had call
Comparable Acquisition	• Comp 1 • Comp 2	• Head of CVC • CEO	• Revisit • Emailed
IPO	• SPAC	• CEO	• Revisit • Emailed

Exhibit 14: DPI Hit List Template. More columns can be added to contain more information about the PICs for each exit target.

these relationships are built over months or even years, early on in the life of the company, so the decision-makers in these exit targets already become familiar with the portfolio company when the time comes to act. It is also worth noting that the DPI Hit List also intersects heavily with the fundraising value-add of VC firms. That means the strategic investors the firm can bring in an earlier round could potentially be acquirers down the line.

Finding exits in Southeast Asia is an exercise in creativity

While finding exits in Southeast Asia — and truly profitable ones at that — can be a tough nut to crack, what venture capitalists realize after doing this over time is that it is less a science and more of an art. It requires creativity to be able to find the nonobvious buyers or acquirers that might actually be interested in the capabilities or assets that a portfolio company has, or to be able to pitch the portfolio company in a way that exit targets would find attractive.

The reason VCs would want to find nonobvious exit strategies is two-fold. One is that there can be a lot of noise in a region that is rapidly changing and fast growing and finding the right fit that also reaps in the returns is not as clear as going to the most common destinations for exits.

Two is that there is also a certain level of competition amongst VCs in terms of generating DPI, and this could involve perhaps finding exits that are not as conventional but are still immensely valuable. One example is the increasing interest among second-and third-generation owners of traditional conglomerates and family businesses in technology and digitalization, which open up avenues for buyouts or acquisitions.

The creativity doesn't just play into finding paths to exit, but also forming the relationships that will facilitate these exit strategies into execution. Even if the motivation for finding exits is buried deep in the economics of the fund, how it is done on the ground involves a lot more softer skills than one might expect.

Three Best Practices

1. Avoid exiting your portfolio companies too early. Constantly monitor portfolio companies against benchmark targets to be able to assess when to make the call to divest to start looking for acquirers or secondary sale buyers.
2. Come up with an iterative DPI list of companies for each quarter or year to focus on, in terms of setting up the company towards a target valuation and helping them find exit targets.
3. Set up a DPI hit list of exit targets, and a contact list of decision makers to regularly reach out to and consult on what they are seeing in the market and potentially send them one-pagers on your portfolio companies at the right time.

Chapter 13

Rule #13: There are Rules to Being Good, but No Rules to Being Great

If you've ever played chess, you would be familiar with how easy it is to learn how the pieces move but how hard it is to get good at it. In the past few decades since the Garry Kasparov vs Deep Blue matches, artificial intelligence began to solve for a lot of the best possible moves especially in the opening of the game, and with it came a lot more "rules" or "by the book" ways to play.

This meant a lot more professional players became good at the game by being "good at the book." While it certainly is not the only thing that makes a chess player good at the game, it has certainly helped and even sped up the process to master the game for many. However, because super-grandmasters are already familiar with the book moves and plays, in order to be great, one has to master these "rules" and know when to break them to continue bringing fresh ideas into the game.

So when watching chess games in the era of computers, one will often see masters speeding through the opening and when they go "off the book", commentators will begin to remark that the players *now* "have to play chess."

This idea of mastering the rules and then breaking them does not just apply to chess. The furthering of any human pursuit — from arts to sports to technology — requires the questioning and breaking of convention in order to push this pursuit forward. There's the famous quote attributed to Pablo Picasso, "Learn the rules like a pro so you can break them like an artist" that has also decorated the walls of Google's headquarters.

It also applies to venture capital and more broadly, investing and backing tech startups, as we phrase in Rule #13: "There are rules to being a good VC, but no rules to being a great one." All the "rules" we've introduced in each chapter are meant to capture what we believe are necessary mindset shifts or evolutions for the venture capitalist or startup investor to be effective at various aspects of the VC profession. These rules were crafted and distilled from the wisdom of many seasoned founders and investors, some of whom we've quoted in this book.

However, the hard truth is that there will always be counterexamples and exceptions to whatever rules are promulgated in any instructive format. Many of these rules and forms of guidance you have read in this book, or perhaps in other websites, programs, or courses for venture capital, are indeed useful to get started and navigate the unfamiliarity of the industry, but in order to become a really successful VC, one has to embrace the reality of not having any constant foundation, rules, or structure to stand on.

This is because the venture capital asset class invests in companies that are built and designed to change the status quo — whether that means speeding up or democratizing certain consumer behaviors or business transformations, or creating new markets and disrupting traditional ones. These companies are built around technologies that are continuously changing at an increasing pace, so it goes to reason that any investments made will inevitably be exposed to the risk of change or the "test of time".

The cost of starting a company has decreased significantly with the democratization of programming and product development, and the massive distribution network that is the internet, but at the same time, the window that a company has before it becomes irrelevant or until a new "disruptor" comes into the field is getting shorter and shorter. Even this book will no longer be as relevant in its entirety over the next twenty years.

A corollary of this mindset is that the investments venture capitalists or startup investors make follow this logic: "In spite of the rapidly changing market, economics and technologies underlying this business, the founders and people executing on the vision of the company will be able to steer and grow the business so it stands the test of time."

The various aspects of the VC profession are then designed to reduce the risks of this statement turning out to be false for any specific investment for as long as possible, right from the formation of the investment thesis, all the way through exits and realizing fund returns.

In this book, we collate the wisdom of VCs and founders past and present as of this writing — our meager and humble version of the role AI softwares like Stockfish play in the world of chess — for anyone looking from the outside in to develop their perspective on the industry and acquire the necessary mindsets to break into it. Exhibit 1 below summarizes the mindset shifts at the heart of this wisdom.

But to really build a great career, VCs have to be able to set their own path. This often means thinking less about what the industry *requires or demands* from you, and more about what you *can bring into*

Aspect of the VC Industry	Area	From...	To...
1. Southeast Asia is not Silicon Valley	Southeast Asia	Invest in what has worked	Invest in what works in Southeast Asia
2. If you're aiming big, you need to grow bigger	Investment thesis	Be satisfied with average and above market returns	Never settle. Raise your standards and goals for your investment returns.
3. Diversify, diversify, diversify	LP and GP dynamic, fund setup	LPs are there to provide capital for investments.	LPs can have a lot more value beyond committing capital to funds.
4. Finding the next billion dollar company starts with asking the right questions	Sourcing	Stick to investing in what you know.	Expand what you know and always be learning in order to find great companies and founders to invest in.
5. Approach due diligence with a fresh perspective	Due diligence	DD is just part of the investment process. There's a structured way to go about it.	DD for early-stage investments has to deal with a lot of assumptions (metrics and valuations. Many of these assumptions will change over time after the initial investment.
6. Don't just invest, build companies	Closing	VCs close deals	VCs partner with founders on building the company over the life of the investment.
7. Growth is about de-risking failutre	Portfolio management	Startups fail 90% of the time	Being a VC is not just about finding the 10% that succeed but also increasing the odds for companies that otherwise would have taken longer to grow, stagnated, or even failed.
8. Culture is the leading indicator of startup success	Portfolio management: people	VCs invest in companies and founders	VCs also invest in company culture, and value-add in hiring impacts company culture as well.
9. Scaling is growing by doing more with less	Portfolio management: growth	Growth must be achieved at all costs.	Lean growth is more effective and sustainable long-term for a startup to mature
10. Always be fundraising	Portfolio management: capital	Startups only focus on fundraising when it's time.	Every strategic decision by the startup impacts their ability to fundraise over time.
11. Building a strong board is about balance, not control	Portfolio management: capital	Building and managing a strong board is about taking control early on.	Building and managing a strong board (and even exercising effective control) is about achieveing balance (i.e. everyone aligns on expectations).
12. Finding exits is an exercise in creativity	Driving exits	Startups are built to exit and drive returns.	Startups are built to be great companies, and great companies find themselves in great exits.
13. There are rules to being good, but no rules to being great	VC career	There's a learning curve to becoming a VC that involves embracing rules, structure, market norms.	Becoming a great VC is about embracing that constant uncertainty and change in the industry. What helped you get where you are today will not be what helps you get to tomorrow.

Exhibit 1: The bigger picture of this book — shifting mindsets.

the industry (paraphrasing the famous JFK quote). In the rest of this chapter, we explore various scenarios that VCs have taken to build their careers and how the industry is evolving to open new doors for more people to invest in startups (even without having to be career venture capitalists).

Many Ways to Build a Venture Capital Career, but there are Patterns

VC careers are built on networks and founder trust

Setting one's own path as a venture capitalist stems from the reality that there's no one traditional path to breaking into the venture capital career. While there are hierarchies within firms as we discussed in Chapter 2, many people become GPs, partners, or lead investment teams in specific industries or markets by virtue of the experience, networks, and other advantages they have.

On the *On Call with Insignia Ventures* podcast in 2021, Rajive Keshup, an ex-founder with a massive exit in the US who then went on to be CFO at a couple of Southeast Asia startups before becoming a venture capitalist, cites the importance of (1) building founder respect and founder trust regardless of the path taken.

> "I'd say there's no one traditional path. There's a bunch of paths that you can kind of go to. Any path where you're doing a really good job in building a ton of founder respect and founder trust will get you there faster. And so whether it's being a good product builder, whether it's being a good go-to-market person, the salesperson, there's been so many different careers that have sort of led to VC. If I think about Peter [Kiemper] at Sequoia, slightly a-traditional versus some of the other guys at Sequoia versus Yinglan [Tan] versus a whole host of others, there have been so many different paths to get there, myself included. So I don't think there's one particular path. And so don't try to hone in and [think that] if I check all these boxes, this is going to happen." [1]

As we emphasized throughout the book, relationships are important to the venture capital industry and investing in startups in general, because (1) investments in early-stage companies are essentially investments in people (founders) and (2) being a valuable early-stage investor is a lot about opening doors for the company or unlocking resources that they would not otherwise be able to access, and often the fastest way to do that is through connections and warm introductions.

It is also not uncommon for VCs to ask potential hires for referrals or whom they would consider to be valuable people in their network in order to gauge what kind of network the candidate brings to the table. We've also mentioned in Chapter 3 how some people can even raise funds without necessarily having a track record simply because of the value of their networks.

The value of a person's network is not just the people they know, but also the reputation and trust these people have for them. That is not just built through connections and conversation, often through value exchanges in interactions be it through work or in off-hours. These exchanges could simply be through supporting each other's projects or making introductions.

Specifically for people looking to break into venture capital, having a lot of exposure to founders and interactions with them, or even going through the experience of being one, already sets up an asset or advantage for that person going into the industry. For example, a product manager with a lot of measurable experience helping products scale in various companies would have that product and tech perspective that would be useful in evaluating investments and supporting them. **The idea here is to develop founder empathy, to be able to see things through the founder perspective and factor that into how one would engage with them as a venture capitalist.**

Another more practical reason to build strong networks and accumulate founder trust is to be able to raise capital. This networking ability has been a critical factor in enabling venture capital to be democratized, especially to professionals who may not be able to create substantial funds from their own wealth.

The takeaway here is to increase exposure and keep doors open, as every interaction you have, especially the more related it is to the industry or ecosystem, can add to your advantage as a venture capitalist.

VC careers are built on looking at patterns, and then at the "negative space"

When setting one's own path as a venture capitalist, it's also very important to have strong pattern recognition, and then be able to see beyond the patterns — at the "white spaces" or "negative spaces" in a market or industry. Some of the best VCs in the industry were pioneers in investing in specific markets, be it Don Valentine pushing venture capital into the software industry in the 70s or the likes of Eric Acher and Fabio Igel who set up the first local VC firm in Brazil in 2005. **Successful VCs who have found and led early investments into the eventual fund returners took the risk of going against the grain and pouring their money and ability into founders whom they believed would endure through the future.**

On the *On Call with Insignia Ventures* podcast in 2021, we talked to Eric Acher, managing general partner at monashees, Brazil's first VC firm, about how he and his co-founder Fabio Igel decided to start their own firm. He had just come off a stint at General Atlantic where he earned his first VC stripes going through the dotcom boom and crash in the early 2000s.

> "To understand what's going on [in Latin America] today, I can talk a little bit about what happened in the last 15 years since we started and maybe a bit more, because I believe, just like in Southeast Asia, we are in the first three minutes of the game. It's just starting up — the entrepreneurial revolution, entrepreneurs with technology and capital revolutionizing markets. This is a very recent phenomenon in the region. But it's here to stay. Basically we had an early hype, when there was the dot com boom in the late nineties, there was a little bit of a hype in the region. A few companies were built. No real VCs were present. It was more like financial

investors. And in the end, there was a bubble, but in Latin America, we only had the bursts. A lot of people lost money, very, very few companies really survived. And then we entered a kind of nuclear winter of tech in the region for almost 10 years from 2000 to 2009.

We started right in the middle of this nuclear winter in 2005. And for the first five years, nothing really happened in Brazil and Latin America. Nobody wanted to be an entrepreneur. It was not a viable career. There were no investors, so we were testing the waters, learning, making investments, making mistakes. We could see the trend growing in tech globally with the launch of the iPhone and then Facebook growing and everything and e-commerce. So we knew it was going to get to the region. We basically bet on two things: that the entrepreneurial revolution was going to be global and that Brazil and Latin America were going to be fertile ground for this revolution." [2]

Now, VCs like Eric emerged right as the industry was being democratized across sectors and across geographies, and he and his co-founder took the risk of being a first mover right in the middle of what he considers a "nuclear winter" in Latin America's tech and venture capital landscape. After all, if no one was willing to get the ball rolling, he might as well do it.

Though it may seem like markets are increasingly becoming saturated because of democratization, the nature of where venture capital investments go means that there will always be new opportunities as time goes on — startups setting up in geographies that would benefit from business model innovation (i.e., new forms of distribution), behavioral of process improvement by technological or product innovation.

VC careers are built on full-stack investing experience

Another common thread we see in how successful careers in VC are built is the simplest: climbing up the ladder, learning the ropes, and gaining experience. There are VCs who make early career shifts (after their first or second job, or two to three years after entering the workforce) into venture capital, join firms as analysts, source a successful investment, rise up to become an associate, source a couple more successful investments, and then get promoted to principal then partner for them to focus on a specific industry or market. Then some might choose to go and start their own fund catering to their expertise or area of interest.

Because of how challenging knowledge transfer can be and how competitive it can be in the industry, VC firms are incentivized to facilitate and at times, accelerate, growth through these funnels in order to build up talent and form the next generation of career investors to take the mantles in these firms. There are scout programs, VC accelerators, or internships offered to those who would want to get hands-on experience and see if it is the right career fit for them.

These funnels go even earlier, right into university courses or programs. In the US, First Round set up the Dorm Room Fund for student VCs to invest in fellow student founders, which has emerged to be a funnel for getting people into VC.

Building full-stack investing experience is an important part of becoming a successful venture capitalist, because it requires a specific discipline to be able to align individual sourcing strategy with a fund's mandate, formulate an investment thesis, present a case to an IC to proceed with an investment, and then work on portfolio management aligning with the fund's needs — which is very different from being an angel investor.

All the ex-es intersect

Ex-founder or operator. Ex-banker or finance industry professional. Ex-consulting. Ex-private equity or fund manager. Career venture capitalist. Angel investor. There are a multitude of backgrounds that venture capitalists can come from. Some backgrounds provide more of the networks and founder exposure, like being an ex-operator, angel investor, or career venture capitalist. Other backgrounds give a wider perspective on finding patterns and industry opportunities like being an ex-consultant or working in other non-VC funds that still invest in tech startups. Then being a career venture capitalist sets up that training and additive experience to become a full-stack venture capitalist.

Regardless, the reality is that all these backgrounds or "ex-es" can intersect in various configurations to create that personal "path" and advantage for a venture capitalist, and as mentioned earlier, there is no "one right way" or checklist to becoming a great one, especially based on background. It is ultimately up to you how to leverage the gains from your own background and turn them into advantages and value-adds as a venture capitalist.

The VC Profession: A Recap

So far in this chapter, we've been emphasizing the idea of finding one's own path and that becoming a great VC requires going beyond the convention and breaking the "rules". That said, the asset class in itself has remained unchanged in terms of (1) the role the venture capitalist plays with respect to LPs, founders, and overall ecosystems, as well as (2) the underlying process of making an investment to realizing returns through an exit. In other words, the two things that make venture capital a profession.

Platform

Throughout the book, we took into account the role the VCs play from various points of view:

1. **From the LP or fund perspective**, VCs exist to manage wealth or capital and generate returns by making investments with potentially outsized returns at exit. Inevitably that means increasing the chance of turning a company into a fund returner as much as possible along the way.
2. **From the founder or startup perspective**, VCs exist as an avenue for massive growth financing. This means getting them from simply starting up to scaling up and even into the public markets, where the company can have more liquidity and shore up a more long-term war chest. VCs are also potentially

a strong partner or board member who can help build the business by filling in gaps that would have otherwise been too costly or impractical for the founders to fill on their own — for example, making introductions to the right hires, opening doors for strategic partnerships, and lining up valuable follow-on investors).

3. **From an ecosystem perspective**, VCs are platforms — platforms for capital to go from LPs to startups, platforms for startups to go from zero to the public markets or an acquisition, and platforms for innovation (be it business models or technology) to speed up their go-to-market and widespread adoption.

Process

We also went through the various "steps" that venture capitalists work on as part of the job throughout the life of a fund. We review these steps from the perspective of the VC career and the critical mindset or skills to have at every step of the way.

1. **Investment Thesis:** VCs need to have a starting point from where to begin looking for investment opportunities, even before raising a fund. Of course, investment theses change over time, but VCs are "hired" by LPs because their conviction and perspective convince them that capital commitment in a particular market or industry is worth the risk of investing in the asset class.

2. **Fund Formation:** VCs raise funds from LPs. The critical skill here is to be able to find the best possible LP base that aligns with the investment theses and can be valuable partners throughout the life of the fund.

3. **Sourcing:** VCs will spend a lot of their career doing this, more than any other part of the job, although sourcing is just the top of the investment funnel and many of the meetings and calls will not result in attractive investments.

4. **Due Diligence:** Due diligence is all about finding the answers to the right questions. For early-stage companies, due diligence is used less to resolve assumptions and more to be precise about

these assumptions as a lot of the aspects of the business will have unknowns one can't really go around.

5. **Closing:** Track records are made or left to the wayside because of this step. We often hear of the crazy lengths both founders and investors go to seal the deal with the people they believe should be on their cap table or portfolio. This is the point of no return (mostly), and the quick decisions that have to be made especially in a hot round will have long-term impact, so VCs have to be able to consider the long-term partnership the investment will entail while still moving fast to close the best investments.

6. **Portfolio Management:** This is the long game to an exit at a massive multiple — but the goal is to make this long game as fast as possible while reducing the risk of having to write off the investment, have it returned, or exit prematurely. A tall task, but this is where a VC will often have the help of the firm or other VCs. An investment firm with a global carry, for example, has the benefit of having people in various markets who are all incentivized to work towards the success of the portfolio.

7. **Exits:** There's no success to be considered until the exit — the rest of the metrics are vanity up until this point. The irony is that while everything done up until this point leads to this exit, the exit itself is often beyond the hands of the VC (because there are so many other stakeholders involved), especially for early-stage seed and Series A rounds. The takeaway here is that exits are already being worked on every step of the way.

On the *On Call with Insignia Ventures* podcast in 2021, monashees founder Eric Acher shares the story of Latin America's first venture-backed exit with 99, the "Grab of Brazil", which was acquired by Didi in 2018. Through this story, Eric shows how monashees went through all these steps.

"This company is the first very successful company that really had a great exit. It was 99. 99 was the Grab of Latin America, of Brazil. It really didn't expand pan-regionally. It was active only in Brazil. We invested. We led the seed round in 2013. And then we led the

Series A and then the company continued to grow and was acquired by Didi in early 2018.

So it was a four-and-a-half-year cycle, from a very early stage to a billion-dollar exit. So it was acquired for a billion-dollars by Didi in 2018. That was a big milestone for us because after 12 years, 12 and a half years starting monashees that was really the first, first big exit. So it took time and I think that you have to be resilient.

And this was a very special company. I think it was a milestone for the whole market, because it was the first unicorn of Latin America, a VC backed billion-dollar tech company in Latin America that started with entrepreneurs raising rounds from the beginning. I have to say at the same time that looking at what's happened in other countries, 99 could have been a larger company and could have been more of a significant leader in the market, but that's exactly the point I was mentioning before.

99 was built at a time when there was no access to growth capital. So when Uber entered Brazil in 2014 with infinite cash and infinite pockets, it was very hard. 99 did such an incredible job, not only surviving, but becoming profitable and competing with Uber until it was acquired by Didi. That was an unbelievable journey, unbelievable journey. If the same thing happened in the last five years and 99 had more access to capital, it could surely be a Grab and be a much bigger company, but anyways, very successful, entrepreneurs are incredible, and we're very happy with that, but I think it's important to note how the timing made a difference here.

We ended up helping 99 on many fronts. We were very much involved, significant equity and the board seat from the beginning of my partner Carlo. And we helped with our knowledge about marketplaces. In the beginning, we had invested for a few years in marketplaces. We knew how important it was to start on the supply side. It was very important to reduce friction, to bring the drivers, start it only with the taxi drivers and then migrate to the other drivers. That knowledge of marketplaces helped entrepreneurs think about it. Also, we helped bring Tiger as a follow-on investor. That was another help. And then finally we helped bring talent. We brought a very important COO that became the CEO of the company, Peter Fernandez. We helped him join the company. And so talent, capital, and some market and industry knowledge. Those were the points that we were able to help entrepreneurs in building, but it's their merit in building an incredible company, that was our first unicorn." [2]

Skills

Apart from looking at the role and the process, we've also covered a number of the important skills that a VC needs in order to be effective across their career. These skills may seem to be standing in opposition with each other, so we juxtaposed these "contrasts" and cover them as skills that actually work in conjunction with each other.

1. **Empathy and Radical Candor:** VCs build founder trust and respect with empathy, but one can't always take up the side of the founder and excuse perspectives or practices if they threaten to exacerbate risks to the company's growth. VCs are in a position to help founders face the hard truths while they still have the time and resources to face it, and not when it's too late. So VCs need to have radical candor in order to confront these situations with founders. This is a level of honesty that does not just end with acknowledgment or even result in conflict, but positively transforms leadership and the company as well.

   On the *On Call with Insignia Ventures* podcast in 2021 with Rajive Keshup, he shares how he balances being a cheerleader or supporter of his portfolio with some tough love.

   "To the outside world, I'm like a cheerleader. I might as well have pom-poms on like I'll retweet, tweet. Anywhere I talk to, my founders can walk on water, but like underneath, I'm kicking their butt. I'm constantly saying things like, "Where the hell is this? Why is this?" And I'm like a torrent for a lot of them. So I feel like this is a good dichotomy of good luck, bad love, or hard love, not-so-nice love. but it comes from a place of "Hey, let's execute faster. Let's build bigger. Let's go faster." And I'm trying to drive cultures of accountability within our portfolio across the board, and bring a little bit of PE discipline to our startups a little bit earlier and in governance a lot earlier." [1]

2. **Playing to Strengths and Building on Gaps:** VCs all have their own advantages they bring to the field, but because of the nature of these investments and the underlying economics and technology, they also have to continuously evolve these advantages — that can range from expanding their network into new industries to bringing people into their team who can better meet the needs of their portfolio.

3. **Catering to Specific Needs and Leveraging on the Scalability of Value-Adds:** VCs have to deal with investments on a case-by-case basis, but at the same time, there are learnings and practices that can cross cases and be scaled so the VC becomes more effective as a whole. For example, learnings a VC gained from working with one founder running a post-Series B company could benefit a founder who is running an earlier-stage company, as shown in Exhibit 2 below.

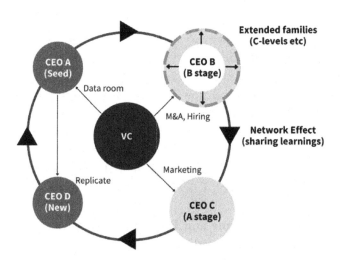

Exhibit 2: A sample illustration of how a VC can scale their value-add across the various kinds of founders they work with. Illustration of a framework or approach shared by Joolin in an article published in *Insignia Business Review* in 2020. [3]

In an interview with Joolin Chuah in 2020, the first investment hire of Insignia Ventures, she shares how she has leveraged playing to her strengths and scaling her value-add in working with founders.

"It's three things that I really do to this day. First is playing to my strengths — my expertise in fintech and banking, and experience dealing with seed stage companies and first-time founders. I started small and niche and supported founders in fintech and insurtech by leveraging my knowledge and network, before moving into new sectors such as logistics and commerce. I was also laser focused on helping first-time founders and seed stage companies in financials and strategy.

Once I have done it at length, I started to see a strong network effect where I can share learnings I gained from one founder to another. I also started to see a powerful ripple effect when founders speak highly of me in their community. This helped to build my personal branding and confidence in the industry. To this day, I am truly grateful and need to give all my founders full credit for putting their trust in me.

Second is respecting the time of founders. Their hours are expensive. This means every minute I spend with them needs to be valuable. That said, in order to spend time more effectively with founders, I need to be constantly learning and picking up useful information and new insights. I also need to build connections with industry veterans.

Third is delivering results and replicating that success across the founders I'm handling over time. Ensuring my founders meet their targets and have a healthy balance sheet and runway are insufficient. In fact, I need to ensure consistency in delivering results." [3]

4. **Playing the Long Game and Playing it Fast:** Venture capital is a profession that requires discipline, resilience, and patience. It can take time and a lot of hoops, especially in an emerging market like Southeast Asia, to get a startup from seed to exit. It can also take time to find that fund returner. VCs need to stay focused on the long-term, all the more in a hot sector or market,

and have that resilience to continue innovating their approach and making that everyday 1% increase. At the same time, opportunities come by in the blink of an eye and VCs also need to be able to recognize when they need to make fast decisions, all the while considering the long-term implications.

Eric Acher shares what he considers to be the top three skills of a venture capitalist, and these are underlined by a long-term perspective, which was likely influenced by how long it took for Latin America to get into gear after monashees was first started.

"First is resilience and patience. The first cycle for any VC will take 10 years and you have to really want to do it and help entrepreneurs. And not really think about the rewards too soon. Of course, you can win the lottery in two years, have an incredible exit, but it takes time. And so resilience and patience to go through good times and bad times are key.

Second I'd say it's very important to have a collaborative approach to build lasting relationships with founders and always thinking about maximizing the long-term not maximizing the short term. It's not being transactional, being collaborative. You may lose here and there in a short time, but it will really build the relationships and the reputation that you need in the long run as a VC and especially in Latin America, where traditionally financial investors had all the bargaining power and were never collaborative. That makes a big difference.

The last one is the ability to move fast, make decisions fast, identify patterns, make connections across many parallel channels. There's a sea of information but you have to move fast and that's very important." [2]

Tech stack

While venture capital is a profession that revolves around relationships, and will remain this way, there are a lot of aspects of the job that are increasingly being taken over by technology, either to (1) free up more time for the VC to focus on more high-touch aspects of the job or (2) scale the ability of the VC.

The tech stack evolves from year to year for obvious reasons, but it is worth looking at a snapshot of what this tech stack looks like. Sometimes VCs will also invest in startups because of the tools they can provide for the firm specifically. For example, they might invest in a job marketplace to help them gain better access to talent for themselves and their portfolio companies.

Venture Capital's Constant Evolution

Having emphasized the point on the importance of charting one's own path to build a venture capital career, and recapping the aspects of the VC profession we've covered over the course of this book, we now look at how the venture capital industry has been evolving over the past ten years up until the turn of the decade, especially in the context of Southeast Asia and what these developments could mean for the future of the profession.

1. **Democratization of venture capital fund management/fund strategy.**

We've covered this more in depth in Chapter 3, but the main idea here is that **venture capital funds are being created to cater to earlier and earlier growth stages (seed funds).** One of the pioneering, successful examples of this shift in Silicon Valley is Floodgate, which was built up specifically to target seed stage startups. Now, even firms that are typically investing in Series A or Series B or even Series C are going into seed rounds as well. Another part of this is also that there are more methods for investors to participate in early rounds through angel syndicates or rolling funds or crowdfunding platforms. These shifts in investment strategy have resulted in the rapid rise of angel and seed activity over later rounds of fundraising, as shown in Exhibit 3.

What this means for the VC industry is that there are more opportunities to create a career built on the "negative space" or the niche spots in the market or segments that are not being captured by the larger, later-stage firms or funds. These segments might even be considered risky by the generalist VC firm, mainly because of the

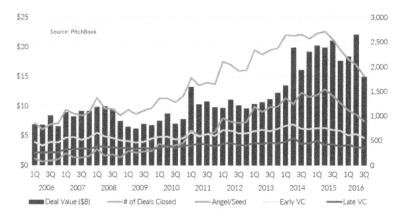

Exhibit 3: Angel and seed investment activity have overtaken Early VC and Late VC activity post 2010 as documented by Pitchbook. [4]

lack of expertise in these areas. This is especially true for an emerging market like Southeast Asia, where one could argue that there are still a lot of "negative spaces" in the industry in terms of opportunities that firms may not be paying much attention to as of this writing (e.g., applications for crypto or blockchain in the region, SaaS investments, Islamic finance, green investments etc.) A VC professional could either position themselves to lead investments in these areas as part of a well-resourced VC firm, or start a fund focused on that niche themselves.

It is important to note though that while democratization means more opportunities to invest in, it also means more competition. Global marquee investors and many late-stage players have extended their capabilities to invest earlier, especially in Southeast Asia, raising the prices for other investors to enter as well. The increasing density of investors presents the challenge for investors, whether angels or venture capital firms, to be able to develop and sell concrete differentiators.

2. Democratization of Sourcing through VC Scouts.
A parallel trend to funds being set up to target earlier stage startups and more niche segments has been the democratization specifically of the "sourcing" step in the venture capital investment process.

Specifically, scout programs are set-ups where a venture capital firm offers professionals (typically operators with deep networks in the ecosystem) profit-sharing on deals these professionals can source. The ticket size, mechanics, and depth of commitment of the scouts vary from program to program, and some programs have emerged which are independent of the VC firms themselves (more like angel investor syndicates). The creation of scout programs is credited to Sequoia Capital, though the mechanisms themselves have evolved as more firms began adopting the model.

As we write in an article in *Insignia Business Review* in 2021, larger firms can cast a wider net by virtue of a formalized network and program where individuals can share carry with the firm with companies or founders they introduce that make it through to closing.

> "VCs benefit primarily from being able to expand their horizon for deal flow without having to commit too much, especially from the perspective of the partners.
>
> The logic here is that in order to find fundmaking deals, investors want to cast a wide net over as many early-stage founders and companies as possible. The problem is that the firm can't spend so much in terms of time or check size (imagine the inefficiency of having a partner having to choose writing $10–15m checks for 100 companies over supporting a billion-dollar deal) in order to make each potential catch worthwhile, especially for firms that handle a massive portfolio. So a scouts program, at its core, enables these firms to discover early-stage deals at scale, funneling more options for partners to work with and develop.
>
> For the scouts, the benefits range from purely financial (i.e. profit-sharing with the fund) to career-building (e.g. getting hired by the fund, or eventually becoming a fully-fledged angel or seed investor). Most VC scouts programs often involve former leadership of unicorns or ex-founders for example who have built the relevant networks over time who then send over referrals to VC firms running the programs." [5]

An evolution of the scout program has been not just scale sourcing, but scale sourcing education (and even the full stack of venture capital investment skills), and building up the talent pool of venture capital professionals in the market. So firms could even offer training and courses as a funnel into their scout program, or set up an entirely separate "VC accelerator" that increases the talent pool for the entire ecosystem.

Just as we discussed in the previous point, democratization leads to greater competition, and the same holds true as more scout programs and communities emerge in Southeast Asia. From a sourcing perspective, there's also the challenge of having an increasing top-of-funnel but having difficulties taking advantage of this pool of startups or a misalignment with the kinds of the startups that are coming in the pipeline.

3. Platformization of Venture Capital into Venture Building.

As we mentioned earlier, venture capital (firms) are platforms in the industry. The trend has been to beef up the capabilities of VC firms as platforms, creating as many channels for connections in the industry and ecosystem as possible, be it through talent development or thought leadership. This is most apparent with firms like First Round or a16z that have built out nearly independent publications to put their thought leadership in the spotlight.

In Southeast Asia, the past ten years from 2010 to 2020 saw an increasing shift towards platformization of firms as they began to expand their "value-adds" and network effects within their portfolio to meet as many needs of portfolio companies at various stages of growth as possible. Of course, platformization is not a surefire approach to success. There are firms like Benchmark that have thrived on being lean and simply focusing on building a strong investment team with diverse industry expertise. But it comes as no surprise that the incentive to stack up on services for VC firms in Southeast Asia is much higher given the emerging market nature of the ecosystem and various challenges that come with scaling a startup in the region.

Going one step further is the venture building approach where VC firms will actively take part in the formation of the founding team, the execution of the initial go-to-market of the company, or a critical pivot for the company by providing them with the right leadership and tools. Of course, not all VC firms will have the expertise to do this (a firm would need engineers and market launch experts as well as the ability to bring in co-founders), and just like the "service agency" approach, it does not automatically make a firm or fund successful. The advantage though is that a VC can tap into opportunities where they see no existing companies that check all the boxes for them or for the IC.

4. Data-Driven Venture Capital.
As we covered in the tech stack section, more VCs are making use of various tools to be able to scale their abilities across the whole investment process, especially when it comes to the steps that heavily require networking (e.g., fundraising, sourcing, portfolio management).

But more than just using tools, the main evolution of the VC here is that instead of simply going out into the world with an investment thesis and trying to meet as many founders as possible, they would build or buy tools that can cast nets for them and curate their investment funnel through various sourcing indicators — app performance, hiring and team size, past fundraising, etc.

Apart from sourcing, there are also a variety of data aggregation platforms that can help VCs in hiring as well as connecting with investors across the value chain to either fundraise from or support their portfolio companies in fundraising.

That said, the effectiveness of data-driven VC depends on the quality of the data. For a market in Southeast Asia entering the 2020s, the industry still has a lot of opaqueness in terms of data availability and accessibility, but the more an ecosystem matures, the more reliable these data sources can become.

5. ESG and Sustainability.
An important evolution in the venture capital industry has been the greater focus towards the ESG (environmental, social, governance) impact of their investments.

This intuitively aligns with the kind of long-term mindset that VCs would have in supporting value creation, at the same time, they would want these long-term solutions to be able to move fast and generate returns.

This ESG focus does not just mean setting up funds focused on investing in green startups, startups addressing social inequalities, or regtech startups, but simply taking this into account in the due diligence so it applies to any investment made, or even making it part of the fund mandate. Some of these considerations are already part-and-parcel of a standard due diligence process, like gaining visibility into a company's governance structure.

VCs may also include ESG consulting in their portfolio management strategy, diagnosing how their portfolio companies could improve across sustainability, diversity, and accountability and equipping them with professionals and resources to be able to act on the diagnosis.

VC associations across the world are also promoting this focus by offering incentives for firms that can concretely follow through on this ESG focus on their portfolio.

6. Embracing greater exposure to liquidity through public markets and web3.

Venture capital throughout history has almost exclusively been focused on very illiquid investments, but two shifts have made VCs rethink their level of exposure to liquidity.

First is the venture-backed tech IPO boom, with both the influx to the public markets and the performance of tech companies when they get there having reached new highs over the past decade. VCs will typically exit most if not all of their position in a company upon its entry in the public markets, mainly to safeguard their returns and the returns of their LPs from price volatility. With the increasing upside of holding on to these positions even as they go public, VCs have been exploring ways to create more flexibility for them and their investors to keep investing (or not) in these companies.

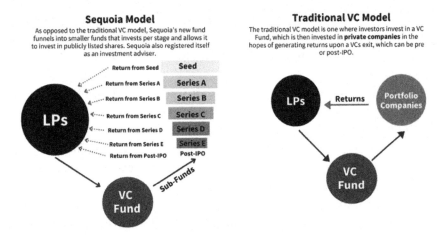

Exhibit 4: Sequoia Fund model vs traditional VC model.

One way is to decouple the ability of the VC fund to invest in companies from the expectations and commitments of LPs. In 2021, Sequoia Capital launched the Sequoia Fund to take on an open-ended approach to venture capital, no longer bound by the pressure to deliver returns for the fund within a specific time period. This model is compared to the traditional VC model in Exhibit 4 above.

Another shift that has been changing the way VCs look at liquidity is the rise of decentralized finance adoption, where transactions are done using tokens or cryptocurrencies, which in themselves are backed by their very users. Investing in these types of solutions can no longer be done using the traditional cash-for-equity setup. VCs have had to learn (in many cases, the hard way) to adjust their fund structures to invest in these ventures, from token sales and air drops to crypto-native funds and a mix of these various strategies. Funds are also being set up by operators "born-and-raised" on these decentralized technologies, and the returns of these funds have been outperforming traditional funds in a shorter period of time.

These adjustments are being motivated by the reality that tokens and cryptocurrencies are no longer just limited in adoption to trading and investing. They are increasingly becoming a concrete transaction layer for what is called "web3" or the "decentralized internet" where internet platforms are disintermediated by the ability of asset creators to fully own and manage their assets and transactions.

While both the draw of the public market returns on tech companies and the future of a decentralized internet are forcing VC funds to rethink their exposure to liquidity, the latter is likely to have a more long-term and permanent effect on the way VC is done, as opposed to the former which is likely to have a more cyclical effect as these public market performances have tended to ebb and flow (and one could even argue the 2010s has been an outlier period in the history of tech investing).

7. web3 protocols as new infrastructure for democratization of venture capital.

A potential long-term implication of the rise of web3 is the very decentralization of venture capital itself. One of the applications of decentralized technology is the formation of decentralized autonomous organizations, or DAOs. At its core the governance and management of a DAO is done through highly transparent token-based voting, where the tokens are minted and exchanged within the DAO itself. On the surface, the allure of a DAO with respect to venture capital or investing in web3 in general has been the ability for the crypto-native masses to participate, but as of this writing, the jury is still out on the mechanics, governance, and regulation that will truly make this sustainable for VCs, given that decentralization also exposes an organization to management risks, manipulation, and unsecured volatility — all risks which VCs have traditionally been set up to protect against.

So, the way to look at DAOs is less a replacement for VCs and more an entirely new infrastructure for people to raise money for funding their assets, creations, or ventures, which could take up a slice of the internet and software companies in a decentralized, web3 future. In general, web3 implications for venture capital is the next chapter to the overarching narrative of the democratization of venture capital, where the means to invest are no longer consolidated by a handful of funds housed in a certain geography. The democratization itself is already happening with angel syndicates, niche funds, and fractional investing, but web3 protocols offer a more transparent and secure infrastructure to facilitate these transactions. Exhibit 5 below illustrates how a DAO might work especially in the context of funding web3 projects.

Even with all these developments, emerging models for investing in tech companies, and new arenas on which VCs are competing summarized in Exhibit 6, it is important to remember that venture capital is less of an infrastructure or specific way of investing, but more of the very act of backing those creating value where none previously existed, before anyone else believes in them. The methodology has evolved over time, and will continue to evolve, but the act of venture capital existed long before the internet or software and it will exist long after, as long as there are people willing to put capital into the high-risk, high-reward ventures that create value at scale.

Decentralized Autonomous Organizations (DAOs)

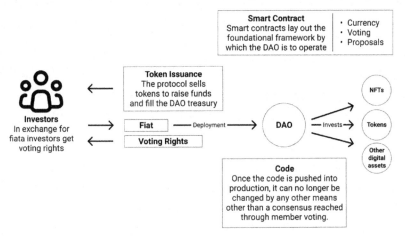

Exhibit 5:   How Decentralized Autonomous Organizations work.

Aspect of the VC Industry	From...	To...
Fund Formation	Investing in companies with initial product and PMF Generalist investing	Investing in founders pre-product and pre-revenue NIche investing (separate funds for specific industries)
Sourcing	Venture capitalist leveraging networks for sourcing	Formalizing and scaling networks through scouts programs
Involvement in Earlier-Stage Companies	Investor and board member	Venture builder
Networking (Sourcing, Fundraising, Due Diligence)	Opportunistic or manual networking	Curated and scaled networking through data platforms
Fund Mandates	No accounting for environmental, social, or governance impact	Including ESG considerations in every investment
Liquidity	All illiquid investments	Greater liquidity exposure through public markets and tokens
Infrastructure	Centralized platform between LPs and portfolio companies	Decentralized structures facilitating direct capital flows from investors to startups on web3 protocols

Exhibit 6: Summary of Evolutions in VC we discussed that have been ongoing in the last decade leading up to the 2020s.

The Outlier Business

No matter how many startup bibles are consumed, VC courses are taken, or internships and work experience are accumulated, VCs will, at many points in their careers, face decisions that require them to go "off the book" and really play the game. Whether or not they are willing to embrace these decisions is already half the journey.

Venture capital is not the only way to invest in startups — one can be an angel investor, join a more institutional fund, or join an accelerator. It is worth reflecting on whether or not a VC career will truly enable one to maximize the value they want to bring into the world. One can easily fall into complacency in the industry (especially in more saturated markets) considering it simply a job, or on the other end of the spectrum, get overwhelmed by the demands of working in it. This is why Rule #13 exists — because in order to really thrive as a VC, one has to really internalize what they want out of being a VC. One can be a good VC at the job, but becoming great and successful is another matter altogether. The best founders do the same thing day in and day out because this is not just a job for them that they can easily sell or pass on — it is their life's work. VCs that can work on this same wavelength as the best founders they back can put themselves in a "great" rather than "good" mindset.

Venture capital is an outlier business. Just as successful VCs made their money from the rare investments that beat the odds and the curve, **in order to become great, VCs need to be able to raise and manage funds that perform way above their peers and the market indexes.** That said, the chances of VCs funds gaining a 2 to 3x return is much more spread out, but the ambitious VC is likely not to settle for that.

Another reason VC is an outlier business is not just because of the odds working against the asset class itself but also because of what it demands from the VC professional. In chess, in order to become grandmaster, chess players spend hours and years training, learning from the best, sharpening their intuition, and playing the best to gain rating points. There's also the element of luck —because games and tournaments are decided in the shortest of moments in comparison to the vast amount of time needed to get to those games and tournaments. The learning curve for a VC is not as steep, but becoming great will require a lot of patience — as we've mentioned before — and working day and night for the long haul, all while being able to make those split-second decisions that could make or break a fund. Even if stories abound of the massive returns to be made, these returns have all taken time and entailed a lot of work behind the scenes, from hiring the people to deciding the right time to exit. Not many people would be comfortable or well-suited with this level of drawn-out uncertainty and variability, and may be more content simply working as part of the firm and not managing their own portfolio.

Finally, a venture capitalist is only as great as what motivates them. It's relatively easier to be a VC who simply rides the bandwagons, stays in the industry for a while, but doesn't really leave their mark. One can be content with that path, but at the same time, the best only get to where they are because of a combination of opportunity and preparation (mindset) — luck is not worth anything if no one's there to take advantage of it.

In Southeast Asia the motivations abound given how vibrant and fast-moving the ecosystem is — from the problems of fragmentation, inequalities, and inefficiencies that are calling out to be solved to the inspiring founders who are working against the grain to build great companies. What will keep you going as a venture capitalist? Eric Acher shares what drives him and his team at monashees on the *On Call with Insignia Ventures* podcast in 2021.

"I know probably several VCs say things along these lines, but what we do is basically we want to generate, you know, attractive returns to our investors as a consequence of helping entrepreneurs build world-class tech companies in Latin America. This is what we do, but I have to say, this is not why we do it. Both Fabio and I from the beginning, we really believe in this entrepreneurial revolution as a possibility to change the region. Every time I look around and I see the deep inequality that exists in Brazil and Latin America, it gives us incredible motivation to continue to — together with the other players — democratize access to capital, to the best entrepreneurs with the right values, from any background so they can solve the important problems and the inefficiency in the region, create jobs, improve people's lives, inspire other entrepreneurs and young people. And of course generate attractive returns. So we continue this virtuous cycle and we can reshape our region. I think behind everything that's the force that motivates the whole team of Monashees." [2]

What will keep you going as a venture capitalist?

Three Best Practices

1. Define your focus and expertise as an investor, based on your background and interest.
2. Maximize exposure to founders, even if the interactions do not involve directly investing in them.
3. Build long-lasting relationships with founders — their contact numbers and what they say about you is your CV/track record.

Afterword: Venture Capital's Neverending Dance with Uncertainty

Venture-backed tech startups are by nature built and grown in the context of constantly heightened uncertainty, relative to any other type of business. There is the uncertainty in a startup's ability to secure enough resources in time to bring a product to market, or whether the lack of resources would be enough to make a dent in the market. There is uncertainty in a startup's ability to scale amidst incumbents or status quo behaviors and processes. Then there is uncertainty in a startup's ability to lead the market and endure as a mature company.

This uncertainty is inherently tied into the nature of venture capital as a funding vehicle for such startups and business models designed for rapid scale. As we discussed in Chapter 1, "Venture capitalists back those creating value where none previously existed, before anyone else believes in them." This adds greater meaning to the gains of both these companies and their early investors, which is also why these stories of "first checks" always manage to capture the imagination of people.

Uncertainty is Also an Uncertain Variable

This relationship between venture capital and uncertainty has fluctuated over time. Every time the bandwagon effect, which we also covered in Chapter 1, reached its peak, that's when uncertainty and venture capital are furthest apart, and on paper returns, the illusion becomes prevalent that anything venture capital touches becomes gold. Business models and organizations then that are not suited to venture capital or at least not prepared for it are then pumped up with this highly volatile, highly demanding fuel.

But the reality is that this isn't the case, at least not for long. Uncertainty somehow always finds its way back to venture capital with market corrections, when the true quality of investments is put to the test. Both startup founders and investors who never left the side of uncertainty by being disciplined and building cash flow flexibility and processes around their hypergrowth, even in a bull market, are better prepared to ride the waves of price adjustments and fundraising winters when they come.

The conclusion here is not that these bandwagons, bubbles, or hype cycles can be avoided. In fact, they may be necessary in a highly competitive market, at least with respect to making any venture capital returns meaningful. As we brought up in Chapter 13, "Just as successful VCs made their money from the rare investments that beat the odds and the curve, in order to become great, VCs need to be able to raise and manage funds that perform way above their peers and the market indexes." The harsh reality of the market is winners are defined by how far apart they are from everyone else, hence becoming a business of outliers and rarities.

Instead of trying to find some way out of the ebb and flow of the market, a more sustainable, and frankly simpler, way to look at venture capital is as a constant dance with uncertainty. And this is something not only for investors to keep in mind in every investment decision, but founders as well when they take in this hypergrowth capital and progressively give up ownership of their company.

Keeping Up with the Changing Music of the Market

This published first edition of *Backing the Bold* was written and revised over the course of what can be described as a historical upheaval in the global tech startup and venture capital landscape. And the difference was the most striking in Southeast Asia. With the region's digital economy just coming off a record year of funding and valuations bolstered by the pandemic-induced digitalization wave narrative, the first half of 2022 saw a near-180 in the fundraising climate, driven by inflation and supply chain strains first hitting public market valuations, then drying up private market activity as well.

Pushing the dance analogy further, one can think of this market impact in Southeast Asia as the market dancing at the bpm of an EDM song then having to slow down to a ballad in a split-second. Add in the fact that many of those dancing to the EDM song have not experienced what it's like to dance to a ballad.

Those companies able to quickly match their pace to the whiplash of this market shift likely have a path to profitability (if not already profitable) or a long enough runway to focus on monetization (or able to quickly lengthen its runway) or both. Then for investors, their pace is only as good as majority of their portfolio's. If they are unable to support their companies in staying afloat or have a portfolio mostly of companies unable to stay afloat, then it is easy to drown.

Of course, dancing to rapidly changing beats is easier said than done and implies that many of the factors that have led to the challenges in this bear market are actually rooted in decisions made during the bull run.

So you Think you Can Dance (with Uncertainty)?

The good thing is, and I hope you agree having reached this essay, that *Backing the Bold* was not written with the quick buck or purely the gold rush in mind, but long-term value creation from both Southeast Asia investors and founders, regardless of the weather.

While written amidst hype and edited amidst caution, the insights and mindsets imparted in these pages are meant to dance with uncertainty — the examples use to illustrate these insights, admittedly only time can tell, but that's also part of the dance.

And as mentioned in the Acknowledgments in the beginning of the book, *Backing the Bold* is a living organism, and while this first edition will largely remain unchanged in its foundations and key message, the finer points are already evolving as I write.

This reason this is the case is because *Backing the Bold* is a companion primer to the Insignia Ventures Academy program, where people from a diverse range of backgrounds come together to learn hands-on with real companies and the support of seasoned investors and founders how to dance with uncertainty from the venture capitalist's perspective.

And if there is anything I have learned over the course of seeing several cohorts come together, go through the rigor of the program, and then go on to leverage their newfound learnings and networks to play a variety of roles in the ecosystem, it is that the music of the market is never the same twice, and by implication, every cohort experience is different.

There are patterns and melodies that are useful to keep an ear out for, and some dancers might disagree about how they break down beats (e.g., quality vs quantity in investment allocation), but the best ones are learning the music as it evolves. And they are only able to do this because they have built an internal rhythm (i.e., an investor instinct), built over time with many experiences, many conversations with founders, and foundational principles and values.

Just as the venture fellows who have gone through Insignia Ventures Academy do not necessarily come out going into a venture capital career (some become founders, others shift industries, etc.), the mindset of dancing with uncertainty and in a constantly changing music, even if learned in the context of venture capital, can also apply to many journeys in life.

So if you think this dance is for you, or want to try it out, check out how you can find your own rhythm with Insignia Ventures Academy at www.insignia.academy.

Finally, I would like to thank you, the reader, for making it this far into *Backing the Bold,* or even opening it if you happened to pass through this page. Wherever you are, and whatever your dance is in life, I hope you are dancing with uncertainty no matter how the music changes.

Paulo Joquiño
Manila
17 June 2022

Appendix A: References

Chapter 1

1. Rajive Keshup and Yinglan Tan. 2021. *Unpacking the VC: Yinglan Tan.* Clubhouse Session.
2. NextUnicorn Ventures. 2021. *The Full List of Unicorn Startups in Southeast Asia.* https://nextunicorn.ventures/the-full-list-of-unicorn-startups-in-southeast-asia/CB Insights. 2021.
3. CB Insights. *Unicorn Exits Tracker.* https://www.cbinsights.com/research-unicorn-exits
4. Paulo Joquino. 2021. *ASES Stanford Panel: Notes for the aspiring venture capitalist taking a leap into Southeast Asia.* Insignia Business Review. http://review.insignia.vc/2021/04/27/ases-stanford-panel-notes-for-the-aspiring-venture-capitalist-taking-leap-into-southeast-asia/
5. Paulo Joquino. 2020. *Leadership matters but will it change the game for Alibaba and Lazada.* Insignia Business Review. http://review.insignia.vc/2020/08/20/leadership-matters-but-will-it-change-the-game-for-alibaba-and-lazada/
6. Iprice Group. 2021. *Southeast Asia's Map of E-commerce.* https://www-emis-com.libproxy.smu.edu.sg/php/search/docpdf?pc=ID&doc_id=715920309

Chapter 2

1. Manish Singh. 2021. *Gojek and Tokopedia merge to form GoTo group.* TechCrunch. https://techcrunch.com/2021/05/16/gojek-and-tokopedia-merge-to-form-goto-group/

2. Yinglan Tan and Paulo Joquiño. 2020. *Navigating ASEANnovation: The Reservoir Principle and Other Essays on Startups and Innovation in Southeast Asia*. World Scientific Publishing Company.
3. Bill Roosman. 2020. Riding The K12 Learning Cycle In Southeast Asia. Insignia Business Review. http://review.insignia.vc/2020/07/14/riding-the-k12-learning-cycle-in-southeast-asia/
4. Paulo Joquino. 2021. *Mapping The Waves Of Innovation In Southeast Asia's Food System*. Insignia Business Review. http://review.insignia.vc/2021/03/09/mapping-the-waves-of-innovation-in-southeast-asias-food-system/
5. Insignia Business Review. 2021. *Ecommerce Logistics: The Wind Beneath The New Normal's Wings*. http://review.insignia.vc/2021/05/11/ecommerce-logistics-the-wind-beneath-the-new-normals-wings/
6. CB Insights. 2015. *Disrupting Banking: The Fintech Startups That Are Unbundling Wells Fargo, Citi and Bank of America*. https://www.cbinsights.com/research/disrupting-banking-fintech-startups/

Chapter 3

1. Robin Wigglesworth. 2021. *'Game over': Investors hunt for a new model after years of broad gains*. Financial Times. https://www.ft.com/content/bfc51c7a-e009-4ef1-ae9a-3545f76cf2fd
2. Giacomo Mollo. 2019. *David Swensen's Yale Endowment shows how Venture Capital is good for your portfolio asset allocation*. Medium. https://giacomomollo.medium.com/david-swensens-yale-endowment-shows-how-venture-capital-is-good-for-your-portfolio-asset-98bab7ffc1f
3. Luke Antal. 2019. *Venture Returns Outperform Public Markets Over Many Periods*. Alumni Ventures Group. https://cdn2.hubspot.net/hubfs/3925488/White%20Papers/Venture%20Returns%20Outperform%20Public%20Markets-AVG.pdf
4. Deal Street Asia. 2021. *SE Asia's VC Funds: Q1 2021 Review*. https://www.dealstreetasia.com/reports/se-asias-vc-funds-q1-2021-review/
5. Paulo Joquiño. 2021. *SuperReturn China 2021 Panel: Dissecting the influx of foreign capital into Southeast Asia*. Insignia Business Review. http://review.insignia.vc/2021/05/18/superreturn-china-2021-panel-dissecting-the-influx-of-foreign-capital-into-southeast-asia/

6. Paulo Joquiño. 2019. *From Betting On The Future To Charting Its Course: Venture Building With LPs*. Insignia Business Review. http://review.insignia.vc/2019/12/13/from-betting-on-the-future-to-charting-its-course-venture-building-with-lps/
7. Cristiano Bellavitis and Natalia Matanova. *Do Interest Rates Affect VC Fundraising and Investments?*. https://www.efmaefm.org/0EFMAMEETINGS/EFMA%20ANNUAL%20MEETINGS/2017-Athens/papers/EFMA2017_0125_fullpaper.pdf

Chapter 4

1. Michael Seibel. *Why does your company deserve more money*. Y Combinator. https://www.ycombinator.com/blog/why-does-your-company-deserve-more-money/ (page 106–107)
2. Platform Revolution. 2022. *PayPal, Reddit and the power of fakin' it*. https://platformthinkinglabs.com/materials/seeding-youtube-megaupload-paypal-reddit/
3. On Call with Insignia Ventures. 2021. *Sustaining The Pandemic's 10x Digitalization With Lifepal's Giacomo Ficari, Intellect's Theodoric Chew, And Finhay's Huy Nghiem*. Insignia Business Review. http://review.insignia.vc/2021/05/11/s03e05-e06-sustaining-the-pandemics-10x-digitalization-with-lifepals-giacomo-ficari-intellects-theodoric-chew-and-finhays-huy-nghiem/
4. Paulo Joquiño. 2021. *5 Lessons On Building A Global AI Marketing Company: Case Study On Appier's Road To IPO*. Insignia Business Review. http://review.insignia.vc/2021/03/30/5-lessons-from-appier-road-to-ipo/
5. On Call with Insignia Ventures. 2020. *Building Southeast Asia's First Digital-Only Bank In The Philippines With Tonik CEO And Founder Greg Krasnov*. Insignia Business Review. http://review.insignia.vc/2020/07/16/building-southeast-asias-first-digital-only-bank-in-the-philippines-with-tonik-ceo-and-founder-greg-krasnov/
6. Vcstarterkit. Twitter. https://twitter.com/vcstarterkit/status/1275444501348323331

7. Connie Loizos. 2019. *A peek inside Sequoia Capital's low-flying, wide-reaching scout program.* Tech Crunch. https://techcrunch.com/2019/06/07/a-peek-inside-sequoia-capitals-low-flying-wide-reaching-scout-program/
8. Paulo Joquiño. 2019. *From Betting On The Future To Charting Its Course: Venture Building With LPs.* Insignia Business Review. http://review.insignia.vc/2019/12/13/from-betting-on-the-future-to-charting-its-course-venture-building-with-lps/
9. On Call with Insignia Ventures. 2021. *On Call With Insignia 3: Hendra Kwik, CEO Of FazzFinancial Group On Going Regional, People-First Leadership, And The Future Of Fintech In Southeast Asia.* Insignia Business Review. http://review.insignia.vc/2021/04/07/on-call-with-insignia-3-hendra-kwik-ceo-of-fazzfinancial-group-on-going-regional-people-first-leadership-and-the-future-of-fintech-in-southeast-asia/
10. Insignia Ventures Academy. 2021. One Pager-Sample. App.

Chapter 5

1. CleverTap. 2020. *Cohort Analysis: Beginners Guide to Improving Retention.* https://clevertap.com/blog/cohort-analysis/
2. On Call with Insignia Ventures. 2021. *On Call With Insignia 3: Aaron Tan, CEO Of Carro, On Future Of Southeast Asia's Automotive Retail Industry, Artificial Intelligence, And Leading APAC's Top High Growth Company For 2021.* Insignia Business Review. http://review.insignia.vc/2021/04/13/on-call-with-insignia-3-aaron-tan-ceo-carro-southeast-asia-automotive-retail-industry-artificial-intelligence-apac-top-high-growth-company-for-2021/
3. Wall Street Prep. 2020. VC Valuation. https://www.wallstreetprep.com/knowledge/vc-valuation-6-steps-to-valuing-early-stage-firms-excel-template/

Chapter 6

1. On Call with Insignia Ventures. 2020. *Shaping the future of Southeast Asia's Car Industry with Carro Group CFO Ernest Chew.* Insignia Business Review. http://review.insignia.vc/2020/12/04/shaping-the-future-southeast-asia-car-industry-cfo-on-call-carro-group-cfo-ernest-chew/

2. Catherine Shu. 2021. *Founded by former Carousell and Fave execs, Rainforest gets $36M to consolidate Asia-Pacific Amazon Marketplace brands.* TechCrunch. https://techcrunch.com/2021/05/05/founded-by-former-carousell-ovo-and-fave-execs-rainforest-raises-36m-to-aggregate-asia-pacific-amazon-marketplace-sellers/amp/
3. Patrick Gordan. 2012. *Venture Debt: A Capital Idea for Startups.* Kauffman Fellows. https://www.kauffmanfellows.org/journal_posts/venture-debt-a-capital-idea-for-startups
4. SVCA. 2021. *VIMA Kit.* https://www.svca.org.sg/publications/vima-kit
5. Kirk Coburn. 2020. *The Latest Changes in VC Deal Terms — Pay-to-Play.* https://kirkcoburn.com/2020/07/23/the-latest-changes-in-vc-deal-terms-pay-to-play/
6. Insignia Ventures CapTable Calculator. https://www.insignia.vc/captable

Chapter 7

1. Velocity Ventures. Preqin. https://caia.org/sites/default/files/wp-content/uploads/2021/07/SE-Asia-VC-Table-3-1024x768.png
2. Nicolas Cerdeira & Kyril Kotashev. 2021. *Startup Failure Rate: Ultimate Report + Infographic.* Failory. https://www.failory.com/blog/startup-failure-rate
3. Saul Singer. 2018. *Timeline of a Startup.* Twitter. https://twitter.com/saulsinger/status/948554355640340481/photo/1
4. On Call with Insignia Ventures. 2021. *S03E05-E06: Sustaining The Pandemic's 10x Digitalization With Lifepal's Giacomo Ficari, Intellect's Theodoric Chew, And Finhay's Huy Nghiem.* Insignia Business Review. http://review.insignia.vc/2021/05/11/s03e05-e06-sustaining-the-pandemics-10x-digitalization-with-lifepals-giacomo-ficari-intellects-theodoric-chew-and-finhays-huy-nghiem/
5. Paulo Joquiño. 2021. *Zero To Sea: 5 Lessons From Southeast Asia's First Tech Unicorn In The Public Markets.* Insignia Business Review. http://review.insignia.vc/2021/03/16/zero-to-sea-5-lessons-from-southeast-asias-first-tech-unicorn-in-the-public-markets/
6. On Call with Insignia Ventures. 2021. *On Call With Insignia 3: Hendra Kwik, CEO Of FazzFinancial Group On Going Regional, People-First Leadership, And The Future Of Fintech In Southeast Asia.* Insignia Business

Review. http://review.insignia.vc/2021/04/07/on-call-with-insignia-3-hendra-kwik-ceo-of-fazzfinancial-group-on-going-regional-people-first-leadership-and-the-future-of-fintech-in-southeast-asia/

7. On Call with Insignia Ventures. 2020. *Linh Thai, Aaron Tan, & Yinglan Tan On COVID-19 Strategies For Startups In Southeast Asia*. Insignia Business Review. http://review.insignia.vc/2020/04/06/on-call-with-linh-thai-aaron-tan-yinglan-tan-covid-19-strategies-for-startups-in-southeast-asia/

8. On Call with Insignia Ventures. 2021. *On Call With Insignia 3: Aaron Tan, CEO Of Carro, On Future Of Southeast Asia's Automotive Retail Industry, Artificial Intelligence, And Leading APAC's Top High Growth Company For 2021*. Insignia Business Review. http://review.insignia.vc/2021/04/13/on-call-with-insignia-3-aaron-tan-ceo-carro-southeast-asia-automotive-retail-industry-artificial-intelligence-apac-top-high-growth-company-for-2021/

9. On Call with Insignia Ventures. 2020. *Unlocking The Future Of Smart Access And Smart Cities: On Call With Igloohome CEO And Co-Founder Anthony Chow*. Insignia Business Review. http://review.insignia.vc/2020/09/18/unlocking-the-future-of-smart-access-and-smart-cities-on-call-with-igloohome-ceo-and-co-founder-anthony-chow/

10. Yinglan Tan and Paulo Joquiño. 2020. *Navigating ASEANnovation: The Reservoir Principle and Other Essays on Startups and Innovation in Southeast Asia*. World Scientific Publishing Company.

11. On Call with Insignia Ventures. 2020. *Unstoppable Founders And Enduring Platform Companies With Yinglan Tan*. Insignia Business Review. http://review.insignia.vc/2020/05/19/unstoppable-founders-and-enduring-platform-companies-with-yinglan-tan/

Chapter 8

1. Yinglan Tan and Paulo Joquiño. 2020. *Navigating ASEANnovation: The Reservoir Principle and Other Essays on Startups and Innovation in Southeast Asia*. World Scientific Publishing Company.

2. On Call with Insignia Ventures. 2021. *S03E12: Igloocompany CEO Anthony Chow On Expanding Into The US, Singapore Startups Going Global From Day One, And Building A Global Distribution Network*. Insignia Business Review. http://review.insignia.vc/2021/06/22/igloocompany-ceo-anthony-chow-on-expanding-into-the-us-singapore-startups-going-global-from-day-one-and-building-global-distribution-network/

3. On Call with Insignia Ventures. 2021. *Fostering Indonesia's Next Generation Of CEOs And Investors: On Call With Ajaib CPO And Co-Founder Yada Piyajomkwan.* Insignia Business Review. http://review.insignia. vc/2021/01/21/fostering-indonesias-next-generation-ceos-and-investors-on-call-with-ajaib-cpo-and-co-founder-yada-piyajomkwan/

4. On Call with Insignia Ventures. 2020. *Growth Hacking Indonesia's Interbank Transfer App With Flip CEO And Co-Founder Rafi Putra Arriyan.* Insignia Business Review. http://review.insignia.vc/2020/06/30/growth-hacking-indonesias-interbank-transfer-app-with-flip-ceo-and-co-founder-rafi-putra-arriyan/

5. On Call with Insignia Ventures. 2020. *Graduating From Gojek Executive To Proptech Startup Founder: On Call With Pinhome Co-Founder Dayu Dara Permata And Ahmed Aljunied.* Insignia Business Review. http://review. insignia.vc/2020/10/08/graduating-from-gojek-executive-to-proptech-startup-founder-on-call-with-pinhome-co-founder-dayu-dara-permata-and-ahmed-aljunied/

6. On Call with Insignia Ventures. 2020. *Neobanking For SMEs In Southeast Asia: On Call With Aspire CEO And Co-Founder Andrea Baronchelli.* Insignia Business Review. http://review.insignia.vc/2020/09/24/neobanking-for-smes-in-southeast-asia-on-call-with-aspire-ceo-and-co-founder-andrea-baronchelli/

7. On Call with Insignia Ventures. 2020. *Paving The Ecommerce Road For Indonesia's Rural Economy With Super CEO And Co-Founder Steven Wongsoredjo.* Insignia Business Review. http://review.insignia. vc/2020/07/07/paving-the-ecommerce-road-for-indonesias-rural-economy-with-super-ceo-and-co-founder-steven-wongsoredjo/

8. On Call with Insignia Ventures. 2021. *On Call With Insignia 3: Aaron Tan, CEO Of Carro, On Future Of Southeast Asia's Automotive Retail Industry, Artificial Intelligence, And Leading APAC's Top High Growth Company For 2021.* Insignia Business Review. http://review.insignia. vc/2021/04/13/on-call-with-insignia-3-aaron-tan-ceo-carro-southeast-asia-automotive-retail-industry-artificial-intelligence-apac-top-high-growth-company-for-2021/

9. On Call with Insignia Ventures. 2021. *S03E05-E06: Sustaining The Pandemic's 10x Digitalization With Lifepal's Giacomo Ficari, Intellect's Theodoric Chew, And Finhay's Huy Nghiem.* Insignia Business Review. http://review.insignia.vc/2021/05/11/s03e05-e06-sustaining-the-pandemics-10x-digitalization-with-lifepals-giacomo-ficari-intellects-theodoric-chew-and-finhays-huy-nghiem/

10. Paulo Joquiño. 2019. *Developing Effective Local Teams For Cross-Border Companies.* Insignia Business Review. http://review.insignia. vc/2019/08/23/developing-local-teams-for-cross-border/

11. On Call with Insignia Ventures. 2020. *Remote Productivity with Carro co-founder Kelvin Chng, WIZ.AI chairman Jianfeng Lu, Insignia Ventures Head of Tech Ridy Lie.* Insignia Business Review. http://review.insignia. vc/2020/09/03/remote-productivity-carro-co-founder-kelvin-chng-wiz-ai-chairman-jianfeng-lu-insignia-ventures-head-of-tech-ridy-lie/

12. Pranav Balakrishnan. 2021. *Gojek's Indian engine got it to US$10 billion. Now it wants to change gears.* The Ken. https://the-ken.com/story/ gojeks-indian-engine-got-it-to-10-billion-now-it-wants-to-change-it/

13. On Call with Insignia Ventures. 2020. *Shaping The Future Of Southeast Asia's Car Industry Through The CFO Lens: On Call With Carro Group CFO Ernest Chew.* Insignia Business Review. http://review.insignia. vc/2020/12/04/shaping-the-future-southeast-asia-car-industry-cfo-on-call-carro-group-cfo-ernest-chew/

14. On Call with Insignia Ventures. 2020. *Establishing Thought Leadership In Southeast Asia's Logistics Part 1: On Call With Janio Asia Co-Founder And Head Of Marketing Nathaniel Yim.* Insignia Business Review. http:// review.insignia.vc/2020/10/22/establishing-thought-leadership-in-southeast-asias-logistics-part-1-on-call-with-janio-asia-co-founder-and-head-of-marketing-nathaniel-yim/

15. Jesse Choi. 2021. *Episode 3: Decoding entrepreneurship with Phil Opamuratawongse.* Going Southeast. https://medium.com/ going-southeast/episode-3-decoding-entrepreneurship-with-phil-opamuratawongse-71af6fe111bf

Chapter 9

1. On Call with Insignia Ventures. 2021. *On Call With Insignia 3: Hendra Kwik, CEO Of FazzFinancial Group On Going Regional, People-First Leadership, And The Future Of Fintech In Southeast Asia.* Insignia Business Review. http://review.insignia.vc/2021/04/07/on-call-with-insignia-3-hendra-kwik-ceo-of-fazzfinancial-group-on-going-regional-people-first-leadership-and-the-future-of-fintech-in-southeast-asia/

2. Paulo Joquino. 2020. *Revisiting The Rural Economy.* Insignia Business Review. http://review.insignia.vc/2020/03/16/revisiting-the-rural-economy/

3. Bill Roosman. 2020. *Riding The K12 Learning Cycle In Southeast Asia.* Insignia Business Review. http://review.insignia.vc/2020/07/14/riding-the-k12-learning-cycle-in-southeast-asia/

Chapter 10

1. Yinglan Tan and Paulo Joquiño. 2020. *Navigating ASEANnovation: The Reservoir Principle and Other Essays on Startups and Innovation in Southeast Asia.* World Scientific Publishing Company.
2. On Call with Insignia Ventures. 2021. *On Call With Insignia 3: Hendra Kwik, CEO Of FazzFinancial Group On Going Regional, People-First Leadership, And The Future Of Fintech In Southeast Asia.* Insignia Business Review. http://review.insignia.vc/2021/04/07/on-call-with-insignia-3-hendra-kwik-ceo-of-fazzfinancial-group-on-going-regional-people-first-leadership-and-the-future-of-fintech-in-southeast-asia/
3. On Call with Insignia Ventures. 2020. *The New Normal Part 1 With Dianping's Zhang Tao And JAMM Active's Chih Cheung.* Insignia Business Review. http://review.insignia.vc/2020/04/20/the-new-normal-with-dianpings-zhang-tao-and-jamm-active-limiteds-chih-cheung/

Chapter 11

1. Brad Feld and Mahendra Ramsinghani. 2013. *Startup Boards: Getting the Most Out of Your Board of Directors (Techstars).* Wiley. https://www.amazon.com/Startup-Boards-Getting-Board-Directors/dp/1118443667
2. Bryan Schreier. *Preparing a Board Deck.* Sequoia. https://www.sequoiacap.com/article/preparing-a-board-deck/
3. Jon Callaghan. 2016. *Let's Fix Startup Board Meetings.* True Ventures. https://trueventures.com/blog/lets-fix-startup-board-meetings

Chapter 12

1. Jon Russell. 2019. *Go-Jek buys fintech startup Coins.ph for $72M ahead of Philippines expansion.* TechCrunch. https://techcrunch.com/2019/01/18/gojek-coins-ph-philippines/
2. Paulo Joquino. 2021. *5 Lessons On Building A Global AI Marketing Company: Case Study On Appier's Road To IPO.* Insignia Business Review. http://review.insignia.vc/2021/03/30/5-lessons-from-appier-road-to-ipo/

3. Paulo Joquino. 2019. *Beyond the Gong: Succeeding in the Public Markets.* Insignia Business Review. http://review.insignia.vc/2019/11/25/beyond-the-gong-succeeding-in-the-public-markets/
4. CBInsights. 2021. *From Alibaba To Zynga: 45 Of The Best VC Bets Of All Time And What We Can Learn From Them.* https://www.cbinsights.com/research/best-venture-capital-investments/
5. Miguel Cordon. 2020. *A cheat sheet of tech acquisitions in Southeast Asia.* Tech in Asia. https://www.techinasia.com/tech-merger-acquisition-southeast-asia
6. Catherine Shu. 2021. *Payfazz invests $30M in Xfers as the two Southeast Asia fintechs form Fazz Financial Group.* TechCrunch. https://techcrunch.com/2021/03/03/payfazz-invests-30m-in-xfers-as-the-two-southeast-asian-fintechs-form-fazz-financial-group/
7. Paulo Joquino. 2021. *Zero to Sea: 5 Lessons from Southeast Asia's first tech unicorn in the public markets.* Insignia Business Review. http://review.insignia.vc/2021/03/16/zero-to-sea-5-lessons-from-southeast-asias-first-tech-unicorn-in-the-public-markets/
8. Jamin Ball. 2020. *What it Takes to Become a Public SaaS Company: Part 2.* Clouded Judgment. https://cloudedjudgement.substack.com/p/what-it-takes-to-become-a-public-ea2
9. Victor Koch. 2020. *What Is A SPAC? Simple Explanation.* Seeking Alpha. https://seekingalpha.com/instablog/50309069-victor-koch/5484131-what-is-spac-simple-explanation
10. Rob Go. 2018. *How VCs Get Measured.* Better Everyday. https://bettereveryday.vc/how-vcs-get-measured-fbfc4d513436
11. Saheli Roy Choudhury. 2021. *Indonesia's internet start-ups Gojek and Tokopedia announce merger.* https://www.cnbc.com/2021/05/17/goto-indonesia-internet-start-ups-gojektokopedia-announce-merger.html

Chapter 13

1. On Call with Insignia Ventures. 2021. *S03E16: Cathay Innovation Investment Director Rajive Keshup On Southeast Asia's Gold Rush From A Global Investment Firm's Perspective.* Insignia Business Review. http://review.insignia.vc/2021/07/20/cathay-innovation-investment-director-rajive-keshup-on-southeast-asias-gold-rush-from-a-global-investment-firms-perspective/

2. On Call with Insignia Ventures. 2021. *S03E15: Parallels And Synergies Between Latin America And Southeast Asia From Eric Acher, Founding Managing Partner Of Monashees, Brazil's First Venture Capital Firm*. Insignia Business Review. http://review.insignia.vc/2021/07/13/parallels-and-synergies-between-latin-america-and-southeast-asia-from-eric-acher-founding-managing-partner-of-monashees-brazils-first-venture-capital-firm/

3. Joolin Chuah. 2020. *Driving Value As A Venture Capitalist, After The Vows*. Insignia Business Review. http://review.insignia.vc/2020/03/02/driving-value-as-a-venture-capitalist-after-the-vows/

4. Joshua Mayers. 2016. *The current state of venture capital in 18 charts*. PitchBook. https://pitchbook.com/news/articles/the-current-state-of-venture-capital-in-18-charts

5. Gail Lau. 2021. *The Hidden Driver Of Southeast Asia Venture Capital's Meteoric Rise*. Insignia Business Review. http://review.insignia.vc/2021/04/20/the-hidden-driver-of-southeast-asia-venture-capitals-meteoric-rise/

Appendix B: Insignia Ventures Portfolio Companies Mentioned

Listed below are companies mentioned in the book that are part of the Insignia Ventures portfolio. For more on Insignia Ventures' portfolio, head to www.insignia.vc/portfolio.

Chapter 4

1. Finhay (Huy Nghiem)
2. Appier (Chih Han Yu)
3. Tonik (Greg Krasnov)
4. Payfazz, Shipper, Super

Chapter 5

1. Carro (Aaron Tan)

Chapter 6

1. Carro (Ernest Chew)
2. Rainforest (JJ Chai)

Chapter 7

1. Finhay (Huy Nghiem)
2. GoTo Group
3. Payfazz (Hendra Kwik)
4. Carro (Aaron Tan)

Chapter 8

1. Carro, Pinhome, AwanTunai
2. igloocompany (Anthony Chow)
3. Ajaib (Yada Piyajomkwan)
4. Flip (Rafi Putra Arriyan)
5. Pinhome (Dayu Dara Permata, Ahmed Aljunied)
6. Carro (Aaron Tan)
7. Aspire (Andrea Baronchelli)
8. Super (Steven Wongsoredjo)
9. Carro (Aaron Tan)
10. Lifepal (Giacomo Ficari)
11. Intellect (Theodoric Chew)
12. Intellect (Theodoric Chew)
13. igloocompany
14. Janio (Junkai Ng)
15. Flip (Rafi Putra Arriyan)
16. Carro (Kelvin Chng)
17. Carro (Ernest Chew)
18. Janio (Nathaniel Yim)
19. Ajaib (Yada Piyajomkwan)
20. Lifepal (Giacomo Ficari)

Chapter 9

1. Carro, Ajaib, Appier
2. Flip
3. GoTo

4. igloocompany (Anthony Chow)
5. Shipper, Super, Lifepal, Payfazz

Chapter 10

1. Payfazz (Hendra Kwik)

Chapter 12

1. Appier
2. Carro (Aaron Tan)
3. Carro
4. GoTo
5. Payfazz

Appendix C: Best Practices List

Chapter 1

1. Invest early. Avoid the bandwagons and gravity wells, unless you started it.
2. As a venture capitalist, it's important to figure out your value-add, not just on a firm level but also on an individual level. How can you create value for your portfolio companies?
3. It's valuable for venture capitalists to help their founders embrace Rule #1, whether that means connections or better understanding the nuances of a local market or industry.

Chapter 2

1. Schedule time every month to check your misses and sharpen your investment approach.
2. An investment thesis can be general but still comprehensive. It's important to cover all angles from the market to technology, business models and founders.
3. Schedule time to regularly check your deal flow funnel.

Chapter 3

1. It's very useful to get a feel of the market by talking to as many GPs in the same target market and growth stage as possible to

decide whether or not to embark on this journey and get practical tips from those who have already gone through all the work.
2. Optimize time, but maximize outreach. Treat fundraising like a sales process.
3. Do not underestimate the value of a strong and diversified LP base.

Chapter 4

1. Come up with your own sourcing strategy tailor fit to your investment thesis. Certain channels and contacts apply better to a specific vertical or market.
2. Spotting the right signals and reaching out at the right moment can better lubricate initial communication with a founder. Push strategies with "brand" recognition from pull strategies (thought leadership) is an ideal mix.
3. Win investments in IC with conviction, which should be backed by a deep understanding of the ins and outs of the company.

Chapter 5

1. Beware of the blended and empty numbers in running due diligence. Ensure that numbers tie to what the business actually does in reality.
2. It is important to find the right comparable to base exit values to ensure valuations are realistic and justifiable.
3. It is a good practice to set SOPs in place to run due diligence with your portfolio.

Chapter 6

1. Be transparent in dealing with the founders and co-investors throughout the process of closing the investment round.
2. Get yourself on the side of (majority of) the founders when it comes to negotiations.
3. Always put the interests of the fund and company first.

Chapter 7

1. Avoid giving too much value-add, and where applicable, try to find people who can commit to helping the company and have the specialty to do so for the long-term.
2. Have a dashboard with north star metrics for your portfolio companies to quickly view how they are performing, with notes on action points being taken to achieve specific goals.
3. Have a list of exit scenarios, potential new investors and strategics for each of your portfolio companies that are regularly revisited and updated. Keep in touch with these investors and strategics to get a sense of how their view of the market is evolving and tell them stories of your companies when the opening arises.

Chapter 8

1. Focus on executive hires for portfolio companies where the fund has high ownership.
2. Organize your network to be able to easily find people whom you can introduce to founders if they are looking for specific hires.
3. Do not just liaise with the CEO — work with the rest of the leadership team to get a better sense of company culture and how the company is growing and developing as an organization.

Chapter 9

1. Segment portfolio companies under your purview into different levels of priority and schedule update meetings with founders depending on the level of priority.
2. Don't just work with the CEO. Get to know the rest of the management team and build working relationships with them to easily coordinate any support provided.
3. VCs are not meant to run the company. Avoid crossing the lines in intervention and instead enable change rather than managing it. Any level of support in terms of growth strategy begins from the context of the founder and company.

Chapter 10

1. Always fundraise with the next funding round in mind. Keep tabs on your portfolio companies and air concerns in regular meetings, but keep a healthy distance as well and let the founders come to you for help as much as possible (certain scenarios this may not apply).
2. Regularly revisit and iterate investor pipelines for fundraising.
3. It's always better to get a CFO or strategic development lead than to spend a lot of your time on supporting specific companies with their fundraising. This way you can focus more on the origination and introductions rather than the communication or coordination.

Chapter 11

1. Enable the founder-CEO to take ownership during meetings.
2. It's less about sharing what you know and more about asking the right questions.
3. Board meetings are only as effective as what happens in between them. Maximize board meeting prep in update meetings with founders and management.

Chapter 12

1. Avoid exiting your portfolio companies too early. Constantly monitor portfolio companies against benchmark targets to be able to assess when to make the call to divest to start looking for acquirers or secondary sale buyers.
2. Come up with an iterative DPI list of companies for each quarter or year to focus on, in terms of setting up the company towards a target valuation and helping them find exit targets.
3. Set up a DPI hit list of exit targets, and a contact list of decision makers to regularly reach out to and consult on what they are seeing in the market and potentially send them one-pagers on your portfolio companies at the right time.

Chapter 13

1. Define your focus and expertise as an investor, based on your background and interest.
2. Maximize exposure to founders, even if the interactions do not involve directly investing in them.
3. Build long-lasting relationships with founders — their contact numbers and what they say about you is your CV/track record.

Printed in the United States
by Baker & Taylor Publisher Services